Praise for *From the Dress-Up Corner to the Senior Prom*

"A brave, lucid, and insightful exploration of the intersections of gender, sexuality, and the experiences of K-12 students. Informed by scholarship and years of school experience, Jennifer Bryan has written a superb manual for faculty, administrators, and families on how to navigate safe passages for all students. Following Bryan's advice not to run from these issues, but to embrace them conscientiously, will help educators and parents meet the challenges of raising healthy children in a nation where gender and sex have become tools of commerce." —**Arthur Lipkin** EdD, chair, MA Commission on GLBT Youth

"What we teach in our school curriculum helps shape the minds, attitudes, and identities of children. Conversely, what we omit or leave unexamined matters as well. In this carefully researched, courageous book, Jennifer Bryan cogently argues that despite the centrality of gender and sexuality to our core relationships and identity, schools rarely contend with these topics. Bryan is persuasive, forthright, and sensitive in challenging us to formulate a more inclusive and complex approach to addressing gender and sexuality diversity in school. As a teacher, I have often shied away from topics of gender and sexuality. I fear that I don't know enough or that traversing these topics is too fraught and dangerous. Reading this book challenged me to re-think my tendency to sidestep these issues and provided me the conceptual vocabulary and practical strategies to be a better teacher for all my students." —**Sam Intrator** PhD, Department of Education and Child Study, Smith College, professor of Education and Child Study, Smith College

"The issue of safety for GLBTQI students in our schools today is a matter of life and death, not a matter of politics. Jennifer Bryan's book is essential reading for anyone directly or indirectly involved in the education of children today. As the Head of a pre-K through 8th grade independent school, I found valuable information contained in this book for faculty, parents, and trustees alike. Whatever your role is in the process of education, Jennifer Bryan's book provides real life examples along with excellent solutions, making it a useful tool in the classroom and at home. Bryan does not shy away from the conflict, rather she encourages us to face the prejudices and inequities that exist with confidence, candor, and even humor. This book is a must read now!" —**John Peterman**, Head of School, Brookwood School, Manchester, MA

My children, Noah and Claire, are the inspiration for this book.

FROM THE DRESS-UP CORNER TO THE SENIOR PROM

Navigating Gender and Sexuality Diversity in PreK–12 Schools

Jennifer Bryan

ROWMAN & LITTLEFIELD EDUCATION

A division of
ROWMAN & LITTLEFIELD PUBLISHERS, INC.
Lanham • Boulder • New York • Toronto • Plymouth, UK

Published by Rowman & Littlefield Education
A division of Rowman & Littlefield Publishers, Inc.
A wholly owned subsidary of The Rowman & Littlefield Publishing Group, Inc.
4501 Forbes Boulevard, Suite 200, Lanham, Maryland 20706
http://www.rowmaneducation.com

10 Thornbury Road, Plymouth PL6 7PP, United Kingdom

British Library Cataloguing in Publication Information Available

Library of Congress Cataloging-in-Publication Data
Bryan, Jennifer, 1961–
  From the dress-up corner to the senior prom : navigating gender and sexuality diversity
in preK-12 schools / Jennifer Bryan.
    p. cm.
  Includes bibliographical references.
  ISBN 978-1-60709-978-9 (cloth : alk. paper) — ISBN 978-1-60709-979-6 (pbk. : alk.
paper) — ISBN 978-1-60709-980-2 (electronic)
  1. Sex differences in education—United States. 2. Gender identity—United States.
3. Teachers—In-service training—United States. I. Title.
  LC212.9.B79 2012
  370.15'1—dc23

                                                                        2012000236

∞™ The paper used in this publication meets the minimum requirements of
American National Standard for Information Sciences—Permanence of Paper
for Printed Library Materials, ANSI/NISO Z39.48-1992.

Printed in the United States of America

CONTENTS

ACKNOWLEDGMENTS

On January 1, 2009 my partner Markie suggested our family take a sabbatical year in Boulder, Colorado. In spite of being a homebody, I said yes, because Markie has always been the visionary in our relationship, and she knew that every member of our family—including the 80 year-old cat—might be transformed if we altered the status quo of our lives in a big way. The challenges we faced were of modest and grand proportions: learning to ski (Noah); studying Eco-Psychology (Markie); adopting a puppy (Claire); submitting a book proposal (me). I would never have been able to begin the brick-by-brick construction of this book without the gift of time that the year in Boulder offered. For this and so much more, I am grateful to Markie.

I have been blessed by the great generosity of others throughout this project. Some of the help I received was quite unexpected, actually. For instance, I sent editor Susan McEachern one of those "cold-call" emails, hoping she might spare a few minutes of her time to give me the skinny on book publishing. In spite of not knowing me even a little, she forwarded the email to Tom Koerner, editorial director of the Education Division at Rowman & Littlefield. After some hefty cajoling on my part, Tom agreed to publish this book.

I had no idea that writing and publishing a book of this magnitude is the literary equivalent of a steeplechase (the kind without the horses), and I am grateful to Liz Meyer who offered no-nonsense advice about how to complete the course without getting stuck in one of those ditches of water. When I asked her how long my project would take, she said, *You figure out how much time you need and then add a year.* In addition to accurate predictions of this sort,

Liz brought the wisdom of her own scholarship to bear on the content of my book, reading drafts of chapters, offering opportune suggestions and asking just the right questions.

David Campos and Ian MacGillivray read early versions of the manuscript and offered a forgiving balance of constructive criticism and encouragement. Via the internet I put out a call to teachers who would be willing to read draft chapters, and eight educators from Alaska to Iowa to New York came forward. These busy teachers, strangers to me, took time to help. No surprise, really, because year after year I am inspired by the generosity and good-heartedness of the PreK-12 teachers I have the privilege to work with and learn from.

My funny, smart college friend Mary Burchenal also read several chapters, and to tell you the truth, she was my most hard-nosed critic. Mary is a long-time teacher/administrator at Brookline High School in Massachusetts, and she enlightened me about the bottom-line realities of school administrators, teaching me about the pivotal "or else" factor.

Mary: *Or else what? What if they don't?*

Me: *Don't what?*

Mary: *Don't do all this great stuff you suggest. Administrators ask themselves five times a day--- 'what catastrophe will occur if I don't deal with this issue right now?' You have to lay out the 'or else.' As in, 'you better do this* **or else**...'"

I have the highest regard for Mary's life-long career as a teacher, so I took her advice to heart.

What was my greatest bit of good luck? Renee DePalma Ungaro. While researching my book, I discovered Renee's work as Senior Researcher on the UK-based *No Outsiders Project.* The project investigated approaches to addressing lesbian, gay, bisexual and transgender equality in primary schools. The articles and books based on this research offer some of the best practical scholarship on the role of gender and sexuality in primary schools available today. When I first emailed Renee and asked if she would look at my manuscript, I had no idea I would end up with such a brilliant, witty and steadfast reader.

Renee offered vital feedback on the manuscript, demonstrating time and again her keen grasp of all those knotty places where gender, sexuality, and education intersect. Her curiosity and "musings" inspired deeper and different kinds of thinking on my part. When I would sink into maudlin despair about ever finishing the book, or I would wonder if anybody actually understood a word of what I was writing, an email from Renee would arrive just in time. Not only did she understand what I was writing, she was excited about what I was writing. Having Renee pen the Foreword to this book is a true honor and thrill.

I offer a special thank you to Sebastian Barr, another unbelievable "find" in the journey of writing this book. Sebastian contacted me right about the time I needed to find a research assistant in Northampton. In addition to being a skill-ful researcher, table-maker, and web sleuth, Sebastian is a first-rate scholar in his own right. He is smart-smart, curious, enlightened beyond his years, and a natural teacher. I am grateful for his intellectual and emotional companionship during this journey; it is hard to imagine completing the project without him. I know that as Sebastian pursues his own graduate studies, the future of gender and sexuality research is in exceptional hands.

My posse of supporters has been diverse and strong all along, and I am par-ticularly grateful to and proud of the elders in my corner. Elizabeth "Babs" Conant has been a key patron of my efforts from the beginning and also, an inspiration, as she and her partner Camille have modeled a lifetime of advocat-ing for GLBTQ rights and equality for all. My in-laws, Ed and Cynny Babbott and my parents, Marny and Fred Smith, have also been pioneers. Over the years they have stood beside me and Margaret, blessing our first home, our family wedding, and our children. Their wisdom, grace and generosity blessed this book project long before it even started.

The central core: David, Sarah, Joe, the women of MOTE (mothers on the edge), my brother Ed. Thank you to Debbie Roffman, Barbara Swanson at NY-SAIS, Gill Cook, Mary McMenamin at RLP, Maggie Bittel, Walter DeMelle, Carol Gilligan, Manuel Garcia, the good folks at Paradise Copies, John Collins, Kathleen Boucher and my kind reviewers Elizabeth Meyer, Arthur Lipkin, Pat Basset, Sam Intrator, John Peterman and Mike McCarthy. To all the educators, students and parents whose stories and lesson plans appear in this book, I honor you.

FOREWORD

Have you ever been asked to imagine whom you would invite to a fantasy dinner party? Well, psychologist and educational consultant Jennifer Bryan has answered this question in book form: she has invited French philosopher Michel Foucault and American philosopher Judith Butler to sit down at the table with a Catholic school teacher, a five-year-old and her two moms, a gender-neutral puppet called "Nat," a mixed-race, same-sex adolescent couple who wish to attend their senior prom together, a man who first "knew" he was a man at the age of twenty-one, and a couple of male penguins who happen to be in love with each other. Among others. And we, the readers, have been invited as well. And our host, the author of this book, has found a way for all these guests to talk to each other and, best of all, to listen to each other.

The fish is the last to discover water. Or so the old adage goes. This is one of the first things I tell my students, who are studying to be school teachers. One might wonder why teachers would be interested in such philosophical proposals about fish and their relationship to water. Jennifer's book will definitely clear that up.

In fact, this pithy fish adage can actually be traced to a statement made by anthropologist Clyde Kluckhohn in 1949, "Ordinarily, we are unaware of the special lens through which we look at life. It would hardly be fish who discovered the existence of water" (cited in Wolcott 2005, 123). Kluckhohn was talking about the study of culture, and how much easier it is to see the "strange" things that others do than it is to recognize the everyday assumptions, rituals, and taboos that constitute our own society. He may not have had twenty-first-century understandings of sex, gender, and sexuality specifically in mind, but clearly this wisdom is applicable here. And Jennifer's application of this wisdom has resulted in a book that artfully depicts a world of complex problems, real people, and creative responses—all of which will seem quite familiar to anyone who has ever stepped foot in a school.

As a heterosexual person who has always, more or less, fit rather neatly into the categories of girl and woman, provided by my society, I would naturally be one of the last to discover what Bryan in this book defines as Gender and Sexuality Diversity (GSD). I would be the last to notice the myriad ways in which the glorious biodiversity of GSD is shaped and contained by my own culture. Kluckhohn's apparently simple statement about the awareness of fish suggests lots of things that are explained in more detail, with an admirable clarity and concrete examples, in this book.

For example, like water, sexuality and gender are everywhere. It's who our parents are (*What if I have two moms?*). It's the clothes we put on in the morning (*Can I wear this skirt? Well, that depends . . .*). We tend to forget about everyday experiences of gender and sexuality, unless something happens to muddy up the waters. And for some people, these waters can get muddy pretty early on (*Some of the other children tease me when I mention my moms*).

The water is an important discovery for those of us who have been swimming along in a transparent sea. We have the luxury *not* to wonder what sex and gender really are, and how they come about, and what happens when they don't line up like most people expect. And for those of us who fail to discover the water we swim in, it's still there. And it shapes our lives and the lives of others, whether we notice it or not.

Teachers[1] have a particularly important role in the lives of others. I don't want to claim that they are the only ones, and I certainly don't want to add superhuman powers of detection to the already-too-long list of things that teachers have a "special responsibility" for in our society. But if anybody is in a position to become more observant than the average fish, and to achieve a clearer understanding of GSD that can make a difference in the lives of others, it's teachers.

I know, because I spent a few years working with teachers who were doing just that. As the senior researcher of an initiative in the UK called The No Outsiders Project, I had the enormous pleasure to work with a team of primary school teachers who had taken it upon themselves to investigate how GSD was relevant to their children's lives, and how this might inform their teaching. One teacher, for example, noticed that students "corrected" her stick figure drawings when the figures failed to conform to gender stereotypes. Other teachers noticed that reading stories that included gay, lesbian, and gender nonconforming characters made it easier to challenge homophobic insults (see DePalma and Atkinson 2010).

I first learned of Jennifer's existence because of her children's book *The Different Dragon*, and when I discovered that she was writing a book for teachers, I was excited to know more. I had the privilege of readings drafts of all the chapters, and the whole time I was secretly wishing she had just got around to this about five years earlier so we could have used it in our project.

One of the ideas that inspired the No Outsiders Project was that we wanted to find ways to work together, teachers and academics, to bridge that all-too-common divide between theory and practice. I actually believe there is theory behind everyone's practice, and the question is whether we recognize it. If we do manage to recognize our implicit theories, then we can make adjustments to how we understand our world and improve how we act upon it. Jennifer Bryan has managed to write a book that helps us to do just that. Her clear explanations and engaging examples are enough to help any fish discover water, and even to enjoy the process.

Renée DePalma
September 19, 2011
University of A Coruña, Spain

REFERENCES

DePalma, Renée. 2010. The nature of institutional heteronormativity in primary schools and practice-based responses. *Teaching and Teacher Education* 26: 1669–76.

———. 2009. Sexualities equality in all primary schools: A case for not waiting for ideal conditions. *Sexuality matters: Paradigms and policies for educational leaders.* James W. Koschoreck and Autumn A. Tooms, eds. Plymouth, UK: Rowman & Littlefield.

DePalma, Renée, and Elizabeth Atkinson. 2009. "No Outsiders": Moving beyond a discourse of tolerance to challenge heteronormativity in primary schools. *British Educational Research Journal* 35(6): 837–55.

———, eds. 2010. *Undoing homophobia in primary schools.* Stoke on Trent: Trentham Books.

Wolcott, Henry. 2005. *The art of fieldwork*, 2nd ed. Walnut Creek, CA: Alta Mira Press.

NOTE

1. I use this term broadly to include, as Jennifer describes in her introduction, "anyone who works with children and adolescents in an educational capacity."

INTRODUCTION

1971

I grew up as the only girl with four brothers in a very athletic family. I was an energetic tomboy, and what I thought about sometimes was how much easier life would have been if I had been born a boy. There could have been just five brothers. If I were a boy, then my wanting to play with the boys, dress like the boys, act like the boys wouldn't have been a problem. My mother was over the moon when she finally had a girl, and she was excited about my being a particular kind of girl: dolls, bikinis, jewelry, ladylike behavior in church. I was interested in hockey pucks, bb guns, and riding my Sting Ray bicycle.

I won that bike at the elementary school fair in fourth grade. It was the end of a glorious day of riding the Scrambler and eating cotton candy and sticking my head through the hole of the plywood sponge toss board. I was pretty grubby. The rides began to shut down in the late afternoon, and Miss Grayson, our petite, stern principal, took her place atop a step stool at home plate on the baseball diamond to announce the winners of the big raffle.

Two bicycles were lashed up on the chain-link backstop for everyone to admire. There was a girls' bike, robin's egg blue with a white basket in front and red, white, and blue streamers tied to the handlebars. The boys' bike was a black Sting Ray with a banana seat, roll bar, and a three-speed stick shift. Red flames roared across the chain guard.

When Miss Grayson called out the first number and I saw it matched the one on my soggy orange ticket, I began shouting and pushing my way to the front of the crowd. "I've got it! I have it! That's my number!" As Miss Grayson looked down at me from her home-plate perch, the expression on her face seemed strained. I imagine she had hoped for a less disheveled and muddy winner, or at least someone wearing shoes.

She checked my numbers carefully and then nodded her head. "Yes, Jenny, this is the winning ticket." And then she turned toward Mr. Stanley, our custodian, who was up on a ladder by the backstop. She gestured for him to take the girls' bike down, and I shouted, "No, No! I want that one!" and pointed to the Sting Ray. Miss Grayson scowled, and then promptly found her wooden smile. A wave of uneasy laughter twittered across the throng of families gathered on the infield grass. The look on Miss Grayson's face, or the murmuring of the crowd. I wasn't sure what it was but I knew that somehow I had made a mistake.

2007

A problem began at recess.[1] The boys were not letting the girls play kickball. *"Kickball is for boys! Girls can't play!"* A cry went up. The teachers didn't know what to do. They tried to integrate the kickball game and appeal to fairness but found that many of the girls (and a few of the shyer, less athletic boys) didn't know the rules and didn't have the skills to play. *"You should only be able to play if you know how and you are good!! Girls should be jumping rope or swinging on the swings! Kickball is for boys!"* More cries went up. Gender role stereotypes were running wild and running the dynamics at recess.

This began to spill over into the classroom. Toby loved the color purple. He loved *High School Musical*. Classmates began to interrogate him about his *High School Musical* lunch box, with its pink border and pink stars circling the smiling face of Zach Efron. These exchanges were uncomfortable and began to interfere with the sense of community and cooperation that Ms. Bellini and Ms. Sugarman, the second grade teachers, were working so hard to build.

So I loaned Ms. Bellini a copy of *Oliver Button Is a Star*, a film that features the book by Tomie dePaola *Oliver Button Is a Sissy*. Oliver, for those of you unfamiliar with the story, doesn't like playing ball. He likes to tap dance. The boys call him a sissy. The girls stick up for him. His father is worried about what will become of his son. Oliver enters the talent show and wins third place for his tap dancing. In the eyes of many, he is transformed into a star.

The film also features a second grade teacher, Mary Cowhey, using the Oliver Button story to do a comprehensive module on gender stereotypes. Ms. Bellini decided to try the same lesson with Classroom 2F. When she asked her students to make a list about "What Boys Do and Like" and "What Girls Do and Like," the results were unnerving. *Shopping* is for girls, *cute things* are for girls, *pink* is for girls. Touching *slimy things* is for boys, *history* is for boys, *cars and motorcycles* are for boys.

Ms. Bellini asked Classroom 2F who made up these rules about what's okay for boys and girls to do. They paused, and then Philippe called out, "George Bush!" Loren chimed in, "Congress!" Ms. Bellini surveyed the circle of expectant, slightly puzzled faces. "Let's draw some pictures of our ideas," she suggested.

The group talked about and defined the word "stereotype." Then Ms. Bellini asked the kids to draw pictures of themselves doing things that they like that don't necessarily follow the "rules" or stereotypes of "What Boys Do and Like" and "What Girls Do and Like." They drew a boy cooking, a girl in a football uniform, a girl driving a racecar. For almost all the students, the drawings were autobiographical.

Next, brilliantly, Ms. Bellini made challenging gender stereotypes the theme of special sharing; she invited the kids to bring in things they like to do or play with that might not conform to the list they had made. The sharings would provide "proof" that the stereotypes don't always apply (finding "proof" was a concept being used in other parts of the curriculum). A letter went home explaining the theme and intention to the parents (see box 2.1).

Each day several children shared. Andy brought in a pink unicorn, his favorite stuffed animal. He said it was proof that boys can like unicorns *and* pink. (Toby clapped loudly and asked several questions.) John brought in a boy doll named Ken who, according to John, is a friend of Barbie's. His sister lets him play with it. He said it was proof that boys can like dolls. Courtney brought in her New England Patriots jersey, proof that girls like football too. Toby proudly shared his poster of the cast of *High School Musical*. Marisol shared her tool belt, proof that girls can be good at fixing things. Oscar brought in a Beanie Baby rabbit that was really cute and said it was proof that boys can like cute things. Then he told everyone in the sharing circle to scoot back. He stepped into the circle and did a snappy dance move. He said that was proof that boys like to dance sometimes too.

Ms. Bellini also made a selection of books available in the classroom library over the next two weeks and watched as every child in the group explored the stories of *Pugdog* and *Max the Stubborn Little Wolf*; *Elena's Serenade*; *A Fire Engine for Ruthie*; *Rough, Tough Charlie*; *Ballerino Nate*; *The Princesses Have a Ball*; and *Pinky and Rex and the Bully*. The conversations about the characters in those books carried over into snack time, and more than once during the school day, a child in Classroom 2F would pronounce, "I think what you just said is a stereotype. I don't have to do it that way."

Ms. Bellini returned to the question of who made up all these rules for girls and boys, and this is what she said to the circle of second graders. "I've got news for you. WE, all people, kids, grown-ups, teachers, parents, make up these rules for ourselves and each other. The president didn't decide that pink is for girls and blue is for boys. *We* did." She moved her hand in a sweeping gesture around the circle. "Congress didn't vote in a law that says boys can't like dolls and girls can't play kickball. We did." The children were still and quiet. "So if you or we in Classroom

Box 0.1

Friday October 26, 2007

Dear Classroom 2F Families,

We've been talking this week in our community meetings about stereotypes of boys and girls. As a group, we've defined stereotype as, "What some people say that boys like/do _____ or girls like/do _____." The conversations have been rich with different ideas from the students about ways girls and boys like and do the same things, even if "some people say" one thing is for girls and another for boys. We've found many, many examples of "proof" that something isn't just for boys or just girls by talking about what the kids themselves like or do. Today a suggestion was made that next week's sharing could be sharing a way that you are different than what was "on the boys' or girls' side of the list" of stereotypes generated by Group 2F.

Here's the list Group 2F came up with:

Boys
- play kickball, baseball, sports
- like cars, motorcycles
- like big jewels, chains
- like blue
- play four square
- like superheroes, swords, wild movies
- like slimy things—bugs, frogs, worms
- like history
- like tennis
- like math

Girls
- like dancing
- do ballet
- do art
- like jump rope
- like shopping
- like pink
- like horseback riding
- play with dolls, Barbies
- like princesses
- like cute things
- like hula hooping

In response to this suggestion, there will be two options for next week's sharing starting Monday October 29th. Your child can share a way that they feel they are different than a girl/boy stereotype—it can be from the list above or not—or they can just share something they like to do. I've included the sharing schedule on the back. Please let me know if you have any questions.

Many thanks,
Ms. Bellini

2F don't agree with these stereotype rules, we have the power to change them." "Really?" asked Alysha. "Really," said Ms. Bellini.

Later in the school year, after someone brought in a children's clothing catalog to show how stereotyped it was, Classroom 2F decided to make their own clothing catalog. They cut out pictures of shirts, shoes, pants, dresses, sports clothes, and accessories from all the kids' catalogs they could find. Each child got to create two pages of his or her "style." Some kids absolutely matched up with the gender stereotype. Stevie was all Patriots, all Celtics, all Red Sox, both pages. Lillian could hardly choose among all the beautiful spring dresses for girls.

Then there were kids who had a mixture of stereotypically masculine and feminine images, though this was more true for the girls. It was Andy, who shared his pink unicorn back in the fall, who approached Ms. Bellini during catalog making day and asked her quietly, "Do you think I should use this shirt?" He held up the clipping of a gorgeous pink polo shirt. "Absolutely," she said, "If that's the right shirt for you, that's the shirt you should put on your page." And he did.

IT'S GOOD THAT YOU'RE HERE

If you have picked up this book, you may be approaching these pages with great eagerness or a modest dose of curiosity or perhaps even deeply held skepticism. Regardless of your predisposition, *From the Dress-Up Corner to the Senior Prom* was written for you. This book will help you know more about Gender and Sexuality Diversity in schools and offers suggestions about how to apply what you learn here to your own work. Though readers will not all share the same opinions, I believe everyone who is committed to healthy, positive educational experiences for children and adolescents will find useful information in the chapters ahead.

It has been my good fortune and great privilege to collaborate with so many people who have dedicated their lives to the enterprise of "schooling." Many educators are working hard to sort through the place of gender and sexuality in the preK–12 setting. The truth is, however, that there is much more work to do, *and* we need more people to do it. In light of the pervasiveness of gender and sexuality related harassment, and the trend that some students would rather take their own lives than endure daily torment at school, educators and parents must act intelligently and compassionately right now.

So it's good that you are here.

WHAT INFORMS MY PERSPECTIVE

As a senior in college, I did not possess a vision of my professional or personal path in life. I would learn several years later in graduate school that Freud identified love and work as "the cornerstones of our humanness." At the time, I felt pretty confused about both domains. My more assured peers at Princeton were destined for Wall Street, medical school, and the Peace Corps. Instead of making career plans, I was preoccupied with writing my senior thesis and plagued by questions about my own sexuality. I had wrestled with my sexual identity since adolescence, and now, on the eve of leaving the (relatively) safe confines of college, I still felt unsure about who I was or, more importantly, who I could be in the world of love.

Fortunately for me, Blair Torrey knew that I should be a teacher before I did, so questions about the world of work were answered when he invited me to teach

English at the Hotchkiss School in 1983. Teaching high school and coaching sports for four years led to a growing interest in the emotional lives of my adolescent students. I identified with their vibrancy and longings, their boldness and hesitations. When I immersed myself in counseling psychology at Teachers College, Columbia University, I quickly understood that in order to know my students deeply, I must also know myself.

It took far more time to come out as a lesbian back then than I imagine it would take me today. The first person I had to come out to was myself, which meant reworking a confusing gender and sexuality narrative that began with being "the only girl" in a family with lots of boys, and had dead-ended in grim images of lonely lesbians drinking too much in a dark New York City bar. Good therapy and the personal work of earning a degree in psychology helped me unpack and discard some of the constricting gendered expectations I had grown up with. It was still difficult to envision a fulfilling, lifelong partnership that involved family and community but that too would come with time.

Ultimately I left teaching and pursued a doctorate at Columbia. It's true that I was quite intrigued by the study of psychology at that point, but I also struggled with how to comfortably integrate my lesbian identity into my role as a classroom teacher. Leaving the classroom was my choice, yet it also felt unavoidable. Being out as a teacher in that environment did not seem possible at the time. Only now can I see my ambivalent exit from teaching as the "official" beginning of my search for understanding the role of gender and sexuality in schools. The unofficial beginning was probably my experience with Principal Grayson back at that elementary school fair (see 1971).

As any good teacher or psychologist knows, the pursuit of knowledge, the willingness to be curious, the capacity to think critically, and the ability to bring emotional intelligence to bear on all matters of the head and heart serves students of every age well. These tenets inform my current work as an educational consultant. However, there is an additional crucial component of my formal training: being a parent. Raising a son and daughter with my longtime partner for the past fifteen years helps me to empathize and identify with parents who want what is best for their children and who instinctively protect them against the unknown. Parenting is a humbling, glorious, nerve-wracking endeavor; our children need and deserve so much from us.

Writing the children's book *The Different Dragon* was absolutely inspired by my firsthand experience of reading to the kids each night and yearning for a magical tale, one with fabulous illustrations, spirited characters, singing, a bit of melodrama, and a family that looked like ours. I wanted a book that did not explain our family or defend our family, a book that was not even about our family, really. So I ended up writing one.

It is pretty exciting that *The Different Dragon* has found its way to some bedside tables and to the bookshelves in some elementary classroom libraries. Even though my wonderful publisher, Two Lives Publishing, is no longer in business, the book is now available through CreateSpace.[2] My hope is that more children's book authors will take a matter-of-fact approach to stories that include gay, lesbian, bisexual, transgender, queer, and intersex (GLBTQI)[3] people or families.

A NEW CONSTRUCT: GENDER AND SEXUALITY DIVERSITY

I have created a construct that I call **Gender and Sexuality Diversity** (GSD) to describe this "area of inquiry." GSD is a broad construct that includes everyone and recognizes the centrality of gender and sexuality in all human beings. In the school setting, everyone from the history teacher to the crossing guard to the assistant principal to the nurse have a gender and a sexuality. And these essential aspects of our identity are inherently **diverse**. The "diversity" in gender and sexuality diversity stands for **biodiversity**, the natural variation that characterizes all species on the planet. Variations in shoe size, hair color, body type, skin color, and handedness. Variations in genders and sexualities.

Recognizing this natural biodiversity is a starting point, and the GSD construct makes conversations about gender and sexuality inclusive and real. This framework has evolved and been refined by my work with hundreds of teachers, administrators, parents, and students who have shared their own questions and experiences with me over the past thirteen years. You will hear many of their stories in the pages ahead; this is their book too.

CONCERNS ABOUT DEVELOPMENTAL APPROPRIATENESS

Every teacher is concerned about conducting age-appropriate conversations and using age-appropriate materials with their students. I view such developmental considerations as a given, regardless of the topic at hand. My experience suggests that the concern about "age-appropriateness" around *this* subject matter is often driven by anxiety; teachers are worried about bringing something "sexualized" to children. In reality, you as a teacher, educator, counselor, coach, or mentor are in a position to bring desperately needed information and context to the gender and sexuality quandaries of all your students. This book will help us see that whether they are in kindergarten or eighth grade or seniors in high school, students are in the midst of developing and evolving as gendered, sexual beings, and they need the steady hand of teachers—in concert with parents—to guide them along the way.

THE CENTRAL QUESTION AND HOW TO ADDRESS IT

❖ *The school community needs a point of view on these issues. Then we all need to support this view.*[4] —fourth grade teacher

How exactly do you discover, establish, and act upon that "community point of view"? Most schools are made up of teachers, administrators, parents, and students who have shared goals, and yet, predictably, differing points of view. For example, everyone agrees that a fundamental goal for kindergartners is to successfully transition from home into the world of school. Not everyone necessarily agrees on the best way to accomplish that transition. With regard to matters of gender and sexuality in school, there can be a staggering number of differing points of view, with some even questioning the validity of gender and sexuality diversity as an "educational" issue at all. This book wades right into that swampy, ubiquitous debate. Put on your waders and come along.

ESSENTIAL FRAMEWORKS

I propose two conceptual frameworks for individual educators and whole school communities to apply to this central question and to all matters related to gender and sexuality diversity.

Framework 1: Educators must have a thorough, contemporary understanding of gender identity development (GID) and sexual identity development (SID) in children and adolescents, paying particular attention to the impact of heteronormative[5] expectations on GID and SID.

Framework 2: School mission and educational philosophy must be the central reference points for establishing policy and best "good" pedagogical practices for addressing gender and sexuality diversity. (GSD)

Answers to your questions about how to address GSD in schools can be found at the intersection of (1) your understanding of *gender identity development* and *sexual identity development* in children and adolescence, and (2) your particular *educational philosophy* as a school community (see graphic 2.1). The foundations

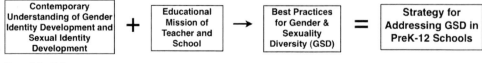

Graphic 0.1.

of human development, pedagogy, and educational values anchor this approach and are referenced repeatedly throughout this book.

CHARTING NEW TERRITORY

There is no universal or time-tested protocol available for this work. Using the frameworks proposed here, a single school, one community at a time, one district at a time, must clarify its pedagogical rationale and intention regarding the "teaching" and "learning" that relates to gender and sexuality diversity. This clarity of intention is absolutely necessary in order to navigate such complex terrain, and it will take more than an "external mandate" (e.g., upcoming accreditation review; new antibullying legislation) for members of a school community to genuinely, deeply engage in this effort. The learning process is not always comfortable but it is absolutely vital and often quite rewarding.

WHOM IS THE BOOK FOR?

I believe teachers are uniquely qualified to help students and parents learn about gender and sexuality diversity, and yet they are in a precarious position when it comes to applying their skills to this highly politicized issue. On these pages preK–12 educators will recognize their own central questions, common school-based scenarios, and the high stakes involved in determining the "right thing to do" with regard to GSD. This book provides anyone who works with children and adolescents in an educational capacity (e.g., administrators, teachers, school psychologists, coaches, preservice teachers, religious instructors, camp counselors) the concepts and tools needed to engage their students, parents, and fellow educators in productive conversations and learning about gender and sexuality diversity. I hope teachers and practitioners of all stripes will take what is relevant and useful here and apply it to their own work.

WHAT ABOUT PARENTS?

For children and adolescents, parents are the preeminent source when it comes to instilling values of all kinds. Certainly the way children view themselves, others, and the world at large is in some measure a by-product of how they were raised at home. Children benefit from a collaborative partnership between home and school on every level, and learning about gender and sexuality diversity is no exception. A vocal minority of parents insists that school is not the place for their children to see, hear, talk, or learn about their own gender and sexuality, or the gender and sexuality of others. Yet my experience affirms, year after year, that most parents are hungry for this information, because they too want to understand GSD and teach their children accordingly.

If you are a curious or concerned parent, reading this book may help you better fathom the gender and sexuality of your own child. These chapters will also shed light on the shape and scope of GSD issues at your child's school. There is a Hebrew proverb that might be helpful as you venture forth: *Do not confine your children to your own learning for they were born in another time.* This is indeed a different time that many adults are disoriented and dizzied by. It often feels as if "The Media"—whoever and whatever that is, exactly—has taken over and is influencing our children in ways that we are powerless to control.

If parents and educators avail themselves of the resources provided here, the crucial partnership between parents and school in addressing gender and sexuality diversity will be supported and fortified. When parents and teachers share conceptual frameworks and use a common "language," collaborating is easier. Even when the inevitable disagreements arise, outcomes are more productive. And as much as students are influenced by The Media, what important adults in their lives have to say matters most.

WHAT'S IN THE BOOK?

Adequate, accurate, and current information about the process of *gender identity development* (GID) and *sexual identity development* (SID) in human beings is an essential starting point in understanding school-based manifestations of gender and sexuality diversity. Thus, the book begins in chapter 1 with an examination of gender identity development and sexual identity development from biological and sociological perspectives, providing updates and challenges to our understanding of how and when children and adolescents develop these fundamental aspects of human identity. Chapter 2 examines the influence of heteronormative assumptions and expectations on these developmental processes.

Chapter 3 establishes the centrality of educational mission and school philosophy in shaping best "good" pedagogical practices for addressing gender and sexuality diversity. Chapter 4 offers a mosaic of what GSD actually looks like in the preK–12 setting. Through examining real-life scenarios, the issues and student needs in each vignette are highlighted and translated into developmental terms. Readers are invited to consider new ways of seeing these common situations. Anyone who is skeptical about the ubiquity of gender and sexuality diversity in day-to-day school life will find chapter 4 particularly revealing.

Chapter 5 identifies the learning needs of preK–12 educators in relation to gender and sexuality diversity and outlines critical approaches to their professional development. Chapter 6 looks at the GSD strategies and curricula that are best suited to early childhood and elementary education (ECEE) and chapter 7 does the same for middle school and high school education. Both chapters are full of models, sample conversations, lesson plans, and a wide array of resources. Chapter 8 profiles comprehensive sexuality education as an essential part of preK–12 school curriculum, and Chapter 9 identifies the educational programs and school policies that best support addressing gender and sexuality diversity. Chapter 10 examines the unique opportunities and challenges for GLBTQI and straight educators, with an emphasis on the intersection of personal and professional identities and teaching with the whole self. The "coming out problem" is also explored, as well as ways for colleagues to work effectively together.

CASE EXAMPLES AND QUOTATIONS

In every chapter you will find quotations and case examples taken from real life, from real people, from real schools across the country. In addition to illustrating and affirming a variety of perspectives, these quotations and cases provide opportunities for learning. There is no single right answer, no single correct approach to the questions and concerns that can arise from gender and sexuality diversity. Rather than just "going on instinct"—which in plenty of cases is a fine way to go—readers are encouraged to apply theory to practice, to apply the frameworks offered here, to try on contemporary language, explore new ways of thinking about common/complex issues, and take risks in their teaching. My hope is that this material will inspire active grappling rather than passive ingestion!

A WORD OF CAUTION; A FEW WORDS OF ENCOURAGEMENT

The first three chapters of the book are challenging, with an abundance of information, terminology, and concepts to take in. When I solicited readers for the first six chapters of this manuscript in its draft form, I was lucky enough to find willing participants in Alaska, California, Montana, Nevada, Iowa, Minnesota, and New York. To a person, they identified the demands of the initial chapters as being ultimately advantageous. The conceptual foundations established in chapters 1 through 3 permit readers to work in new ways with the case studies, lesson plans, classroom dynamics, administrative challenges, and curricular dilemmas that appear throughout the rest of the book.

Persevere, dear Reader. Press on!

WHY YOU ARE SO IMPORTANT

Children and adolescents are bombarded daily with highly gendered and sexualized messages from mercenary marketers, mainstream media, and vast, unregulated sources on the Internet. Any conversation or learning about gender and sexuality diversity that takes place in school with a thoughtful, informed, and well-trained teacher in charge is a desperately needed counterweight to what students—whether we want them to or not—are "learning" everywhere else.

Do I want Ms. Bellini to help her second graders sort out the gender stereotypes percolating under the kickball dynamics at recess? You bet, and not just by enforcing a rule that says "everyone gets to play." Do I want Classroom 2F to figure out that they can challenge gender expectations and dance or play as they like? Yes! Am I grateful that Andrew was given an opportunity to express his love of pink with his classmates and teacher? Absolutely. Because every child is unique. And whether this was Andrew's Sting Ray bike moment or not, all students need safety and affirmation in order to find themselves and flourish in school.

NOTES

1. Based on a true story. Some names and details have been changed to protect the innocent.
2. https://www.createspace.com/3557692 (Don't go to Amazon. Please.)
3. I use the GLBTQI acronym throughout the book, though the acronym appears in different configurations in quotations from other authors, scholars, and lay people. For some the ordering of these identities matters with regard to hierarchy and privilege. For others, additional identities such as Questioning are important. In my view, using this acronym is expedient at best. It allows us to conveniently identify certain people but it only minimally enhances what we really know about them.
4. Direct quotations are denoted by these symbols:

    ❖ = teachers/administrators
    ➢ = students
    ☐ = parents

5. Heteronormativity is defined and discussed at length in chapter 2. It is also in the glossary of terms.

❶

GENDER AND SEXUALITY DIVERSITY AT SCHOOL

What Educators Need to Know and Then Some

When, where, and how do gender and sexuality emerge in human beings? What do *gender identity development* and *sexual identity development* look like in preschoolers, school-age children, and adolescents? Is gender all about genetics? Sexuality all about hormones? What about the "nature versus nurture" debate? The developmental story that we are most familiar with goes like this: a particular *biological sex* determines a particular *gender identity* that, in turn, determines a particular *sexual orientation*. The End. Is this an accurate narrative? Probably not, given the importance of socialization. It is actually impossible to know anyone's entire developmental story for sure.

The language of this developmental tale is full of scientific, psychological, and sociological terminology. Some educators can define these terms and some cannot. Some educators think they know what these terms mean only to discover that somewhere in the last ten years, the definition—or the science behind the definition—has changed. So establishing a shared and accurate language[1] for discussions of gender and sexuality diversity (GSD) is a critical first step for preK–12 educators and parents.

Gender and Sexuality Diversity[2] (GSD) is a broad construct that describes the continuums of biological sex, gender identity, gender expression, sexual orientation, sexual behavior, and sexual identity. GSD recognizes that gender identity and sexual identity are essential aspects of human identity for all people, and that gender and sexuality are inherently diverse. "Diversity" refers to the concept of **biodiversity,** signifying the variety of genders and sexualities in the human species throughout the world. Thus, discussions of gay, lesbian, bisexual, transgender, queer, intersex (**GLBTQI**) identities in this book are part of the larger consideration of gender and sexuality diversity.

GSD: TERMINOLOGY, "DATA," AND CONSTRUCTS

This chapter defines the central terms and presents the primary constructs related to gender identity development (GID) and sexual identity development (SID) in children and adolescents. Grasping the inherent complexity of GID and SID requires that we

- integrate multiple sources of "data" (i.e., biology, genetics, sociology, psychology).
- understand separate yet interrelated aspects of the self (i.e., body, mind, psyche).
- challenge the **binary**[3] thesis that organizes much of our "either/or" thinking about gender and sexuality in many cultures (i.e., two sexes, two genders, two sexualities).

You can see, then, that there is much more involved here than merely learning the definitions of certain words. Having definitions that are multilayered, and "meaning" that is constantly influenced by context, reflects the shifting terrain of present-day conversations about gender and sexuality diversity.

Use the Glossaries; Refer Back Often

The "data" in this book is presented primarily through scenarios, case studies, and anecdotes. As the terms defined and the constructs reviewed here in chapter 1 "come alive" in the real-life situations described throughout the book, you may want to refer back to this chapter for clarification of terms and reminders of developmental benchmarks. If you find yourself midway through chapter 6 wondering "What is the difference between *transgender* and *queer* again?" head back to the glossary of terms, and do not be too hard on yourself. The language of gender and sexuality diversity is fluid and not always easy to assimilate.

Note: There is an extensive glossary at the end of the book, with comprehensive definitions of relevant terms. Because there are so many terms in chapter 1 that readers may or may not be familiar with, there is an abridged glossary with basic definitions at the beginning of each section in this chapter.

Voices from the Field

In addition, you will also find direct quotations from teachers, administrators, counselors, trustees, parents, and students throughout the book.[4] These quotes come primarily from the preK–12 school communities with whom I have worked. Since 1999, participants at my workshops and seminars have provided me with evaluations; I have had many verbal and Internet exchanges, and in March 2011 I gathered additional data in an online survey. Taken together these voices offer an audio mirror of the diverse opinions, concerns, and experiences in private and public school communities across the country.

The Debate over "Developmental Appropriateness"

In order to take a close look at GID and SID in students of every age, we must first understand the factors that influence our beliefs about what is truly developmentally appropriate. The multiple views on development are the by-product of academic background, professional training, selective interpretations of theories and research, and cultural values. In this chapter and throughout the book, an emphasis on **pedagogical**[5] responsibility (e.g., meeting the intellectual, social, and emotional needs of every student) can help teachers prioritize what developmentally appropriate instruction looks like—even when this view might clash with other beliefs, values, and philosophies.

Gender and Sexuality: "Nature Is a Slob"

Gender and sexuality are naturally complex and diverse elements of human identity. This chapter provides educators with the basic information they need to work with the GSD of their students, parents, families, colleagues, and communities. However, providing "basic information" does not mean there are simple answers and ready formulas for untangling the naturally occurring variance, ambiguity, patterns, and inconsistency that characterize gender and sexuality. Alice Dreger, professor of medical humanities and bioethics at Northwestern University, puts it this way: "Biology does not fit neatly into simple categories . . . science actually tells us sex is messy." She says, "Humans like categories neat, but nature is a slob" (Clarey 2009, B9).

SECTION I
GSD: DEVELOPMENTALLY APPROPRIATE PRACTICE

❖ *While talking about these issues is important, we must be sensitive at all times to developmental appropriateness.*

DEFINING DEVELOPMENTALLY APPROPRIATE PRACTICE (DAP)

Nearly every conversation about early childhood, elementary, middle, and high school pedagogy centers on the concept of **developmentally appropriate**

practice (DAP). Understanding child and adolescent development is a compulsory reference point for building educational philosophy, practice, and curricula. The "development" in DAP refers to the (1) cognitive, (2) physical, (3) social, and (4) psychological aspects of the child. However, despite this standard definition, there is much debate about what is developmentally appropriate in relation to gender and sexuality diversity (GSD) in the context of preK–12 schooling. Consider these varying perspectives from elementary and middle school teachers:

- ❖ *Kids are thinking about sexuality at a much younger age than we want to accept.*
- ❖ *It seems a bit ridiculous to address sexuality in kindergarten.*
- ❖ *It is important to talk about gender/sex at a young age, before opinions are fully formed.*
- ❖ *I worry that elementary students are not mature enough to accept and consider this topic.*
- ❖ *We have a Gay Straight Alliance in our middle school—is this too young?*
- ❖ *How do we deal with the widely varying perceptions of "readiness" in the school? Many people believe young kids are just not ready for discussions about gender and sexuality.*

In truth there are no purely objective measures to assess readiness for this topic, or any other for that matter. As a result, our beliefs about "appropriateness" and "readiness" are often driven by history and culture, rather than by sound, research-based understanding. Historically, teachers have *not* been trained or encouraged to explicitly engage with the gender and sexuality of their students. In the fall of 2010, when I asked a group of one hundred and twenty preK–8 teachers at a progressive independent school in New York City how many had received specific training in this area, six people raised their hands. At many schools, fewer hands than that go up.

For the teacher who deems a conversation about sexuality with kindergartners "a bit ridiculous," it is likely that she imagines **sexual behavior** will be part of the discussion, rather than conversations about love, relationships, and configurations of different families. The teacher who worries that elementary students are not mature enough to consider GSD must not be familiar with the questions fourth graders pose when given permission to ask about sexuality (see chapter 4, p. 100). The administrator who is concerned that middle school students are "too young" for a Gay Straight Alliance lacks a basic understanding of (1) when gender identity development (GID) and sexuality identity development (SID) begin, and (2) where eleven- to fourteen-year-olds are in that developmental process.

Gender/Sexuality Terms and Definitions: Section I

comprehensive sexuality education
program that provides children and adolescents with comprehensive information about human sexuality, from abstinence to birth control. The goal is help students make healthy choices in relation to their sexuality.

gender
a socially constructed system of classification that ascribes qualities of *masculinity* and *femininity* to people. Gender characteristics can change over time and are different between cultures. Gender is not the same as *biological sex*, though the two are often conflated with each other.

gender expression
the way people externally communicate their *gender identity* to others through behavior, clothing, hairstyle, voice, and so on.

gender identity
our innermost concept of self as male, female, queer— what we perceive and call ourselves.

gender identity development
a process of determining and consolidating one's gender identity, manifest first in toddlerhood, continuing through adulthood. Actual development of GI likely begins prior to toddlerhood.

gender roles
the set of roles and behaviors assigned to females and males by a given society.

sexual behavior
what one actually does sexually. Sexual behavior is usually, but not always, consistent with one's *sexual identity* and *sexual orientation*.

sexual orientation
traditionally defined as the direction of one's sexual attraction to the same sex (homosexual), the opposite sex (heterosexual), both men and women (bisexual), or any sexual identity (pansexual). Asexual describes those who have no sexual attraction.

sexuality
a broad construct that refers to the totality of sexual identity, orientation, and behavior.

sexual identity
how we view ourselves sexually; what we call ourselves (e.g., gay, bi, queer, straight).

sexual identity development
a process of determining and consolidating one's sexual identity that is manifest first in early childhood and continues through adulthood.

Fear and Research

There is a long-standing fear that discussions between teachers and students about gender and sexuality will "sexualize" innocent young children. In reality, children are sexualized by marketers interested in selling products of all kinds, not by elementary school teachers (Lamb, Brown, and Tappan 2009; *Sexy* 2007; Lamb and Brown 2007). When it comes to middle and high school, people still cling to the mistaken contention that **comprehensive sexuality education (CSE)**[6] leads to premature sexual activity. Numerous studies conducted under the science-based-research guidelines of No Child Left Behind (NCLB) demonstrate that, in fact, comprehensive sexuality education actually delays sexual experimentation and reduces high-risk sexual behaviors (SIECUS 2010; Oster 2008; Hayes and Walters 2007; American Psychological Association 2005).

It is clear, then, that many of the practices that have been deemed developmentally "inappropriate" for preK–12 students are based not on valid data but on fear and misinformation. These erroneous ideas about what children are "ready for" have circulated long enough and often enough that they have become unquestioned "facts." We should not be surprised then, that teachers who avoid this material and redirect GSD issues believe they are acting in the best interests of their students.

Cultural Diversity Dilemmas

The varying perceptions of developmental readiness that educators and parents have are also clearly influenced by cultural beliefs and values related to GSD. Review these teacher comments.

❖ *What about those families for whom issues of gender and sexuality bring up religious conflicts?*

❖ *We have to help our students become responsible citizens in diverse communities beyond our walls.*

❖ *I don't want to exclude other forms of diversity. In other words, this shouldn't take center stage over race, religion, ethnicity, etc.*

❖ *The school should not embrace these controversies but rather develop a tolerance for all types of diversity.*

❖ *It might be helpful for parents to have a workshop like this. Then again, that might open a "can of worms."*

Within different ethnicities, races, religions, and regions of the United States, there is a wide range of attitudes toward the different elements of GSD:

- gender
- gender expression

- gender roles
- sexuality
- sexual orientation
- sexual relationships
- sexual behavior
- family configuration
- family roles

Clashing religious beliefs and conflicting cultural norms can indeed be a "can of worms" when it comes to attitudes toward GSD. Teachers try to work equitably with every student and every family, yet are understandably confused about when "values" and "ideology" should or should not outweigh what is known to be a developmental "truth."

> What formal sources influence your professional understanding of developmentally appropriate practice?
>
> In what ways might your own personal and/or cultural values influence your professional beliefs about developmentally appropriate practice?

Pedagogical Responsibility

As you read the science and theory that follows, remember that educators are in a unique position to provide accurate information and facilitate thoughtful conversations about all the different aspects of self that children bring in to school every single day. If there is a philosophical and pedagogical commitment to working with the whole child (i.e., attending to cognitive, social, and emotional development), then educators must be prepared to work with their students' gender and sexuality at every grade level. Whether they are watching family films, prime time television, commercials, print ads, or music videos, children and adolescents are repeatedly exposed to hazardous media portrayals of just about anything having to do with gender, sexuality, and intimate relationships. The most effective strategy for countering media messages is for parents and teachers to educate young people about gender and sexuality diversity at every opportunity.

WHAT TO REMEMBER: SECTION I

Gender and Sexuality Diversity and Developmentally Appropriate Practice

1. There are many different views about developmentally appropriate practice (DAP) in relation to gender and sexuality in preK–12 schooling.

    a. In addition to scientific understanding, determining developmentally appropriate practice (DAP) is influenced by history, culture, and values.

    b. Teachers lack specific training in determining DAP as it relates to gender and sexuality diversity.

2. The fear that elementary teachers will "sexualize" their students is misplaced. Media and marketing promote the sexualization of children; teachers do not.

3. Some educators continue to ignore research-based evidence that comprehensive sexuality education is

    a. developmentally appropriate.

    b. an effective way to delay sexual experimentation and reduce high-risk sexual behaviors.

4. The pedagogical responsibility of working with the cognitive, social, and emotional development of all students requires that teachers address gender and sexuality diversity at every grade level.

SECTION II
(BIOLOGICAL) SEX:
DEFINING THE TERMS; LEARNING THE LANGUAGE; GRASPING THE CONCEPTS

Gender/Sexuality Terms and Definitions: Section II	
affirmed gender	a classification based on an individual's gender identity, which may be different/separate from assigned birth sex.
assigned birth sex	a classification ("it's a boy"/"it's a girl") based on reproductive anatomy and physiology.
biological sex	the biological state of having (1) female or male genitalia, (2) female (XX) or male (XY) chromosomes, and (3) a mixture of hormones: estrogen, progesterone, and testosterone.
female	one of the two recognized, primary biological sexes.
gene	a segment of DNA; a unit of heredity.
intersex	a range of physiological conditions in which a person is born with reproductive and/or sexual anatomy that do not conform to binary definitions of female or male biological sex.
male	one of the two recognized, primary biological sexes.
reproductive sex organs	internal and external parts of the body that are involved in reproduction, e.g., penis, vagina, uterus, testicles, ovaries.

sex	the identification of biological and assigned sex.
"sex" hormones	hormones associated with uterine development of sex and gender (estrogen, progesterone, testosterone). A contested term.
sex reassignment surgery	surgical procedures that modify one's primary and/or secondary sex characteristics.
surgical correction	refers to an increasingly contested early treatment option for intersex individuals born with ambiguous genitalia.
transsexual	individuals who does not identify with their birth-assigned gender and alter their body hormonally and/or surgically.

An assortment of words that come from a variety of sources, including science, medicine, sociology, psychology, literature, and popular culture, make up the lexicon of gender and sexuality. Having a basic grasp of the language is a significant step toward being able to think intelligently and communicate sensitively about GSD issues. The student who says of her teachers, "*I get mis-gendered all the time. I don't think anybody has a clue that this isn't about sexual orientation*," expresses the way that being seen and identified accurately is fundamental to one's experience in the world.

BIOLOGICAL SEX

Though *sex* and *gender* are often used interchangeably in common discourse, these terms are not synonymous. **Sex** or **biological sex** is determined by three factors:

1. Internal and external **reproductive sex organs** (e.g., ovaries, testes, penis, vagina, uterus)
2. **Genes** (XX chromosomes for females, XY chromosomes for males)
3. **Hormones**[7] (estrogen, progesterone, testosterone)

In Western culture we recognize two primary biological sexes, **male** and **female**. At birth, the majority of infants are labeled male or female by virtue of the clear external appearance of a penis or vagina. Yet, without special testing, we cannot know the exact chromosomal makeup of an infant at birth. We do not know whether a full complement of reproductive sex organs exist, nor do we know the combination and levels of various hormones present. It is based on appearance alone that most of us are declared female or male.

Intersex[8]

A small percentage of infants are born with ambiguous or combined external female and male genitals; medical professionals typically **assign** these intersex individuals a sex/gender at birth. This assignment is based on a perceived cultural need to be either a male or a female, and surgical correction is often performed not out of medical necessity but to achieve a clear gender identity (see section III). Genetic testing and an assessment of internal sex organs can provide additional information about the "maleness" or "femaleness" of the infant, yet the surgical procedure—to create a vagina or penis—can still be based on appearance alone and/or by inconsistent standards (Karkazis 2008).

> What impact does recognizing only two dominant sex categories have on certain individuals? If there is no medical risk involved in an intersex condition, is "surgical correction" necessary? What exactly is being "corrected"?
>
> What stops us as a culture from recognizing nonpathological variation within the biological sex category?

It is also possible to have an intersex condition that is not readily detectable, as some intersex people are born with "normal" external genitalia. For some the discovery of having an intersex condition occurs in adulthood and coincides with a manifest irregularity related to reproductive sex organs (e.g., infertility) or when an outside authority requests testing (see What Makes a Woman a Woman?).

What Makes a Woman a Woman?

At age eighteen South African athlete Caster Semenya won a gold medal in the 800 meters at the 2009 World Championships in Athletics and was immediately subjected to sex-determination testing by the I.A.A.F., the governing body of Track and Field. Claims were made, based on Semenya's masculine appearance and outstanding performance, that she was not biologically female. Competitors protested. One said, "These kind of people should not run with us. For me, she is not a woman. She is a man" (Clarey 2009, B9).

Prior to this international incident Semenya's sex was regularly questioned at track competitions; she grew accustomed to visiting the bathroom prior to a race with a member of the opposing team. She would pull down her shorts to show her external female genitals and thereby verify her sex/gender. The I.A.A.F. testing ultimately revealed that Semenya has no uterus or ovaries, and has a pair of undescended testes. Alice Dreger, a professor of medical humanities and bioethics at Northwestern University, commented on Semenya's case, "There isn't really one simple way to sort out males and females. Sports require that we do, but biology doesn't care. Biology does not fit neatly into simple categories" (Clarey 2009, B9).

After almost a year "testing" the I.A.A.F. ruled that Semenya could compete as a woman (Clarey 2010), but have now enacted a new policy that Semenya and other females whose functional testosterone and androgen levels are in the typical male range must have their levels chemically "adjusted" to be in the typical female range. To date, there has been no call for male athletes with above average functional hormone levels to undergo this regulation process, which Dreger calls "biochemical policing" (Dreger 2011).

Transsexual

Transsexual is the term for those whose gender identity (see section III) does not match their biological or assigned birth sex[9] and who undergo physical changes through the use of hormones and/or reconstructive surgery (**sex reassignment surgery**). Hormones and surgery allow a transsexual person to live as the biological sex and **affirmed gender** with which they identify (see From James to Jenny). It is important to note that these medical interventions are extremely expensive, not typically covered by insurance, and not available in certain parts of the country. Therefore, not all people who wish to physically and hormonally change their sex and gender in this manner can do so.

From James to Jenny

In her 2003 best-selling memoir, She's Not There: A Life in Two Genders, *Jennifer Finney Boylan recounts her experience of growing up biologically male yet identifying as female. For forty years Boylan lived as a man, successfully authored several books, fathered two children and served as the chair of the English Department at Colby College.* She's Not There *chronicles her transition psychologically and physically, including sex reassignment surgery, from James Boylan to Jenny Boylan.* She's Not There *is in its eighth printing and in addition to her professorship at Colby, Boylan speaks internationally about transgender and transsexual issues. www.jenniferboylan.net.*

WHAT TO REMEMBER: SECTION II

Biological Sex

1. **Biological sex** and **gender** are not the same.
2. Biological sex = reproductive sex organs + chromosomes + hormones.
   a. There is more variability in biological sex than commonly acknowledged.
   b. There is variance within each (female, male, intersex) sex category.
   c. Variance does not necessarily indicate deviance or pathology.

3. **Intersex** is a condition characterized by ambiguous or combined external and/or internal reproductive sex organs.

   a. Surgically correcting **intersex** conditions and **assigning** a gender at birth is a highly contested and potentially damaging protocol that is still practiced by some medical professionals in the United States at present.

4. A **transsexual** person is an individual whose gender identity does not match his or her biological or assigned birth sex and who undergoes medical treatment (e.g., hormones, surgery) in order to live in his or her affirmed sex and gender.

SECTION III
GENDER:
DEFINING THE TERMS; LEARNING THE LANGUAGE; GRASPING THE CONCEPTS

One is born with a body that is immediately ascribed a male or female identity (usually on the basis of fairly unambiguous physiological evidence, the possession of a penis or vagina) but one becomes a man or a woman through social interactions within a set of cultural understandings about femininity and masculinity. (Bradley 2007, 21)

Gender/Sexuality Terms and Definitions: Section III

androgynous	having both male and female characteristics.
cisgender	a term describing individuals whose gender identity and gender expression match their biological and assigned birth sex. A cisgender person is someone who is *not* transgender.
continuum of genders	a way of describing more than two genders.
continuum of masculinities/ femininities	a way of describing more than two discreet forms of gender expression.
femininity	commonly understood to refer to a collection of qualities or attributes associated with women, as distinct from men; what qualities qualify as feminine is subject to debate, as is whether such qualities should be considered innate essences or cultural norms.
gender identity instruction	the conscious and unconscious ways that teachers, parents, media teach children the "right" way to "be" a particular gender.

genderqueer	a rejection of the gender binary (man/woman) in favor of a more fluid, nontraditional gender identity.
gender variant	a more contemporary term to describe those whose gender identity or expression differ from cultural expectations based on biological sex; it is increasingly applied to gender nonconforming children who may or may not develop a transgender identity. Gender variance does *not* indicate pathology.
masculinity	commonly understood to refer to a collection of qualities or attributes associated with men, as distinct from women; what qualities qualify as masculine is subject to debate, as is whether such qualities should be considered innate essences or cultural norms.
socialization	the process by which people are taught or made to behave in a way that is acceptable to their society.
trans	often used as substitute for transgender but it can also be used to include other gender identities, such as genderqueer and two spirit.
transgender	a broad term describing the continuum of individuals whose gender identity or gender expression, to varying degrees, do not conform to stereotypical masculine or feminine norms. Also used to describe those whose gender identity does not match their biological sex.
two spirit	in Native American culture, this term generally means a person born with one biological sex who fulfills at least some of the gender roles assigned to both sexes; considered part male, part female.

GENDER IDENTITY

Birth sex is a by-product of anatomy, genetics, and biology. **Gender** is a broad construct that places those "sexed bodies" into discreet categories, most commonly *girl/woman/feminine*, or *boy/man/masculine*. Psychologist and sexologist John Money introduced the modern term "gender" in the 1950s in relation to his study of intersex individuals (Rosin 2008; Colapinto 2001). Because his subjects could not be readily classified as male or female, Money wanted to investigate the development of their gender in relation to

1. individual expression
2. self-identification

3. social patterns
4. relational characteristics

Eventually Money sought to prove that after genital surgery, **socialization** could successfully shape gender identity development (GID). If parents raised their child in the **surgically assigned gender** (see "Correcting" and "Assigning" Gender), the child would develop a congruent, healthy **gender identity**.

Money's theory of "socialization over biology" has been roundly discredited in the past twenty years (Blakemore, Berenbaum, and Liben 2009; Colapinto 2001), yet his thinking influenced decades of treatment of gender and sexual disorders, and his legacy continues to this day. What we know is that the interplay between and among **biological, psychological,** and **social factors** determine the various aspects of gender. The debate about whether gender is "naturally" versus "culturally" determined is specious and harmful, as if it could be one without the other.

"Correcting" and "Assigning" Gender

What slowly began to dawn on me, however, as I did some research on the subject, was that all the other surgeries I had gone through were unnecessary; they were the consequence of the scar tissue produced by the first surgery I underwent. Worse, that first surgery was fundamentally cosmetic. It was not presented as a cosmetic option, however, but rather as a necessary correction—a surgical fixing of gender, and of a sexed body, that might otherwise remain ambiguous, and thus disturbing, at least to some. The assumption was that it would be more traumatic to leave the body unchanged than it would be to endure the surgeries and scarring.

—Christopher Breu, "Middlesex Meditations:
Understanding and Teaching Intersex"

Gender identity (GI) is the way we feel and view ourselves as a particular gender. Because American culture is built on binary notions of gender, there are only two commonly accepted gender identities: **girl/woman** and **boy/man**. In reality, gender identities exist on a continuum. There are people who identify as

- a woman
- a man
- a combination of woman and man
- something in between woman and man
- something other than woman or man

There is historical evidence that this range of identities has existed across cultures and throughout time (*Middle Sexes* 2008), yet it is only in the recent past in the

United States that modern terms such as **transgender**, **two spirit** (see Excerpts from Documentary Film), and **genderqueer** have emerged to describe a variety of gender identities.

Excerpts from Documentary Film *Two Spirits* by Lydia Nibley

In Navajo teaching, in the old, traditional world, there were four basic genders. The first one was that women are the first gender because Navajo is a matrilineal society. Men is the second gender. And the third gender is the Nadleehi, born as a male person but functions in the role of a girl in early childhood. And functions more in the role of a woman in adulthood. And it's just the opposite for the fourth gender, where they were born biologically female, but function in the role of a boy in early childhood and matured into a man, and conducts their life in that gender identity.

—Wesley Thomas

The masculine and feminine together are sometimes reflected so completely in the body of one person that it's as if they have two spirits.

—Richard LaFortune

Transgender Identity

Transgender is a term used to describe those who adopt a range of behaviors associated with the "other" or different biological sex, and who, in some manner, transcend their assigned gender (Blakemore et al. 2009). For example, people can

- wear clothes associated with a different sex.
- adopt a grooming style associated with a different sex.
- participate in activities primarily associated with a different sex.
- change to a name associated with a different sex.
- undergo medical treatments (e.g., hormones, surgery) to acquire physical characteristics of a different sex (this is associated with transsexual identity).

Not surprisingly, such a broad definition leads to misunderstanding and misinterpretation of what transgender may mean in a particular instance. Additionally, there is enormous variety among those who identify as transgender. Some transgender people embrace traditional forms of gender and subscribe to conventional definitions of masculinity and femininity. For others, identifying as trans is a way to challenge, subvert, or expand traditional gender categories (Meyer 2010).

Gender variant is the current term used by many professionals in medicine, psychology, and education to describe children who have a persistent pattern of **gender expression** that is nonstereotypical. However, categorizing children who express their gender in a natural and fluid way with a label that connotes pathology seems inherently biased. The term *variant* is an accurate descriptor, and reflects an essential concept in terms of the biodiversity of the human species, yet its application in this context is problematic. It implies "deviation" from an accepted "norm." In this case, the norm is restrictive and does not allow for the type of variation that is not only predictable but (should be) acceptable.

Gender variant preschool and early elementary age children may not have language or be given language to describe this aspect of their identity in a more fluid way. Even in these early years of development, narrow perceptions of "normal" gender dominate; "variations" are often corrected and behaviors redirected. While a small percentage of gender variant children may ultimately identify as transgender, most do not (Brill and Pepper 2008).

Transgender children and teens. Current treatment protocols (see Additional Resource 1.1) for those children who are transgender include allowing them to live full-time, at home and at school, in their preferred gender (Brill and Pepper 2008). As the child matures a decision can be made about whether to use hormones to block the onset of puberty. Transgender teens who are forced to endure puberty in their nonaffirmed gender suffer significant adverse psychological consequences. Hormone blocking also permits more time for the teen and family to engage in intensive psychological counseling and testing before making a permanent decision to undergo a hormonally induced gender transition (Children's Hospital Boston 2010; Brill and Pepper 2008).

> How can schools recognize and integrate intersex, gender variant, transgender, and transsexual students, teachers, and parents into the preK–12 community? What is the pedagogical risk in recognizing the spectrum of gender identities?

GENDER IDENTITY DEVELOPMENT (GID)

Gender identity is strongly influenced by biological sex and begins to emerge in the first year of life. Given that a majority of biological females develop a gender identity of girl/woman and a majority of biological males develop a gender identity of boy/man, some conclude that gender identity is naturally determined by biological sex alone (Blakemore et al. 2009). There is a wealth of research, however, that demonstrates the sizable impact of socialization on GID, in every culture around the world (Blakemore et al. 2009; see Lessons from the Samoan Fa'afafine'). It is the interplay between (a) the genes, sex organs, and hormones we are born with and (b) how we are raised culturally that determines (c) who we are and (d) how we live in the world (diagram 1.1).

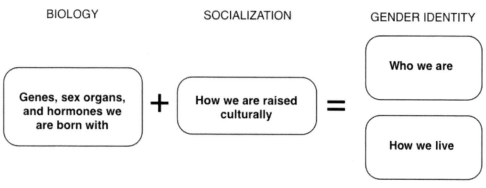

Diagram I.I.

Lessons from the Samoan Fa'afafine'

The question of whether gender-atypical behavior causes inherent distress (one of the diagnostic criterion for gender identity disorder in the DSM-IV) or is the by-product of social condemnation, led Vasey and Bartlett (2007) to study the Samoan Fa'afafine'. The word fa'afafine *means "in the manner of woman" and is used to describe biological males who identify as men and whose gender expression is predominantly feminine.*

In this Samoan culture, where there is a high degree of social tolerance for and acceptance of feminine males, the Fa'afafine' do not experience distress, nor is their behavior considered unacceptable or disordered. There is no "category" in Samoan culture that correlates with the Western concept of "gay." The Fa'afafine' have sex with men who, in Western terms, would be seen as bisexual. In this particular environment, it is not socially incompatible for a Fa'afafine' to have a penis, to identify as a man, and to have sex with straight men and live in the manner of a woman.

Are You a Boy or a Girl?

Most children can identify themselves, and others, as a boy or a girl by the age of two; this "knowledge" is communicated externally by the toddler through language and/or gestures. Yet an internal experience of gender likely begins in infancy. What we know at present is that gender development is not linear, and not the by-product of a single domain of influence (Trautner et al. 2005; Ruble et al. 2007; Blakemore et al. 2009). It is a dynamic and evolving process.

GID is characterized by (1) a process of shifting gendered behaviors and gender-related attitudes and (2) periods of greater fluidity or rigidity. It is also influenced by age and environment. Students of every age manifest this dynamic developmental process every day of their lives, and as a result, teachers bear witness to the biological, psychological, social, and environmental matrix of gender identity development all the time at school.

The nature vs. nurture trap.   We cannot determine how much of the toddler's emerging gender identity is innate and how much is being shaped by external influences. Asking "How much of this? How much of that?" does not really further our understanding of GID in children. Rather, asking *In what ways does socialization impact GID?* points us in the direction of multiple processes whereby adults explicitly and implicitly teach, shape, direct, and acculturate children in relation to the child's own gender identity, and the gender identity of others.

Gender Identity "Instruction" (GII)

Parents, teachers, and other primary caregivers are crucial reference points as the child absorbs social cues about who and how to be in terms of gender. From the clothes they are dressed in, to toys they are given, to the way they are lined up for P.E., children are constantly immersed in what I call **gender identity instruction (GII)**. For example:

- A boy wearing pink crocs is teased; the teacher intervenes, affirming the boy's right to wear pink if he wants to.
- A girl who has been excluded from the boys' stickball game is encouraged by her teacher to join the girls who are jumping rope instead.
- The girls' cheerleading coach negotiates the "style" of the squad's uniform in the direction of something less "provocative."
- The head of the science department okays an advanced independent chemistry project led by two girls.
- Football players running laps are berated by the coach who tells them they look like "a bunch of girls."

Teachers consciously and unconsciously engage in GII with students every day.

> If a biological boy feels himself to be a girl, yet is perceived by everyone else as a boy, what is his gender identity?
>
> What changes can schools make to create greater acceptance and safety for gender nonconforming children and adolescents?

GENDER EXPRESSION

People communicate gender in various ways, including through their mannerisms, clothing, body language, hairstyle, behavior, and tone of voice. These external behaviors express an internal sense of gender identity and are typically labeled

masculine, **feminine**, or **androgynous**. These labels are cultural assignments, and it is not clear whether labeling child care as a "feminine" activity, for example, is **descriptive** or **prescriptive**. Is investment banking something men "naturally" do and is therefore labeled a masculine profession, or is there a cultural *prescription* that men should be in charge of the financial world and therefore investment banking is "masculine"? Consider the example in "Men Who Change Diapers and Men Who Don't."

Men Who Change Diapers and Men Who Don't

In his study of gender meanings and practices, Gutman (1996) found that economic changes in Mexico City impacted gender roles and perceptions of masculinity and femininity. In certain lower-class families, women found work outside the home and men assumed childcare duties. This economic necessity influenced the acceptability of men engaging in the traditionally "feminine" job of caring for children. Within their own community culture, these working class fathers were not seen as men who were "less than" because of "carrying their babies." However, men in the upper social classes did attach a feminizing stigma to any male who does women's work.

There is a bedrock cultural expectation that one's **gender expression** will reflect one's gender identity which reflects one's biological sex. For example, a biological male should identify as a man and behave in a culturally prescribed masculine manner. The binary framing of sex and gender denies not only a continuum of biological and gender identities but also a **continuum of femininities and masculinities.** Culturally driven ascriptions of masculine and feminine to certain activities and roles are unquestioned by many and resisted by some.

The Rules for Girls and Boys (Women and Men)

Our expectation of gender expression as being "one or the other" (i.e., not masculine and feminine alternately, or integrated) results in our rejection in boys and men that which we call femininity. To a lesser degree, we censure expressions of that which we call masculinity in girls and women. Remember Ms. Bellini and Classroom 2F (from the introduction)? The list of "What Boys Do" and "What Girls Do" is a convincing example of the degree to which second graders have already corralled and categorized acceptable expressions of femininity and masculinity (see also "The Story of the Pink Monkey").

The Story of the Pink Monkey

It's time to go pick up her older brother at school. Claire, age five, has been playing with her stuffed animal, which is a bright pink monkey. According to Claire, Monkey is a boy, and on this particular occasion she has him in a dress that she has borrowed from a stuffed bear. When it is time to get in the car, Claire takes the dress off Monkey and leaves the dress behind.

Didn't Monkey want to wear the dress to pickup? *I ask.*

No.

How come?

He didn't want to.

Was he embarrassed about the dress?

Yup.

Boys can wear dresses if they want to, you know.

They can? *Claire is surprised, and skeptical, because as a five-year-old, her cognitive development is beginning to allow for a clearer perception of reality versus fantasy. In reality, she's never seen a single boy wear a dress to pickup at her brother's school. She is protecting Monkey from the ridicule he is sure to endure if he's seen in a dress.*

GENDER SOCIALIZATION/GENDER ROLES

For children and adolescents, gender identity development and gender expression are part and parcel of everyday life. Children learn from the moment they join the culture that gender identity and expressions of masculinity and femininity are linked to certain social roles. In imaginary play and dress-up young children try on different social identities and **gender roles**. Daddies shave like this; Grandmas wear hats like that. Tia Felicia bakes peanut butter cookies, and Uncle Romeo sharpens knives and carves the turkey. Men are pilots; women are nurses (see Gender Role Socialization: A Study of Gender and Jobs).

Gender Role Socialization: A Study of Gender and Jobs

Early and pervasive gender identity instruction impacts not only the individual child but also the broader social milieu. Wilbourn and Kee's (2010) research on children's perception of gender and various occupations reveals how early and deeply children learn the rules about (1) appropriate gender roles for men and women and (2) what the gendered world of work should, or does, look like. Eight- and nine-year-olds completed several tasks (e.g., memorization, sentence completion) with stereotypical pairings of the following categories as prompts:

- male names and male occupations (e.g., Frank, plumber)
- female names and female occupations (e.g., Debbie, housewife)
- and nonstereotypical pairings (e.g., James, babysitter; Susan, auto mechanic)

Results showed that the students (1) had more difficulty recalling nonstereotypical pairings, (2) took longer to create sentences using nonstereotypical pairings, and (3) distorted the research prompt or changed the nonstereotypical pairings to fit with conventional norms. The conscious and unconscious reflection and reinforcement of "traditional" gender norms is clear.

- **Julie, Police Officer:** *Julian the police officer fights crime.*
- **James, Babysitter:** *James the babysitter likes babysitting because she likes kids.*
- **Henry, Nurse:** *Henry the nurse is a children's doctor.*
- **Patricia, Janitor**: *Patricia the janitor is a pretty janitor.*

Gendered Job Roles; Gendered Values

Research consistently reveals how early in life children learn (1) to value males over females, (2) to attribute more power and importance to masculine traits over feminine qualities, and (3) to perceive boys and men as having more agency than girls and women in the world of work and elsewhere (Wilbourn and Kee 2010). Vocational development, the process by which people chose occupations and their life's work, begins during play in childhood as children pretend to be a mail carrier, a veterinarian, or the captain of a sailing ship (Hartung, Porfeli, and Vondrack 2008). This early role-playing sows the seeds of perceptions about what is possible for girls and boys later in life in the world of work.

Gender Role Models

Late elementary kids and adolescents also "try on" different roles and styles, turning to celebrities, fashion models, professional athletes, rappers, and pop stars for cues about how men and women "do" masculinity and femininity. Marketers of fashion, toys, and gear populate and dominate consumer culture with grossly exaggerated images of femininity and masculinity. Whether it is through parenting, schooling, media, or marketing, children and adolescents have their gendered behaviors mirrored and affirmed—or discouraged and redirected—all the time.

Rigidity or flexibility: Does it matter? Educators and parents have been influenced over the past fifty years by biological, social learning, and cognitive learning theories of gender socialization and gender roles. Some theories emphasize the "hardwired" conceptualization of gender role development, and others underscore the importance of environmental factors (Blakemore et al. 2009). Studies indicate that when children are raised or taught in an environment that supports flexible gender expression and gender roles, kids tend to demonstrate greater flexibility at every age (see The Story of Two Boys and Nail Polish). A more rigid environment produces more stereotypical expressions of gender (Davies 2004). Yet such generalizations are helpful only up to a point; one of the hallmarks of biodiversity is that there are always variations and exceptions to most "rules."

The Story of Two Boys and Nail Polish

Two eight-year-old boys are kicking the soccer ball in the back yard.

First Boy: Is it okay that I'm wearing nail polish?

Second Boy: Where did you get it?

First Boy: My sister painted her nails and then she painted mine. She painted my mom's and dad's too.

Second Boy: Really? Your dad too?

First Boy: He kind of liked it.

Second Boy: What color is it?

First Boy: It's kind of a silver-gray.

Second Boy: (Pause) Yeah, that's okay.

As an educator, how does your own gender identity and gender expression influence your work with students?

Do the students "see" your gender as you want them to? What gender roles do you model intentionally? Inadvertently?

What assumptions do you make about your students based on their gender identity and gender expression?

Gender "Norms" and Consequences in School

Gender expression and gender roles are fixed for some and more fluid for others; this is true for children, adolescents, and adults. Many school-age children express their gender largely in accord with societal expectations; those who do not, however, are frequently teased and bullied, experiencing confusion, shame, and anxiety as they discover that something fundamental about who they are is unacceptable. For adolescents who live outside the boundaries of acceptable gender expectations, physical, psychological, and sexual harassment are the norm (see diagram 1.2). In the 2009 GLSEN survey almost half of all transgender students reported missing at least one day of school in the past month due to feeling unsafe (Greytak, Kosciw, and Diaz 2009). These are among the students whose physical and emotional safety is at greatest risk in middle and high school settings.

The ultimate consequence. The killing of college student Mathew Shepard in 1998 drew national attention to the lethality of hate crimes against GLBTQI adults. Ten years later the murder of eighth grader Larry King offers stark evidence that gender- and sexuality-based violence may now be a part of middle school life. Prior to the shooting, King had begun dressing in women's clothing and wearing makeup, which prompted bullying from a group of male students. King also told people he was gay. "'They teased him because he was different,' said Marissa Moreno, thirteen, also in the eighth grade. 'But he wasn't afraid to show

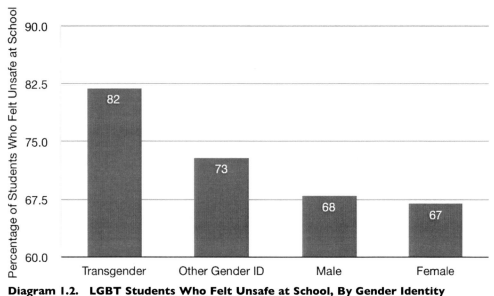

Diagram 1.2. LGBT Students Who Felt Unsafe at School, By Gender Identity
Data compiled from the 2006-2007 GLSEN National Climate Survey, which sampled 6,209 LGBT Students, grades 6-12,
as presented in the GLSEN report *Harsh Realities: The Experience of Transgender Youth in Our Nation's Schools* (Greytak,
Kosciw, and Diaz 2009).

himself'" (Cathcart 2008). Brandon McInerney, the classmate who shot King, is currently standing trail as an adult. Prosecutors have added a hate crime allegation, arguing that McInerney's actions were partially motivated by his alleged neo-Nazi sympathies (Saillant 2011).

The multiple functions of "gender" in the school setting may be difficult to fully grasp. When does the play toy a boy or girl chooses become a stepping stone to future professional aspirations? Is sitting boy-girl-boy-girl in class reinforcing "differences" that could be damaging to some children? When does a boy wearing nail polish as part of his gender expression become a rationale for peer violence? These are not simple questions, yet a broad, accurate understanding of "what gender is" will serve you well as you search for answers.

WHAT TO REMEMBER: SECTION III

Gender

1. **Gender** is a broad social construction that organizes identity, expression, and roles.
    a. There are two commonly accepted genders, girl/woman and boy/man.
    b. Some people (e.g., genderqueer) do not identify as girl/woman or boy/man.
2. **Gender identity** is the way one views oneself as woman, man, transgender, two spirit, genderqueer, or something else.

    a. Transgender describes those who adopt a range of behaviors associated with the "other" or different biological sex, and who, in some manner, transcend their assigned gender.

    b. Gender variant describes children whose gender expression is fluid and variable. Gender variance is not a sign of pathology. A very small percentage of gender variant children and teens end up being transgender.

3. **Gender identity development** is influenced by the interplay among biological, environmental, and social factors.

    a. Toddlers begin explicitly articulating gender identity around the age of two, but it is likely that an internal experience of gender begins sooner than that.

    b. Gender identity "instruction" refers to the socialization process by which children are instructed (explicitly and implicitly) about acceptable behaviors for boys and girls.

4. **Gender role** is the social expectation and demand that one should behave in a certain way based on gender identity.

    a. In environments that have fewer rigid expectations, children express their gender more expansively and flexibly.

    b. School-age children engage in a kind of "career identity development," establishing strong ideas about acceptable jobs and careers based on gender.

5. **Gender expression** is the external communication of gender identity through dress, manner, voice, style, and behavior.

    a. Children who express their gender in nonstereotypical ways are frequently subjected to teasing and bullying, and suffer social rejection.

    b. Adolescents who express their gender in nonstereotypical ways are among the most at-risk students in terms of physical, psychological, and sexual safety in school.

SECTION IV
SEXUALITY:
DEFINING THE TERMS; LEARNING THE LANGUAGE;
GRASPING THE CONCEPTS

Gender/Sexuality Terms and Definitions: Section IV

asexual   sexual orientation of an individual who does not feel sexual attraction or sexual desire.

bisexual   sexual orientation for an individual whose romantic, emotional, and sexual attractions and connections are with both males and females.

continuum of sexual orientation	a way of describing more than two sexual orientations.
gay	an adjective describing an individual whose primary romantic, emotional, and sexual attractions and connections are with someone of the same sex. Specifically refers to men; also used as an umbrella term to describe all people with same-sex attractions.
heterosexuality	sexual, emotional, and/or romantic attraction to a biological sex other than one's own.
homosexuality	sexual, emotional, and/or romantic attraction to someone of the same biological sex.
lesbian	a woman who feels romantically, emotionally, and sexually attracted to other women.
pansexual	describes those who are attracted to people across a spectrum of genders and sexes.
polyamorous	refers to having honest relationships with multiple partners based on different types of intimacy, including sexual and/or romantic love.
queer	formerly a derogatory term and recently reclaimed as a positive umbrella term by many to describe those who do not conform to binary notions of gender and sexuality.
queer theory	an approach to literary and cultural studies that rejects traditional categories of gender and sexuality.
straight	a slang term for a person with a heterosexual orientation.

In addition to prevailing assumptions in American society about "naturally" occurring aspects of gender (i.e., woman/feminine—male/masculine paradigm), there are similar assumptions and expectations about sexuality (Farrell, Gupta, and Queen 2005). **Sexuality** is a broad construct that encompasses orientation/attraction, identity, and behavior, and as with gender, it is important to examine these distinct components, in addition to the whole. Controversies about "sex in schools" are often the result of misinformation and misunderstanding about what aspects of sexuality are actually being addressed with primary, middle, and high school students.

SEXUAL ORIENTATION: TRADITIONALLY DEFINED

Sexual orientation describes the "direction" and intensity of our sexual and romantic attractions. Through the pioneering research of Alfred Kinsey in the 1950s,

Box 1.1.   Kinsey and Associate's Seven-Point Continuum of Human Sexual Behavior

Kinsey, Pomeroy, and Martin (1948) developed the following scale for human sexual behavior and psychological response, positing that every person falls somewhere along a continuum between heterosexual and homosexual behavior.

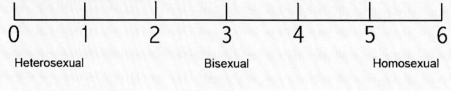

0   1   2   3   4   5   6

Heterosexual   Bisexual   Homosexual

0 = Exclusively heterosexual with no homosexual behavior and psychological response
1 = Predominantly heterosexual, only incidentally homosexual
2 = Predominantly heterosexual, but more than incidentally homosexual
3 = Equally heterosexual and homosexual
4 = Predominantly homosexual, but more than incidentally heterosexual
5 = Predominantly homosexual, only incidentally heterosexual
6 = Exclusively homosexual with no heterosexual behavior and psychological response

we know that sexual orientation and romantic attraction exist on a continuum (box 1.1), with people experiencing a range of intensity in their attractions to others (Gathorne-Harty 1998). In Kinsey's paradigm one who is sexually attracted to a person of a different biological sex has a **heterosexual** orientation; people attracted to those of the same biological sex have a **homosexual** orientation; those attracted to males and females have a **bisexual** orientation. For example, a person who locates herself as a 0 on Kinsey's scale (box 1.1) would be exclusively heterosexual and a person who locates himself as a 6 would be exclusively homosexual in attraction to others.

Kinsey and Biodiversity

Males do not represent two discrete populations, heterosexual and homosexual. The world is not to be divided into sheep and goats. It is a fundamental of taxonomy that nature rarely deals with discrete categories. . . . The living world is a continuum in each and every one of its aspects (Kinsey et al. 1948, 639).

Through his data collection from thousands of human subjects, Kinsey came to understand sexuality to be nuanced and diverse. He created a numbered scale to reflect varying degrees of erotic response to others and determined that people engaged in a much wider range of sexual behaviors with different kinds of partners than previously assumed. In addition to **sexual behavior**, he paid attention to people's fantasies, relationships, and dream life. He determined that sexual behavior is best understood as the by-product of multiple factors, and that differences in orientation, identity, and behavior are part of the natural variation of the species (Kinsey, Pomeroy, and Martin 1948; Kinsey, Pomeroy, Martin, and Gebhard 1953). "The living world is a continuum in each and every one of its aspects" (639).

The Battle Over Bisexuality

The legitimacy of bisexuality as an orientation has been and continues to be debated, even by supposed experts. According to Dr. Ruth Westheimer, the sex therapist and popular talk radio celebrity, "Everyone is either straight or gay. Some people go through an in-between stage where they are perhaps, not sure, but eventually they fall into one category or the other, so that there really is no such thing as being bisexual—though some people lead a bisexual lifestyle for a certain time in their lives." Bisexuality challenges the preferred binary structure of gender and sexuality. The idea that someone could experience "both," or more than one kind of orientation or attraction, flies in the face of categorizing identity and behavior as "either/or."

It is also worth noting that more women than men identify as bisexual (LeVay and Valente 2002). Thus, the skepticism about and dismissal of bisexuality as a bona fide sexual orientation may also, in some measure, be the by-product of sexism.

> We shall not really succeed in discarding the straitjacket of our own cultural beliefs about sexual choice if we fail to come to terms with the well-documented, normal human capacity to love members of both sexes. —Margaret Mead

Whatever the source of bias may be against those who "love members of both sexes," we know that this "capacity" is accepted and even honored in other cultures around the world.

Sexual Orientation: New Conceptualizations

In spite of the additional scientific support of Kinsey's findings over the years (Masters, Johnson, and Kolodny 1997), contemporary science does not consistently or readily recognize a continuum of sexual attraction/orientation. Instead the fixed categories of heterosexual, bisexual, and homosexual are often used to organize these aspects of sexuality. New conceptualizations of human sexuality (e.g., feminist theory) and new terminology (e.g., genderqueer), however, have emerged in response to this dominant, limiting **heteronormative**[10] paradigm. For example, *queer* as an identity rejects both linear and categorical schemas, requiring a fluid and flexible model. If we believe that gender and sexuality are inherently diverse, then our frameworks must reflect the natural varieties of identity, attraction, expression, and behavior (see chapter 2, diagram 2.1).

New terms. The use of contemporary scientific terminology influences how people are categorized, and only certain identities and practices, namely, those that conform to heteronormativity, are privileged. Yet social dynamics and behaviors also influence taxonomy. Increasingly, the language of gender and sexuality (e.g., queer, cisgender, transgender, polyamorous) is emerging from contemporary culture, rather than the research lab or medical clinic, and there is increasing recognition that "science and society are mutually informed by one another" (Nehm and Young 2008, 1176). Thus, educators need to understand not only the definitions of these terms but the social and political positions that "words" can represent or imply as well.

SEXUAL DEVELOPMENT

When Does Development Begin?

In utero the fetus is exposed to varying amounts of chemically related sex steroid hormones (e.g., androgens, estrogens). These hormones influence the development of sex traits and behavior in males and females. Research suggests that higher levels of androgens produce an attraction to males, and lower levels of androgens produces attraction to females, regardless of the chromosomal makeup of the fetus (LeVay and Valente 2002). In addition to varying hormone levels, genetics also play a role in determining sexual orientation (Rosenthal 2005; Kendler, Thornton, Gilman, and Kessler 2000; see "What We Can Learn from the Fruit Fly").

It is worth noting that there is some debate about the dualistic framework of "male sex hormones" and "female sex hormones." Scientific evidence shows that "'sex hormones' are neither sex-specific nor restricted to sex-related organs or functions," yet the binary concept persists in science, medicine, and popular culture (Nehm and Young 2008, 1178). Some, such as Fausto-Sterling (2000) argue that science is not entirely objective when "*biological* results do not match *cultural* notions of sex and gender." This is an area of inquiry worthy of further attention.

What We Can Learn from the Fruit Fly

In her New York Times *article "For Fruit Flies, Gene Shift Tilts Sex Orientation," Elisabeth Rosenthal (2005) summarized the unexpected discovery that the manipulation of a single gene could influence the sexual orientation of a fruit fly. By isolating a "master sexual gene" that can create and change patterns of sexual behavior, scientists demonstrated what is typically understood as "instinctive behavior" as having a firmly genetic basis.*

Dr. Michael Weiss, chairman of the department of biochemistry at Case Western Reserve University, commented, "Hopefully this will take the discussion about sexual preferences out of the realm of morality and put it in the realm of science. . . . I never chose to be heterosexual; it just happened. But humans are complicated. With the flies we can see in a simple and elegant way how a gene can influence and determine behavior" (Rosenthal 2005).

How Does Development Progress?

We know that children are sexual and sensual beings, and that they are curious about bodies and body parts, their own and others'. Toddlers and preschoolers take pleasure in exploring their bodies, figuring out what is what and how everything works. They discover that there are different kinds of bodies in the world and that people can touch each other in ways that feel good: a mother breastfeeds an infant, a father gives a toddler a bath, a preschooler plays "doctor" with a friend, a child sees a romantic couple kissing. Children learn that there are "private parts" of the body that should not be shown or shared in public, and it does not take long for them to realize that these "parts" are implicated in something called "sex."

The Battle over "Awareness" and "Innocence"

Children's early experiences of the body and human relationships are part of their developing sense of their own sexuality. Children are not "sexually active" in any kind of grown-up fashion, nor do they have a mature sexual identity. However, not knowing the word "masturbation" or what it "means" does not keep young children from touching themselves in ways that feel good. It is the adult need to think of children as "innocent" (i.e., not aware of sexuality in self or others) that interferes with recognizing and supporting the natural, ongoing physiological, social, emotional, and behavioral exploration and development of sexuality that progresses throughout childhood and beyond (see "The Story of Tasha in the Tub").

The Story of Tasha in the Tub

The bath is full of soapy bubbles and lots of toys. Four-year-old Tasha finds a medicine dropper and tries to fill it with water. Her mom shows her how to submerge the tip of the dropper in the water and pull back the plunger. Tasha delights in squirting the dropper and watches the stream of water arc across the tub. She does this several times. The water stays inside the tub, *reminds her mom.*

Then Tasha stands up, holds the dropper in front of her vagina and squirts water into the tub. This is how Gabe pees, *she says. (Gabe is her seven-year-old brother.)* One time he peed in the back yard. *Sasha "pees" like this again, this time spraying the water back and forth.* Did you pee in the back yard too? *her mother asks in mock surprise.* I sit when I pee. *Tasha seems to lose interest in the medicine dropper and begins to play with a boat. Then she says,* Some day

I am going to push Gabey's penis right back into his body and then he'll have a bagina like mine.

What makes talking about sexual identity with children and adolescents in a school setting controversial?

In what ways can teachers and parents collaborate in helping children of every age develop a healthy sexual identity?

What Do You "Know" and When Do You "Know" It?

There are no definitive markers or behaviors that predict the "what" and "when" of sexual orientation, yet a child as young as age five may "know" that something essential about her is different from her peers. How does she "know"? Heteronormativity is like the water that fish swim in. If the water suits you, you may not even notice that it is there. You swim along; you fit into heteronormative models of gender and sexuality; life is copacetic. But if your identity and orientation are not heteronormative, the water does not feel quite right. You notice that some of your fundamental attitudes, impulses, and behaviors do not correspond with the cultural norms for gender and sexuality.

"Knowing" about your sexuality is a highly personal and individual experience. For example, consider the following accounts from Robert Trachtenberg's book *When I Knew* (2005). Though intended to be wry and humorous, these stories also illustrate the subjective and idiosyncratic nature of knowing; watching a movie, wearing a piece of clothing, or meeting a particular person can be the catalyst for understanding this central part of one's identity.

> *I was sitting next to my mother, munching on popcorn, watching* The Sound of Music, *and I wondered in my little five-year-old brain if it was wrong to want to be Christopher Plummer, a.k.a. Captain von Trapp. It was the only way, as a girl, that I could imagine being able to be with the beautiful Julie Andrews. . . . I made my mother take me back to see the movie several times that summer, which she was more than happy to do as she just assumed it was because I wanted to be a nun—not that I wanted to be with a nun.*
>
> —Kate Nielsen

> *When I was six, my mother got me a Batman Underoos costume with a cape and mask to play in because my neighbors had similar Super Friends costumes. However, when I traded my friend Stephanie for her Wonder Woman Underoos costume, I was grounded and scolded.*
>
> *The experience taught me two things: I knew I was different, and I knew that I looked much better than Stephanie in that costume.*
>
> —Matt Brubaker

I knew I was gay when the most exciting part of my Bar Mitzvah was meeting with the party planner.

—Howard Bragman

You don't just "know." You know. Then you know-know. Then you really, really, KNOW.

—Brian Leitch

In addition to being subjective, knowing can happen at any age. For example, this young salmon (see cartoon) is on his way upstream to spawn, just like the rest of his peers. The onset of puberty awakens sexual urges in the species, and the majority of the male cohort are intent on mating with a female salmon. Yet the protagonist here realizes that he does not want to mate with a female. He lacks the innate urge to spawn. Rather than feel left out, he appears to be quite excited by the fact that (a) he has figured out he is gay and (b) he gets to turn around and swim downstream. What would a bisexual salmon do?!

A child who grows up to be a gay adult can have early experiences (between ages five and nine) of not fitting in, yet he may or may not "know" that this experience of feeling different is directly related to sexual identity and sexual orientation until

"I'm gay! I'm gay!"

Graphic 1.1.
© New Yorker

"later." Similarly, the heterosexual child may "know" about his sexual attraction all along, yet this may not even come into consciousness—*Hey, I'm swimming in water!*—until puberty or even later.

"Romance" First; Puberty Second

While puberty marks the beginning of physiological, psychological, intellectual, and social advances in sexual development, *awareness* of sexual attraction occurs *before* the onset of puberty (Davies 2004). Girls mature earlier than boys, so it is often the girls who impose a presexualized, "romantic" structure to the social world of elementary school. Some male peers comply with this role-playing and rehearsal, yet many would rather throw food at the sixth grade party than dance with the girls. The social milieu of fourth, fifth, and sixth grade is typically awash in the real and imagined flirtations of "boyfriends" and "girlfriends."

The Inevitability of "Pairing" (Before, During, and After Puberty)

Regardless of who is truly "ready" for an intimate, sexual relationship of any kind, all school-age children are confronted with the question: *Who will I pair with?*

❖ *Children are bombarded with sexual stereotypes from all the forms of media, and many of the girls (not so much the boys) feel they "need" a boyfriend or girlfriend. I just wish English had a set of words to denote a friend who happens to be a boy, as opposed to a "boyfriend," or a friend who happens to be a girl, as opposed to a "girlfriend." I've had several seven-year-old children tell me they are dating, when what they mean is that they are playing together at recess.*

For younger students the pairing question is not urgent, and is often addressed in pretend play, where a "mother" and "father" are "married" yet not particularly intimate. As older elementary students move toward the prepubertal phase, curiosities and concerns about sexual identity and sexual orientation become more prominent. The movement from *awareness* to the actual *experience* of sexual attraction typically coincides with the hormonal changes that are the hallmark of puberty. The fact that children and adolescents enter puberty at different ages and mature at different rates wreaks havoc on the social milieu of late elementary and middle school.

SEXUAL IDENTITY/SEXUAL BEHAVIOR

For most people, sexual orientation/attraction is a strong predictor of **sexual identity** and **sexual behavior**. Sexual identity refers to how a person self-identifies in terms of sexuality (e.g., gay, bisexual, straight, queer, asexual), and sexual behavior is what one actually does sexually and with whom. The development of sexual identity is intimately connected with biological sex, gender identity, and sexual orientation, though it is impossible to know the exact apportionment of each factor. As with other aspects of identity development (e.g., racial identity, cultural identity), some adolescents (or adults) may experiment with a range of sexual behaviors based on different attractions, while others will identify exclusively with a particular sexual orientation and never vary. Again, this variation in individual processes is natural and to be expected.

What's Okay to "Know"?

Cultural expectations of sexual identity, orientation, and behavior also have a strong influence on how readily and comfortably people become aware of and express these aspects of themselves. Social and legal approval is a potent force in "normalizing" certain identities and rejecting and/or criminalizing others. With greater visibility and acceptance of gay people in contemporary culture, adolescents have been "knowing" and coming out earlier (e.g., middle school) than in the past (Denizet-Lewis 2009). At the same time, the stigma of being GLBTQI remains intense in most school contexts (Kosciw et al. 2010).

Coming in and coming out. What is crucial for educators to recognize is that the heteronormative structure of school allows preadolescents and early adolescents who are straight to develop *gradually*, to "come in" to a more public and active expression of their sexuality at a natural pace. "Coming out" allows GLBTQI students to claim participation in the intra- and interpersonal process of sexual identity development, yet it forces these adolescents to make declarations about identity at a time and in a manner that may or may not suit the natural course of their individual development. If the heteronormative bias did not exist, GLBTQI students would have the same developmental options that straight kids do with regard to sexuality: meandering, waiting, abstaining, dabbling, or charging full speed ahead.

Stereotypes and Predictions

Popular cultural stereotypes suggest that feminine men are more likely to be gay and masculine women are more likely to be lesbian. Research in this area, however, has not established that gender expression is a reliable predictor of sexual orientation (Garcia and Slesaransky-Poe 2010). What we do know is:

- Some children who express their gender in nonstereotypical ways grow up to be GLBTQ and some do not.

- Some children who demonstrate same-sex attractions just before and during puberty grow up to be GLBTQ and some do not.
- A small percentage of gender variant children grow up to be transgender but most do not.

Yet, however solid these research findings may be, **the cultural stereotypes that link gender expression and sexual orientation have a powerful influence over how students of every age are perceived and treated at school.**

> As an educator, how does your own sexuality influence your work with students?
>
> How do your students perceive your sexuality? Do the students "see" your sexuality as you want them to?
>
> What assumptions do you make about your students' sexual orientation? What are these assumptions based on?

WHAT TO REMEMBER: SECTION IV

Sexuality

1. **Sexuality** is a broad construct that encompasses orientation, identity, and behavior.
2. **Sexual orientation** is the direction and intensity of romantic and sexual attraction.
   a. Sexual orientation and romantic attraction exist on a continuum; people experience a range of intensity in their attractions to others.
   b. Gender expression is not necessarily a predictor of sexual orientation.
   c. The language of science reflects a more limited view of sexuality; contemporary culture is creating expansive terms and constructs (e.g., queer) to capture the diversity and fluidity of sexuality.
3. **Sexual identity** is how we view and identify ourselves sexually.
4. **Sexual behavior** is what we actually do sexually and with whom.
5. Controversies about "sex in schools" are often the result of misinformation and misunderstanding about what aspects of sexuality are actually being addressed.
6. Cultural approval is a potent force in "normalizing" and privileging certain identities and behaviors and rejecting/criminalizing others.
7. Children are sexual, sensual beings and are naturally curious about bodies and intimacy.
   a. Preschool and primary students' expression and exploration of their sexuality is ongoing throughout childhood.

   b. Young children (five–nine) who grow up to be a GLBTQ may have an early experience of knowing that they do not "fit in"; it may or may not be until later that they relate this feeling to sexual identity.

8. **Puberty** is the process of physiological, psychological, intellectual, and social advances in sexual development.

   a. Awareness of sexual attraction occurs before the onset of puberty.

9. All school-age children and adolescents are faced with and engaged with the question of with whom they will ultimately partner.

10. Gender expression is not a reliable predictor of sexual orientation.

11. Stereotypes that link gender expression and sexual orientation influence how children are perceived and trained at school.

ADDITIONAL RESOURCE

Additional Resource 1.1:
Standards of Care for Children and Adolescents with Gender Dysphoria, Adapted from the World Professional Association for Transgender Health's "Standards of Care for the Health of Transsexual, Transgender, and Gender Nonconforming People" (2011)

Before physical intervention is considered, the child or adolescent and his or her family must undergo counseling with a mental health professional to explore the nature and characteristics of the child's or adolescent's gender identity and dysphoria. Therapy to treat distress the child or adolescent experiences related to gender dysphoria, as well as any comorbid psychological or life issues, is necessary, and for adolescents should include discussion of the possibilities and limitations of medical treatments/interventions.

For children and adolescents, the first step may be a social transition, when the child or adolescent experiencing gender dysphoria assumes the gender role with which he or she identifies. Families will vary on decisions regarding the timing (i.e., how soon) and extent (i.e., a family could allow a partial transition in which the child assumes a different gender role only on vacation), but it is critical that in all cases the child or adolescent understands this transition does not have to be permanent.

There are three stages of physical intervention available to adolescents for whom such interventions are necessary. The first stage is **fully reversible interventions (FRI)**—hormone blockers that delay pubertal changes. To be eligible for FRI, the adolescent must (1) have demonstrated a long-lasting and intense pattern of gender nonconformity or gender dysphoria (whether suppressed or expressed), (2) have experienced emerging or worsening gender dysphoria with the onset of puberty, (3) be in a stable situation and be considered well-functioning (after addressing any coexisting psychological, medical, or social problems), and (4) have given informed consent (or have legal caretakers give consent if the adolescent is a minor).

The second stage is **partially reversible interventions (PRI)**—hormonal interventions that masculinize or feminize the body. Adolescents can enter PRI with informed consent either from the adolescent (if of legal age) or from the adolescent's legal caretaker. Ideally, even if the adolescent is not a minor, the decision to enter this stage will be supported by the family.

The third stage is **irreversible interventions (II)**—surgical intervention. Genital surgery should not be carried out until the adolescent reaches legal adulthood (though this age threshold is not itself grounds for surgical intervention) and has lived continuously for at least one year in the gender role that matches his or her gender identity. Transgender male adolescents (who were female-assigned at birth) may undergo chest surgery before legal adulthood after they have lived in their desired gender role for a significant period of time and have been on hormone therapy for a year, if this earlier intervention is necessary.

These guidelines are to be considered as well-researched suggestions and clinicians may customize them as needed to fit the individual situations of children/adolescent patients and their families. While the guidelines discuss eligibility for interventions, it is also important that clinicians and families understand the significant physical and mental risks of withholding medical treatment (www.wpath.org/publications_standards.cfm).

NOTES

1. Rules of conventional grammar are not always followed in relation to gender/pronoun agreement. The reason for this will (hopefully) become clear as you read further.

2. Terms and concepts are bolded when first defined.

3. *Binary* is a term used to describe that which relates to, is composed of, or involves *two* things.

4. Direct quotations are denoted by these symbols:

   ❖ = teachers/administrators
   ➢ = students
   ☐ = parents

5. *Pedagogy* has several meanings. In this book pedagogy refers to (1) the art and science of teaching and instruction, and (2) a particular approach to teaching based on educational theory.

6. See chapter 8 for more on comprehensive sexuality education.

7. For further discussion of sex hormones see Sexual Development in this chapter.

8. Nomenclature related to intersexuality is under debate, with *disorders of sex development* (DSD) emerging as a preferred term in some medical circles and *intersex* preferred in others. The

term *intersex* is more widely recognized and understood. It is also less pathologizing than DSD, thus I use the term *intersex* here.

9. In the trans community some people now refer to birth sex as "assigned" rather than "biological." This shift is due to the growing number of trans people who assert that they have always been male or female, and that their original assignment to the opposite sex—which typically occurs at birth—was erroneous. The shift in terminology is also an attempt to move beyond using "biological"—which is often interpreted as "real"—when distinguishing between the genders and sexes of trans and nontrans people. In this book "biological sex" refers to a person's genes, hormones, and sex organs.

10. The binary view of gender and sexuality that assumes and privileges heterosexuality in individuals, couples, and families, and supports traditional masculine and feminine gender roles and expression (see chapter 2).

2

HETERONORMATIVITY AT SCHOOL

Questioning the "Natural Order" of Things

When someone with the authority of a teacher, say, describes the world and you are not in it, there is a moment of psychic disequilibrium, as if you looked into a mirror and saw nothing.

—Adrienne Rich, *Blood, Bread and Poetry*

A book about two people who fall in love, two penguins raising a chick or a teenage boy deciding whether and how to "fit in" can become a dangerous presence if the two people both happen to be princes, the two penguins both happen to be male and the teenage boy happens to be gay.

—DePalma and Atkinson (2010),
Undoing Homophobia in Primary Schools

Think of the last time you filled out an information sheet at the doctor's office. It is highly likely that you had two choices on the form for "gender," a box labeled "male" and a box labeled "female." You probably checked one of the boxes and moved on, without thinking twice. This chapter explores the power and influence of **heteronormativity**, which is our cultural and social "management" of gender and sexuality. Heteronormativity relies on forms with boxes; it disallows the natural variations in *biological sex*, *gender identity*, *gender expression*, and *sexual orientation*—as illustrated in chapter 1—that exist in the human species.

Heteronormativity reinforces those identities that conform to "traditional" expectations of sex, gender, and sexuality, namely, the heterosexual pairing of a biological, cisgender, masculine man and a biological, cisgender, feminine woman.

Individuals, cultures, and institutions promote heteronormativity, and preK–12 schools are explicitly and implicitly organized to reinforce "normative" ideals and interpretations of gender and sexuality. This chapter examines the impact of heteronormativity on the identity development of all children and adolescents.

HETERONORMATIVITY: THE "NATURAL ORDER" OF THINGS

When we experience the biodiversity of a given species, whether it is the bird, the cat, or the rose, we revel in its variation and beauty. Different songs, myriad patterns on coats of fur, a wide palette of colors. Conversely, the diversity of genders and sexualities in the human species is experienced by many as a threat to what they perceive as the "natural order" of things. Instead of being *part of* the full expression of that natural order, gender and sexuality diversity (GSD) is viewed as an aberration.

Different aspects of the human species, be it skin color, eye color, height, or shoe size, vary across individuals; this is true of gender and sexuality as well. The New Diagram of Sex and Gender (diagram 2.1) challenges binary thinking about gender

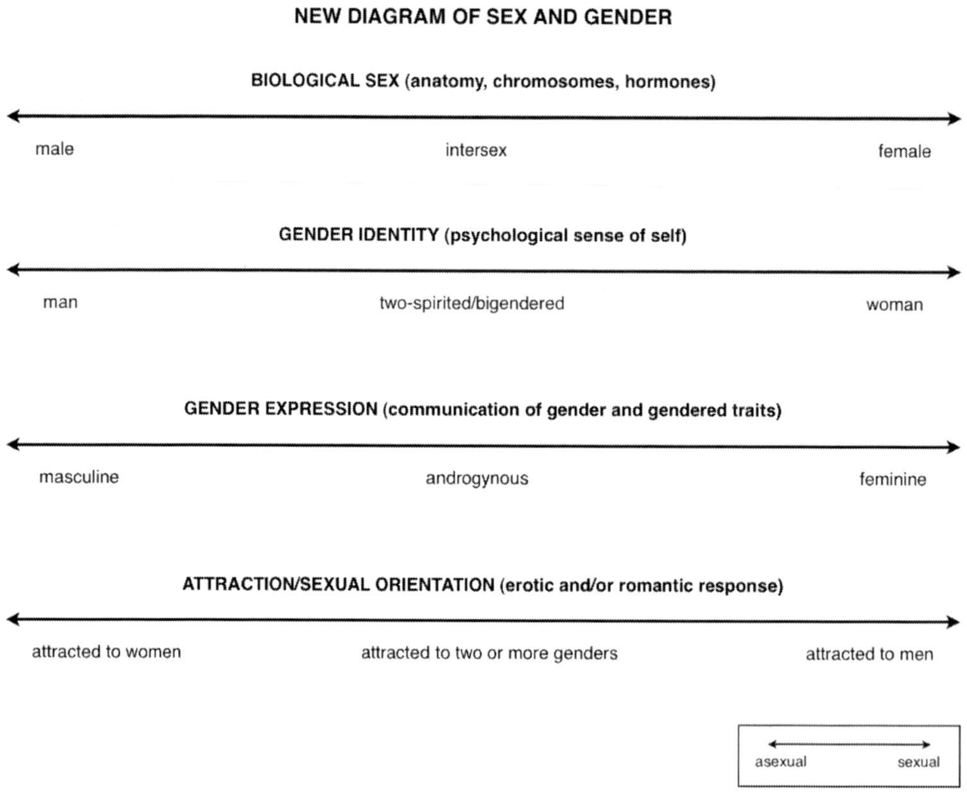

NEW DIAGRAM OF SEX AND GENDER

BIOLOGICAL SEX (anatomy, chromosomes, hormones)

male   intersex   female

GENDER IDENTITY (psychological sense of self)

man   two-spirited/bigendered   woman

GENDER EXPRESSION (communication of gender and gendered traits)

masculine   androgynous   feminine

ATTRACTION/SEXUAL ORIENTATION (erotic and/or romantic response)

attracted to women   attracted to two or more genders   attracted to men

asexual   sexual

Diagram 2.1.

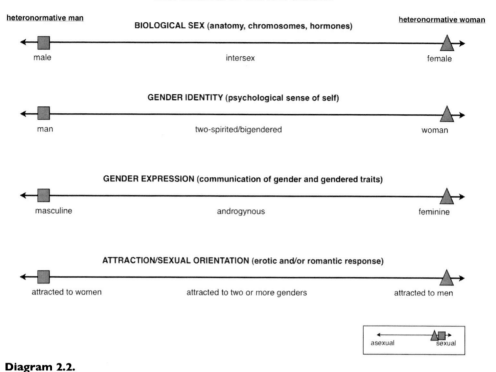

NEW DIAGRAM OF SEX AND GENDER

Diagram 2.2.
Copyright Pending 2011 Jennifer Bryan & Sebastian Mitchell Barr; Modified from Diagram of Sex and Gender © 2000 Center for Gender Sanity

and sexuality and presents a schema of five separate yet related continuums. The biodiversity of gender and sexuality is more fully captured in this model; it is a distinct improvement over discreet boxes of binary identities.

At the same time, this schema still does not fully represent all contemporary gender and sexual identities, nor does it adequately depict the interrelationship of the five continuums. Identities such as transgender, genderqueer, and queer (see chapter 1) require a schema that is less linear and "fixed." Some individuals occupy multiple spots on a given continuum and need a more fluid way to identify. In addition, the concept of "movement" along any continuum(s) is not captured by this two-dimensional diagram.

Despite these limitations, however, the model is useful in illustrating several central aspects of sex and gender. It challenges the idea that these aspects of identity can be reduced to binary options. Diagram 2.2 also provides a visual depiction of heteronormativity, highlighting the purported superior "locations" on these continua, namely, those that conform to traditional expressions of sex, gender, and sexuality.

Heteronormative Beliefs

Heteronormativity is one way of trying to "simplify" and organize the messiness of biology. As such, heteronormative standards are based on the belief that

- there are two distinct gender categories (man/woman).
- there are two distinct forms of gender expression (masculine/feminine).
- men are/should be masculine.
- women are/should be feminine.
- men and women are heterosexual.
- male/female heterosexual pairing is the ideal

This narrow view of gender identity (GI) and sexual identity (SI) is based on the belief that biological processes naturally "lead to" this heteronormative standard and that reinforcement of heteronormativity merely affirms what nature intended—*This is how we were meant to be*—in the first place.

This perspective discounts the variations of gender and sexuality that occur as part of normal identity development for many individuals. It also denies the social and political constructions of gender and sexuality that are imposed by society, reinforced by parents, and ultimately perpetuated by children themselves (see The Story of Nat the Puppet). For example, is purple being a "girl color" the natural order of things? Is redirecting boys away from ballet merely reinforcing something that nature intended? Indeed, the consistent presence of different genders, sexualities, and behaviors in all human and animal species over the course of history suggests that GSD is undeniably part of an "intended order" of some kind (Roughgarden 2004), just not the heteronormative order.

The Story of Nat the Puppet

Nat is a puppet I use when I work with my 1st graders to talk about things like being an ally, hair, and how we're different and how we're the same. I got Nat a few years ago to help 1st graders talk about gender and gender stereotypes, and designed Nat to be what I thought was "gender neutral." I dressed Nat in a red hoodie sweatshirt and made the hair from yellow feathers. When Nat arrived with me in class, students immediately connected to Nat, and began interacting with him (more on the pronoun in a moment) as if he were one of them.

The first conversation about gender that Nat joined us for followed a discussion about gender stereotypes. We had already introduced the idea by using Jennifer's book, The Different Dragon, *to talk about stereotypes related to dragons. Kids quickly saw how there are stereotypes about boys and girls too, and they shared some that stood out for them: girls have long hair, boys' hair is short, boys like sports, girls like to play dress-up. They also shared many examples of people they know who break those stereotypes, including themselves.*

When Nat came along, one of the first questions children had was, "Is Nat a boy or girl?" Nat was feeling a little shy and wasn't ready to talk yet, but nodded when I asked if the kids could share what they thought. Hands shot up, and one child said, "Nat has short hair, so he's a boy." Nat spoke up and said, "But I don't have hair, I have feathers. And girls can have short hair too, you said so!" Kids nodded in agreement and waved their hands in the air with more ideas. "Nat is wearing a red sweatshirt, and it looks like a boy sweatshirt," and "Nat looks like a boy," came next. Nat looked at me and whispered in my ear. I then pointed out that one of their teachers, a girl, has short hair and was wearing blue jeans and a dark green T-shirt, so did that make her a boy? "NO!" they all laughed. "Nat, do you like princesses or Spider-Man?" asked a little girl sitting next to me. "I like both," Nat pronounced. A little boy raised his hand and shared, "One thing makes boys different from girls, and that's their private parts." After the giggles died down, I agreed that girls and boys have different parts, but because Nat is a puppet, he doesn't have those parts. So we talked about how girls and boys feel that they are a boy or a girl on the inside, and that for most people, their inside feelings match up with their parts.

As we all talked together, and I talked about Nat, I found it incredibly difficult to avoid using pronouns. I thought for a long time about why Nat seems so clearly a boy to the kids, and asked them what it would take for them to see Nat as a girl. The changes they suggested included visual changes that would "feminize" Nat—longer hair feathers, a headband, maybe some earrings, a different outfit. One little girl lent Nat her blue, feathered headband, and we put it on Nat's head. The kids mostly thought it was funny, as if one of the boys in the class put it on his head. So there it was, Nat became a boy, a he, him. But Nat still likes princesses, and cooking and playing dress-up, and soccer and building with blocks, and the color pink. As Nat says, "I'm just Nat."

—Laura Stewart, ethics teacher, Ethical Culture Fieldston School

Heteronormative Bias at School

Children learn at a very early age that it is not biological sex that communicates one's gender to the rest of society; rather it is the signifiers we choose to wear that will identify us as male or female. These choices are informed by codes that are explicitly and implicitly taught to children. (Meyer 2007, 19)

❖ *Dads never want their boys playing with dolls; this might make their son gay.*

School is a major site of identity development and identity "negotiation." The intentional and unintentional *gender identity instruction* (GII) and *sexual identity instruction* (SII) that most children receive at school is fundamentally biased in the direction of heteronormative beliefs and assumptions.

❖ *At a parent conference a mother told me her daughter liked to wear boys underwear. I was surprised that she allowed this and that she told me about it. I didn't know what to say, so I just smiled and went on with my report.*

This bias affects everything from classroom curricula and athletics, to school policies and the designation of restroom spaces in the school building. Thus, recognizing, challenging, disrupting, and ultimately transforming heteronormative bias is a vast undertaking.

For most schools, the challenge begins with (1) recognizing that heteronormative bias exists and (2) understanding its impact on all members of a school community (see The Story of the Heterosexual Matrix and Mundane Classroom Moments). In chapter 1 we examined the power of gender "norms" and roles on students of every age. There is a similar normative assumption in relation to sexuality in that **children are treated as and assumed to be heterosexual when they begin school**. Most educators know that, statistically speaking, a small percentage of their students will identify as gay at some point in their lives. However, this factual knowledge does not typically change the initial assumption that students in the class are heterosexual until proven otherwise.

The Story of the Heterosexual Matrix and Mundane Classroom Moments

Judith Butler developed the idea of the heterosexual matrix to describe the ways in which heterosexuality is constructed and maintained as the norm. I realized that this matrix is being created and maintained each day in my classroom through interactions between myself, the teaching assistants, and the children. Actions and events which seem insignificant become the sites where this happens, from where the children sit on the carpet, to who interrupts lessons, to who plays kiss chase on the playground and how; from the coat colours worn by the children to the language I use to address them, to the presentation of homework. In these everyday, mundane moments of life in my classroom, the children and staff, including myself, are creating and policing what it means to be a boy or a girl.

—Elementary teacher, quoted in DePalma and Atkinson (2010, 56)

The Inevitability of "Pairing"

Children understand at an early age that when any kind of romantic coupling occurs, it is "supposed to" involve a boy and a girl, a man and a woman. Adults project these heteronormative expectations, which often reflect parental beliefs and cultural values, onto toddlers and preschool playmates freely (see The Story of Boyfriends for Girls of Every Age).

- *Is Tommy your boyfriend?*
- *Do you have a little crush on Lila? Give Lila a big hug.*
- *You are dressing up as a family—are you the mommy? Is Teddy going to be the daddy?*

Our very youngest students are immersed in a school world that typically reflects and reinforces heteronormative genders and sexualities, exclusively.

The Story of Boyfriends for Girls of Every Age

"So do you have any boyfriends?" "I bet she's got so many boyfriends." "Any boys catching your eye this year?"

I think I must have been three when people first thought it was cute to ask if I was dating anyone—specifically if I was dating any boys. At three does anyone want a boyfriend?! But that's not the point is it? The point is that boys and girls together are cute. The point is that it is assumed a girl is eventually going to want and have a boyfriend. And that point wasn't lost on me.

As a small child I just laughed and said no. And in actuality, when we played house, I had a girlfriend. Boys were my friends, but girls were something different. I knew I liked girls. But each year multitudes of people asked if I had a boyfriend so it isn't any wonder that I hit middle school and had a whole slew of boyfriends—sometimes we even held hands. And in high school, as people kept asking "So any new boyfriends in North Carolina," I kept dating guys, with mild interest at best.

We wonder why it takes us so long to figure out something so simple as whom we are attracted to . . .; it's because since we are three years old, no one else even leaves room for the possibility of us being anything but heterosexual! Please, I knew whom I liked from early childhood. I just thought it didn't matter because all girls dated guys anyway. And it took me 16 years (and some honest media portrayal of lesbians) for me to realize it didn't have to be like that.

—S. Barr

Heteronormativity and Early Elementary Age Children

Heterosexual pairing dominates board books, coloring books, picture books, and early readers. The exclusively heterosexual images in *Pat the Bunny, Goodnight, Gorilla, Where's Spot?* and *The Berenstain Bears* is not the problem. It is the **absence of alternative images** that promotes bias in the classroom environment.

❖ *A few years ago, our librarian put a storybook about the gay penguins at a zoo in the library. Our administrator was very upset. Although the book remains in the collection, I think she requested that it be put behind the librarians' desks and only available upon request. I found this very discouraging.*

Having time-tested favorite books in the classroom creates a familiar environment for teachers, students, and parents alike. *We have this book at home, too!* Yet the challenge of recognizing the potentially negative impact of exclusive heteronormativity on children requires questioning the status quo. It means pursuing the unfamiliar; it means keeping a book about gay penguins on the shelf where children can find it.

As this teacher observes, validating same-sex pairing is an important aspect of supporting a range of sexual identities.

❖ *I think the best thing that I have seen coworkers do (and have done myself) is to affirm for children that they can marry who they want to—at the preK and Kindergarten levels this kind of conversation happens all the time and inevitably a child will say something like, "Well I want to marry (child of same gender)." In all cases, I have observed teachers acknowledging this as a possibility and affirming that statement. I live in Massachusetts and have also acknowledged and seen coworkers acknowledge that yes, it is possible for "a boy to marry a boy" (or girl to marry a girl) in this state. I think it's important for kids to know that's a possibility, and I would probably say that even if I didn't live in a state where it was technically legal.*

Children experiment with gender roles and sexual roles all the time in pretend play. At this age when a child explores the idea of a girl marrying a girl, she is not asking about state law. Some day she may be interested in the legal aspects of GSD; but right now the child just wants to know if a girl can pair with a girl in the special way that is associated with marriage.

Young Children and Sexuality

❖ *Every year kids who are 5 announce "crushes" and "boyfriends/girlfriends," and we've even had kissing/pinching butts before.*

Pretend play about marriage does not necessarily include overly sexualized elements, yet it is important to recognize that five- and six-year-old children can also engage in play that strongly connotes sexuality (Blaise 2009). In her qualitative study of a kindergarten classroom, Blaise observed interactions among children that actively manifest their gender identities and sexual identities (see box 2.1). As noted in chapter 1, there is a cultural press to view children as "innocent," nonsexual beings, yet children's engagement with everyday culture—which includes television, pop music, and music videos—invites them to explore sexualized adult identities.

The Wonderful Heteronormative World of Disney

The invitation to explore sexual identity is served up in children's media as well. Consider, for a moment, that timeless parenting staple: G-rated Disney movies. What is the impact of Disney's heteronormative (and often sexist) model on the gender identity development (GID) and sexual identity development (SID) of children? Contemporary theories of gender and sexuality have deconstructed and made more explicit the negative impact this bias has, particularly on those children who do not identify with the heteronormative standards of a masculine male pairing with a feminine female (Fausto-Sterling 2000; Kimmel 2000; DePalma and Atkinson 2009).

Box 2.1. Sexuality in the Kindergarten Classroom

In her field research Mindy Blaise (2009) observed the play of three kindergarten students. At the back of the classroom, Mary performed a Christian Aguilera pop song for her peers Felipe and Maggie. Mary's rendition included the refrain: *What a girl wants is beauty beyond belief.* Mary sang the song while fluttering her eye lashes, tossing her hair, and running both hands down the sides of her body, as if to emphasize her shapely figure. All three children appeared to be experiencing great pleasure in this performance, and Blaise interviewed the class to learn how much they "understood" this behavior.

Felipe: Well, she's singing about getting boyfriends. All girls want and need boyfriends.

Mindy: Is that true, everyone?

Whole class: Yea . . .

Mary: She is singing about getting lots and lots of boyfriends, that's what girls want, not just one (putting up one finger).

Mindy: Why do girls want lots and lots of boyfriends? Why is this important?

Kim: First, girls have to get pretty, before they can get a boyfriend.

Mindy: What do you mean? How do girls get pretty?

Kim: Well, pretty is like, you know, it's like looking a certain way, having good clothes, you know, they have to match and everything, and having long hair.

Elena: No. Pretty can be more than just that.

Mindy: What do you mean, Elena?

Elena: Well there are lots of ways you can be pretty and I don't think that Christina Aguilera is pretty.

Mary: (Turning her body towards Elena) What?

Mindy: Does Christina Aguilera have good clothes and nice hair?

Kim: Oh yes. She has really, really, really good clothes.

Felipe: No, Christina Aguilera has sexy clothes (laughter from the class) that shows her body off. (Blaise 2009, 454)

The dialogue among these five- and six-year-olds reflects all the contemporary "adult" complexities of gender roles and sexuality "norms." These students are not "innocent" nor are they naïve about the prevailing heteronormative expectations for girls and boys, women and men.

G-rated films are by definition supposed to be devoid of "sexuality," yet the promotion of heteronormativity is central to most children's movies (Martin and Kazyak 2009). We know that many young children watch G-rated films multiple times, learning that men and women with certain types of bodies and certain types of gender expression end up together, "kissing" and living happily ever after. And the kissing in some of these films is plainly sexual, not merely an affectionate peck on the cheek.

Consider these Disney pairs and then take a short quiz:

- Robin Hood and Maid Marian
- Pongo and Perdita

- Aladdin and Jasmine
- Tramp and Lady
- Woody and Bo Peep
- John Smith and Pocahontas
- Simba and Nala
- Tarzan and Jane
- Shrek and Fiona
- Ginger and Rocky
- Eric and Ariel
- Mickey and Minnie
- Beast and Belle
- Thomas O'Malley and Duchess

What do these pairs have in common? They are (a) sibling pairs who overcome great adversity, (b) superheroes with special powers, (c) heterosexual couples who fall in love during the movie, or (d) characters on Sesame Street. (If you did not answer "c," you must proceed directly to Disney World.)

As Martin and Kazyak demonstrate, the following themes are featured in most Disney films:

1. Heterosexual relationships are portrayed as magical and transformative for the main characters.
2. Gendered behavior is often sexualized behavior (e.g., bare-chested men almost "catch" the heroine naked and ogle her curvaceous female body).
3. Humor is often related to men's crotches, butts, and genitals.
4. Romantic scenes move more slowly and are accompanied by a certain type of music.
5. The "happy ending" often involves a kiss or embrace between the heterosexual hero and heroine.

However, the potentially negative influence of the Disney ideal is not limited to nonheteronormative children. Recently various authors have addressed the impact of the "princess identity" on all young girls (Wohlwend 2009; Orenstein 2011; Schwyzer 2011), noting the overt and covert shaping of an identity that is based primarily on appearance.

For many adults, little girls dressed up as princesses are genuinely "cute," and telling a young girl that she looks "pretty" is a standard compliment. Yet as Peggy Orenstein, author of *Cinderella Ate My Daughter: Dispatches from the Front Lines of the New Girlie-Girl Culture,* notes, this early, frequent message that being the "Fairest of Them All" is more important than being competent, strong, or creative has a tremendous impact on the identity development of all girls (Orenstein 2011).

Can't girls be princesses anymore?! Most adults do not mean to sexualize young girls by complimenting their "beauty." They participate in this long-standing reinforcement of fairy tales and make-believe as a way to show love and affection, to make girls feel special. As Mary's rendition of "What a Girl Wants" (box 2.1) demonstrates, the porous boundary between what is true make-believe and what is the ubiquitous, highly sexualized imaging of only slightly older girls and young women makes promoting the young princess culture problematic.

> While all children want affirmation, princess culture teaches little girls to get that approval through their looks. Little girls learn quickly what "works" to elicit adoration from mom and dad, as well as from teachers, uncles, aunts, and other adults. Soon—much too soon—they notice that older girls and women get validation for a particular kind of dress, a particular kind of behavior. They watch their father's eyes, they follow their uncle's gaze. They listen to what these men they love say when they see "hot" young women on television or on the street. And they learn how to be from what they hear and see (Schwyzer 2011).

Schwyzer encourages fathers and other men to provide the important girls in their lives with plenty of attention for kindness, athleticism, intelligence, and other qualities unrelated to looks. Men must also be mindful of how they talk about older girls and women when little girls are listening in, which is just about all the time.

What about Disney and the boys? The heteronormativity sponsored by Disney offers boys an equally limited repertoire of gender and sexual identities. Consider these "packages" offered at Disney World's Bibbidi Bobbidi Boutique. Parents can purchase varying packages for "girls 3 years old and above" that include hairstyling (Fairytale Princess, Disney Diva, or Pop Princess), hair extensions, "shimmering" makeup, nail color, princess costuming and accessorizing, and a full set of photos. Prices range from $49.95 to $189.95. Girls can also choose the Secret Star Makeover package, which transforms them into pop stars "just like Hannah Montana." For boys 3 and older there is the Knight Package, which includes hairstyling and a "mighty" sword and shield, for only $15.00 (http://disneyworld.disney .go.com/tours-and-experiences/bibbidi-bobbidi-boutique).

The princess makeover offered to girls includes makeup, costumes, several hairstyles to choose from, and a boatload of accessories for as much as $189.95. The boys' Knight Package for $15.00 includes hairstyling and a sword. That's it? Boys and men in Disney films are brave and physically strong; they overcome adversity (e.g., hyenas, wicked spells, capitalists) and rescue girls or women who are in distress. When boys/men are not acting courageous and toting weaponry in the film, they are invited to act dopey and disoriented at the first sign of an attractive female (e.g., Mowgli in *The Jungle Book*, the Seven Dwarfs in *Snow White,* Aladdin in *Aladdin and The Magic Lamp*).

Disney's influence is vast, and children bring the heroine and hero "package" with them to school. Of course they want to emulate the cartoon characters that populate their world, from the designs on their pajamas, to commercials advertising the latest Disney release, to the toys at McDonald's (*Do you want a girl toy or a boy toy with that Happy Meal?*). How should a teacher respond? The challenge is to work with children's natural affinity for these fairy-tale identities, and at the same time, teach students to think critically about who these figures are and what they stand for. Teachers can ensure that at least while students are at school, these are not the only models available to them.

The other part of this challenge is for teachers to create an environment that allows for nonheteronormative pretend play and fairy-tale exploration. A teacher involved in the No Outsiders project responded this way when he found children dividing themselves into boys' tables and girls' tables: *"I'm a boy-girl; where do I sit?"* (DePalma and Atkinson 2010). In her "Story of the Boy Who Wore a Tutu," the teacher demonstrates how allowing children to express fluid gender identities bumps up against rules and policies that are intended to regulate behavior in helpful ways. *The lines were blurry for me and I often felt conflicted.* There is no neat protocol that will readily clarify this blurry picture. What matters is the teacher's awareness and ongoing examination of what will best serve the interests of her student.

The Story of the Boy Who Wore a Tutu

There was a male student who attended our school for many years. From early on, he always wanted to wear a tutu to school and frequently found ways to cross dress. Generally, the school and the student body were very accepting of his choices. We found ourselves torn, at times. We had a very clear policy that there was no costume wearing at our school and we also observed a practice of grace and courtesy in our school. He was often coming in with a variety of outfits and behaved overly dramatic which, at times, caused disruption in the classroom. It was hard, at times, to find a way to address the underlying issues without feeling like we were being discriminating of his differences. I felt consistently challenged to figure out where to draw the line and how to make this child understand that despite his differences, there were still protocols to follow. The lines were blurry for me and I often felt conflicted. These are the same challenges I face when I put an adult spin on something a child is doing and don't know where to draw the lines.

—Elementary teacher

Heteronormativity and Family Life

The heteronormative standard also influences perceptions of "family norms," with children in the school setting being exposed repeatedly to exclusively heterosexual parents who produce exclusively heterosexual offspring. This image of "standard" family life is reinforced by everything from the books that teachers and students read, to displays in the hallway and foyer of the school, to forms that parents must sign, to the creation of holiday cards (see graphic 2.1). In elementary social studies, children study different famous figures at different times in history; family life in this part of the curriculum is usually firmly heteronormative. This bias makes it hard for children, whether they are from GLBTQI families or not, to see GLBTQI lives reflected matter-of-factly in the everyday images and messages at school.

Talking about families; talking about "sex." It is also true that recognizing and talking about *gay* families means acknowledging more explicitly that different sexual identities exist in the world. Conversations about "a mommy and a daddy" are not seen as or experienced as being sexual, even though a heterosexual pair is at the center of the conversation. Conversations about gay parents are

"I have two mommies. I know where the apostrophe goes."

Graphic 2.1.
© New Yorker

seen as sexualized, because to identify anything other than the heteronormative standard draws unwanted attention to the heretofore "invisible" (hetero)sexuality of straight parents (Youdell 2009). Talking about a married heterosexual couple is a conversation about family. Talking about a married/partnered gay couple can be construed as a conversation about sex. Referencing gay families must become commonplace and integrated matter-of-faculty into discussions in order to disrupt this stereotype.

> What changes could be made to your particular classroom environment that would challenge exclusively heteronormative ideals? What changes in your curriculum?
>
> To what degree do you embody heteronormativity? How might you use your own identity—regardless of what it is—to talk about the impact of hetero-normativity?

Heteronormativity and Elementary School Culture

Think about all the components of elementary school "culture." There is no way to list them all but here are a few, in no particular order of importance:

- how involved parents are
- what teachers wear
- how brightly lit the cafeteria is
- the administrative approach to disciplinary issues
- the installation of a fabulous new climbing structure on the playground
- the annual craft fair
- the role of standardized testing
- the fifth grade trip to Nature's Classroom
- Thanksgiving assembly

The "Letter from a Sixth Grade Student to the Chorus Teacher" was an unexpected referendum on an age-old fixture of elementary school culture: the chorus. In truth, there may be many long-standing "institutions" of the school environment that need to be reassessed with heteronormativity in mind. What books are available at the annual book fair? Is field day organized by gender alone? Does the celebration of Black History Month include notable GLBTQI black people? What costumes are acceptable at the Halloween parade (see The Halloween Costume Controversy)?

Letter from a Sixth Grade Student to the Chorus Teacher

I wanted to tell you about the way you set up some of the chorus songs based on gender. There is a song that all of the boys are going to sing, and there is a song that all of the girls are going to sing. The separation is based on the context of the songs: falling in love with someone of the opposite gender. This is heterosex-ist and can make homosexual or bisexual kids uncomfortable. This can also be sexist, depending on the kinds of songs the boys and girls are going to sing. This can be uncomfortable for kids who aren't sure about their gender identity and want room to explore it.

Singing parts are often divided by gender because it's a convenient way to split. This classifies everyone in ways that they don't necessarily want to be classified. At this point, we all have basically the same singing range: there are boys with high voices and girls with low voices. It also ends up as a competition between boys and girls to see who can sing better.

I know that you are not doing this on purpose but I don't feel comfortable discriminating against LGBT people. By separating songs by gender, we are as-suming that everyone in this chorus is heterosexual. If you could please have the all-boy songs and the all-girl songs sung by everyone, I personally would be a lot more comfortable, not to mention the potential LGBT people in the chorus. I'd be happy to talk about this in person if it is unclear.

P.S. If you do change the songs, please tell the chorus why, because I think kids should be aware of these issues.

—Sixth grade boy (with some help from his transgender older sister)

The Halloween Costume Controversy

In 2010, a five-year-old boy in the Midwest dressed up as his favorite character from the TV show "Scooby-Doo," the redheaded Daphne who wears a bright pink dress, purple leggings, pink boots, a neon ascot, and accessories to match. The boy was scared that his classmates would make fun of him and almost changed his mind, but it was Halloween, and his mother, Sarah, assured him that his costume was fine. He should wear what he wanted.

His mother was right; not a single child said anything negative about his Daphne costume. Sarah was shocked, however, by the response of some mothers who expressed "concern." They suggested that allowing a boy to look like that at school was confusing for other children. Sarah took issue with the reasoning behind the attitudes and behavior of these parents. "If my daughter had dressed as Batman," Sarah said, "no one would have thought twice about it."

She argued that her son's choice of costume did not necessarily have anything to do with his gender or sexual orientation and certainly would not "make him gay" as others had proposed. She defended his right to be who he is. "My job as his mother is not to stifle the man that he will be, but to help him along his way. Mine is not to dictate what is 'normal' and what is not, but to help him become a good person" (Ferran 2010).

The Heteronormativity That Children Bring to School

Imagine that you are a third grade teacher with a particularly "boy crazy" group of girls in your class this year. Not only are you grappling with the impact their "energy" is having on the classroom dynamics, you wonder if these girls are uniquely precocious, or do they, in fact, represent the new normal for third grade girls? The research of Myers and Raymond (2010) demonstrates that many young elementary age girls organize their interests and identity around heteronormative ideals, and in addition, they reject gay and lesbian identities.

The Girl Project.   Girls, mostly age nine and under, were invited into focus groups to discuss their interests, and the researchers quickly discovered that a majority of the girls wanted to talk about boys.

> These girls performed heterosexual desire long before adolescence: It was an everyday issue for them. Girls as young as first grade brought their preexisting boy-centered language to focus groups: "hotties," "crushes," and "dating." These girls measured themselves and each other according to their perceptions of boys' interests, even when no boys were present. All three groups of girls did this, with the second/third graders—seven- and eight-year-olds—being the most expressive. (Myers and Raymond 2010, 184)

The topic of "boyfriends" was initially introduced by a girl in the focus group, and at first the girls protested: "Are we going to talk about boys? Because if we do I'm going to freak out." Yet the group quickly decided that talking about crushes was desirable and okay, as long as they did not tell the boys. Even though not all the girls in these focus groups identified themselves as "boy crazy," and even though some objected to conversations about the "X word" (i.e., sex), the group nonetheless organized itself around heteronormative themes (see excerpt in box 2.2).

The researchers noted the intense pressure that all of the girls experienced—and perpetuated—to achieve the heteronormative ideal (i.e., a feminine sexy girl pairing with a masculine hottie boy). Regardless of their true developmental readiness, many girls narrated and rehearsed boy/girl pairing while the others listened and bore witness. When the conversation turned to male homosexuality and lesbianism, the girls made it clear that being gay was not an acceptable part of boy or girl identity. The tabloid rumor that one of their celebrity "hotties" was gay was met with horror and disgust; being gay was compared to "eating boogers."

Heteronormativity and Nonheterosexual Children

As mentioned in chapter 1 children whose fully developed sexual identity and sexual orientation is not heterosexual may understand at an early age (five to nine) that something fundamental about their "self" is different from the majority of people around them. Heteronormative culture has a major impact on a child's *process* of self-discovery. How is the classroom performance of "What a Girl Wants" (box 2.1) experienced by the nonheteronormative child? Where would the author of "The Story of Boyfriends for Girls of Every Age" locate herself in the Girl

> **Box 2.2.   Excerpt from *Elementary School Girls and Heteronormativity: The Girl Project***
>
> When we asked the girls about favorite TV shows, we learned that many of the kindergarten and first-grade girls were not allowed to watch shows on which the characters kissed, but they all seemed to know about them. When asked about kissing on TV, the second and third graders squealed, "Eww! It's gross!" Molly (second grade) said, "Kissing is gross!" Most said they were allowed to watch shows containing kissing, though. Ariana (third grade) said, "My dad makes me cover the TV when they're kissing."
>
> Some of these "kissing shows" were actually adult programming, as Brooke (second grade) explained: Brooke said, "I watch a show with my parents and sometimes by myself, but I can't tell you what it's called because you'll be shocked." Kristen said, "Just tell us." Brooke said, "No" and put her hands over her mouth. Several girls yelled, "Tell us!" Brooke said that she watches *Sex and the City*. Alicia (third grade) shrugged and said, "It seems bad because of the X word, but it's not about that. It's about women talking about their problems and stuff." Girls nodded. Brooke thought that she would shock the group, but based on many girls' reactions, *Sex and the City* was common viewing. These girls defended it as not inappropriately sexual—the "X word"—but as gender appropriate—"women talking about their problems." Thus, despite the programming's being for adults, the girls believed it was not "inappropriate" for them. (Myers and Raymond 2010, 178)

Project dynamics? When these children do not respond to the heteronormative images, language, and constructions of the culture in the same way their peers do, they know that something essential about their understanding of and place in the world is different. The lack of mirroring and positive reinforcement of their non-heteronormative experience has a profound impact on their identity development.

> What might make the overall social environment of your school more inclusive and welcoming of nonheteronormativity?
>
> Think about traditions, decorations, and holiday celebrations at your school. What are the intentional and unintentional messages they convey?

Heteronormativity and Children from GLBTQI Families

Children with GLBTQI parents are also affected by a school culture that does not readily accept and/or acknowledge their family structure. In 2003 in Louisiana, when a seven-year-old boy told a classmate that his mother was "gay," he was punished by his teacher and the school principal for using a "bad word." This may be a reflection of ideology in a conservative state almost ten years ago. However, in 2007 a third grade girl in Massachusetts—the first state in America to legalize same-sex marriage in 2004—was verbally bullied and physically threatened by classmates because of having lesbian parents (Kosciw and Diaz 2008). In their 2008 study of the school-based experiences of LGBT families, GLSEN found:

> A small percentage of students reported being directly mistreated by or receiving negative comments from a teacher because of their family (11% and 15%, respectively). However, many students with LGBT parents may experience

more subtle forms of exclusion from their school. More than a quarter (30%) of students in our study reported feeling that they could not fully participate in school specifically because they had an LGBT parent, and 36% felt that school personnel did not acknowledge that they were from an LGBT family (e.g., not permitting one parent to sign a school form because he or she was not the student's legal parent or guardian). In addition, about a fifth of students reported that they had been discouraged from talking about their parents or family at school by a teacher, principal or other school staff person (22%) and felt excluded from classroom activities because they had an LGBT parent (20%). For example, some students described incidents in which representations of LGBT families were not included in class activities, such as when constructing a family tree. (Kosciw and Diaz 2008)

In what school-based situations would a teacher, principal, or staff person discourage a student from talking about his gay parents or family? Based on climate surveys, we know that the use of homophobic language in schools is epidemic (Kosciw et al. 2010), yet the focus of concern in relation to this trend is typically those students who themselves may be GLBTQI. Is this advice to hide the truth about one's family an attempt to protect children? What message does that advice send?

It is clear that children with GLBTQI parents bear the bias of heteronormativity, whether they openly discuss their parents or not. "Letters from Camp" illustrates the negative impact that hearing homophobic language can have. This ten-year-old is reflecting the particular reality of boy culture as lived out at this camp, where kids use antigay expressions to assert their masculinity and dominance.

Letter From Camp 1

(10 year old boy to his 7 year old sister)

Graphic 2.2.

Letter From Camp 2

(10 year old boy to his moms)

Dear MoMs
Camps okay, but theres a lot
of talk about gays and faggot
Some examples, when a kid was
in the changing room they said if
you look at me your gay.
And who is more of a fagott.

Love

Graphic 2.3.

Heteronormativity and the "Authority of a Teacher"

Because elementary school is a powerful socializing force in presenting and maintaining heteronormativity, teachers have tremendous clout in their role as a primary "identity instructor." It is easy for teachers to forget that **while school-age children may not be sexually mature or sexually active, they are developing this aspect of their identity in an ongoing way**. The teacher can either support, mirror, and validate an emerging, nonheteronormative identity, or deny, stigmatize, and suppress it. The Adrienne Rich quotation that begins this chapter speaks to the profound impact a teacher has when she truly "sees"—or does not see—her student in the world.

Heteronormativity and Nonheterosexual Teens

The elementary student moves on to middle school and enters early adolescence, a developmental stage that is characterized by enormous physiological, cognitive, social, and psychological changes. As students enter puberty and move closer to becoming sexually active, heteronormative expectations become more intense. Students do not all mature at the same time or rate, yet the social milieu demands that students "declare" their identities on many dimensions. *Are you a jock or a musician? A partier? Skater? A geek? Gay? Straight? Queer? What is queer anyway?*

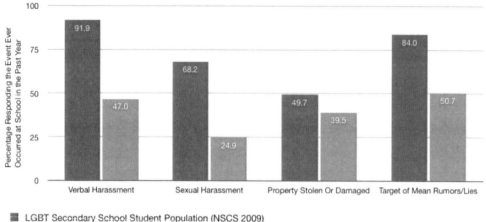

Diagram 2.3. LGBT Secondary School Student Population vs. General Secondary School Student Population: Victimization Experiences at School
Data from the 2009 GLSEN Climate Survey as presented in Kosciw, Greytak, Diaz, and Bartkiewicz (2010). The sample consisted of 7,216 non-heterosexual U.S. students, grades 6-12, 9.7% of which identified themselves as not cisgender (e.g. transgender, genderqueer).

For students who are heterosexual there are social structures in middle school (MS) and high school (HS) within which they can explore, experiment, and ultimately, consolidate their sexual identity. Under the very best of circumstances, students who are gay, lesbian, bisexual, transgender, queer, or intersex (GLBTQI) are supported, yet they still experience a level of conspicuousness that carries an enormous added burden to the already challenging task of sexual identity development (see chapter 7 for detailed discussion). Under the worst of circumstances, GLBTQI students—or those perceived to be GLBTQI—experience ongoing verbal, physical, and sexual harassment every day at school (Kosciw et al. 2010; diagram 2.3).

Differently Gendered Teens

> ➤ *More than 90 percent of the students at my school have no information about gender diversity, but tons about sexuality.*
> ➤ *Everybody knows about the LGB but nobody knows about the T.*
> ➤ *A few teachers are good with sexuality, but none even know the basics about gender diversity.*
> ➤ *I'm trans in a very transphobic school. I get on the bus every day forcing myself to think of reasons why I shouldn't drop out.*

Many educators have worked hard over the past thirty years to inform themselves about different sexualities; engaging with students who have different gender presentations is a more recent area of inquiry. Those educators who support

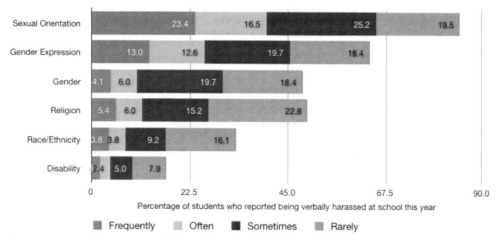

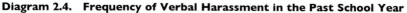

Diagram 2.4. Frequency of Verbal Harassment in the Past School Year
Data from the 2009 GLSEN Climate Survey as presented in Kosciw, Greytak, Diaz, and Bartkiewicz (2010). The sample consisted of 7,216 non-heterosexual U.S. students, grades 6-12, 9.7% of which identified themselves as not cisgender (e.g. transgender, genderqueer).

their gay students may find understanding, supporting, and educating others about the fluidity of *transgender* or *genderqueer* identities new territory.

> ❖ *My biggest challenge is helping elementary, middle school, and high school students and their parents understand the difference between sexual identity and gender identity. It is my belief that a narrow view of gender identity is one of the primary reasons some children are teased by others and assumed to be lesbian or gay. For example, the boy with long hair who is not athletic or the girl with short hair who enjoys basketball and wears ties are sometimes asked (and teased) about being gay or lesbian because of their gender expression or gender roles.*

This is an important area of professional development for teachers, as the research demonstrates that the school experiences of teens who express their gender differently than expected can be very negative (Kosciw et al. 2010; diagram 2.4).

WHAT TO REMEMBER: CHAPTER TWO

Heteronormativity

1. **Heteronormativity** is the assumption that everyone is or should be heterosexual, that men should be masculine and women should be feminine, and that male/female pairing is ideal.
2. In spite of data that demonstrates the natural variability of gender and sexuality, heteronormativity is perceived as normative and preferable.

3. School is typically a heteronormative institution.

4. Educators must recognize heteronormativity and understand its impact on student development.

5. Books, television, movies, and other forms of media that are marketed to children and adolescents emphasize and privilege heteronormative behaviors and images.

6. Young children explore sexuality through their pretend play.

7. Pressure for girls to conform to/perform heterosexual pairings begins as early as kindergarten and first grade.

8. Families, as well as individuals, are typically portrayed as heteronormative.

9. Exclusively heteronormative environments make healthy gender identity development and sexual identity development extremely difficult for GLBTQI youth.

10. GLBTQI youth—and those perceived to be GLBTQI—are at highest risk for harassment and victimization in schools.

11. Typically educators are more familiar with the notion of different sexualities than different gender identities, such as genderqueer.

3

A FRAMEWORK FOR ENGAGING GSD AT SCHOOL

Educational Mission; Best "Good" Pedagogical Practices

Any program studying sexuality must address a common charge: that such programs are motivated by the "political agenda" of promoting the social acceptance of homosexuality as an acceptable "lifestyle," and that its faculty are not inquiring as scholars but are "proselytizing" for this lifestyle. The response should be that the primary motivation for such studies is to gain knowledge that we need if we are to think well about a crucial area of human life. An ancillary motivation is indeed one of fostering respect, tolerance, and friendship. These are fine aims for a curriculum in a democracy to have.

It is not clear why learning about a subject should be associated with the erosion of moral judgment on the subject.

—Martha Nussbaum, *Cultivating Humanity*

A comprehensive understanding of gender and sexuality developmental, as outlined in chapter 1, is the first framework that educators need in order to engage with gender and sexuality diversity at school. This chapter offers a second framework for "teaching and learning" about gender and sexuality diversity (GSD) and guides educators as they prepare to work directly with GSD in the classroom, hallways, and every other corner of school life. While there are many political, legal, social, religious, and medical directives about gender and sexuality diversity, in a school setting, it is **educational mission** that must serve as the primary guide.

Using the school's mission as the second central framework ensures that the same educational goals and pedagogical practices that inform teaching in other areas will inform engagement with GSD as well. Best "good" practices in relation to GSD must be based on the predominant values and goals espoused in the mission. They must be established with the same thoroughness and rigor that characterizes best practice development in all other areas.

Educators are trained to assess methodology, build and revise curricula, and explore new ways of teaching old material and old ways of teaching new material. This dynamic, ongoing process of assessment and evaluation ensures that children are the beneficiaries of best practices in every subject year after year. It also affirms the pedagogical integrity of the school's efforts. Simply put, there is no better approach than this for addressing gender and sexuality diversity in the preK–12 setting.

SECTION I
EDUCATIONAL MISSION

WHAT'S IN A MISSION?

The school mission statement provides a succinct summary of what the institution stands for and strives to be. Schools define themselves according to particular values and points of emphasis, from *promoting a culture of mutual trust and respect* to a *commitment to working with the "whole child."* Consider these examples from public and private preK–12 schools across the United States.

Mission Language from Public School Districts

- *Every student must be educated in a safe, welcoming, effective and innovative learning environment . . . that supports civility, respect, and academic achievement.* (Dallas, TX)
- *Core Values: Trust, Respect, Integrity, Diversity, Excellence.* (Clarke County, GA)
- *All schools can and must be a safe learning environment where every student and adult is valued and respected.* (Duval County, FL)
- *Create a collaborative school climate that improves student learning, promotes student engagement, and builds on prior knowledge and experiences.* (Boston, MA)
- *Develop the potential of each pupil so that he/she will be informed, prepared and capable of assuming full responsibility for making his/her own decisions.* (Laguna Beach, CA)
- *Maintain safe and orderly school environments for all students and employees . . . and promote a culture of mutual trust and respect.* (Santa Barbara, CA)

- *Provide relevant, integrated and meaningful learning experiences for students that will prepare them for life.* (Helena, MT)
- *Administration, teachers and staff are united in a common goal to develop all students to their highest level of performance.* (Syracuse, NY)
- *Everybody is somebody.* (Midland County, AR)

Mission Language from Independent Schools across the United States

- *Promote the full development of mind, body, and spirit . . . ; cultivate respect for diversity and engender habits of moral and ethical leadership and a sense of responsibility to the broader community.* (Baltimore, MD)
- *Promote educational excellence, personal responsibility, and balanced growth, and thereby help . . . students discover their talents and develop their best potentials.* (Houston, TX)
- *Provide a culturally diverse environment in which students develop a love of learning, a strong social conscience, and a spirit of discovery as they pursue their full academic and personal potential.* (Morristown, NJ)
- *Mutual respect is the foundation of our School community, and that respect for others leads us to serve them and to embrace diverse peoples and cultures.* (Charlotte, NC)
- *Values of faith, community, justice and respect provide the foundation for students to be powerful agents of change.* (Englewood, CO)
- *Values inclusion . . .; we deliberately seek ways to recruit and retain a diverse board of trustees, faculty, staff, and student body, broaden our worldview, and become more involved in our larger community.* (Gainesville, GA)
- *Empower students to develop intellectual curiosity, the courage to lead, and the confidence to thrive in a complex and changing world.* (Grosse Point Woods, MI)
- *Prepare students for college and life by inspiring achievement, integrity, confidence, and compassion in an academic community dedicated to nurturing mind, body, and soul.* (Jacksonville, FL)
- *Partners with families and the community to prepare students for socially responsible, values based leadership in a culturally and religiously diverse world.* (Kansas City, MO)
- *A vibrant and diverse community whose purpose is to promote personal and intellectual growth.* (Los Angeles, CA)

For both public and private preK–12 schools, articulating and implementing a clear mission is not just a matter of principle but a requirement for accreditation in every region of the country. For example, the New England Association of Schools and Colleges (NEASC) states that there must be "**congruence between the schools' stated mission and core values and its actual program, policies, planning and decision-making**" (2007). (emphasis mine)

Loosely translated, the NEASC requirement means schools must walk the walk, not just talk the talk. Here's the challenge. In the mission statement, idealism (i.e., "vision") and practicality (i.e., "program") meet. Clarifying and establishing values and educational philosophy is one task; implementing and putting these values into practice is another. As this teacher notes

❖ *The more explicit we are, the more practiced we will be in welcoming and supporting ALL students, which is our mission.*

For every school that explores approaches to gender and sexuality diversity, this grappling with the gaps between word and deed is a central and critical part of the process by which best practices can be determined.

Mission in Relation to "Diversity"

In 2011 it is rare to find a preK–12 school in the United States that does not mention "valuing diversity" as part of its educational philosophy and community ethos. The history and evolution of "diversity" as a concept and construct is beyond the scope of this chapter. Suffice it to say that there have been many incarnations of racial, religious, and ethnic integration in American public and private schools over time. As the comments from these teachers attest, it is unclear today whether diverse genders and sexualities represent the kind of "diversity" that educational institutions seek to integrate, value, and respect.

❖ *Addressing gender and sexuality is important. It is part of our mission; it is the right way, the ethical way.*
❖ *This is important but let's not overdo it—it's respect, that's all it is.*
❖ *The strength of the white male culture is such that little emphasis is put on recognizing and/or addressing issues of GSD. While the school is in the process of increasing the diversity of the student and adult population, it does not seem that GSD would be considered part of that picture.*

Some schools refer to *diversity* in the most general terms (i.e., hard to tell what the word actually stands for) and some define exactly what they mean, enumerating the demographics and experiences that fall under the diversity signifier. Review the language in the samples provided in Additional Resources 3.1 through 3.3. Which statements make the school's intention clear? **Clarifying**

**what the school's "commitment to diversity" actually means *in practice*
is essential.**

Though the mission may assert "respect for the individual" or "valuing differences," people may interpret those statements very differently.

❖ *We need to make sure the whole community knows that discussion of gender
and sexuality is within our mission and can take place any time.*

❖ *I don't see this as being the same as race. Racial diversity makes sense to me;
"gender diversity" does not.*

❖ *In the Resource Group 175 Strategic Report done for the school last year,
this observation was shared: "There was no consistent agreement as to what
diversity means at the school or as to what it should mean."*

It can be a common assumption—by parents, teachers, and students alike—that
gender and sexuality diversity is not included in broad endorsements of "respect
for others."

Therefore, explicitly identifying the components of GSD that are respected, valued, and protected provides a key reference point for all community members. For
example, the phrase "valuing differences such as age, race, sex, gender identities,
sexual identities, religion . . ." leaves no doubt that sex, gender, and sexuality are
valued and protected categories.[1] In addition, research indicates that enumeration
is a critical feature of policies that successfully support a safe school environment
for all students, not just those who are GLBTQI (Kosciw et al. 2010).

> Given the explicit endorsement of "equitable and just treatment for all" in most
> school missions, why do many educators doubt that inclusion of gender and
> sexuality diversity is part of their school's agenda?
>
> What does your own mission statement say? How often do you use it as a peda-
> gogical reference point for what and how you teach?

Mission and Politics

In discussions about (a) mission, (b) values, and (c) gender and sexuality diversity, teachers often raise questions about *ideology, politics,* and *"neutrality."*
Among the thousands of educators I have worked with over the years, there is a
striking degree of trepidation and ambivalence about taking a personal *or* professional stand in relation to GSD. For example, while most teachers are personally
and professionally emphatic about the immorality of racism, sexism, or anti-Semi-
tism, many are less certain—as this teacher observes—about whether discrimination and bias related to gender and sexuality diversity should be viewed similarly
in an educational setting.

❖ *We need constant reassurance from administration that this topic is integral to school's mission.*

If a teacher asserts, for instance, that racism is reprehensible, she is not likely to be accused of having some kind of "political agenda" (though if she is a person of color, she might well be perceived by some as "pushing her own issues"). More importantly, she never doubts that this assertion about racism is in keeping with the educational mission and values of the school (even if racism is an ongoing issue at her school). The teacher who questions antigay bias, heterosexism, or homophobia, however, fears being tagged with the "political agenda" label. She is vulnerable to backlash from angry parents and sanction from her administration. In some schools, she may fear losing her job.

Most mission statements include a declaration to the effect that "all children and families are welcome in our community." However, the elementary teacher who uses books and conversation with his students to affirm, for example, that same-sex parents are "acceptable" and welcome, can be unclear about the school's support of this instruction.

❖ *The administration needs to clarify what is appropriate for a teacher to discuss and then have our backs!*
❖ *We need a school philosophy that gives institutional support to teachers and students to ask/teach freely about these issues. This is an "educational" agenda, not a political one!*
❖ *I find it fascinating that GSD is still treated like the outlier in inclusion work. It is last on the list to be tackled in most initiatives. Somehow as a country we shamed folks into at least feeling like they can avoid the work on ableism, race, religion, etc. But it still seems legal in school environments to allow community discomfort with GSD to prevail so that no work gets done.*

The teacher may even have a child with same-sex parents right in his classroom, yet he still questions whether discussing gender and sexuality diversity in a positive light is in keeping with the school's values and district policy. So, in spite of the child's enrollment at the school, and despite assertions in the mission statement about "valuing diversity," fear of parent disapproval and administrative reprimand are potent and commonplace obstacles for classroom teachers (DePalma and Atkinson 2010, 56).

> What in your school mission statement does or does not support explicitly including gender and sexuality diversity in your educational program?
> Do you have your own questions or concerns about whether GSD should be an explicit part of the school program in the same way that other aspects of identity (e.g., race) are?

Mission and "Neutrality"

In the face of this philosophical uncertainty and pedagogical fear, it is not surprising then that some schools and teachers seek safe ground by adopting a "neutral" stance.[2]

❖ *What is the role of a teacher relative to issues of gender expression, sexual identity and working with GLBTQ families in the classroom and school community? Can you, should you take a neutral stance on these issues?*

❖ *While we don't want to promote any specific ideology, it will be important for all our students to leave our school with the tools to talk honestly and respectfully about gender and sexual identity and to be responsible citizens in diverse communities beyond our walls.*

❖ *I don't think it is my role as a teacher to give an opinion about this.*

At first glance, the I'm-not-taking-a-stand-one-way-or-another position seems legitimate; educators will often argue the importance of allowing "both sides" to be heard in any conflict. Yet as I have watched this conversation unfold over and over again among educators, it is only a matter of time until someone observes that the school has rendered opinions and taken nonneutral, moral stands on other diversity issues: *We don't tolerate racism; why should we be "neutral" toward heterosexism?*

In actuality there is very little neutrality in creating and pursuing *any* educational mission. Values of all kinds serve as indispensable philosophical and pedagogical guideposts (see, for example, NAIS Principles of Good Practice, Additional Resource 3.4, and National Association for the Education of Young Children Code of Ethical Conduct, Additional Resource 3.5), and there are multiple "authorities" involved in shaping educational vision, such as parents, school boards, trustees, superintendents, and state legislatures. There are various practical factors to contend with like (a) finances, (b) student performance, (c) attrition, and (d) compliance with state mandates, none of which are "neutral" in their impact.

Then there are long-standing traditions or community activities that explicitly and implicitly convey a variety of mission values. For example, consider the "values" that are expressed via (a) the formal graduation dress code, (b) the senior prom, (c) rival athletic contests, and (d) the annual Maypole ceremony. These rituals (and many more like them) are associated with school spirit and community building (see chapter 7). They are rarely perceived as being exclusionary or offensive in relation to gender and sexuality diversity. So questioning whether the school is fulfilling its mission in relation to GSD means questioning the status quo on multiple levels.

Do your own professional values line up with your school's stated mission and philosophy in relation to gender and sexuality diversity? Your personal values?

Do you consider your personal and professional values as being different and/or separate? How do you define the boundary between what is personal belief and professional obligation? (See chapter 10 for more on personal/professional identity.)

Religious schools.   Those schools with religious affiliations face a unique obligation when articulating their mission in relation to gender and sexuality diversity. They must answer to the standards set by educational accreditation authorities *and* to the doctrine on which their faith is based. For example, since the ordination of openly gay bishop Gene Robinson in 2003, and the more recent ordination of openly lesbian bishop Mary Glasspool in 2010, schools with Episcopal affiliations have had to contend with a profound theological rift in relation to GSD that has divided the Anglican Church worldwide. Similarly Catholic, Quaker, and Jewish schools must attend to the ways matters of educational mission and religious doctrine inform and are influenced by each other.

WHAT TO REMEMBER: SECTION I

Mission

1. The school's educational mission is one of two primary frameworks for addressing gender and sexuality diversity. (The other is comprehensive knowledge of GID and SID in children and adolescents. See chapter 1.)
2. A mission statement is where ideology and practicality meet.
3. "Valuing diversity" is included in most mission statements, yet schools vary widely in whether/how they enumerate what "diversity" stands for.
4. The shape and scope of a school mission is influenced by many factors, including professional guidelines, economic realities, state law, and long-standing school traditions.
5. Out of fear and pedagogical uncertainty, teachers may try to maintain a "neutral" position in relation to GSD.
6. The National Association of Independent Schools (NAIS) includes Equity and Justice as part of their Principles of Good Practice.
7. The National Association of Educators of Young Children (NAEYC) includes Commitment to Inclusion and Diversity as part of their Core Competencies.
8. Religious and military schools may be particularly challenged to honor potentially competing value sets in relation to GSD.

SECTION II
STANDARDS OF GOOD PRACTICE

Educators have a responsibility to make schools into places that are for, and that attempt to teach, all their students. To fail to work against the various forms of oppression is to be complicit with them. (Kumashiro 2002, 37)

WORKING WITH ALL CHILDREN;
WORKING WITH WHOLE CHILDREN

The standards of good practice for private and public school teachers emphasize understanding and working with the "whole child" in a developmentally appropriate manner (NAEYC Advanced Standards of Practice, Additional Resource 3.6; NAIS Principles of Good Practice, Additional Resource 3.4). At each grade level, therefore, educators must meet the *cognitive, social, emotional*, and *physical* needs of children and adolescents. As established in chapter 1, gender identity and sexual identity are central to human development at every age and thus *should* fit squarely within the "whole child" concept. Unfortunately, the aspects of development related to gender and sexuality are often sidestepped out of ignorance, fear, and bias.

In order for all students to feel affirmed and thrive, their learning environment must be safe and free of bias. The prevalence of gender and sexuality based harassment in preK–12 schools across the United States reflects a widespread failure to affirm and protect students whose gender expression and sexual identity do not con-

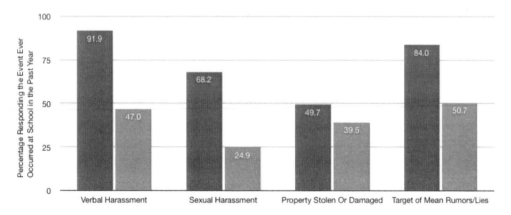

Diagram 3.1.   LGBT Secondary School Student Population vs. General Secondary School Student Population: Victimization Experiences at School
Data from the 2009 GLSEN Climate Survey as presented in Kosciw, Greytak, Diaz, and Bartkiewicz (2010). The sample consisted of 7,216 non-heterosexual U.S. students, grades 6-12, 9.7% of which identified themselves as not cisgender (e.g. transgender, genderqueer).

form to heteronormative standards (see diagram 3.1). In addition to being subjected to emotional, physical, and sexual harassment, these students do not perform as well academically—despite being just as qualified—as their straight peers, and some foreclose on plans to finish high school and/or attend college (Kosciw et al. 2010).

Rethinking "Best Practices"

The concept of "best practices" is front and center in any conversation about preK–12 educational policy. However, here, and throughout this book, I emphasize the best "good practices." Kumashiro (2002; 2008) rightly underscores the importance of concepts and resources rather than singular strategies that "work." The term "best practices" implies that there is a "best way" and one need only find it and use it to be successful. **Good practice** in relation to GSD education challenges a teacher to engage with new language and constructs; she must then adapt and modify those constructs along the way.[3] Chapters 6 and 7 are full of models and examples of good practice.

The Problematic "Celebration" Approach

In an attempt to create more inclusive and safe environments, some preK–12 schools engage diversity by "celebrating" anyone who is not white, not male, not Christian, not American, and, very occasionally, not heterosexual. While the intentions here may be good, there is little pedagogical credibility to this approach, as these celebrations or special programs are typically

- isolated events.
- not well integrated into the intellectual and social fabric of the school.
- based on superficial understandings of a given "minority" group.

The let's-celebrate-those-who-are-different tack also perpetuates a "dominant vs. other" paradigm. Diversity celebrations or programs are about *them*; the rest of the year is about *us*.

Another pedagogical flaw in the celebration approach lies in the assumption that all types of "different" can be comfortably accommodated within a single construct. If *diversity* is defined by a school as including race, religion, ethnicity, age, sex, gender identity, sexual orientation, and nationality, what will the focus of the celebration be? What will be the common element among those being celebrated? And how do they all feel being lumped together as the honored guests at the annual Martin Luther King Jr. Day assembly?

What the "diverse" invitees may have most in common is the experience of being the object of prejudice, of being used by society to contain or represent that which is "other," dirty, inferior, exotic, foreign, dangerous, even perverse. Beyond that, the histories of these celebrants are profoundly different; their respective fights for equity and justice do not share the same dimensions and trajectories. While the aim of these celebrations is to create inclusivity, they can actually perpetuate division. Best good practices require true integration of "difference" into the community and ongoing representation in the curriculum.

In addition to marginalization being a difficult rallying point for celebration, some of the groups who are gathered under the Diversity or Multicultural umbrella have historically adversarial relationships. There is a risk here of overgeneralizing about the attitudes and behaviors of certain groups, and at the same time, the animosity and conflict between certain categories of people are well documented. It is crucial to recognize that attitudes toward gender and sexuality are strongly influenced by any number of additional identifiers, including (but not limited to) race, age, ethnicity, nationality, and religion. The assumption that a racial minority will "understand" or be "identified with" a sexual minority because they share second class status in society is a belittling and facile perspective.

Trying to understand the complex interplay of different cultural values in relation to GSD is tricky going. On the one hand, a story like "The View of 'Other' Countries" provides a particular perspective on how GSD is viewed globally by some. Yet the story can also create the impression that it is those "other" countries like Russia, Korea, and South Africa that are "barbaric" while the United States is "civilized." **Clarity about sameness and otherness is best achieved by understanding that we are all alike and we are all different.** This dual reality makes generalizations inherently risky.

The View of "Other" Countries

I am working with a group of 9th grade boys at a boarding school in the South. We are meeting in a science lecture hall after dinner, and most of the boys look rumpled, having removed their jackets and ties. Some appear incredibly young, little boys with fresh faces and buzz cuts. Others sport stubble and deep voices. We are talking about adolescence, puberty, gender, sexuality, stereotypes. The boys are predictably rowdy, and the discussion is peppered with jokes and mild put-downs. At one point, when we are talking about attitudes towards gay people, a tall, Slavic-looking boy raises his hand and volunteers, "In my country, we kill you!" I raise my eyebrows, take a step back and say, "Whoa." There is quite a bit of laughter, and a boy in the front row explains to me, "He's from Russia." While the boy from Russia is smiling, it is clear that his comment is sincere, not merely provocative. "What about other countries?" I ask. Another boy offers, "In Korea we do not have this conversation. I do not understand why we are talking about such things." In the front row, a boy with very dark skin who has been silent until now says in a soft voice, "These people are punished in my country. They are beaten."

"And what about in this country? The United States?" I ask. "Not as bad,"
someone says. Another boy counters: "What about all the gay-bashing, Dude?
What do you call that?" "Well, that's not as bad as killing." I raise my eyebrows
again and say, "Looks like we have different points of view about what goes on
right here in this country. Who is right?" I gesture to the two boys who spoke
last, "And, are we even asking the right question?"

Multicultural Practice

In the mid-1970s multicultural education (MCE) emerged as an educational
paradigm aimed at promoting social justice for racial and ethnic minorities in
schooling. MCE builds curricula that reflect the social, economic, and racial diversity that exists within schools. It also challenges prevailing pedagogical approaches,
which have failed to close the achievement gap between white and nonwhite students in public education (Pollock 2008). While certain models of MCE emphasize
social justice and equity for all, fundamental disagreements remain regarding the
types of cultural differences that should be included in MCE, particularly those
related to GSD (Jennings and Macgillivray 2011; Meyer 2010; Asher 2007).

The question of whether gender and sexuality belong within a MCE frame is
seemingly legitimate.

❖ *Is someone being transgender a "cultural" issue in the same way that being*
   African American or a first generation immigrant is? I don't really think so.

❖ *I would be sad to see us actively promote a gay and lesbian culture. I would*
   rather see the school be quietly appreciative of people's life choices. I think
   that we're already very welcoming and open.

We use demographic variables such as age, race, ethnicity, biological sex, gender
identity, sexual identity, religion, class, ability, and nationality to create categories
of people. Which of these variables represent a *cultural* identity and which represent a *human* identity? Are they inherently linked? Or are they one in the same?

People of certain racial, ethnic, and religious identities have long histories of
shared existence, common language, communal living, unique traditions, rituals,
and struggles. Though a variety of genders and sexualities have existed throughout
history; across every culture, religion, and region of the world, GLBTQI people as
a *group* are not connected through heritage, language, or place of origin. In the
past twenty-five years, through scholarship and film, the history of gay and lesbian
people has been and continues to be told (*Out of the Past* 1998; D'Emilio 2002;
Bronski 2011). Yet current popular notions of "gay culture" refer to shared behaviors and characteristics that can be based primarily on stereotypes and superficial
understandings of what it means to identify as GLBTQI. There are as many "within
group" differences among GLBTQI people as there are among, say, Jewish people.

In an attempt to bring the troubled relationship between MCE and LGBT issues to light, Jennings and Macgillivray (2011) reviewed the strengths and weaknesses of a dozen popular multicultural education textbooks. The majority of the texts that did address LGBT issues emphasized harassment of LGBT youth without balancing this view with accounts of well-adjusted, successful teens. As a result, most texts did not mention the positive role of Gay Straight Alliances in the lives of LGBT youth. In addition, most of these texts also conflated terms/concepts related to *gender* with terms/concepts related to *sexuality*. However, Jennings and Macgillivray also noted a number of improvements in the depth and breadth of LGBT content as compared to previous reviews. They conclude that "there is room under the umbrella of multiculturalism" for LGBT education (58).

Transformative or expedient? The values of MCE support challenging the oppression of any group or class of people. As employed by some teachers, a MCE approach provides a pedagogical framework for transforming prejudicial views and challenging social injustices related to gender and sexuality. However, for other educators, "adding" gender and sexuality diversity to an existing multicultural curriculum is expedient and far less disruptive to classroom norms, traditional language, and standard pedagogical approaches.

> Multiculturalism actually disturbs the traditional classroom far less, for two reasons. First, when dealing with questions of sexual identity or same-sex parents, much of the traditional language, many of the conventional approaches, require radical change. Tense local debates often accompany those changes. Second, teachers often address multicultural issues by simply introducing special lessons into an established curriculum. This additive approach, while admittedly insufficient, requires no fundamental reconceptualization of classroom methods, values and goals. (Birden 2005, 122)

Thus, there are ways that teachers can use the MCE framework to include GLBTQI concerns in the discourse, yet **never really deeply challenge the dominant status of heterosexuality and traditional gender roles.**

For example, a teacher who reads *And Tango Makes Three* to her class to illustrate "a different kind of family" (i.e., two dads, one baby penguin) is not necessarily engaging in a comprehensive reevaluation of the countless ways heteronormativity informs behavior and instruction in the school setting (see chapter 2). Certainly, reading *Tango* is a very important step toward creating a more inclusive curriculum and showing students that there are many ways to be a family. Dismantling systemic, heteronormative structures and assumptions in the curriculum and classroom, however, requires a much deeper, comprehensive process.

To deeply question heteronormative standards may lead right into the fray of conflicting cultural norms and values. For example, if upholding traditional

gender roles is viewed as unquestioned in a particular ethnic group, the classroom teacher who supports a more expansive interpretation of gender roles and
expression may be seen as disrespecting one set of cultural beliefs while acknowledging another. Yet the interactive and dynamic nature of "culture" creates a
minefield for any teacher trying to predict the "values" of a particular group or
category of people. There are too many exceptions to all those cultural rules.
Basing pedagogy on *educational values* is the soundest approach to establishing
best good practices.

> In your professional role, how do you define "culture?" How do you work with
> cultural differences in your teaching?
>
> Does your school mission support questioning and possibly transforming hetero-
> normative structures? What might this kind of transformation look like in your
> classroom, on your team, or in your work as an educator?

Pedagogy and Good Practice

> ❖ *My job is to help students communicate effectively and "think" for them-*
> *selves, and I realize that this is just as true with these issues. And I know*
> *how to do that.*

Educators are relieved when I remind them that *they* are the experts in teaching
the skills students (and adults) need to make sense of complex issues:

- intellectual curiosity
- critical thinking
- empathy
- openness to the unfamiliar
- acceptance of contradictions and complexity
- unbiased research
- effective communication
- a broad view of the world

These are the very skills that are at the heart of good practice for teaching and
learning about gender and sexuality diversity. Yet in order for educators to teach
students how to grapple with the complexities of gender and sexuality, educators
themselves must be given multiple opportunities for professional development
in the domain of GSD. Until they have their own quality learning experiences,
teachers cannot be expected to offer best good practices to students. Chapter 5
explores in depth the various components of successful professional development
for educators in this area.

Conflict as Catalyst for Learning

Most individual educators and school communities prefer to avoid conflict. Yet for schools to find an authentic approach and relationship to gender and sexuality diversity, they must contend with the tensions and differences that exist within their own community. Teachers, parents, administrators, school boards, and trustees tend to have shared goals (e.g., *Let's offer our kids the best education possible*) but plenty of differences in experience and opinion. This is true whether people are debating the wisdom of having a school dress code, switching to a different math curriculum, adopting a block schedule, or addressing gender and sexuality diversity. It is impossible to sidestep these value-driven conflicts, yet it *is* possible to frame such conflicts as natural, inevitable, and potentially useful. Consider this statement by the Wheeler School in Rhode Island.

The Wheeler School Statement on Diversity

At Wheeler we actively seek students, faculty and staff from diverse backgrounds in the belief that a broad range of experiences and viewpoints enhance learning, enrich life on campus, and better prepare us all for full participation in a pluralistic, democratic society.

We also are working toward an inclusive curriculum and pedagogy that recognizes that we live in a multicultural nation and world. To reach this goal we know we must confront overt and hidden biases, such as racism, sexism, and homophobia, in ourselves and others.

*We believe that these goals cannot be reached without an open and continuous dialogue between all members of the Wheeler community, including families and students. We recognize that our diversity—whether based on race, ethnicity, religion, economic status, gender, sexual orientation, or some other source—**can sometimes lead to conflict, but we also believe that such tension can provide the catalyst for the growth and change we seek**.* [emphasis mine]

We are supported in the pursuit of diversity by Wheeler's long tradition of respect for the dignity of the individual and our shared sense of responsibility for the well-being of each other and the larger community.

No pain, no gain.   If genuine change in attitudes, policy, and practice is going to be possible, there must be a realistic acknowledgment of the discomfort involved in examining and questioning long-held truths about gender and sexuality.

❖ *Learning what my colleagues think/feel was not always easy but it was so important. In spite of our differences, I feel more confident now that we can move forward as a community.*

As educators we know that important learning often includes some measure of intellectual and emotional tension and discomfort. Using educational mission and sound pedagogy, each school can offer "teaching and learning" about gender and sexuality diversity that benefits and involves every community member.

WHAT TO REMEMBER: SECTION III

Pedagogy and Best Practices

1. The school's educational mission and pedagogical approach (i.e., best good practices) is one of two primary frameworks for addressing gender and sexuality diversity. (The other is comprehensive knowledge of GID and SID.)
2. The Standards of Good Practice for both public and private schools involve working with the whole child at every age.
3. Best good practices include providing a bias-free learning environment for all students at every age.
4. Pedagogical approaches that involve "celebrating" diversity can foster a climate of "otherness" rather than inclusivity.
5. Schools must be explicit about what *diversity* stands for.
6. Combining various "minorities" under the broad construct of diversity assumes affinity and cohesion among groups that may not be allied.
7. A multicultural education approach to gender and sexuality diversity can be transformative rather than expedient only if heteronormative structures and systems in school are deconstructed.
8. The essential skills for engaging GSD in preK–12 schools are the same as those required for many types of intellectual and emotional learning (e.g., critical thinking, curiosity, empathy, values clarification, etc.)
9. Professional development for teachers must offer multiple opportunities for intellectual and emotional learning about GSD.
10. Differences in opinion, values, and perspective about GSD are inevitable. A process approach to teaching and learning for all community members—teachers, parents, administrators, students—creates a safe, pedagogically consistent framework.
11. Schools can frame the "conflict" about gender and sexuality diversity as a necessary catalyst for learning, growth, and change.

ADDITIONAL RESOURCES

Additional Resource 3.1

Defining and Addressing "Diversity": Independent Schools

- *Students flourish in a diverse community.*
- *Strives to maintain a culture of diversity with respect to income, race, ethnicity, gender, sexual orientation, and religion.*

- *Welcomes students, faculty, staff and board of trustees from nontraditional families, multicultural families, and immigrant families.*
- *Immersion in a diverse school culture as well as educational training that helps students learn more about and appreciate differences on a continuing basis.*
- *This approach fosters respect for differences, enhances personal growth and development, and provides essential preparation for the increasing diversity of higher education, community life and the workplace.*
- *Preconceived notions are often dispelled through activities and discussions about differences, leading to a more open and caring culture that celebrates diversity.*
- *Values geographic diversity and socioeconomic diversity, which brings a variety of perspectives and enables students to debate, discover, and expand upon their knowledge of the world.*
- *Embracing diversity and the pursuit of excellence, we create a community in which individuals flourish.*
- *In keeping with the Quakers' longstanding commitment to respect for differences . . . strives to maintain a culture of diversity with respect to income, race, ethnicity, gender, sexual orientation and religion.*

Additional Resource 3.2

Defining and Addressing "Diversity": Public Schools

- *Every student can be . . . successful by participating in a learning community where all members understand and respect each other. . . . Diversity includes but is not limited to race, ethnicity, language, culture, sexual orientation, disability, gender, socioeconomic status, age, national origin, and religion.* ("Multicultural Philosophy," Clarke County, GA)
- *We value the diversity of people, perspectives and practices* ("Strategic Plan 2006–2011," Cincinnati, OH)
- *The Charlotte-Mecklenburg Board of Education defines multicultural education as that which recognizes, values and affirms diversity in a pluralistic environment . . . and fosters acceptance and appreciation of diversity, development of greater understanding of cultural patterns, respect for people of all cultures, development of positive and productive interaction among people and experiences of diverse cultural groups, and understanding of historical, political and economic bases of current inequalities.* ("Multiculturalism," Charlotte-Mecklenburg, NC)
- *We believe in taking into consideration each child's special needs and cultural background; therefore the nature of each individual, along with their cultural beliefs, must be recognized as unique intellectually, physically, socially and emotionally.* ("Beliefs," Coral Gables Senior High School, FL)

- *Our greatest strength as a school district is the racial, gender, ethnic, and socio-economic diversity of our students and community. . . . We encourage diversity as a vital component of educational value that includes our parents, community partners, civic and faith based organizations.* ("Core Beliefs and Commitments," Duval County, FL)
- *To develop in each individual a respect from himself/herself and the capacity to maintain his/her individuality and to respect the same right for every other individual* ("Philosophy of Education," Laguna Beach, CA)
- *We value student and staff diversity in our schools and classrooms and will promote equal access across all educational programs and activities* ("Core Beliefs and Commitments," Santa Barbara, CA)
- *Exposure to a broad range of ideas and experiences is necessary to prepare students for a life of responsible citizenship* ("Freedom to Teach, to Learn and to Express Ideas," Helena, MT)
- *[We] recognize the value of sustaining and advancing a safe and welcoming learning environment, and thus, strive to treat both employees and students with respect and dignity.* ("Diversity, Equity and Inclusion," South Washington County, MN)
- *Our students will perceive the District as a place of hope, where cultural diversity and individual differences are appreciated and where all students, regardless of socio-economic background, can achieve their highest potential.* ("Educational Philosophy," Syracuse, NY)

Additional Resource 3.3

National Association for the Education of Young Children Advanced Standards: Depth of Commitment to Inclusion and Diversity

Although all areas of professional education share this commitment, early childhood education has traditionally had a special concern with these issues. Much of the history of the field has been an effort to prevent later social, emotional, and academic difficulties through high-quality intervention, especially for those young children living in poverty or experiencing developmental challenges. Traditionally, but to a growing extent in recent years, equity and justice concerns, antibias approaches to early education, and cultural competence have influenced the early childhood field's position statements and standards. NAEYC's Governing Board has identified as its overarching priority the creation of a "high performing, inclusive organization" that draws from and attracts diverse perspectives and cultures to create excellence.

Additional Resource 3.4

NAIS Principles of Good Practice

The NAIS Principles of Good Practice for member schools define high standards and ethical behavior in key areas of school operations to guide schools in becoming the best education communities they can be. Accordingly, membership in NAIS is contingent upon agreement to abide by "the spirit" of the PGPs. Principles are precepts grounded in an ethic and ethos of "doing the right thing." Practices are common activities.

From **Early Childhood Educators** (Revised and approved by the NAIS board in 1994):

- Early childhood education emphasizes the development of the whole child, providing for each child's social, emotional, physical, and intellectual needs.
- Early childhood programs are developmentally appropriate, in that they are based on an understanding of general patterns of growth in the early years as well as children's individual development.
- Early childhood educators engage parents as partners in understanding the unique characteristics and needs of young children.
- Early childhood educators, in observing and interpreting children's behavior, use bias-free assessment tools based on developmental norms.
- Early childhood educators promote equity and justice by creating a community that fosters respect, understanding, and an appreciation of differences.

From **Elementary Educators** (Revised and approved by the NAIS board in 2001):

- Elementary school educators create a safe and secure environment in which students grow in both autonomy and the ability to work and play together.
- Elementary school educators support the child's emerging identity by respecting and providing for each student's voice.
- Elementary school educators build relationships with their students in which each child feels understood, nurtured, and challenged.
- Elementary school educators work to create a relationship with parents that facilitates the exchange of information necessary to ensure the child's progress.
- Elementary school educators defend the dignity and worth of each member of the community and create an environment that fosters respect, understanding, and acceptance of differences.

From **Middle School Educators** (Revised and approved by the NAIS board in 2008):

- Middle school is a unique period in the educational life of a student. Youngsters experience a variety of significant changes, both individually and collectively. The range of academic ability and physical and emotional development is huge. Relationships among adolescents, not to mention with their parents, change on a daily basis. Middle school educators have the responsibility to respond to and provide for the unique developmental needs and characteristics of their students.
- Middle school educators provide specific programs aimed at creating a bias-free environment, safe and inclusive for all, which focuses on eliminating cliques and establishes a climate where bullying is unacceptable. Programs should support each student's need to develop a distinct self-concept and to be recognized as an individual and as a member of the group.

From **Secondary School Educators** (Revised and approved by the NAIS board in 2003):

- Secondary school educators take responsibility for being role models.
- Secondary school educators affirm and defend the dignity and worth of each member of the community and maintain an environment that fosters respect.
- Secondary school educators help students take more and more responsibility for themselves and the multiple communities in which they live.
- Secondary school educators prepare students to take advantage of subsequent opportunities for learning and to take their places as members of a democratic society and the global community.

Additional Resource 3.5

National Association for the Education of Young Children Code of Ethical Conduct: Guidelines for Responsible Behavior in Early Childhood Education

I. *Ethical Responsibilities to Children*

Childhood is a unique and valuable stage in the life cycle. Our paramount responsibility is to provide safe, healthy, nurturing, and responsive settings for children. We are committed to supporting children's development by cherishing individual differences, by helping them learn to live and work cooperatively, and by promoting their self-esteem.

Ideals:

- To be familiar with the knowledge base of early childhood education and to keep current through continuing education and in-service training.
- To base program practices upon current knowledge in the field of child development and related disciplines and upon particular knowledge of each child.
- To recognize and respect the uniqueness and potential of each child.
- To appreciate the special vulnerability of children.
- To create and maintain a safe and healthy setting that foster children's social, emotional, intellectual, and physical development and that respect their dignity and their contributions.
- To support the right of children with special needs to participate, consistent with their ability, in regular early childhood programs.

Principles:

- Above all we shall not harm children. We shall not participate in practices that are disrespectful, degrading, dangerous, exploitative, intimidating, psychologically damaging, or physically harmful to children. *This principle has precedence over all others in this Code.*
- We shall not participate in practices that discriminate against children by denying benefits, giving special advantages, or excluding them from programs or activities on the basis of their race, religion, sex, national origin, or the status, behavior, or beliefs of their parents.
- We shall involve all of those with relevant knowledge (including staff and parents) in decisions concerning a child.
- When, after appropriate efforts have been made with a child and the family, the child still does not appear to be benefiting from a program, we shall communicate our concern to the family in a positive way and offer them assistance in finding a more suitable setting.
- We shall be familiar with the symptoms of child abuse and neglect and know and follow community procedures and state laws that protect children against abuse and neglect.
- When we have evidence of abuse or neglect, we shall report the evidence to the appropriate community agency and follow up to ensure that appropriate action has been taken. When possible, parents will be informed that the referral has been made.
- When another person tells us of their suspicion that a child is being abused or neglected but we lack evidence, we shall assist that person in taking appropriate action to protect the child.
- When a child protective agency fails to provide adequate protection for abused or neglected children, we acknowledge a collective ethical responsibility to work toward improvement of these services.
- When we become aware of a practice or situation that endangers the health or safety of children, but has not been previously known to do so, we have

an ethical responsibility to inform those who can remedy the situation and who can keep other children from being similarly endangered.

II. *Ethical Responsibilities to Families*

Families are of primary importance in children's development. (The term *family* may include others, besides parents, who are responsibly involved with the child.) Because the family and the early childhood educator have a common interest in the child's welfare, we acknowledge a primary responsibility to bring about collaboration between the home and school in ways that enhance the child's development.

Ideals:

- To develop relationships of mutual trust with families we serve.
- To acknowledge and build upon strengths and competencies as we support families in their task of nurturing children.
- To respect the dignity of each family and its culture, customs, and beliefs.
- To respect families' child rearing values and their right to make decisions for their children.
- To interpret each child's progress to parents within the framework of a developmental perspective and to help families understand and appreciate the value of a developmental perspective and to help families understand and appreciate the value of developmentally appropriate early childhood programs.
- To help family members improve their understanding of their children and to enhance their skills as parents.
- To participate in building support networks for families to interact with program staff and families.

Principles:

- We shall not deny family members access to their child's classroom or program setting.
- We shall inform families of program philosophy, policies, and personnel qualifications, and explain why we teach as we do.
- We shall inform families of and, when appropriate, involve them in policy decisions.
- We shall inform families of and, when appropriate, involve them in significant decisions affecting their child.
- We shall inform the family of accidents involving their child, of risks such as exposures to contagious disease that may result in infection, and of events that might result in psychological damage.
- We shall not permit or participate in research that could in any way hinder the education or development of the children in our programs. Families shall be fully informed of any proposed research projects involving their children and shall have the opportunity to give or withhold consent.

- We shall not engage in or support exploitation of families. We shall not use our relationship with a family for private advantage or personal gain, or enter into relationships with family members that might impair our effectiveness in working with children.
- We shall develop written policies for the protection of confidentiality and the disclosure of children's records beyond family members, program personnel, and consultants having an obligation of confidentiality shall require familial consent (except in cases of abuse or neglect).
- We shall maintain confidentiality and shall respect the family's right to privacy, refraining from disclosure of confidential information and intrusion into family life. However when we are concerned about a child's welfare it is permissible to reveal confidential information to agencies and individuals who may be able to act in the child's interest.
- In cases where family members are in conflict we shall work openly, sharing our observations of the child, to help all parties involved make informed decisions. We shall refrain from becoming an advocate for one party.
- We shall be familiar with and appropriately use community resources and professional services that support families. After a referral has been made, we shall follow up to ensure that services have been adequately provided.

Additional Resource 3.6

NAEYC Advanced Standards

Core Standards

1. *Promoting Child Development and Learning*:
   Candidates use their understanding of young children's characteristics and needs, and of multiple interacting influences on children's development and learning, to create environments that are healthy, respectful, supportive, and challenging for all children.
2. *Building Family and Community Relationships*:
   Candidates know about, understand, and value the importance and complex characteristics of children's families and communities. They use this understanding to create respectful, reciprocal relationships that support and empower families, and to involve all families in their children's development and learning.
3. *Observing, Documenting, and Assessing to Support Young Children and Families:*
   Candidates know about and understand the goals, benefits, and uses of assessment. They know about and use systematic observations, documentation, and other effective assessment strategies in a responsible way, in partnership

with families and other professionals, to positively influence children's development and learning.

4. *Teaching and Learning:*
Candidates integrate their understanding of and relationships with children and families; their understanding of developmentally effective approaches to teaching and learning; and their knowledge of academic disciplines to design, implement, and evaluate experiences that promote positive development and learning for all children.

   a. *Connecting with children and families:*
   Candidates know, understand, and use positive relationships and supportive interactions as the foundation for their work with young children.

   b. *Using developmentally effective approaches:*
   Candidates know, understand, and use a wide array of effective approaches, strategies, and tools to positively influence young children's development and learning.

   c. *Understanding content knowledge in early education:*
   Candidates understand the importance of each content area in young children's learning. They know the essential concepts, inquiry tools, and structure of content areas including academic subjects and can identify resources to deepen their understanding.

   d. *Building meaningful curriculum:*
   Candidates use their own knowledge and other resources to design, implement, and evaluate meaningful, challenging curriculum that promotes comprehensive developmental and learning outcomes for all young children.

5. *Growing as a Professional:*
Candidates identify and conduct themselves as members of the early childhood profession. They know and use ethical guidelines and other professional standards related to early childhood practice. They are continuous, collaborative learners who demonstrate knowledgeable, reflective, and critical perspectives on their work, making informed decisions that integrate knowledge from a variety of sources. They are informed advocates for sound educational practices and policies.

Additional Resource 3.7

NAIS Principles of Good Practice: Equity and Justice

Creating and sustaining an inclusive, equitable, and just independent school community requires commitment, reflection, conscious, and deliberate action, as well as constant vigilance based on the overarching principles of inclusivity, diversity, and multiculturalism. The following Principles of Good Practice for Equity and Justice provide the foundation for such a community.

- The school establishes the foundation for its commitment to equity and justice in its mission statement and strategic planning.
- The school respects, affirms, and protects the dignity and worth of each member of the school community.
- The school establishes, publishes, implements, and reviews policies that promote equity and justice in the life of the school.
- The school supports the ongoing education of the board, parents, students, and all school personnel as part of the process of creating and sustaining an equitable and just community.
- The school ensures an antibias environment by assessing school culture and addressing issues of equity and justice in pedagogy, assessment, curriculum, programs, admission, and hiring.
- The school values each and every child, recognizing and teaching to varied learning styles, abilities, and life experiences.
- The school uses inclusive, antibias language in written and oral communication.
- The school complies with local, state, and federal laws and regulations that promote diversity.
- The school provides appropriate opportunities for leadership and participation in decision making to all members of the school community.
- The school includes all families and guardians as partners in the process of creating and sustaining an equitable and just community.
- The school expects from its students and all members of the community an appreciation of and responsibility for the principles of equity and justice.

—National Association of Independent Schools, 2004

NOTES

1. Chapter 9 explores in greater depth those written statements, policies, and programs that best support gender and sexuality diversity in the school setting.

2. See chapter 9 for case examples related to neutrality policies.

3. Chapter 5 explores in detail the kind of transformative learning and teaching demanded of teachers who wish to effectively engage GSD.

4

GSD AT SCHOOL

Understanding What You See;
Thinking Critically About What You See

I was regarded by many as kind of sissyfied, which I resented because I really was not a sissy. I was not a tough guy, but . . . I was good at any sport where you threw things, or hit them, or caught them, or something like that. I hated things like swimming and tumbling and those kinds of things, so I was really not a sissy. [But] the coaches were so intolerant and there was no program for all of us. So I never regarded myself as being much and I never regarded myself as being good looking and I never had a date in high school, because I thought, who'd want to date me? So I didn't bother.

—Charles Schulz, *Peanuts* cartoonist

This chapter addresses first, our difficulty in "seeing" gender and sexuality diversity (GSD) fully at school, and second, the challenge of thinking more broadly and deeply about the role of gender and sexuality in students' lives. What follows are examples of GSD in day-to-day school life. Each real-life scenario is accompanied by a developmental and pedagogical analysis that suggests new ways of seeing and thinking about behavior. This mosaic of scenarios invites you to understand more fully those students, teachers, parents, and administrators whose school experience is powerfully influenced by gender and sexuality diversity, heteronormativity, and antigay bias.

SECTION I
WHAT WE SEE; HOW WE SEE

FRAMING THE BIG PICTURE

❖ *School is not the appropriate place for these issues. It is the role of parents to educate their children about this.*

❖ *It seems like a bit much to be talking about sex with kindergartners.*

Misconceptions about what gender and sexuality diversity actually is and how it is manifest in preK–12 schools abound. People hear the word "sexuality" and recoil, assuming that children are being taught about "sex" and sexual behavior. Using mature sexual and gender identities such as gay, lesbian, bisexual, transgender, queer, and intersex (GLBTQI)—which are connected to sexual behavior—to frame discussions of gender and sexuality with younger children has contributed to concerns about the developmental appropriateness of such conversations and lessons.

Using a pedagogical framework like the one established in chapter 3 of this book makes reflecting on the *gender identity development* (GID) and *sexual identity development* (SID) in preK and elementary students entirely possible. Using educational missions (e.g., working with the whole child) and values (e.g., respect for the individual) as the primary reference point permits educators to do their job. Considering GID and SID for four- to twelve-year-olds is a fully appropriate and indispensable component of working with children this age. In fact, addressing gender and sexuality in the school setting is an important component of educating *all* preK–12 students. **The developmental issues may change from year to year, but the relevance of gender identity and sexual identity remains consistent over time.**

A Wider Perspective, a Layered Perspective

The gender and sexuality diversity (GSD) construct allows us to consider a broad range of students at every age and pay attention to critical aspects of their identity development. Too often the focus of conversations about gender and sexuality in middle and high schools is on "the gay kids" and how to keep other students from bullying "the gay kids." As demonstrated in chapter 1 *biological sex*, *gender identity*, and *sexual orientation* are building blocks of identity for every member of the human species. Sex, identity, and orientation combine, overlap, remain distinct yet intertwined. Thus we need an expansive and layered lens to help us with what we see and how we see it, in all members of the school community.

Consider this. A problem, like Childhood Obesity for instance, comes floating down the river. Overweight children of all ages are struggling in the water;

someone eventually notices and has the skill to haul them out. Financial and human resources are then devoted to treating all the medical, emotional, and social problems that obese children encounter. However, there is a remarkable and problematic lack of curiosity about what is happening upstream: *Where did Childhood Obesity come from?* Interventions are myopically directed at the problem in the present moment.

Public health researchers often use this metaphor to prove a point: the only way to prevent public health crises is to determine what is going on *upstream.*

What if school is the river?   Students of all ages with a range of gender presentations and sexualities are flailing in the river. It is unclear whether anyone at school (1) notices, (2) cares enough to fish them out, and (3) knows what to do once the kids are on shore. School climate surveys over the past ten years (Kosciw et al. 2010) have consistently identified the multiple ways that school is a hostile environment for

- kids whose gender expression/identity is different from accepted norms.
- kids who are perceived to be differently gendered and/or gay.
- kids who identify as differently gendered and/or gay.

Yet, despite years of data, there is still shock at the plight of these children struggling in the water. Most adults on the banks of the river have very few substantive ideas about what is going on upstream, and they have surprisingly little clarity about what to do in the present moment.

In the fall of 2010 alone there were half a dozen teen, male suicides linked to chronic GSD-related harassment that occurred at school (Hubbard 2010). In light of these highest of stakes, it is confounding that many schools continue to avoid addressing this particular cohort of vulnerable students, except in the most remedial ways. They devote scant resources to training school personnel about who these children are and what they need. And there is a bewildering lack of big-picture curiosity:

- *How did these particular students end up in the river? Why these students and not others?*
- *Did they fall or were they pushed?*
- *How far upstream did this happen? Preschool? Sixth grade?*
- *Do they know how to swim?*
- *What factors contribute to their difficulty in staying on dry land?*
- *Were/are teachers aware? Did/do they try to help?*
- *How many other kids are there like them?*
- *Shouldn't they be in class? They are missing a lot of school.*

If we do not ask and answer these kinds of systemic, contextualized questions, we will not be able to provide safety and affirmation of all students, at every age, in our schools. It is that simple.

SECTION II
GSD AT SCHOOL

GUIDELINES FOR SCENARIOS

Quotations[1] in this chapter (and throughout the book) are from real teachers, parents, and students; their names and identifying details have been changed to protect their privacy. Their statements and actions reflect a range of opinions, perspectives and questions, and are not meant to serve as "right" or "wrong" answers. The case examples here are organized by developmental stage, beginning with early childhood and ending with late adolescence.

You may be naturally drawn to and most interested in reading about the age group with whom you work, yet I encourage you to take in all the scenarios, in the spirit of understanding upstream and downstream, in addition to right where you are. As you read, place yourself "in" each situation (e.g., in the role of the teacher) and reflect on both your personal and professional reactions. In particular, consider the following:

- Your own emotional response in the moment
- Developmental issues related to gender and sexuality embedded in each situation
- Explicit and implicit impact of heteronormative expectations on the people in the scenario
- Mission values and educational philosophy that might shape the teacher's (your) response
- Good practices involved in engaging this "teachable moment"

Many different and valuable outcomes are possible for each scenario. Rather than jump quickly to a solution or "answer," you are invited to have an emotional and intellectual experience of these situations. Try to observe yourself and your reactions as much as possible, without filtering them.

Warning!

Along with feeling compelled by these stories, you may find yourself getting frustrated reading this chapter. Most teachers are glad to be invited into a learning experience as long as they ultimately "get some answers." If this were a lively professional development program (rather than a book), you would have the opportunity to engage with these scenarios as part of a small group of teachers working together. Indeed, the small group learning process allows for dialogue, collaboration, mutual understanding, values clarification, and problem solving.

> However, before this result is reached, *an introspective dialogue* has to be completed. Understanding a situation is not enough: the situation must make personal (emotional) sense *for the individual*, so that he or she is motivated and able to act. (Geijsel and Meijers 2005, 425; emphasis mine)

Wait! Did you just exhale deeply with exasperation? Are you rolling your eyes? I think I hear you saying: *Introspective dialogue? Give me a break. Who has time for introspective anything?*

The analysis provided after each scenario, while not an "answer" per se, is intended to help you, as an individual, understand your emotional response and to help you reflect on your "introspective narrative." Turn the page and keep reading. If you learn these critical thinking skills now in relation to GSD, you will be better prepared for whatever comes along. Onward!

THE VIEW OF EARLY CHILDHOOD

I. Preschool—*Acceptable Playmates*

- ❖ *What do we do with parents who only want their child to play with children of the same sex?*
- ❖ *Not so much in Nursery but in Pre-K and above we begin to hear "boys are stronger," "all girls like jumping rope," etc.*

Connie and David are parents of four-year-old Kyle, a curious, gregarious preschooler who loves imaginary play. At pickup time for the past month these parents have been commenting on how Kyle is "always playing with the girls" and doesn't seem particularly drawn to the boys and their style of play. Over time Connie and David's observations become concerns, and at some point they ask the teacher to encourage Kyle to play with the boys more often. David says, "If you could just direct him to the boys and make playing with them sound like a good idea, that might help him get out of this pattern of only playing with girls."

2. Preschool—*Boys and Pink*

- ❖ *How do we fight against the stereotypes that are already dictating the play of our students? The kids are constantly talking about "girl" colors or "boy" clothes. It feels like we are the only ones challenging those ideas.*

❖ *In Pre-K I am surprised that "boy" toys and "girl" toys is already an issue. I want them to have freedom to explore without restrictions.*

As children are settling down on their mats for rest time, the teacher, Ms. Gomez Munoz, hears two girls whispering loudly. She bends over next to them and says softly, "You girls need to quiet down. It's rest time." Raya asks, "Did you know that Maxine's stuffy is a boy?" Her tone is accusatory. Ms. Gomez Munoz says, "No I didn't, but thank you for telling me." Raya says, "I don't think Maxine's stuffy is a boy because he is big and pink and he's an elephant." Ms. Gomez Munoz looks at Maxine who says with certainty, "He's a boy." Maxine then scowls at Raya. Raffi whispers loudly from his nearby mat, "I don't think it's a boy either." Now Maxine looks injured, like she's about to start crying. Ms. Gomez Munoz says, "We can have a conversation about this after rest time but for right now, I need you to be quiet and take care of your own stuffy." Raya and Raffi share a triumphant look before settling onto their mats.

3. Preschool—*Who's in Your Family?*

☐ *I just think that talking about all of this is too confusing for young kids. . . . They don't need to get all mixed up in our latest "social experiment."*

Annie, five, and Isabella, four, are in the same Montessori class, and in this moment they are sharing a rug and playing some combination of vet clinic, hospital, and school. They are also excited about having a play date after school. "Giraffe is going to need an operation," says Annie. "His leg is broken."

Isabella says, "Maybe we can take care of him at your house later."

"No," Annie replies. "We can't take our work out of school. But we can play something else. I have more animals at home."

Then Isabella says, matter-of-factly, "When one of your moms dies, then maybe your Dad can come over."

After a slight pause, Annie says, "I don't have that kind of Dad. I have a donor dad who helped make me."

A longer pause. Isabella says, "Oh." And then, "Giraffe is going to need *two* operations because this leg is broken too."

Analysis of Scenarios 1–3

Developmental tasks for preschoolers. What these three scenarios have in common is that they are about the social and cultural "rules" that shape our expectations about gender and families. Kyle's parents are worried about their son's seemingly atypical preference for playing with girls rather than boys in his preschool cohort. Children at this developmental stage are exploring and trying on multiple behaviors, skills, roles, and identities. The world of school, versus the world of home, invites children to expand their repertoire of interests and explore their capacities. Most preK teachers want their students to revel unselfconsciously in the process of "discovery" about Self, Others, and the World.

Gendered expectations. Yet in schools we see that at the earliest ages children are directed and redirected toward acceptable gender expression and roles. What are these parents concerned about? It is possible that they are worried Kyle will become overly "girly" in his play and in the company he keeps? This could be the beginning of a slippery slope for a young boy who "needs" to be masculine. Who established these gendered expectations for children? Nobody seems to know exactly who made the rules but everybody clearly knows what the rules are, even some of the preschoolers themselves. And everyone knows the rules about "gender" are much stricter for young boys than for young girls.

Gendered norms. It is unlikely that Raya heard someone say directly, "Big pink elephants can't be boys," but she is troubled by the seeming incongruity between "boy" and "pink." The preschooler's cognitive development is beginning to allow for a clearer perception of reality, and in reality, most boys are not associated with pink. Pink is associated with girls. Her cognitive capacities and increasing social awareness allow her to "learn" the behavioral norms for boys and girls. Day after day she soaks up multiple implicit and explicit cultural messages about what is and is not acceptable for boys and girls to wear, to do, to be.

Heteronormative family norms. Isabella is trying to sort out the difference between what Annie's family looks like (i.e., two mothers, two children, two pets) and what her own family and most families she is familiar with look like (i.e., a mom, dad, kids, pets). What has she learned through the picture books she reads, the movies and television shows she watches, the advertisements on billboards and in magazines at the pediatrician's office? The heteronormative standard for family life requires a mother and a father.

So for Isabella, one way to bring a dad into Annie's family is to get rid of one of the moms (she knows that *three* parents are not allowed). While her four-year-old brain may not get the larger existential meaning of death, she is old enough to know that dying is one way that someone might "go away." When informed about this exchange after the fact, Isabella's parent was embarrassed and concerned by her daughter's seeming insensitivity to Annie's family configuration. "Oh, dear. That's not a very nice thing to say. I hope Annie's feelings weren't hurt." To scold Isabella for her logic is to deny the ubiquitous messages in a preschooler's world about what a "normal" family looks like.

What to "See"; Questions to Consider

There is an important learning process occurring between Annie and Isabella, and with a teacher's thoughtful facilitation both of these girls (and the rest of the class) will begin to see and know each other and the inherent diversity of gender, sexuality, and family life in the world more accurately. Isabella's application of concrete thinking to solve this "problem" creates a prime opportunity for the teacher to help her students "think about thinking" and "problem solving." In addition to teaching about different kinds of families, the teacher identifies flexible thinking and curiosity as useful approaches for taking in that which is unfamiliar.

THE VIEW OF EARLY ELEMENTARY

4. Kindergarten—*Where's Your Mom?*

❖ *I don't feel prepared because I don't know what's acceptable to bring up with such young children. I don't want to get "in trouble."*

In September kindergarten students are in morning circle discussing the question of the day: *Who is in your family?* Children are sharing about parents, grandparents, siblings, pets. When it is Sheila's turn, she announces proudly, "I have a Papa, a Daddy, and a dog named Hank."

Carlos says, "I didn't know two boys can get married."

Sheila replies, "My dads aren't married but they want to be."

Lily is curious: "Can two girls get married? Who gets to wear the white dress?"

Before anyone can answer, Carlos asks another question. "If you have two dads then where is your mom? Everyone has to have a mother to be born."

Molly agrees. "That's true because you're born from your mommy's tummy."

Peter says, "My baby sister was in my mom's tummy for a long time before she was born."

5. First Grade—*Boy Colors/Girl Colors*

❖ *I wonder if students at our school feel pressure from teachers and parents to be more feminine or manly.*

❖ *How do teachers work with parents who are telling their child that, in effect, he is a sissy?*

First graders are working in small groups, coloring with crayons at their clustered desks. They are illustrating the covers of their poetry journals and talking quietly. In one group a boy named Charlie is drawing big arcs of color. He has already colored a yellow arc, a purple arc, and is starting on a pink arc when Amanda, a girl in his cluster, says loudly and excitedly, "Charlie is using girl colors!!" All the children turn and look at Charlie and Amanda, curious about this blatant girl-color/boy-color infraction. Charlie is blushing, and the teacher intervenes, reminding

Amanda and the rest of the class that there is no such thing as a girl color or a boy color. "You can use any color for your illustrations that you want," she says. The children go back to work, except for Charlie who seems uncertain about whether to finish the pink arc or start his drawing all over again.

Analysis of Scenarios 4 and 5

Family as primary reference point.   The primary concerns for this age group relate to Self, Other, and Family. They evaluate these elements of relational life all the time, both consciously and unconsciously. Kindergartners have internalized many images and "facts" about family life. They know that parents are typically a heterosexual couple, and they know that babies grow in mommies' tummies. Sheila's family configuration creates cognitive dissonance for many of these students; they react to Sheila's noncompliance with *social norms* (i.e., two dads) and *biological norms* (i.e., no mom).

Meet the gender police.   So too with Charlie's choice of colors for his poetry journal cover. As noted in chapter 1, the assimilation of gender roles begins at birth, and these first graders already have seven years of learning the gender rules under their belts. Amanda knows that Charlie is not in compliance with the girl colors/boy colors rule, and she points that out. Peers of every age police each other's behavior, ensuring that gender and sexuality norms are maintained (Pascoe 2007).

What To "See"; Questions to Consider

Kindergartners and first graders already demonstrate gender role stereotyping and "norms," but it is important to remember that children at this developmental age are also open to considering "new" or "other" rules. This openness to broader understandings of gender and sexuality will wax and wane, as the students get older. **The fundamental developmental message, however, should be the same at every age: there are many different ways to express gender and many different ways to express sexuality.** Rigid rules and stereotypes interfere with people expressing their gender identity and sexual identity freely and authentically. (Chapter 6 contains lesson plans that are designed to address these issues.)

THE VIEW OF ELEMENTARY

6. Second Grade—*P.E. and the Gender Police*

❖ *Boys don't want to dance in P.E. because that is a girl thing to do.*

❖ *I was taken aback when a boy in my class acknowledged that teasing was wrong, yet he insisted that Oliver (in the story Oliver Button is a Sissy) really shouldn't be dancing. I felt like our adult version of "blame the victim" had already begun.*

It is P.E. for the second graders, and this is the first class in a series involving square dancing. Most of the boys are grumbling about the activity, though not all, and a few of the girls are also complaining that they would rather do the obstacle course from the previous week. One of the protesters is Martha (Marty), a proud "tomboy," very athletic, a regular in kicker (soccer), touch football, and stickball. She prefers wearing sports shorts and T-shirts to school each day and can name every player (and position) on her beloved Colorado Rockies.

As the class forms two lines facing each other, children keep switching places so that they will be across from a desired partner. Most of the second graders choose a partner of the same sex; girls want to dance with their best friends and boys don't want cooties from the girls. Marty appears uncertain about where to stand and finds herself opposite Max, a slight, uncoordinated boy. The class wise guy, Bennett, calls out, "Hey look, Marty and Max are together, except Marty is the boy and Max is the girl!" Several of the students laugh at this. The P.E. teacher blows her whistle and calls for the group's attention.

Analysis of Scenario 6

Girls as tomboys.   Marty's challenge to the gender code is more significant than Charlie's selecting the wrong color marker. As interpreted by her peers— and likely some of the grown-ups at school too—she "acts like a boy." The term "tomboy" has been used for decades to characterize girls whose gender expression is considered "masculine." In chapter 2, the New Diagram of Sex and Gender (diagram 2.1) depicts gender expression on a continuum, yet instead of allowing for a broad range of gender expressions, behaviors, and dress, these kinds of preferences—whether long-term or fleeting—are labeled as *either* masculine *or* feminine. And masculine is better.

What Does "Tomboy" Mean?

The word "tomboy," I don't even know what it means. What is a "tom" "boy?" Why is a spirited girl who is very physical, why is she called a boy? It doesn't really make any sense to me. I guess I would call her a resister, because she's doing things that have been labeled "boy" in our society, which means "not girl."

—Carol Gilligan, in the documentary film
Tomboys! Feisty Girls and Spirited Women

If Marty likes so many "masculine" things, then she must "be" a boy. Marty has never identified herself as a boy or male, nor has she expressed a desire to be a boy. She is clear about the activities she likes and the clothing that suits her, yet these expressions of self are met with resistance. She cannot be a *girl* who likes these activities; she must be at least part *boy*. What part of Marty's identity is being suppressed and regulated here? And to what end?

Boys as sissies. Max's small physical stature and lack of athleticism leave him open for the label of "sissy," a word that has none of the positive connotations that "tomboy" might. Masculine is preferable to feminine, especially in boys. School-age boys express their masculinity primarily through demonstrations of physical strength and agility, along with dress, manner of relating, and hobbies (e.g., collecting matchbox cars, baseball cards, Transformers, Airsoft guns). Max's lack of stereotypical "masculine" gender expression leaves him vulnerable to ridicule and denigration. In the heteronormative culture of this second grade class there seems to be little room for identities or expressions that challenge narrow prescriptions for how boys and girls should "be."

What to "See"; Questions to Consider

In chapter 1 I expressed my discomfort with labeling children like Marty and Max as *gender variant*, a term currently used by some pediatricians, psychologists, and educators to describe nonstereotypical gender expression. The process of categorization itself suggests that (1) even though Marty and Max are expressing their gender in a natural and fluid way, and (2) even though this expression fits with the concept of a continuum for *gender expression*, they still need a "label." Variance is an essential concept in terms of the biodiversity of the species, yet its use in situations like this locates the "problem" (i.e., gender expression that does not conform to traditional norms) in individuals rather than in the environment, where discomfort with or unawareness of the continuum model (diagram 2.1) dominate.

7. Third Grade—*Valentines for All*

❖ *Third and fourth graders will call each other gay, or laugh when they hear the word gay. I wish we had more books or discussions.*

❖ *We are not really allowed to discuss issues related to sexual orientation in the classroom.*

Third graders are making special decorative bags for collecting valentines. As the children work at a table together, the teacher overhears them talking about whom they are going to give valentines to. Amy announces proudly, "I'm going to make *BLING!* valentines for everyone in the class." Diego chimes in and says, "I'm giving everyone candy in mine. And besides, that's the same rule as before. You have to give one to everybody in the class." Ben responds, "Well, actually, boys shouldn't send valentines to boys because that says you're gay." Amy makes a silly face and says, "I don't think so." "Yeah, well, it's true," insists Ben. "Valentines are girly anyway and I only care about the candy." Diego does not say anything and has stopped working on his project. "I like chocolate kisses the best," says Amy.

Analysis of Scenario 7

What does "gay" mean in third grade? Clearly the landscape of gender and sexuality diversity has gotten more complex, as children in middle childhood are capable of grappling with big concepts and are thinking about them now in both personal and abstract terms (see cartoon). Conversations about two moms or gay families back in kindergarten was one thing. The third graders' conversation about "gay" comes at a pivotal developmental turning point, as they explicitly question for themselves: *who is it okay to be?* (i.e., gender expression) and *whom is it okay to love?* (i.e., sexual orientation). These third graders have not entered adolescence, yet as we learned in chapter 2 (see The Girl Project) their questions and concerns about sexual identity and sexual orientation have begun. They understand that "pairing" will ultimately become central to their relational lives, and as a result, they are paying more explicit attention to the "rules" about pairing.

The bridge from gender to sexuality. Clearly the policing of gendered social behavior by peers continues, as Ben holds himself in check in relation to making valentines and encourages Diego to do likewise. In addition, Ben has gotten the cultural message—from an older brother? parents? church?—that "gay" is not

"This is Donovan. He's pretty sure he's gay, too."

Graphic 4.1.
© New Yorker

okay, especially for a boy. He makes the link between rules about gender and rules about sexuality explicit. This bridge between gender and sexuality has been there all along, but third graders can travel it now with greater acumen. Ben identifies the connection between (1) doing things that are "girly" (like sending valentines) and (2) being perceived as "gay."

What To "See"; Questions to Consider

Somehow the gender police have morphed into watchdogs in charge of appropriate expressions of sexual identity! In addition, the locus of "authority" is shifting here. For these eight- and nine-year-olds, it may be more important to follow the rules of the playground (i.e., *don't be gay*) than the rules of kindness in the classroom (i.e., *send everyone a valentine*). If the classroom teacher does not address the reality of these competing sets of rules, she will miss out on a rich opportunity to talk with her students about the bind they are in. The teacher must recognize that for her students, figuring out to whom they should listen can be a sizable ongoing dilemma.

THE VIEW OF LATE ELEMENTARY

8. Fourth Grade—*The Stork Is a Man!*

> ➢ *Is it true that a man had a baby?*—fourth grade student

Some fourth graders are having a discussion at lunch. Fiona says, "Did you hear about that man who is having a baby?"

Akasha scrunches up her face and says, "What?!"

Fiona continues: "My sister saw it on *Oprah* how this man is pregnant and having a baby. He pulled up his shirt and showed his pregnant stomach and everything."

"Ewwwuh," says Keiko.

"No way," Tim declares. "Men can't have babies. This guy must be a freak."

"Where is the baby going to come out?" asks Keiko.

"That's nasty," DeShawn says, and pretends to barf in his lap.

Akasha turns and asks her teacher, "Is this true, Mr. Morris, can a man really have a baby?"

9. Fifth Grade—*Real Parents; Artificial Children?*

> ❖ *I overheard a boy ask Sam, "Which one is your real mom?" He hesitated and then Sam said, "You mean the one who made me?" Sam named his biological mother and that was the end of the exchange, but I could tell Sam was uncomfortable.*

Steven is telling his parents about the sexuality education class he had at school today and is trying to sort through his emotions. "It was all fine until some remarks were made using medical terms, I guess. Mr. Levine said going to a sperm bank is 'artificial,' and that some babies are made that way. At first it kind of passed me by. I didn't know I had my feelings hurt until later." One of Steven's parents asks, "What about it hurt your feelings?" With tears beginning Steven replies, "I think of artificial as being something bad for you, like chemicals in soda or chips. It made me feel like I was worth the same as a soda or something, but I know I'm real and I'm not something manufactured by a company."

Analysis of Scenarios 8 and 9

When "media" sets the context.   The fourth graders are trying to make sense of how a man can have a baby; everything they have learned up until this point has taught them that only women can give birth. Without any understanding of what being *transgender or transsexual* is (see chapter 1), these students have no context for understanding this uncommon circumstance. Thus, their "education" about this aspect of GSD begins on *Oprah*, with a provocative, media-hyped story that sensationalizes this couple's personal decision to create their own family in this particular way.

Real questions; fuzzy answers.   Chapter 1 defined the complex combinations of elements that constitute a range of genders and sexualities. For a small percentage of the population, birth sex and gender identity are not congruent, and these individuals may choose to live in their affirmed gender by making a social and/or medical transition (chapter 1). The man in this story is transgender, with a female biological sex—which includes ovaries and a uterus—and a male gender identity. So yes, a man is pregnant and having a baby.

The sample of sexuality education questions from fourth and fifth graders (see Sexuality Education Questions from Fourth and Fifth Graders) demonstrates that children this age are thinking in both concrete (e.g., *how long is the average penis?*) and sophisticated (e.g., *what is the difference between "having sex" and "making love"?*) ways. They are clearly well aware that "differences" in gender and sexuality exist, including those related to being transgender. In addition, it is important to remember that those fourth grade children who themselves have a "different" gender identity or sexual identity have known for some time that not everyone fits cultural and heteronormative expectations.

Sexuality Education Questions from Fourth and Fifth graders

Is it possible for a girl not to get a period? ** *How long is the average penis?* ** *Why do people smell bad during puberty?* ** *When does puberty start?* ** *Why do people have sex?* ** *Can you have sex and not make a baby?* ** *Why do we talk about this kind of stuff at school?* ** *What are genitals?* ** *What age do people* *start having sex? ✱✱ What emotions would you feel other than being excited when you're having sex? ✱✱ What's the difference between "having sex" and "making love"? ✱✱ Why is it good to shower every day? ✱✱ Why does a boy's voice change? ✱✱ How do gay people have sex? ✱✱ Does pee come out of the same place as the period? ✱✱ Can oral sex cause a woman to get pregnant? ✱✱ What color are cells? In the book it showed purple. ✱✱ How do women sometimes grow beards? ✱✱ What is so great about sex? ✱✱ How many sperms does a man have? ✱✱ What exactly is bisexual? ✱✱ If your bra breaks, does that mean it's too small? ✱✱ I'm still confused about how identical twins begin. ✱✱ Why don't males wear makeup? ✱✱ Can girls have wet dreams? ✱✱ How do "birds and bees" refer to girls and boys? ✱✱ Do you get puberty if you are gay? If so, is it different? ✱✱ Why do grown-ups always get so weird when they talk about sex?*

Keeping up with terminology. While Mr. Levine has nothing but good intentions in talking to his fifth graders about assisted reproduction, his use of an outdated term—"artificial"—affects Steven deeply. The boy wrestles with his feelings about the way he came into the world and the meaning that others ascribe to that. At age eleven Steven's cognitive and emotional capacities enable him to think about his identity and biological origins in increasingly complex ways. It is not just the facts of his conception and birth that matter; the way he is perceived or judged by others because of those facts is also a concern.

What To "See"; Questions to Consider

Here again is the reality of what truly "developmentally appropriate" practice must look like. While it might seem incongruous to discuss transgender and transsexual identities with fourth graders—or even younger children—providing them with information and contexts to understand Self and Other is a critical part of teaching them about the world they actually live in. If the spectrum of genders and sexualities is what children understand from an early age, this conversation with fourth graders has a ready paradigm, and the learning can be contextualized.

In addition, there is a greater variety of how-our-family-came-to-be stories than most teachers recognize. The sex and gender of Steven's parents is deliberately obscured in this scenario because, in fact, parents of all sexes and genders make use of assisted reproductive technology (ART), more so now than any time in the past (Mundy 2008). In her book *Mommies, Daddies, Donors, Surrogates: Answering Tough Questions and Building Strong Families*, clinical and developmental psychologist Diane Ehrensaft chronicles the multiple ways that families are created and addresses the complex questions that arise for all those involved in the effort. Today, more students in preK–12 schools come from families like these; and *all* students can benefit from knowing more about the intersections between identity, biology, and science that pertain to family life.

THE VIEW OF EARLY ADOLESCENCE

10. Sixth Grade—*Who's Who When It Comes to T and Q?*

❖ *Girls who dress in more masculine styles are sometimes questioned about it. I explain that one's clothing is one's choice but I'm not sure that is adequately addressing the issue.*

❖ *I have wondered about the sexuality of several students in the past but have never known when I am making stereotypical assumptions or really actually know.*

Christy is a sixth grader who has been a student at this school since kindergarten. She has always been quiet and on the shy side, considered "boyish" as a result of her masculine gender expression, though she has no interest in sports and is not considered a tomboy. Christy has always been a bit outside of the social circle of girls, and work has been done over the years to integrate her into the social mix of the class with some success. Her classmates have come to appreciate Christy's unique qualities: a gigantic rock and gem collection, a natural affinity for animals, even her boy-clothes wardrobe at times. (She has a huge collection of Keds high tops, all different colors.)

This year, however, she seems particularly set apart from her peers. The social dynamics are challenging for this sixth grade group to negotiate, as the "boy/girl/relationship-thing" typically dominates the interactions inside and outside of class. Though her physical appearance suggests that Christy may have started puberty, she does not join in any casual or formal (e.g., health class) discussions of adolescent development. Her teacher and her peers seem at a loss as to how to understand and engage with Christy about her identity. In addition, the teacher has a conference with Christy's parents coming up and wonders if/how to broach this subject.

Analysis of Scenario 10

What do twelve-year olds "know" about themselves? Christy's manner and behavior could be expressing many things in terms of her gender and/or sexual identity. She may well be fully conscious of having a nonheteronormative gender identity and/or sexual orientation (i.e., she is not a "feminine" girl and/or she may not be attracted to boys), yet she may not be ready to claim a particular "label" for a whole variety of reasons. On the other hand, she may not yet understand fully what her being "different" means for herself and others. We can be sure, however, that she knows she is different in some essential way from most of her female peers, and she has known this for a long time.

Our binary organization of gender (i.e., male/female, masculine/feminine) makes it difficult to place Christy in an accommodating developmental context. Though she clearly fits on the continuum that accurately depicts a range of possibilities with regard to gender identity and gender expression (box 2.1), the **heteronormative organization of school life** does not provide a place for her. She herself is likely to be confused about where she fits in or, even more likely, whether she fits in at all.

Emerging sexuality. We see that this binary ordering of gender and sexuality occurs at every grade level. In sixth grade, however, heterosexual pairing, real or fantasized, is becoming more and more central in social interactions. Some students have begun puberty, and all students are aware of the powerful heteronormative expectations for pairing. They have soaked up and internalized images of heterosexual coupling all their lives. Whether it is the lyrics of a top 20 song (e.g., "let's go all the way tonight") or the theme of a reality show (e.g., *The Bachelor*), the cultural message to children this age is to get ready to "do it."

What To "See"; Questions to Consider

How do sexual concerns about "dating" relate to questions about gender identity? Christy's developmental narrative has emerged naturally over the course of her time at school. She has always been who she is; there is nothing "surprising" about who she is now in sixth grade. Yet the heterosexual, social expectations of boy/girl "dating" further locate the "problem" in her as an individual. The ramifications of problematizing and even pathologizing nonheteronormativity are significant, as students like Christy find themselves at increasing risk for academic, social, and emotional problems. Framing this as an issue for the individual rather than addressing the environmental factors that interfere with the healthy identity development of that individual is a fundamentally biased response.

It is also pedagogically problematic because it reinforces simplistic, narrow, and stereotypical thinking. The only thing we "know" about Christy at this point is that she does not fit in with the heteronormative crowd. We do not know her gender identity or sexual identity, only her gender expression. The inclination might be to make assumptions about who she *is* based on who she appears *not* to be. This would be an easy yet problematic way to contend with the complexity of GID and SID.

11. Seventh Grade—*Scout's Honor*

❖ *We need to give our students the tools to understand the public discourse about these issues. We can't shield them from it, but we can prepare them to approach debate intelligently.*

In seventh grade social studies class there is a productive debate going on about whether money raised at a student-faculty basketball game fund-raiser should be donated to the United Way as originally planned. After a conversation with her parents last night, Caroline speaks up today and suggests that if the money is given to the United Way, which is a supporter of the Boy Scouts of America, then the school will be supporting the Scouts' policy of discriminating against gay people. Dylan says, "I don't think that's such a big deal. The United Way does a lot of other good stuff. That's why we chose them in the first place." Caroline argues that it is a big deal—this type of discrimination is wrong, and Rebecca agrees.

Only a few students are actively participating in the discussion but everyone is listening closely. Eddy says, "I don't think it's a good idea for gay people to be scout masters." This statement is followed quickly by Rosa raising her hand and asking the teacher, "What makes someone gay anyway?" There is a wave of laughter and some groans. Rosa looks defensive and says, "What?! I think it's a good question."

Analysis of Scenario 11

What does "gay" mean in seventh grade? For the seventh grade social studies class, the question of "What makes someone gay?" is posed in a new, real-life context. These middle schoolers must contend now not just with name-calling on the playground or harassment in the locker room, but with the grown-up world of bigotry and the legal/social consequences of antigay prejudice. With a greater ability to make connections between actions and outcomes, and a more complex appreciation for the way a democracy works, these thirteen-year-olds are debating in adult terms the right and wrong of their actions. Caroline may have begun this conversation with her parents, but it is now up to this class and their teacher to sort out the issues at hand.

Running into the law. Rosa wants to be fully informed. Before she decides whether it is right to discriminate against gay people, she needs to know more about them. Let's say she and her classmates have actually learned a fair amount about gender and sexuality diversity in previous years, both formally and informally. Books, projects, health education. Now, at this juncture, the question about sexual orientation takes on new meaning; there is a specific context (i.e., scouting) for considering the inclusion/exclusion of gays. In addition, Eddy's comment introduces a sinister element to the debate, as he gives voice to a popular myth that gay men prey on young boys. So, Rosa is right; it is a good question.

What To "See"; Questions to Consider

With proper training and support (see chapter 5), this social studies teacher can facilitate a thoughtful dialogue and use this opportunity to increase knowledge and enhance the critical thinking skills of her students. Not only do these students need to investigate the biology of sexuality (again), they must research the facts of this particular legal dispute involving the Boy Scouts of America (BSA).

In their research they will find that James Dale, the plaintiff in the case against the BSA, challenges many popular stereotypes about gay men. They will also discover that most people wrongly assume that homosexual men are more likely to be pedophiles than heterosexual men (Clark 2006).

They will find that some local chapters of the BSA support the antigay policy and some do not (see Local United Way Shuns Discriminatory Policies). In their inquiry, students will discover that there is no parallel lawsuit involving the Girl Scouts of America. What will they make of this gender difference? With sufficient information in hand, students will have an opportunity to determine for themselves the legitimacy of the BSA policy. And then they will make an informed decision about what to do with their charitable donation.

Local United Way Shuns Discriminatory Policies

Excerpt from Letter to the Editor, *Daily Hampshire Gazette*, Northampton, Massachusetts (December 2010)

"I was concerned to read the comments of Peter K. Sullivan in his recent letter to the editor ("Says United Way funds 'homophobic' agencies," Nov. 25) and would like to inform readers about the United Way of Hampshire County and its efforts and policies.

"The United Way supports a network of partner agencies that provide vital services throughout this community to our neighbors in need. The UWHC has been proactive on the issue of discrimination and has a nondiscriminatory policy in its bylaws as well as a declaration signed each year by local partner agencies.

"While I cannot speak to the actions or standards of other United Ways or other national organizations, inclusive and respectful service has been a hallmark of our partner agencies for many years in Hampshire County.

"The United Way does not fund the Boy Scouts of America nor has it done so for about 10 years. Locally the United Way does fund the rental assistance program of the Hampshire County chapter of the Salvation Army, whose efforts allow many individuals and families to remain in their homes each year rather than face eviction. We have the Salvation Army's signed non-discrimination certification form on record. If there are issues about which Mr. Sullivan is aware that impact the local chapter, we ask that he bring them to our attention."

—John Ebbets, chief executive officer
United Way of Hampshire County, Massachusetts

THE VIEW OF ADOLESCENCE

12. Eighth Grade—*The Bar Mitzvah*

❖ *I wish we could open up a dialogue more easily with parents. I know I feel defensive when a parent approaches me in a certain way, but the kids need us all to be on the same page.*

The mother of eighth grade Isaiah approaches his teacher, Ms. Rosen, on a Friday after school in the pickup area. She begins to tell Ms. Rosen how excited Isaiah is about his Bar Mitzvah, which is next weekend. Isaiah is well known and well liked, ebullient, quirky, often dramatic, and he has struggled at times over the years with peer relationships with the other boys in his class. He has always been more comfortable socializing with girls, and his closest friendships have often been with girls. If you conducted an informal poll of the teachers who have worked closely with Isaiah, most would venture a guess that he might be gay. This guess is not based on superficial qualities but on knowing Isaiah and observing his overall identity development over the years.

In the midst of talking about the Bar Mitzvah, Isaiah's mother asks Ms. Rosen, "Do you think it is strange that Isaiah has invited so many girl friends to his Bar Mitzvah and almost no boys?" Before Ms. Rosen can reply, the mother continues. "When I pointed this out to Isaiah he said, 'What's the problem with that, Mom? Are you worried that I'm *gay*?'" The mother looks directly at Ms. Rosen, and asks, "Do you think that might be true? Do you think Isaiah is gay?"

Analysis of Scenario 12

The tasks of adolescent development.   Moving into adolescence marks the biggest developmental transition for students since kindergarten, when they made that big step from the world of home into the world of school. The physiological, cognitive, emotional, and social changes that are the hallmark of puberty represent a daunting and exciting challenge for teens to navigate. Childhood is over, and part of "growing up" means figuring out who you are and what you are going to "do" with your more fully developed, more overtly male or female body (Nakkula and Toshalis 2008).

School-age children have crushes and play at having adult relationships. Teens "go out" and experiment with who they are as sexual beings. What might have been explained through a diagram back in fifth grade health class is now a real-life possibility, as adolescents explore the physical and emotional intimacy of romantic/sexual relationships (see Human Relations and Sexuality Comments from Ninth–Twelfth Graders).

Becoming a Bar Mitzvah is a ritual in the Jewish tradition that marks the passage of a boy into manhood. In his comment about being gay, Isaiah may or may not have been making a statement about his sexual identity. Some children/adolescents, though not all, "know" at this age about their romantic and sexual attractions. As noted in chapter 2, the dominance of heterosexual norms, images, and mandates in our culture creates dissonance for those who are oriented differently. Thus someone who is nonheterosexual is likely to "know" this sooner than someone who is heterosexual.

Public vs. private identities. Isaiah may also be speaking the unspeakable, finally making explicit his mother's implicit fear that he might be gay. He offers this possibility at a time when he is literally and symbolically assuming greater responsibility for his actions. Given his lifelong preference for girls as friends and the long-standing issues with his male peer group at school, Isaiah has probably been teased many times over the years about his social behavior and his actual or perceived sexual orientation. The Bar Mitzvah ritual, however, puts all these dynamics on display in a very public and particular way.

What is the teacher's role? The exchange between Isaiah's mother and Ms. Rosen moves the "how-do-you-see-my-child?" conversation into new territory. In conferences, reports, and conversations from preschool to high school graduation, teachers try to help parents "see" and understand their children from many different angles: as a learner, a citizen of the school, a friend to peers, an athlete, an artist. Is Isaiah's mother looking to Ms. Rosen for validation? Support? Disconfirmation? A professional opinion? The question of what Ms. Rosen's role is as *a teacher* in this moment is critical (see chapter 5 and chapter 10 for further discussion).

What To "See"; Questions to Consider

Isaiah's religious celebration is a private event, yet his mother's interaction with Ms. Rosen makes clear how porous the boundary between school and home is. Who "knows" Isaiah best? His parents? His teachers? His peers? All have played a role in Isaiah's identity development; all are mirrors in which Isaiah "sees" himself. If conversations about gender and sexuality were more commonplace, if the processes of gender identity development and sexual identity development were examined and explored throughout preK–12 schooling, this moment of public truth might be easier to navigate for all parties involved.

Human Relations and Sexuality Comments
from Ninth–Twelfth Graders

I've never had sex with anyone but I'm pretty sure I'm lesbian. How, exactly, do you know? ** *I've got a serious boyfriend, but last night I dreamed about kissing my best female friend: does that mean I'm queer?* ** *The whole sex thing is so unfair . . . I don't see how girls can explore their sexuality without getting a reputation as a slut.* ** *At lacrosse camp last year I fooled around with a boy in my dorm and now I'm worried that I'm gay.* ** *I feel like my wanting to remain abstinent until I am older is seen as totally uncool, like I'm a freak or just hiding that I'm a prude.* ** *It feels like the only way to get respect from other guys is to be a player and get as many girls as possible to have sex with you.* ** *I have always been attracted to other boys but do you think I ought to have sex with a girl just to be sure that I'm gay?* ** *I am not attracted to anyone. Everyone else around me, that's all they can think about is sex and girls and maybe guys, but I am just not interested. Is that* *normal?* ❋❋ *Just because I'm athletic and outspoken and don't have a boyfriend, people assume I'm a lesbian. I'm not!* ❋❋ *Just because I'm not athletic and don't have a girlfriend, my friends keep saying I'm a fag. I'm not but they won't believe me until I prove it.* ❋❋ *I have never liked wearing skirts and dresses or makeup, but recently a couple of kids called me a "dyke." I don't think I'm a lesbian but maybe this is a sign and I just don't know yet.* ❋❋ *My brother says that because* Modern Family *is my favorite show, I must be gay. That is so annoying.*

13. Ninth Grade—*Basketball or Kiss Me Kate?*

❖ *Our ninth grade teaching team has encountered some disturbingly insidious homophobia in the students and is looking for ways to best address this.*

Roscoe is in ninth grade at a small boarding school in New England. During the admissions process his talents as an athlete were duly noted, and his father, an alum of the school, was particularly excited about seeing Roscoe follow in his footsteps as a varsity team member in three different sports. After an extremely successful fall season on the soccer team (he was one of two freshmen to make varsity), Roscoe decided he would like to try out for a part in the school's musical production of *Kiss Me Kate* instead of playing basketball. This news spread quickly, and Roscoe found himself being questioned by everyone: peers, teachers, dorm parents, coaches, and his father.

Though his advisor has encouraged him to explore his interest in drama, everyone else clearly thinks Roscoe is making a mistake. The upperclassmen on the basketball team have been teasing him in the dorm, mocking his interest in singing and dancing. The "teasing" begins to feel oppressive and Roscoe tries to avoid this group of boys who call him *wimp*, *gayboy*, *pussy*, and *faggot*, privately and sometimes in front of others.

In addition, the director of the play is a faculty member who is gay but closeted, and the harassers make lewd comments about the director's sexual interest in Roscoe. Even soccer teammates and ninth grade friends have distanced themselves from Roscoe, who feels increasingly isolated and anxious and is seriously reconsidering his participation in the play.

Analysis of Scenario 13

Ideology of "the fag."[2]   With adolescent boys in particular, there is a premium placed on appearing masculine and straight. In her ethnographic research on adolescent boys, masculinity, and sexuality, Pascoe (2007) discovered that (1) asserting masculinity and (2) identifying as heterosexual go hand-in-hand as boys try to become "men."

> The fag epithet, when hurled at other boys, may or may not have explicit sexual meanings, but it always has gendered meanings. When a boy calls another boy a

fag, it means he is not a man but not necessarily that he is a homosexual. (Pascoe 2007, 82)

Boys use "faggot" or the "fag identity" to call other boys' masculinity into question and to promote their own manliness. The use of this slur is as much about policing *gender expression* as it is about challenging *sexual orientation*.

More tasks of adolescent development. As part of maturation into young adulthood, Roscoe and every other high school student considers and tries on various identities. Adolescents locate themselves in individual and group identities through a process of (1) exploration, (2) clarification, and (3) consolidation. Via this intellectual, emotional, social, and behavioral process, the teenager identifies herself as belonging to certain groups (Nakkula and Toshalis 2008). *I am a musician. I am an intellectual. A Republican. Christian. Athlete. Poet. Traveler. Slacker. Environmentalist. Cook. Mechanic. Liberal.* Some of the identities claimed at this developmental stage will become lifelong aspects of self and others will not. Recall your own adolescence and reflect on what your "identities" were back then. (I regret to say that I did not keep up with the piano.)

What adolescents choose to "be" may or may not be in keeping with the values and identities of their parents. In this case Roscoe is living away from home for the first time and moves away from his father's identity as a three-sport-varsity-letter-winner in high school. Roscoe finds himself fighting parental expectations as well as cultural norms that equate basketball with masculinity and singing and dancing in a musical with femininity. What do Roscoe's extracurricular choices have to do with his gender identity development and sexual identity development?

What To "See"; Questions to Consider

Remember Charlie back in first grade? He violated the gender code by choosing a "girl color" marker (p. 94). We do not know the impact that the marker incident (and others like it) have had on Charlie's overall identity development. He may or may not have foreclosed on certain explorations of Self as he grew up. Here, however, we can clearly see that even though Roscoe—unlike the uncoordinated and slight Max in second grade (p. 96)—fulfilled the masculine gender role expectations by being a strong, successful athlete, his desire to explore a different interest suddenly calls his gender expression and sexual identity into question. What do such foreclosures on the developmental task of exploration, clarification, and consolidation cost Roscoe, the individual? His group of schoolmates? Society as a whole?

14. Tenth Grade—*Fairy Tales and Same-Sex Parents*

❖ *What is the place of these issues in the classroom? I can see how they might be part of Health but we have far more important things to teach in traditional classes.*

In sophomore English, students are writing different types of narratives. Some are working on short stories and some are working on children's stories. There is a lesson about plot development in progress. The teacher writes on the board, "Boy meets girl. Boy gets girl. Boy loses girl. Boy gets girl again," and begins to draw a long arc that represents the rise and fall of tension in a story. Alexis raises her hand and says, "Couldn't it be 'boy meets boy' or 'girl meets girl'?" One or two students giggle a bit, some roll their eyes, and Justin says "Awk-ward." The teacher gives Justin a look and says to Alexis, "You're right. It certainly could be. You're the author; you create your characters." Anthony jumps in and says, "Wait a minute, so are you saying that for the children's stories it would be okay to put in gay parents?" This time Justin emits a soft whistle and says, "Dude . . ."

Analysis of Scenario 14

Pairing, parenting, and heteronormativity.   Alexis challenges the hetero-sexist plot development example, a reminder that most tenth graders are preoccupied with sexual pairings, and some are ready to challenge the boy/girl paradigm that most have grown up with. Anthony's question, however, quickly locates the "sexualized" gay pair in the role of parents, and hints that this arrangement may be improper. The concerns expressed back in seventh grade about the safety of having a gay scoutmaster are echoed here in the insinuation that there might be something sexually or morally inappropriate in the conduct of same-sex parents.

For a long time the "fitness" of a gay or lesbian parent has been debated during custody battles in a courtroom, where sexual orientation is often used to legitimize heterosexuals' or delegitimize homosexuals' capacity to parent. Reputable, longitudinal research now demonstrates that children raised by gay parents do not differ from those raised by heterosexual parents on a variety of measures such as social adjustment, self-esteem, and gender identity (Bos and Gartrell 2010; Patterson 2009).

In spite of this evidence that children with gay parents are just as well-adjusted or screwed up as their peers, the appropriateness of having same-sex parents continues to be debated. Consider the actions of Catholic Charities in Boston, Massachusetts, for example (see The Catholic Church and Same-Sex Adoption). While most states now allow a single gay person to petition for adoption, many do not permit *gay couples* to petition (www.lambdalegal.org). One gay person is safe; two gay people are not.

The Catholic Church and Same-Sex Adoption

In 2006, Catholic Charities of Boston (CCAB), one of the largest providers of social services in Massachusetts, stopped facilitating adoptions and foster care placement in response to a state law that required CCAB to place children with same-sex couples. The organization, which began in the early 1900s primarily as an adoption agency, elected to completely remove itself from adoption services rather than accept the state requirements of nondiscrimination against same-sex families. As of April 2011, CCAB maintains its stance with no sign of changes in the future.

The discussion in this tenth grade English class reflects the current, ongoing cultural, political, and legal discourse about the status of gay and lesbian families. What about books for children that feature same-sex parents? The picture book *And Tango Makes Three* is the story of two male penguins that raise a baby chick and form a family at the Central Park Zoo in New York City. *Tango* was at the top of the American Library Association's list of Banned & Challenged Books 2006, 2007, 2008, and second in 2009 (ALA 2007, 2008, 2009, 2010). Challengers, mostly parents, assert that the book promotes homosexuality to young children and is a perverse interpretation of family life (Attempts 2009).

Should these tenth grade students be allowed to write children's stories that feature gay parents? The teacher who questions the place of GSD in the classroom and believes "we have far more important things to teach in traditional classes" thinks he is protecting the rigor and integrity of the school's academic program. Yet the issues that are now on the table in this English class (e.g., censorship, parental rights, bias, role of government) require critical thinking skills of the highest order. The original write-a-story assignment now has the potential to become part of an integrated curriculum project that could include history, ethics, psychology and science (see chapter 7 for more on integrated curriculum).

What to "See"; Questions to Consider

Assigning the teaching and learning about gender and sexuality to health class is a popular approach to "including" gender and sexuality diversity in the curriculum and educational programming of the school. However, the notion that these issues can be contained in a single classroom and a particular unit of study reveals simplistic and wishful thinking. These elemental aspects of our humanity and identity exist everywhere in school life.

In addition, this situation offers a prime opportunity to do more than merely "add" GSD content to the existing curriculum. The topics below require critical thinking skills, mathematical skills, research skills, comparing and contrasting different times and events in history.

- Examining the evolution of the American family in the United States
- Researching statistics/outcomes of adoption placements in the United States
- Studying the history of various civil rights movement in the United States
- Exploring the constitutional rights of parents and children

- Understanding the developmental needs of children with same-sex parents
- Tracking the endurance of certain types of prejudice and stereotypes
- Exploring censorship in children's literature

Regardless of what this tenth grade teacher's "already planned" curriculum is, there are an infinite number of ways, small and large, to explicitly include GSD, ways that support the development of broad-based learning skills and specific content knowledge.

15. Eleventh Grade—*Alfred Kinsey and the Football Rivalry*

❖ *I always strongly respond to the use of "faggot" and the like with a big lecture about how sexuality is inherited, not chosen.*

At the annual rival football game between two high schools, the atmosphere is boisterous, with plenty of fans gathered in the bleachers on both sides of the field. This rivalry goes back almost seventy-five years, and there is a tradition of stealing mascots, making up clever (read: raunchy) cheers, and performing halftime antics intended to dramatize the superiority of one school over the other. Just before halftime, a banner is unfurled at the top of the bleachers on the home team side that says, "Johnson is a Kinsey 6" (NB: "Johnson" is the rival team's quarterback). People begin to notice the banner, and there is some chuckling in the crowd. As the opposing fans begin to boo, the vice principal moves quickly to have the banner taken down.

Later, in a meeting with the boys who were responsible, the vice principal invites them to explain their poor judgment. "We didn't think that anyone, uhm, that they would even know what a Kinsey 6 was. *We* didn't even know until we had that special program last month." The vice principal says, "Well I'm glad you learned something from that program, but you clearly missed the big picture. Calling someone "gay" as a put-down is not okay, it's against our code of conduct, and just because you have changed the terminology doesn't make it any less offensive."

Analysis of Scenario 15

The quarterback is gay! Though the boys in this scenario have cleverly changed the terms, the historical reference to the Kinsey Scale (see chapter 1) in this context is undeniably a direct expression of the antigay prejudice that dominates adolescent boy culture. It is unlikely that these football fans truly believe the rival quarterback is gay. Yet the best way to call his manhood and prowess into question is to pin the gay label on him (Pascoe 2007). If he is "gay," then the quarterback cannot possibly be "manly," tough and skilled.

Boys are typically a full two years behind their female peers in terms of adolescent development, and as a result, young teenage boys are anxious and self-consciousness about their emerging (or lagging) psychosexual development. As puberty progresses, the teenage boy who has a sexual experience with a girl is seen as moving toward manhood. Conversely, the teenage boy who has a sexual experience with another boy is seen as effeminate and unmanly (Pascoe 2007). In many ways, the football quarterback represents the masculine ideal, but if he is gay, his status as an icon of masculinity and virility is shattered.

What To "See"; Questions to Consider

> As discussed in chapter 3, school traditions can be powerful forces in establishing and maintaining gender and sexuality norms. For seventy-five years this football rivalry has been part of a particular "culture" at these schools; the whole town participates in pep rallies, fund-raisers, band boosters. Any step toward questioning or dismantling aspects of this tradition would likely be experienced as an assault on the masculinized culture of high school football and the community support of that culture. The message then is that homophobia and misogyny are the weapons of choice for boys who want to dominate and succeed. Can this rivalry endure; can these teams be supported, without the subjugation of gays and girls? (See chapter 7 for further discussion of the relationship between school sports, GSD, and school climate.)

THE VIEW OF LATE ADOLESCENCE

16. Twelfth Grade—*The Senior Prom*

> ➢ *Is it true about the two boys who couldn't have their picture together as a couple in the yearbook because some people were offended?*

It is time for the prom, and there is quite a buzz at school about two senior girls who are planning to attend as a couple. Nan, who is white, came out as bisexual in tenth grade and has been a leader in the school's Gay Straight Alliance. Chandra, who is African American, recently broke up with her boyfriend, Ray (also African American), and people are "shocked" that she is now dating Nan. The school has explicit rules regarding public displays of affection (PDA), and the two girls have been pushing the boundaries in this area for a week.

The dean of students, Ms. Vasquez, calls the girls in to talk about their behavior. "The rules in the handbook are very clear; only hand-holding is permitted in public. The two of you have been full-body hugging, kissing, lying in each other's laps out on the green. That's not the kind of behavior we expect, especially from two seniors who should know better."

The girls are immediately defensive. Nan argues, "We see straight couples doing the same things all the time, and they don't seem to get in trouble."

Ms. Vasquez shakes her head. "You have no idea which students I may have spoken to."

Chandra says, "I think people just don't want to see two girls together, unless it is some kind of entertainment for the boys."

"Especially if one of the girls is white and the other is black," Nan adds.

Ms. Martinez raises her eyebrows.

Chandra says, "Nobody ever said anything to me when I was with Ray, and we did exactly the same things. With all due respect, you never called me and Ray in to your office."

Analysis of Scenario 16

Heteronormativity and double standards of behavior. While Nan and Chandra's behavior in the public domain is a clear violation of school rules, there is likely some truth in their claims of a double standard. Images of heterosexual couples being intimate are everywhere in society, and part of the acculturation process is to see the sexualized male/female pairing as normative and preferable. Teachers observing a boy/girl couple engaging in the same behavior might think nothing of it, and may or may not intervene because it's "natural" for heterosexual teens to experiment with this kind of intimacy.

Academic, legal, and health consequences. Research indicates that non-heterosexual youth are subjected to "disproportionate educational and criminal-justice punishments that are not explained by greater engagement in illegal or transgressive behaviors" (Himmelstein and Bruckner 2011, 49). The long-term physical, sexual, and psychological health consequences of this bias are significant, with nonheterosexual youth more vulnerable to addiction, promiscuity, and suicidality than their heterosexual peers (Campos 2005). In the situation with Nan and Chandra it is highly likely that the image of two adolescent girls engaging in these explicit public displays of affection registers differently than images of a boy and a girl doing the same thing. If two teenage boys were involved, their behavior would be considered even more transgressive.

Race meets sexuality. Chandra introduces race as an additional variable in this situation, thereby identifying the critical intersection between race and sexuality. In addition to having gendered expectations about sexuality, there are also plenty of stereotyped assumptions about sexuality based on race. Black men are aggressive and hypersexual, Latina women are "hot" and sluttish, and gay culture is seen as largely white, male, and promiscuous. Certainly Chandra's relationship with a black male peer was, for many, more socially acceptable than her pairing with a white female. Teasing out how much the negative reaction to Nan and Chandra is the result of antigay prejudice and how much is related to racial bias will be a challenging task.

There is already so much going on in this situation that Chandra's comment about sexual intimacy between two girls being viewed as a form of "entertainment" for the boys could get lost. Yet it reflects a potent connection between two forms of bias: sexual objectification of women and homophobia. The denigration of Chandra and Nan's lesbian relationship reflects a cultural norm that exists in popular and pornographic entertainment, namely, that two women being sexual together is arousing for men, and in that sense, acceptable (Becker 2006).

What To "See"; Questions to Consider

It is important to note an extremely positive element of this scenario. Because gay teens are often closeted and clandestine in their romantic and sexual activity, there is little opportunity for them to learn about and be "socialized" in the ways of intimate relationships. Chandra and Nan being called in to the dean's office because they are in need of limits regarding their PDA is a wonderful sign of progress. It was not that long ago that Chandra and Nan would have been referred to the school counselor for "help" with their antisocial or perverse behavior.

This situation will test whatever skills the community has developed for leaning into discomfort and grappling with complexity. The school will be better served if conversations about racism, sexism, and homophobia have been plentiful and commonplace prior to this situation. Grappling with the role of intersectionality in both individual identity development and community building requires our best thinking and an open heart.

This is just a small sample of the multiple ways gender and sexuality diversity can be manifest in preK–12 schools. I have focused here on situations that directly involve students, but there are many other moments—in the guidance office, at the annual book fair, in PTO meetings—that involve families, parents, and teaching colleagues as well. This chapter challenges the notion that schools have a choice about whether to "bring in" discussions of GSD or not. These scenarios reinforce our understanding that considerations of gender and sexuality are woven into the fabric of daily life, as a natural by-product of the people who are members of the school community. Simply put, we have met the issues and they are us.

NOTES

1. Direct quotations are denoted by these symbols:

✦ = teachers/administrators
➤ = students
□ = parents

2. George W. Smith and Dorothy E. Smith. 1998. The ideology of "fag": The school experience of gay students. *Sociological Quarterly* 39: 309–27.

⑤

GSD PROFESSIONAL DEVELOPMENT

"Learnings" That Lead to Best Practices

The main question that I would like to have answered came up during a meeting with the Upper School faculty. We asked, "Would it be okay to put up a Safe Zone sticker in the room?" The immediate response was "Well, if we don't put up that sticker, does it automatically mean that it's not a safe zone?" Which indicates to me that there is a sense that people here in this community would not want us to put up such a sticker. Personally, I want to put one up, especially because I think it would be a great conversation starter for kids who ask about it, what it means, etc. Do you have any suggestions about how to proceed here?

—Ninth grade teacher

We need to do much more. I've been here a very long time, twenty plus years, and we have had little to no training in this area.

—Elementary teacher

Can we get a presentation that eschews vilification, oversimplification and patronization?

—Middle school administrator

In many school systems and communities, protected time for in-depth adult learning is rare, and competition for that precious time is keen. Prioritizing professional development needs is nearly impossible when there is always "so much more to be done" in every aspect of school life, from preparing for standardized tests to learning the latest classroom technologies. In the programs and workshops they do have, teachers hope for practical strategies that they can use in their work right away. As a result, professional development programming is often grounded in "informational learning" (i.e., learning new facts). Yet for those educators who are expected to carry out best good practices in relation to gender and sexuality diversity, there must be ample informational *and* "transformational learning" opportunities.

SECTION I
CRITICAL APPROACHES TO
GSD PROFESSIONAL DEVELOPMENT

I am always ready to learn although I do not always like being taught.

—Winston Churchill

No teacher really loves her or his own teacher education.

—Deborah Britzman

HOW TEACHERS LEARN

While there is no consensus about which model of professional development is the most effective, there is abundant literature and research that stress the importance of adult learning in the preK–12 setting. There is a positive link between adult learning and student achievement (DuFour 2007), supporting the belief that adult development is not a "luxury"—as some might perceive it—but rather an effective tool for increasing beneficial student outcomes. Schools should be "learning centers" for administrators, teachers, staff, students, and parents alike (Drago-Severson 2009). In relation to gender and sexuality diversity education, it is key to have all members of the community involved.

Informational Learning; Transformational Learning

Drago-Severson (2009) makes a distinction between two critical forms of learning. *Informational learning* involves gaining knowledge and skills (e.g., getting the latest early reading intervention program efficacy statistics). *Transformational learning* requires engaging one's cognitive, emotional, and interpersonal capacities in such a way that "a qualitative shift occurs in *how a person actively interprets, organizes, understands, and makes sense of his or her experience*" (11). Learning of this magnitude goes well beyond mastering the latest Smart Board technology or experimenting with a new approach to curriculum mapping. For example, the quandary of the high school teacher that begins this chapter (i.e., what to do about Safe Zone stickers) cannot be adequately or effectively addressed with learning new skills and informational instruction alone.

Therefore not only do educators who engage with GSD need professional development, they need a particular approach to adult learning that supports transformational learning across the various subgroups within a school community. The district superintendent or the independent school board of trustees must empower principals and school heads to offer the leadership—and allot the resources—that supports this kind of extended, collaborative learning endeavor. In addition, asking teachers to explore, grow, and change in the realm of GSD requires professional and personal risk-taking that can only occur in a culture of trust. It is critical, then, to address the trust-building needs of adults engaged in this kind of transformational learning.

Content and Process; Finding the Optimal Balance

Chapters 1 through 4 of this book contain a tremendous amount of *content* related to gender and sexuality diversity: concepts, terms, models of development, theories, pedagogical rubrics, research summaries, case examples. For many teachers learning this content (i.e., informational learning) *also* requires fundamental shifts in thinking (i.e., transformational learning) about gender and sexuality. The result? Learning new content or "facts" entails some degree of reshaping perspective as well.

For example, these teachers are looking for updated information (i.e., *content*):

❖ *I could use a good review of adolescent development, gender/sexuality milestones in particular.*
❖ *What does the latest research tell us about inherent differences in boys' and girls' relational styles?*

These teachers are seeking a ***process*** by which learning and change will be made possible:

❖ *The faculty needs more time to discuss our own feelings on these issues and connect before designing curriculum about them.*
❖ *Having an open forum for addressing the school's role, teachers' role and parent's role is key. We need to identify what our real responsibilities and options are.*
❖ *We need to pay close attention to how people are feeling as we proceed with this—this will push a lot of emotional buttons.*

As the last teacher notes, engaging with GSD can "push a lot of emotional buttons." So even the acquisition of basic information in the GSD subject area requires some measure of intellectual and emotional risk-taking. Therefore, professional development (PD) initiatives must be designed to provide GSD content via more "process-oriented" approaches. These approaches (e.g., small group discussion, role-plays, live consultation) allow participants to engage in a blend of instructional-transformational learning. Here is an example of what a balanced PD experience might look like (box 5.1).

Box 5.1. Example of GSD Program Experience

Imagine yourself as this high school teacher, attending a half-day workshop on GSD. You engage in a series of structured tasks that have a mixture of informational learning and transformational learning opportunities, along with a balance of content (passive, facts) and process (active, experiential). The focus for you during the program, for whatever reason, is on the word "queer."

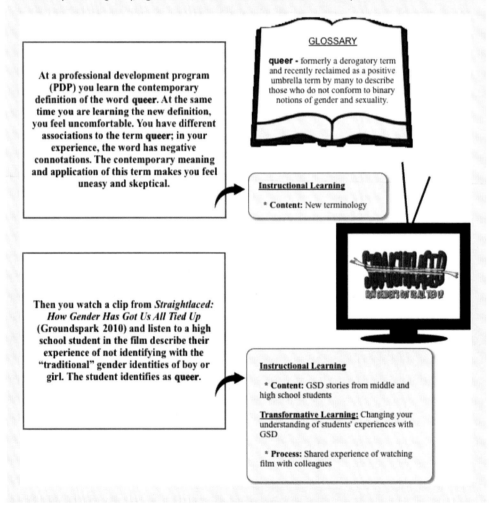

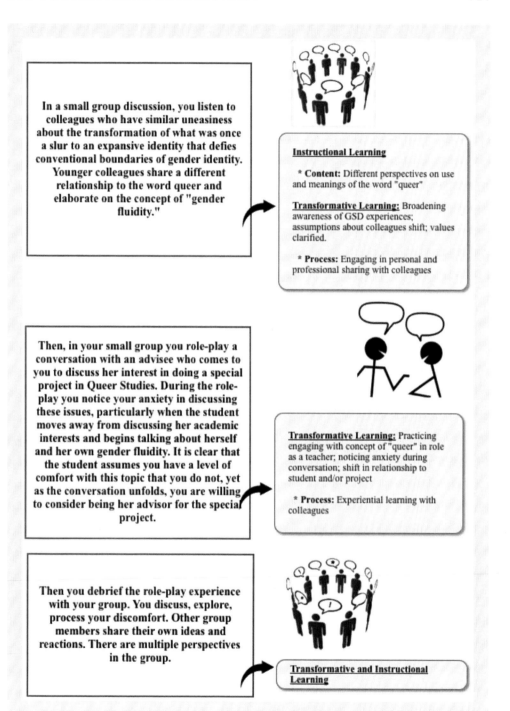

In a small group discussion, you listen to colleagues who have similar uneasiness about the transformation of what was once a slur to an expansive identity that defies conventional boundaries of gender identity. Younger colleagues share a different relationship to the word queer and elaborate on the concept of "gender fluidity."

Instructional Learning

* **Content:** Different perspectives on use and meanings of the word "queer"

Transformative Learning: Broadening awareness of GSD experiences; assumptions about colleagues shift; values clarified.

* **Process:** Engaging in personal and professional sharing with colleagues

Then, in your small group you role-play a conversation with an advisee who comes to you to discuss her interest in doing a special project in Queer Studies. During the role-play you notice your anxiety in discussing these issues, particularly when the student moves away from discussing her academic interests and begins talking about herself and her own gender fluidity. It is clear that the student assumes you have a level of comfort with this topic that you do not, yet as the conversation unfolds, you are willing to consider being her advisor for the special project.

Transformative Learning: Practicing engaging with concept of "queer" in role as a teacher; noticing anxiety during conversation; shift in relationship to student and/or project

* **Process:** Experiential learning with colleagues

Then you debrief the role-play experience with your group. You discuss, explore, process your discomfort. Other group members share their own ideas and reactions. There are multiple perspectives in the group.

Transformative and Instructional Learning

What would happen if the information about contemporary GSD terminology were delivered in a didactic presentation, and you learned about the word "queer" in that format? Teachers could be given hard copies of the PowerPoint slides; they might even have an opportunity to ask questions. Not only is this approach likely to be ineffective, it may well foster confusion and resentment. Without an opportunity to process emotions and reactions, educators feel uncertain about the terminology and resent being expected to "get on board" with this new approach.

Will it take more time and planning and "work" to create an effective program? Yes. However, an expedient approach to gender and sexuality diversity professional development will prove ineffective and far more costly in the end.

CHANGING HOW YOU SEE; CHANGING WHAT YOU DO

It is not so much about to see what no one has seen before, but to think what nobody has yet thought about that which everybody sees.

—Arthur Schopenhauer

The most powerful driver for behavioral change is a change in how one understands the world. If you want powerful ongoing changes in teacher or leadership, you have to get at the underlying beliefs and conceptions that give rise to the behaviors.

—Robert Kegan (1982), "Inner Conflict, Inner Strengths"

Adult development expert Bob Kegan identifies "underlying beliefs" as the locus of control for many adult behaviors (Kegan and Lahey 2002, 70). As noted elsewhere in this book, attitudes about gender and sexuality are highly influenced by cultural beliefs and personal values. Participating in transformational learning opportunities requires educators (and parents and students) to

1. identify/examine *personal* beliefs about gender and sexuality diversity.
2. identify/examine *professional* beliefs about GSD.
3. consider disrupting their foundation of "knowing" about GSD.

We count on teachers to be the purveyors of what is true and right and best. So it is not surprising that they may feel particularly self-conscious about "not knowing" and experiencing the "inadequacy" of their own ideas as part of the GSD learning process.

In addition to increasing what we "know," transformational learning promotes deeper, more intimate connections with others.

What the eye sees better the heart feels more deeply. We not only increase the likelihood of our being moved; we also run the risk that being moved entails. For we are moved somewhere, and that somewhere is further into life, closer to those we live with. They come to matter to us more (Kegan 1982, 16–17).

"The Story of When the Consultant Is Moved" demonstrates the risks and rewards of moving closer to others as we "learn." Sometimes that kind of vulnerability can lead to great pain, and at other times it can lead to great joy. Both are potent sources for transformative learning.

The Story of When the Consultant Is Moved

The invitation to work with a very traditional Episcopal boarding school in the South came as a surprise. As soon as I accepted the job, questions began. A friend asked, "Why are they hiring you? What do they really want?" My brother worried. "I know you're strong and all that, but don't make yourself too vulnerable in that environment. These people may not have your best interests at heart." My mother said, "Make sure you let them know that you were confirmed at Trinity Church in Southport." I began to worry myself about traveling into what everyone perceived as potentially hostile territory for a lesbian from Massachusetts.

After warm welcomes and cordial introductions at the beginning of the professional development program, the Head of School gave the faculty a brief update about a student who was seriously ill and in a nearby hospital. The concern for this boy was palpable. I scanned the worried faces in the room and forgot about my nerves. Instead I wondered about this student, his relationships with these teachers sitting in front of me. Then the Head asked the chaplain to say a prayer for the boy. Everyone stood and so did I. We all bowed our heads during the prayer and at the end of his blessings, the chaplain added, "And send your grace down upon Dr. Bryan and all of us here today, as we search together for ways to give our students the love and support and guidance they need. Amen."

My face flushed. I had not counted on beginning my work with this group feeling caught off guard. In fact I had braced myself for any conflict. Up until this moment I had only experienced people praying for me because of my "sins." How unexpected to feel warmth and welcome from those I had prejudged as adversaries.

Intrator (2006, 236) notes "how valuable it is to provide the structure for teachers to consider how personal values, beliefs, attitudes, and vulnerabilities shape our practice, inform our judgments, and play within our teaching." If you survived the "introspective dialogue" back in chapter 4, then you know that introspection can sometimes elicit disquietude. Deep examination of how we personally and socially construct gender and sexuality diversity invites us to question how we think about, as Schopenhauer puts it, "that which everybody sees."

For example, the graduation dress code has been the same for seventy-five years, and it seems peculiar to now question whether the mandatory requirements of white dresses for girls and jacket and tie for boys are oppressive and violating to some students (see The Story of Dress Uniform Day). Is adding Jeffrey Eugenides's Pulitzer Price–winning novel *Middlesex*, the story of an intersex man's search for identity, to the summer reading list an act of political correctness or is it part of a fundamental paradigm shift in the way the school understands sex and gender? Behavior that used to be understood as "boys being boys" (e.g., senior boys rating how "hot" the freshman girls are) can now be framed as sexual harassment. Is this an overreaction or is it a waking-up to the deeply negative consequences of sexually objectifying young girls? Educators charged with answering these questions must be given an opportunity to engage fully and think critically to find those answers.

The Story of Dress Uniform Day

My Catholic-leaning, independent K–8 school had a uniform, with different rules for girls and boys. For girls, we could wear a combination of a white polo, a light blue blouse, navy shorts, pants, a skort, or a jumper (middle schoolers had the option of a skirt). I am a transgender man but at the time was living as a girl and only knew that I did not want to wear "girls' clothes." Naturally, then, I wore the polo and shorts or pants combination every day. Multiple times each school year, though, the school had "dress uniform days," usually when we had mass or a special event—and for every class picture. On these days I was required to wear the jumper (and the skort and skirt when I was older). I dreaded dress uniform days. I felt like I was being forced into a costume; I felt uncomfortable all day, and even worse—I felt like I was on display in my discomfort and distress.

Rattling the Cage of Certainty

Feminist theorist Judith Butler suggests that in order to engage in and understand the complexity of GSD, we must "pursue the moments of degrounding, when we're standing in two different places at once; or we don't know exactly where we're standing" (Butler 1994). Yet "pursuing" instability feels counterintuitive, foolish even. Educators are oriented toward answering questions; educational systems aim to resolve "problems" as efficiently and quickly as possible. It is awkward (yet ultimately transformative) for a group of educators to experience "degrounding" together. In the example, "Holding Up a Mirror," consider the value of hearing the consultants feedback (box 5.2).

This particular faculty group is representative of most, with individuals having a range of experiences and points of view. Being "all over the place," as one teacher puts it, is disconcerting and tampers with the assumption that everybody on the faculty is pretty much on the same page about important issues. Having "looked" in the mirror via this verbal feedback, this is now an entire group that is, as Butler describes, "standing in two different places at once; or [doesn't] know exactly where [it's] standing" (2006, 533). And throughout the professional development program, participants will struggle with this uncertainty.

Yet, as these teachers attest, there is something comforting in the experience of being lost together.

❖ *It was important for all of us to witness everyone's struggles with finding the right language. None of us have this down.*

BOX 5.2. Holding Up a Mirror

It is the beginning of a professional development program and I have just finished introducing myself to the faculty of an elementary school. In preparation for the program, teachers watched a film last week and completed a questionnaire. Today we will work together, talking about Gender and Sexuality Diversity and how it relates to their particular educational community.

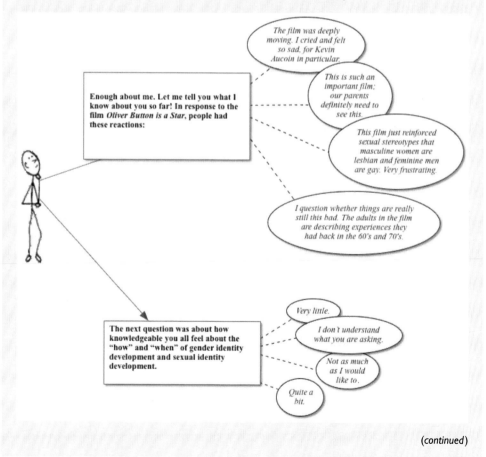

(continued)

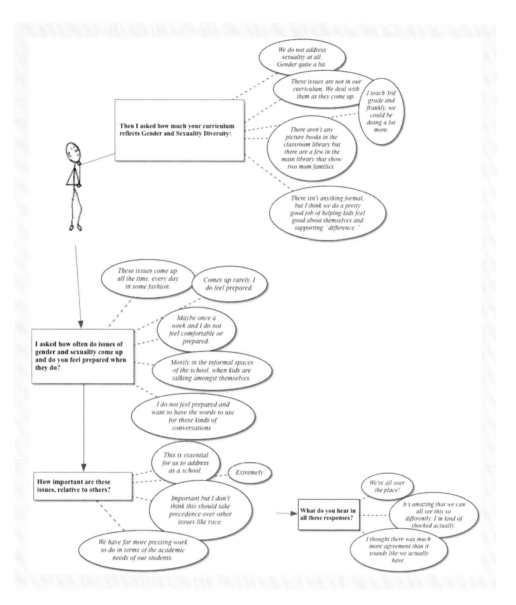

❖ *It made me feel better to see that we are all struggling with this, even the most senior teachers.*

❖ *It felt so awkward to fumble around in front of my colleagues yet it also felt very real, like there wasn't going to be any faking it or posturing.*

"Not knowing" collectively and openly as a group actually makes the learning environment safer, even though the uncertainty of this experience is uncomfortable.

USING WHO YOU ARE TO TEACH

Another critical approach to professional growth in relation to gender and sexuality diversity is encouraging teachers to make use of their most valuable teaching tool: themselves. In spite of not knowing and feeling "degrounded" in the face of GSD, educators should use (1) what they know and don't know, (2) how they feel, and (3) who they are to guide their work.

What You Know

When it comes to GSD teachers must adapt to a combination of knowing and not knowing. The previous chapters of this book offer "knowledge" about gender, sexuality, and heteronormativity, and underscore that sex and gender are inherently messy aspects of identity. As this longtime middle school teacher describes, consistently making room for her knowledge *and* ignorance about gender and sexual identities is a challenging, never-ending process (see The Teacher Who Wished for Tidiness).

The Teacher Who Wished for Tidiness

Society has many subtle and not so subtle ways to say what one "should be." It isn't a very inclusive list. As a teacher I want to be very inclusive. I want all my students to succeed.

I have taught too many "identities" in my 30 year career to think I finally have a comprehensive list. And though I don't have a "complete" list—a tidiness that I really would like to have—I do know that I have to always make a place for both what I do know and what I don't, in my language, teaching, and learning.

If I can lessen my ignorance, just a little each day, then I am doing well. Some days I get it right, some days I don't. Some days I see that it is an accumulation of lots of positive little things that has made the difference. Some days I get tired . . . I've done my part—it's someone else's turn. Other days I plow ahead knocking everyone over in my path and leaving chaos in my wake. Regardless of the yesterday, regardless of all my successes and mistakes, I get up again and say, I am where I am in this gender and sexuality work. *I want my students to succeed. So I keep at it.*

—Middle school teacher, 30+ years

There is a prime opportunity for teachers to model for students how to respond to "not knowing." *I'm not sure I know the answer to that question. I think it has to do with genetics but it could be hormones. Let's find out.* Through her own behavior, the teacher makes not knowing an expected, routine occurrence; she gives her students permission to not know and then go find some answers (or more questions). In addition, those teachers who worry about "saying the wrong thing" in relation to GSD are in a position to model the role of emotions in the learning process. *I'm a little bit nervous about talking about what "transgender" means, because I worry about saying the wrong thing. But let me give it a try anyway.*

What You Feel

Teachers are not typically accustomed to using internal experiences and emotional reactions as pedagogical guides. When faced with a challenge or a problem, teachers would much rather figure out what they are going to "do" than examine how they "feel." Educator Parker Palmer suggests that "the most practical thing we can achieve in any kind of work is insight into what is happening inside us as we do it" (Palmer 2007, 6). Think about that for a moment.

How often do you notice what is "happening inside" while you teach? (Recognizing that you are hungry for lunch does not count.) Paying attention to what is happening *inside* provides a teacher with valuable information about (a) his own emotional response and (b) how the teaching and learning process is going on the *outside*. Think of yourself as a **barometer**. Take barometer readings to learn about yourself and to inform your teaching of others. Checking in with yourself is a form of self-reflection, a valuable tool for integration of learning.

Here is an example of how it works. At a professional development workshop, I give each small group a real-life scenario to work with. I ask participants to

1. assume the role of the teacher in the scenario.
2. place themselves directly in the situation at hand.
3. answer a series of questions.

Remember the third graders back in chapter 4, the ones working at a table making special bags for collecting valentines? (p. 97) Workshop participants are given that same scenario and asked to put themselves in that third grade teacher's shoes, to place themselves in the scene itself. This is the conversation they overhear.

In this moment, when Ben makes his comments, the atmosphere among the students working together at the table shifts. The teacher (i.e., workshop participant who is assuming the role of the teacher) experiences this shift too. Her barometer registers both the external shift (i.e., *The dynamics among the students just changed*) and internal shift (i.e., *I feel something in my gut about what just happened*). In the professional development workshop, the first question participants must answer is: ***How do you feel in this moment?*** Listen in.

Whether we call it intuition, instinct, experience, values, wisdom, empathy, or a gut reaction, a teacher's *professional* response is often shaped by internal, emo-

Graphic 5.1.

tional, and *personal* reactions. When the reaction on the "inside" is negative or complex, as in this valentine scenario, teachers often *ignore* the reading on their barometer. They assume these feelings of anxiety and confusion are "unprofessional" and problematic. Wrong on both counts!

Paying attention to how you feel is part of your professional responsibility, not merely a touchy-feely indulgence. Using yourself as a barometer is a valuable **pedagogical tool**. If you are anxious or afraid in this moment, that is important data. Probably during most moments in the school day, you do not feel anxious and afraid. So something in this situation has triggered your emotional reaction. Or if you feel panicky about saying the wrong thing, again, important data. At the very least, your response tells you that you are not as prepared for this moment as you need to be.

Consider some of the ways a teacher might register her feelings and then respond. There are a dozen possible replies here (see dialogue options). Some responses incorporate the teacher's feelings. One teacher uses his feelings to formulate a plan for consulting with colleagues and opts to come back to the discussion later (see option 3). Another uses her emotional response to model that it is okay for the students to have their own set of feelings (see option 2).

It is also possible for a teacher to feel way over her head in this situation. She checks her barometer, registers her sense of being overwhelmed, and wants to pretend she did not actually overhear the conversation about the consequences of

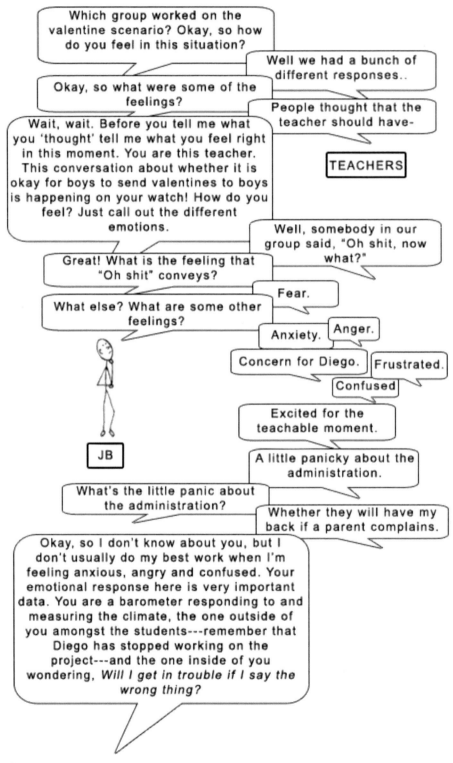

Graphic 5.2.

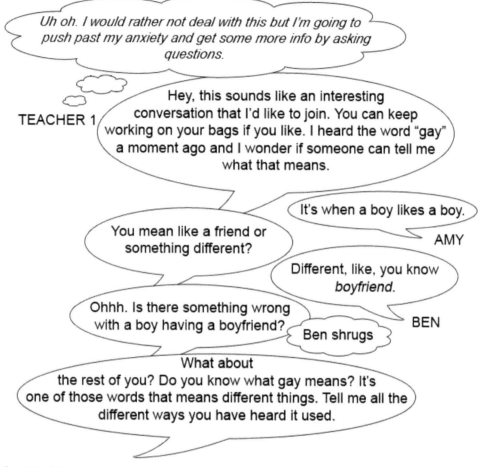

Graphic 5.3. Option I

boys sending valentines to boys. She can take a pass this time around. What matters most is that she follows up with a colleague or teaching team, that she uses reading and other resources to understand what this valentine moment represents in terms of GSD. She can look at her school's mission statement (e.g., respect for differences), identify relevant educational values (e.g., understanding self and others), and consider the climate/community being created in an exchange such as this (e.g., *you're so gay*). All of these resources, along with self-reflection, will help her shape an integrated, professional response (see option 4).

Who You Are

The third element of using who you are to address GSD is explored in chapter 10. Teacher identity—a blend of the professional and personal aspects of self—is examined via the concept that "we teach who we are" (Palmer 2007). What happens

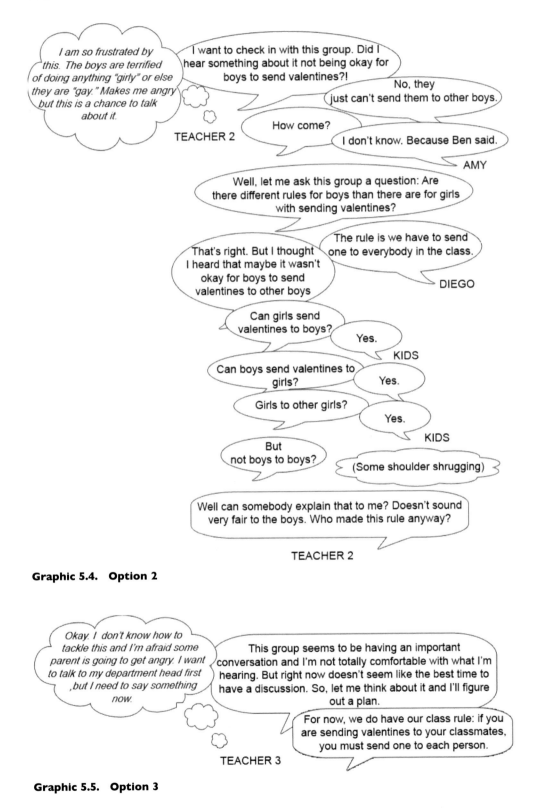

Graphic 5.4.   Option 2

Graphic 5.5.   Option 3

I wanted to come back to something I overheard last week when we were decorating our valentine bags. There was a conversation about the word "gay" and whether it is okay for boys to send valentines to boys, and I got very nervous. I realized that as your teacher, I was not ready to have a conversation with you about "the gay issue." I thought about it a lot later on, and then I talked to some other teachers to get their ideas. Now I feel more ready to have a conversation about what gay means and what it might have to do with sending valentines. I think it is an important conversation to have. I still feel a little awkward but that's okay and however you feel is okay too.

Graphic 5.6.   Option 4

at the intersection of professional and personal identities for educators who are heteronormative? Who are GLBTQI? Chapter 10 examines the question of whether all educators get to bring a "whole self" to the job and identifies the risks and advantages in being fully known as a teacher.

TRANSFORMATIONAL LEARNING (AGAIN)

The notion that teachers must first unsettle their own understandings before they can help students do the same may initially be a tough sell for the professional development program planners. Yet teachers are quite blunt about the degree to which they already feel unsettled and unprepared when it comes to teaching about gender and sexuality diversity.

❖ *There is a student in my classroom possibly grappling with her own gender identity (she's admitted in the past that she wants to be a boy). I don't feel equipped to take care of this and related issues.*

❖ *I have no formal training in how to talk about gender and sexuality in my role as an elementary teacher. I have years of experience and good instincts but I need more to deal with the reality of my students.*

❖ *I am approached often by students in regard to GLBT issues because they see me as "safe" and "cool." I have no formal training in this area and worry that in flying by the seat of my pants, I may be screwing up some poor child.*

Most educators want to learn how to address gender and sexuality effectively and when teachers are given an opportunity and the resources, they welcome the challenges presented by GSD professional development work.

One More "Qualitative Shift" Please

Here is one more challenge, one more opportunity for changing "how a teacher interprets, organizes, understands, and makes sense of" GSD in schools (Drago-Severson 2009, 11). In particular, the invitation here is for **educators to examine their own role in maintaining heteronormativity.** This requires a paradigm shift, a big one. Stay open and take a look.

Currently, conceptualizing homophobia as something that needs to be challenged and eradicated is a standard approach for those who advocate for social justice (i.e., the idea that all people are equal and should be treated as such). Many educators do extremely important work using this approach. Yet a different kind of transformational learning about gender and sexuality diversity involves a new framing of the issues, namely, that **maintaining heteronormative expectations** (i.e., heterosexual feminine women pairing with heterosexual masculine men) **is a collective process of which we are all a part**. If gender is in some measure "socially constructed" (Butler 1994), we must recognize that (1) the construction is ongoing, and (2) we are participants in that construction, whether we are conscious of it or not.

Translation? **We are more comfortable locating the problem in someone else**. Here is a simple example. *It's greedy marketers who are responsible for sexualizing young girls and objectifying women.* True enough, yet purchasing American Apparel clothing for girls supports a company that "is on the hunt for the 'Best Bottom in the World.' . . . We're looking for a brand new bum (the best in the world!) to be the new 'face' for our always expanding intimates and briefs lines . . .; send in a photo of your backside" (http://americanapparel.net/).

Some consumers (i.e., parents) may not be aware of the "best bum" contest, but kids know all about it. Buy the underwear and you tacitly support girls e-mailing photos of their buttocks over the Internet. The message to girls is quite plain: sexy, shapely butts are what matters, not who you are.

PreK–12 schools are primary sites for maintaining heteronormativity. Here is one small example out of hundreds. Read the notice sent home by the school nurse (see Where's Your Bra?). This is a far less provocative example than the "best bum" contest, yet telling in its subtlety.

Where's Your Bra?

Dear Parents of 5th and 6th graders,

   Tomorrow I will begin conducting postural screening for scoliosis during your child's physical education class. For the girls in 5A and 5B, please have your daughter wear the top to a two-piece bathing suit or a sports bra to school tomorrow. For the girls in 6A and 6B, please do the same on Thursday.
Sincerely,
The School Nurse

The nurse is conducting a routine medical exam. It is easier for her to assess the "balance" between a student's shoulders if the student is not wearing a top or shirt. The instructions for girls to wear a bra or a bikini top serve a purely practical purpose. But the request also conveys a gendered assumption, that all fifth and sixth grade girls own a sports bra or two-piece bathing suit top, *and* they are comfortable wearing them to school. This may seem like an issue of very little consequence, yet if you are the ten-year-old girl who purposely does not own a bikini—perhaps because of all it connotes—or who does not need a bra or does not want a bra— perhaps because of what it means culturally to be "ready" for a bra—the official message from the nurse that you must wear one to school stirs panic and dread.

The directing, shaping, requiring of gendered behavior is at the cornerstone of maintaining heteronormativity. It happens everywhere, all the time. *Can you boys move the chairs to the back of the room? Let's get into two lines, boys over here, girls over here.* Heteronormativity is ultimately defined by the pairing of a heterosexual couple, but it also matters very much that the male and female who pair look and act a certain way. A very masculine woman paired with a very feminine man would be viewed as heterosexual, but probably not heteronormative.

Classroom 2F and the Big Paradigm Shift

The big paradigm shift occurs when we understand that **gender norms endure only if they are consented to by the individual, the collective, and the whole**. Remember Ms. Bellini and Classroom 2F and their kickball controversy (see the introduction)? When asked who made all the gender rules, those second grade students guessed that the president of the United States or Congress had created the rules. Ms. Bellini said, "I've got news for you. WE—all people—kids, grown-ups, teachers, parents make up these rules, for ourselves and each other. The president didn't decide that pink is for girls and blue is for boys. *We* did." The message to these second graders was clear: ***The power to change—or perpetuate—the "stereotype rules" lies with us.***

The paradigm shift, the thinking differently about "that which we all see," came when Classroom 2F was invited to (1) see themselves as participants in the rule-making (hence, part of the problem) and (2) transform the rules for the class if they wanted new ones that worked better (hence, part of the solution). A teacher can only facilitate this kind of transformative learning for students if she herself has been challenged to reframe the perennial kickball debate. Ms. Bellini was open to finding a new way to understand and engage the relentless gender stereotypes of second grade recess, so she pursued an unfamiliar path. Being mindful of one's own (innocent? ignorant? unintentional?) participation in reinforcing and maintaining heteronormativity is a critical part of professional development work related to GSD.

WHAT TO REMEMBER: SECTION I

Critical Approaches to GSD Professional Development

1. Adult learning is positively correlated with student achievement.
2. GSD professional development programs (PDP) must include both informational (i.e., facts) and transformational (i.e., new perspectives) learning opportunities.
3. Process-oriented approaches to PDP should be emphasized.
4. Transformational learning involves changing perspectives and paradigms.
5. Transformational learning is intellectually and emotionally challenging.
6. Teachers use of self (i.e., knowledge, emotions, identity) is an effective pedagogical approach to engaging GSD.
7. In order to fully engage GSD, teachers must see that they have both the power to change and the power to maintain heteronormativity in their community.
8. Teachers who engage in this informational and transformational learning about GSD typically find the experience valuable.

SECTION II
CREATING THE CONTEXT FOR LEARNING

CAN SOMEONE REMIND ME WHAT OUR TASK IS?

How often have you been a member of a working group and asked that question, either out loud or to yourself? Establishing goals and identifying desired outcomes is a crucial part of any collaborative learning endeavor, regardless of whether the group is a first grade reading circle, a middle school basketball team, the monthly meeting of department heads, or the school budget committee. Professional development programs that do not establish clear learning objectives may be interesting and even relevant, but they are ultimately ineffective. The "takeaway" means little if the participant is not clear about why/where/how to apply the learning. For GSD programs, these should be among the primary objectives:

- Learn, reflect on, and retain complex "content" related to GSD.
- Examine different attitudes and emotions in Self and Others in relation to gender and sexuality diversity.
- Practice using new language and terms.
- Collaborate with colleagues across similarities and differences.
- Identify structures that facilitate or hinder engagement with GSD.

- Build curricula and policies that support GSD.
- Engage all community members in the learning process.

Because professional development opportunities are rare and coveted, there is always debate about what issue or initiative should be given priority. And there are typically questions about the thinking behind the PDP choice.

❖ *What is the motivation for this initiative at this time? Was it teacher generated? From the administration? It seems to be coming out of nowhere.*

It may be tempting to assume that the person who questions the origins of or necessity for GSD professional development programs is resistant to the effort. Yet the questioner is identifying a compulsory, early group-building task. From start to finish, a working group engages the practical and existential question: *Why are we here?* The context in which GSD programming emerges and takes place must be fully understood by all participants and made transparent to the entire community.

The first step in creating a safe PDP environment is to be clear about the context that inspires and "holds" the learning. Teachers understand that engaging in professional development work is part of their job, yet the attitude they bring to the learning opportunity has an impact on the quality and success of the program. Preparing and informing teachers in advance about the origins, purpose, and scope of the PDP is also an essential first step in creating a trustworthy learning process.

There can be a range of catalysts for formal, structured attention to GSD. Consider the impact that these different contexts have for setting the tone for PDP about gender and sexuality:

- A working committee has been gathering data on school climate in relation to GSD for the past two years; this proposed PDP is the direct result of their recommendations.
- In order to be in compliance with new state legislation related to bullying prevention, the school is engaging in professional trainings as mandated by law.
- The new head of school has a progressive vision of "diversity"; she wants faculty to engage in a series of PDPs related to three primary social identifiers: race, gender, and religion.
- Local and state media coverage of several recent antigay incidents has sparked an interest among a vocal group of teachers, namely, those who have social justice oriented curricula. They have successfully petitioned to have professional development time devoted to GLBTQI issues.
- Administration is mindful of (1) an increased number of same-sex parents with children in the school, (2) an increasingly visible "out" cohort of older

GLBTQI students, and (3) the presence of several gender variant children and one transgender child in the elementary school community. This workshop is an effort to proactively prepare for the needs of these students and families.

- A hazing incident that included sexual and sexual orientation harassment led to the expulsion of two well-liked male students last year. There is widespread disagreement among students, faculty, and parents about whether the administration was justified in dismissing the students. This professional development initiative is intended to provide education on gender, sexuality, harassment, and related legal/policy concerns.

Establish Learning Goals; Invite Teacher Input

Once the context has been clarified, there are additional steps for creating a strong foundation for professional development. Teachers need to know the "what" and the "how" of any PDP. Asking for input also lets people know that this is a collaborative effort, that teachers have an active role in shaping the focus of the program. Here's an example:

1. Define program focus and content
    - We will be looking at Gender and Sexuality Diversity in the preK–6 setting, paying attention to the gender identity development and sexual identity development of students in this age group.
2. Identify learning opportunities and goals
    - Participants will have hands-on opportunities to apply concepts and language to real-life scenarios. They will also explore the ways that our school mission does, or does not, support engaging with gender and sexuality diversity.
3. Invite direct input from participants
    - Participants are encouraged to share any and all questions, concerns, observations about the upcoming program directly with the presenter.

This type of preprogram preparation and communication structures the learning experience in a transparent manner and establishes shared goals. It also lets teachers know that their input is valued.

Where to begin? How to begin? I often suggest that prior to the actual PDP the entire group of participants watch a recommended film (see Additional Resource 5.1) together and then complete a questionnaire afterward. Faculty members work in multiple groups regularly as part of their job. Watching the GSD film as a whole group creates a shared experience that marks the beginning of *this* specific learning endeavor for *this* particular working group. The films typically evoke intellectual curiosity and a variety of feelings; thus, viewers get a taste of the type of informational and transformational learning GSD involves.

Asking participants to complete a questionnaire after the film provides a structured exercise for exploring reactions to the movie and identifying questions for the PDP. This type of introspection, reflection, and sharing is often a precursor to transformational learning. In filling out the questionnaire participants (1) reflect on their level of individual knowledge and preparation, (2) identify their affective responses, (3) consider curricular questions, and (4) examine community-wide attitudes in relation to GSD. Being invited to watch the film and then share questions, concerns, and ideas for the PDP itself increases their investment in the learning process.

Structure, predictability, snacks. In the same way doctors can often be the worst patients, teachers have little tolerance for learning experiences that neglect the basics. Is the space set up correctly and comfortably? Does the technology work? Is there an agenda posted that lets people know the various components of the program, including when the breaks are? How about the coffee? When you ask, PDP participants always have plenty of feedback about the space, time, and important amenities.

- *The room was too cold.*
- *The chairs were uncomfortable.*
- *I liked that the chairs were set up in a way that let us see each other.*
- *There was too much sitting.*
- *The coffee was hot and good. Don't underestimate the value of good coffee!*
- *Why was the film shown at 8:00 a.m. with no opportunity for discussion?*
- *Having a lovely lunch available allowed us to maintain community and continue our conversations more informally. If everyone goes out to get lunch, the group disconnects.*

These may seem like trivial concerns but they are not. When the PDP is well organized and basic human needs are met, participants are more available for the challenging learning tasks at hand.

Learning Styles; Working with Colleagues

There are a variety of adult learning styles and many lenses through which adult development can be viewed (Drago-Severson 2009). The emphasis here is on the importance of using a variety of teaching methods that facilitate transformational learning, for both the individual and the group. In the course of a program, I may use charts, film clips, lecture, pencil and paper surveys, PowerPoint slides, role-plays, large group exercises, live consultation, and more. Adults are no different from children in their favorable response to changes in activities, frequent move-ment, and cookies after lunch.

Drago-Severson (2009) describes "collegial inquiry" in terms of an ideal, bal-anced process of small group work, where members speak, listen, concur, disagree, and clarify solutions.

> Collegial inquiry invites us to reflect internally on our own thinking and to share this in dialogue with others. . . . We are invited to listen carefully; consider diverse points of view; and to work to understand the similarities, differences, and overlapping points of multiple perspectives (which can include theoretical, emotional and political perspectives) . . . not only to listen to divergent points of view but also to listen to new ideas and challenge old ones. Conflict and contra-diction may emerge naturally. . . . When divergent perspectives or solutions are presented, it is best if a person can see the potentially helpful nature of conflict and the ways in which conflict often serves to clarify a solution. (Drago-Severson 2009, 166)

Ah, if only it were that simple. Recall "The Wheeler School Statement on Diver-sity" (see chapter 3). It frames conflict in relation to diversity work as a "catalyst for the change that [we] seek." This statement is absolutely true; it is a much more el-egant version of "no pain, no gain." Yet neither the Wheeler statement nor Drago-Severson's description of "the potentially helpful nature of conflict" adequately conveys the actual stress of this challenge.

The fear of conflict.   When the beliefs, feelings, experiences, and needs people have in relation to gender and sexuality diversity clash, the dissension can be unnerving and profound. Our instinct when conflict occurs is to back away or move the dissent underground. Many, many times I have observed a small group get derailed by participants' fear of naming the source of the tension. And often there is a seemingly compelling rationale not to speak:

- ❖ *He's been here forever; nobody ever confronts him.*
- ❖ *She's the coach and I'm just the assistant coach; I don't feel comfortable ques-tioning her opinion, much less pointing out her prejudice.*
- ❖ *Our group could have gotten a lot more done if we hadn't had one particu-larly conservative member who disagreed with absolutely everything.*

The facilitator must prepare groups for these inevitable dynamics and model ways to address the "unspeakable" disagreements.

Once the tyranny of politeness has been exposed and a group norm for honesty is established, groups feel liberated to do deeper, more meaningful work. It is not a process that is conflict-free going forward, but it is authentic, which is the only way true learning can occur. As this teacher states, "*We had an open dialogue with differing perspectives, a model that is not only possible but preferable to pretending we all agree when we don't."*

Small group process. The program facilitator must help the group hold and contain their affective and intellectual instability well enough—and long enough—so that they can then experience the "qualitative shift" that is the hallmark of transformational learning. The process can be painful as well as joyous, clarifying as well as confounding, confining as well as liberating, and solidifying as well as destabilizing. Moving among and between those intellectual and affective states is taxing for everyone involved, yet the payoff is extremely gratifying.

Critical Tasks for the PDP Consultant

The success of a Gender and Sexuality Diversity PDP rises and falls to a large degree on the facilitator's ability to

1. help participants anticipate and prepare for the ways that "divergent perspectives" can create tension and conflict among colleagues.
2. encourage candor, even if such honesty may expose conflict.
3. model authentic, professional engagement with the material (including not knowing).
4. balance instruction, validation, and empathy with sincere good humor.
5. identify the risk/benefit equation involved in transformational learning.
6. validate (repeatedly) the complexity of the task and the inevitability of discomfort.
7. create a bridge early and often in the PDP between *learning* and *application of learning.*
8. manage the time effectively.

Time management is paramount. Because there is so much material to cover and never enough time, the temptation to rush and collapse the learning process is ever present. Norman Cousins reminds us that ultimately, "Time given to thought is the greatest timesaver of all." It is hard to hold onto that wisdom in the moment. Covering "more" versus going deeply into less is rarely the better pedagogical choice.

WHAT TO REMEMBER: SECTION II

Critical Elements of GSD Professional Development

1. Clarifying the context and learning goals for GSD professional development programs (PDP) is essential. Participants must know why the PDP is occurring and what the purpose is.

2. Teachers should be invited to provide input for the PDP.
3. Begin the PDP process with a shared learning experience, such as viewing a film.
4. The PDP should have multiple components that appeal to different learning styles.
5. The PDP consultant must facilitate the process, contain the affect generated by transformational learning, and model authenticity.
6. Facilitator must prepare participants for inevitable disagreements and model ways to proceed.
7. Facilitator must tend to the structural elements of the PDP, particularly keeping time.

SECTION III
PROGRAM EVALUATION:
WHAT DID I LEARN? WHAT SHOULD WE DO NEXT?

THE VALUE OF ASSESSMENT

At the end of a conference or workshop, participants are typically asked to evaluate the effectiveness of the program itself. Certainly it is valuable for the PDP planners (often administration) and facilitator to know what aspects of the program were most helpful. Yet it is also useful for participants to reflect on the components that facilitated their learning most: (1) *structures* (e.g., large group exercise), (2) *processes* (e.g., role-play), and (3) *content* (e.g., glossary of terms).

❖ *I am always made anxious by role-playing but it is when scenarios are being played out that I find I can grasp what I might do or say. I hate them and I realize they create opportunities for significant learning.*

❖ *I didn't anticipate "language" playing such a big role but it is clear that meanings of some terms have changed and words absolutely do matter.*

❖ *The cone exercise with the whole group was so important in showing us how many assumptions we make about each other all the time. It was a simple exercise but it revealed A LOT!*

People are often surprised by their own learning experience, and in thinking about instruction with their own students, teachers are reminded about the challenges/benefits of certain pedagogical approaches.

What Did I Learn?

An evaluation that emphasizes *self-assessment* provides a structured opportunity for participants to identify new facts, skills, frameworks they have acquired dur-

BOX 5.3

What was the most important learning that occurred for you today?
Informational

That our mission statement is vague and faculty have no real relationship to it.

That there is a continuum for each: biological sex, gender identity, gender expression, and sexual orientation

ALL kids are *somewhere* on each of these spectrums!

Learning that homosexuality is really not a choice.

Awareness of sexual attraction starts before adolescence. While I know that to be true, it was good to have it put so succinctly.

Model of sex and gender provides a clear paradigm.

What was the most important learning that occurred for you today?
Informational and Transformational

That "diversity" and "multiculturalism" aren't necessarily terms that make GLBTQI families feel included.

We need to have these conversations in *every* classroom, not just ones where there is a "different" kid or a "different" family.

I hadn't really looked at our mission statement in this context. It has some critical omissions!

It is way past time to revise my health curriculum.

I learned that hard conversations need to be had. It was also helpful to gain some words for those conversations.

That the world around us isn't as knowledgeable and up-to-date about gender identity issues as I thought.

"What was the most important learning that occurred for you today?"
Transformational

How afraid people are of change.

How I sometimes don't stand up for things I believe.

How open people were willing to be today when given the opportunity.

My lead teacher and I need to sit down and talk about why we don't address GSD. I feel empowered now to initiate that conversation.

I had to acknowledge that in spite of my open-mindedness, I am really doing very little in my classroom in regard to this topic. I feel inspired to change that.

Allowing myself to stretch, squirm, and navigate my way through thinking about these issues.

I realized how irrational some of our cultural "norms" around gender and sexuality really are.

I learned that I'm not prepared to talk about a lot of these issues with my students. I also learned that I still make too many assumptions.

Being forced to stay with the question "What would you say?" That really made us struggle to find words/language to convey our thoughts.

Realizing my own insecurity in talking about these issues with my students in a group setting, versus one-on-one with a child.

How hard it can be to take advantage of teachable moments when we approach them with such apprehension.

That I am incredibly defensive about my own gayness in a largely straight context.

We have to be willing to push ourselves out of our comfort zones more in order to do the learning we need to do.

This has pushed me to think more deeply about my daily interactions with students.

I wasn't sure how relevant this workshop would be for an ECE teacher because we emphasize for kids all the time how we are trying to discover ourselves, our similarities, our differences . . . but I was *wrong*!

ing the PDP. Naming the "most important learning" allows people to reflect on both informational acquisition and transformational experiences. Box 5.3 provides samples of the breadth and depth of learning that typically happens at a successful GSD professional development workshop (full tables are in Additional Resources 5.2 and 5.3). Read through these responses and try to imagine where your own learning experience might fit in.

Application of Learning

The evaluation process also creates an opportunity for people to consider "next steps" for themselves professionally. As participants complete a PDP, they promptly identify ways to *apply their learning* (e.g., integrate new skills, employ new concepts, use different processes and perspectives) to practice.

❖ *I will write up my notes from today and meet with the head of school to discuss them.*

❖ *Integrate some of the books we discussed today into my curriculum.*

❖ *Sit down with my lower school head to look at the systems we have (or don't have) in place that could help us change our approach to these issues in the lower school.*

❖ *I have a student in my class that I need to talk with. Now I feel like I can do that with greater confidence.*

The evaluation can be a place to suggest institutional and systemic "next steps" as well; these suggestions can serve as guideposts for the ongoing professional development process and planning.

❖ *Fill our library with the books displayed today. Put them in places where young children will* <u>*choose*</u> *them for themselves, not just for the teachers to check out for classroom use.*

❖ *We need (1) clear statements from people in leadership, (2) a unified approach to openness in classes and on campus, (3) regular speakers or attention to the issues for the whole community. (We have begun to do this more for issues of race.)*

❖ *Creating a comprehensive Health and Wellness Curriculum for K–12 throughout the district.*

❖ *Optimistically I can see us creating a cross-division curriculum and giving teachers more prep for handling these situations. Pessimistically, I fear we may just resort to lots of talk and meetings and committees that accomplish little.*

Inviting teachers to participate in this process of shaping institutional change increases their ownership of and commitment to that process.

Eschewing the One-shot Deal

As educators we would never consider giving our students just one program to accomplish a complex series of learning tasks. We would not expect them to acquire new skills, understand novel concepts, and integrate new frameworks after a single morning or day of learning. Yet professional development work often follows this pedagogically egregious format, with budget shortfalls and time constraints cited as the primary culprits. Administrators and school boards are forced to make grim decisions about "resource allocation" all the time. If the goal is to prepare educators to effectively engage with gender and sexuality diversity in the preK–12 setting, multiple PDP opportunities must be offered (see The Story of the Light Bulb Moment).

The Story of the Light Bulb Moment

On my second visit to the school, an English teacher approached me just before the workshop was about to begin. "I had a light bulb moment," he said, extending his hand and reminding me of his name. "When you were here last year, I thought I really understood what our conversation about heterosexism was all about. And I did understand it, up here." He pointed to his head. "But I didn't have a feeling of it until we read Romeo and Juliet *last spring. It just happened! I have taught that play for years, but as the kids were talking about love and lust and fidelity and arguing about all that good stuff, this time a little bell went off. This was just such an easy conversation to have. Everybody understood explicitly and implicitly what we were talking about." He made a sweeping gesture with his hands. I nodded and smiled. "This is the archetypal tragic love story, right? But I suddenly thought, 'What if I'm a gay kid sitting in this class? How do I experience this conversation where everybody "gets it" and we're all supposedly on the same page and we're talking about the "universal truths" about Love? What if this were a story about two star-crossed men? Or two women?' There was so much heterosexual privilege in just having the discussion, and I had never noticed that before." I nodded again, with a big smile on my face. "Thanks for telling me," I said. "It's all about the light bulb moments. That's what keeps us going."*

WHAT TO REMEMBER: SECTION III

Individual Assessment/Group Evaluation

1. Participants benefit from evaluating specific components of the PDP in relation to their own learning experience.
2. Participants should identify their informational and transformational learning.

3. Identifying professional "next steps" facilitates participants' application of learning.

4. Identifying institutional "next steps" increases participants' investment in future PD.

5. Effective GSD professional development requires multiple opportunities for learning.

ADDITIONAL RESOURCES

Additional Resource 5.1

Films for GSD Professional Development Programs

Elementary Focus

- *It's Elementary: Talking About Gay Issues in Schools*
- *It's Still Elementary*
- *That's a Family!*
- *Oliver Button Is a Star*
- *Sexy, Inc: Our Children Under the Influence*
- *Kick Like a Girl*
- *Sticks and Stones*

Middle School Focus

- *Let's Get Real*
- *No Dumb Questions*
- *Scout's Honor*
- *Tomboys! Feisty Girls and Spirited Women*
- *Gender Matters: Expression and Identities Beyond the Binary*
- *I'm Just Anneke*

High School Focus

- *Straightlaced: How Gender Has Got Us All Tied Up*
- *For the Bible Tells Me So*
- *Anyone and Everyone*
- *In the Family: Marriage Equality and LGBT Families*
- *Out of the Past: The Struggle for Gay and Lesbian Rights in America*

Additional Resource 5.2

Professional Learning Development Program Evaluation: *Informational and Transformational* Responses to "What was the most important learning that occurred for you today?"

- In listening to others talk about the various questions, I broadened my "library" of positive responses to students' issues and questions.
- Awareness of sexual attraction starts before adolescence. While I know that to be true, it was good to have it put so succinctly.
- Learning the differences between biological sex, gender identity, gender expression, and sexual orientation. I hadn't broken them down that way before.
- That "diversity" and "multiculturalism" aren't necessarily terms which make GLBTQI families feel included.
- Need to have parent education so we can share language, reference points, the challenge.
- That there is a continuum for each: biological sex, gender identity, gender expression. and sexual orientation.
- Model of sex and gender provides a clear paradigm.
- Establishing common language.
- That the world around us isn't as knowledgeable and up-to-date about gender identity issues as I thought.
- I learned that my school is too far behind as far as administrative support and clear mission.
- I learned that hard conversations need to be had. It was also helpful to gain some words for those conversations.
- Starting to understand how to educate the community as a "system."
- The most important concept for me to take away is that you don't have to respond to everything on the spot. You can help the children frame the questions and issues, and then address them over time.
- Learning there are different ways to handle the same situation.
- We need to have these conversations in *every* classroom, not just ones where there is a "different" kid or a "different" family.
- I already know quite a bit about gender and sexuality but having an open conversation about these issues with my colleagues was enormously informative.
- It is way past time to revise my health curriculum.

Additional Resource 5.3

Professional Learning Development Program Evaluation:
Transformational Responses to "What was the most important learning that occurred for you today?"

How afraid people are of change.

How I sometimes don't stand up for things I believe.

How open people were willing to be when given the opportunity.

My lead teacher and I need to sit down and talk about why we don't address GSD. I feel empowered now to initiate that conversation.

Our GLBTQ colleagues feel unsure about how/whether to talk about who they are.

Allowing myself to stretch, squirm, and navigate my way through thinking about these issues.

I need to talk to my son.

I learned that I'm not prepared to talk about a lot of these issues with my students. I also learned that I still make too many assumptions.

Being forced to stay with the question "What would you say?" That really made us struggle to find words/language to convey our thoughts.

Realizing my own insecurity in talking about these issues with my students in a group setting, versus one-on-one with a child.

How hard it can be to take advantage of teachable moments when we approach them with such apprehension.

I had to acknowledge that in spite of my open-mindedness, I am really doing very little in my classroom in regard to this topic. I feel inspired to change that.

Today has been reinforcing rather than learning something new.

I realized how irrational some of our cultural "norms" around gender and sexuality really are.

We had an open dialogue with differing perspectives, a model that not only is this possible but preferable to pretending we all agree when we don't.

Strangely enough, that I still have discomfort talking about these issues. I thought I didn't.

Not really sure why this felt so revolutionary but it did: being asked to consider the *pedagogical* im-

That I am incredibly defensive about my own gayness in a largely straight context.

plications of our reactions to each scenario.

Sometimes it is easier to assume that you're more "with it" than you actually are.

This has pushed me to think more deeply about my daily interactions with students.

To be honest, this is the first program I have even been in where we dealt with such issues and I am just grateful we were able to be a part of it.

The amount of ambivalence that my colleagues have about discussing these issues. We have so much more to learn as a community. This surprised me as I thought we were all more forward-thinking.

For me it was more about grappling with the discomfort about what I said or others said at times and experiencing how we related to each other as faculty in these "mistake" moments. It felt safe somehow.

Having us share what we would actually say, rather than summarizing what we'd say, made me realize how awkward these conversations can be.

I am someone who tends to self-edit before I respond. Today I allowed myself to risk ideas, even though I felt some shame around my answers. I felt as though it made me more sensitive to how students may feel when risking their own ideas.

I had a chance to look at my fear about approaching discussions of different families. I feel less fearful now about "saying the wrong thing."

I really liked simply bringing gender identity issues out into the open. It was helpful to role play these scenarios because I never really thought about how I would deal with these issues.

The cultural conflicts are the most difficult and confusing—they deserve a lot of processing and brainstorming ways to honor conflicting values.

That there are inherent differences of opinion and misunderstanding on these issues and recognizing this is an important part of the process. We can't become more comfortable until we acknowledge the discomfort.

I need to be more explicit in my instruction—not just doing well on the fly" but being intentional in curriculum development.

We have to be willing to push ourselves out of our comfort zones more in order to do the learning we need to do.

I wasn't sure how relevant this workshop would be for an ECE teacher because we emphasize all the time for kids how we are trying to discover ourselves, our similarities, our differences . . . but I was *wrong*! Very interesting—it helped me rethink some of my inhibitions about bringing up certain topics.

I need to keep thinking about how to be out at work with the kids and how the school will support that.

Unfortunately it was hearing my grade partners describe how they are too busy and under too many curricular demands to "fit in" much of this material.

This scenario pushed me to consider whether my actions are due to what I think is best for the student or what I'm most comfortable with.

How truly difficult addressing some of these issues can be and the importance of acknowledging the challenges and conflict involved.

I am so glad we got to role play because we all have these difficult moments and it's great to know I'm not alone.

6

GSD IN EARLY CHILDHOOD AND ELEMENTARY EDUCATION

Strategies, Application, and Curriculum

The problem is not an idea shortage. New approaches can usually be elicited just by asking for them. The average brainstorming session produces lots of fresh thinking. Good ideas surround us. Openness to such ideas does not. What's at a premium is receptivity to innovative suggestions and the vision to pursue them, even if that means reconceiving altogether what we're up to.

—Farson and Keyes, *The Innovation Paradox*

When he found the children dividing themselves into boys' tables and girls' tables, he went to them and asked, "I'm a boy-girl; where do I sit?

—No Outsiders Project Team 2010

What is a mirror for one student is a window for another. We need to be vigilant in our quest to ensure that all students here, no matter what their race, gender, family constellation, or financial situation, are reflected in our curriculum and that they have a mirror in which to see their reality reflected. Likewise, a balanced and thorough education involves looking through windows and coming to know difference, not merely having one's own understanding validated and reinforced.

—Jennifer McLean, former director of studies
Charles River School, Massachusetts

This chapter focuses on early childhood and elementary education (ECEE), highlighting different strategies, approaches, models, and lessons for engaging gender and sexuality diversity with preK–6 students. There are a variety of resources offered in this chapter. Look for **teaching strategies and teaching materials**, **lesson plans**, **school projects**, **book and film recommendations**, along with **organizations** that provide free GSD curricula for ECEE. In addition there are models of conversations about GSD that demonstrate the use of appropriate language.

The resources and approaches presented in this chapter are designed to support community-wide engagement with GSD, involving students, teachers, administrators, and parents. This effort occurs in the classrooms, on the playground, in policy implementation, and during after-school programs. And the success of the effort hinges on effective communication, much of which happens in groups. Thus the chapter begins with a look at common group facilitation strategies and their application to teaching and learning about gender and sexuality in the preK–6 setting.

SECTION I
COMMUNICATION STRATEGIES

THE BENEFITS OF WORKING IN GROUPS

❖ *Is it possible to have effective group discussions with students about this? Seems like an issue better left to individual conversations.*

Effective communication is at the heart of successful engagement with gender and sexuality diversity and much of that communication happens in groups. Teaching students how to be members of productive working groups begins in preK and continues through senior year. If you are acclimating kindergartners to the rules for morning circle for the first time or pushing your varsity basketball team to play as a unit, you are establishing group **norms** and fostering group **cohesion**. Positive group norms contribute to group cohesion; cohesive groups are safer and more productive. It is in cohesive, safe groups that critical learning about GSD occurs.

For most people, being in a group creates different kinds of anxiety. How does one maintain individuality yet also join and be part of the group? How do we make ourselves known and understood when people do not always perceive us the way we intend? Students take on roles in school groups just as they do in their families, and the day-to-day interactions among peers and teachers create a social matrix for learning of all kinds. People tend to be more vulnerable in groups, which makes "injuries" more painful, yet the "repairs" or "transformations" are also more profound.

The teacher who wonders if communication about gender and sexuality diversity is "better left to individual conversations" may be trying to increase the safety of those involved by avoiding group discussion. However, when conversations about GSD are consistently redirected and taken up with individuals rather than discussed openly with the group, students "learn" that

1. *If you say how you really feel about girls playing kickball, you have to talk with the teacher "privately."*
2. *If you say "gay" in front of a coach, you get in trouble and then have to have "a talk."*
3. *When we talked about that pregnant man on* Oprah, *our lunch aide was uncomfortable. She kept trying to change the subject.*

A teacher or coach or paraprofessional who models openness to and readiness for discussions about GSD truly enhances the safety of everyone in the group, **even when that adult may not know exactly what to say.**

Group Process as Strategy

Not everybody is naturally adept at managing group dynamics, and having "individual conversations" with students may feel more comfortable for some teachers, especially if gender and sexuality diversity concerns evoke strong emotions. However, it is in the interactions between and among people—students, peers, teachers, parents—that social development occurs. **Harnessing the power of group process is one of the most important strategies for successfully engaging GSD in schools.** Thus, for some educators, establishing stronger group facilitation skills may be a critical component of GSD professional development efforts.

Certainly there are times when it makes sense to pursue a separate conversation with an individual student. However, even when problems or concerns pertain to only a few students in the class, they still "belong" to the whole group. For example, if a group of boys use "That's so gay" as a put-down, all members of the class or sports team are aware of and affected by this behavior. It may require a meeting with the boys involved *and* a meeting with the whole class or team to bring the issue out onto the table.

The power of the peer group.   Then the classroom community or team can work on this issue together in an ongoing way. A teacher or coach speaking to the boys about their "unacceptable behavior" is one kind of "learning"; enlisting the power of the peer group culture to challenge/change the behavior is another. Some research indicates that peer-driven, group-level interventions are more effective in changing classroom culture than those initiated by adults (Lamb, Bigler, Liben, and Green 2009). As this teacher notes, having students work out some of their own conflicts is a necessity.

The conflicts and jealousies that happen daily between boys and girls within my classroom are a constant disruption, to the point that if the problem isn't broken, bleeding, barfing, burning, or unconscious, then the children need to work it out for themselves, and not during my teaching time.

Exploratory learning and problem solving that students do among themselves is a primary vehicle for academic and social learning in ECEE.

Rules of productive engagement.   Creating an environment where *all questions are welcome* means inviting students to be more transparent about what is on their minds and in their hearts. The rules of group work, particularly with tricky issues, must also be transparent and predictable. Having an explicit contract and expectations about this type of group work spelled out in advance is pedagogically astute on many levels:

1. Teaching students how to engage and talk productively about complex or difficult issues—no matter what the topic is—meets a central tenet of the educational mission of every preK–12 school in the United States.
2. Establishing a format like the Special Group Session (see Teaching Strategy 1) can be part of any group: the after-school playground group, sports teams, extracurricular clubs, special project leaders, etc.

Teaching Resource I

Special Group Session: A Model for Classroom Group Work

Early in the school year, Mr. Bowman introduces his third graders to something called Special Group Session (SGS).

"We are going to spend a lot of time together this year, learning about all kinds of subjects, developing friendships, growing up, discovering new things about ourselves and each other and the world. So there are bound to be times when we get stuck or a problem gets too big or we need to think about changing or addressing something in our class.

"Special Group Sessions are for those times when we need to sit down in our class group and tackle an important problem or issue that has come up. Do any of you have family meetings? It's a little bit like that but with some important differences.

"It is my job, as the teacher, to call a Special Group Session (or SGS), but any of you are welcome to let me know if you think we need one. I can't promise that I will call one each time, but I definitely want to know if you think we need one and why. For example, you could come to me and say, 'Mr. B, there are some mean things happening at lunch, and I think we need an SGS.'

"The ground rules for the SGS are posted right here on the wall."

- Settle into the circle quietly and wait for Mr. Bowman to introduce the topic of the SGS.
- One person speaks at a time. You must have the talking rock in order to speak.
- Speak only for yourself. *I think . . . I feel . . . I saw . . . I hope . . .*
- An SGS is most effective when each member participates and shares. Some of you will have to work at sharing more than usual. Some of you will have to work at sharing less than usual. We all have different styles in a group. We want to create a balance of sharing.
- Try to share both thoughts and feelings. A thought is *Recess is too short.* A feeling is *I'm frustrated when we have indoor recess.*
- Be curious. Have an open mind. The ultimate purpose of the SGS is not to determine who is "right" and who is "wrong." Use an SGS to learn something new or understand something from a different perspective. Use an SGS to consider ways to change.
- It is okay to disagree. Differences of opinion are to be expected; we will not agree about everything in this class.
- It is NOT okay to be disrespectful of another person's ideas or feelings. You may feel very passionately about a topic and you may want everyone to share your opinion. But you cannot put down or tease or be mean to someone who does not share your point of view. Here is an example of what I mean: *"I really really really want* The Bears on Hemlock Mountain *to be our lunchtime story. You are stupid for not wanting* The Bears on Hemlock Mountain." That would not be okay.
- It is okay to talk about the themes or issues from SGS with others outside of the class. It is NOT okay to share what one person specifically said, thought, or felt. For example, you can tell people that the topic of an SGS was "honesty," but you cannot share that *"Tony said such and such about honesty."* Protect everyone's privacy.
- I have responsibilities too. It is my job as the teacher to facilitate the SGS and to make sure the guidelines are respected.
- It is my job as the teacher to keep the SGS discussion safe for everyone.
- At times, I may assign different tasks to students. If it feels like outside research, readings, interviews, etc. will assist the group in addressing the question or problem more effectively, I will add the assigned tasks to the regular homework. Or we may want to know what people's opinions are on a hard topic, so we could interview other kids, teachers, or parents. I will be very clear about this so there won't be any confusion about homework and SGS tasks.
- At times it will be important to continue SGS conversations with your parents at home. Again, I will be very clear about whether talking with parents is part of (a) regular homework, (b) a special assignment, or (c) optional.

HOPE AND DREAD: PARENT COMMUNICATION

❖ *I am afraid to read a book with two moms to my class because of how parents might react.*

❖ *How can I foster open conversation when a student says, "My mom thinks that's wrong"?*

Teachers worry about PARENTS a lot. They worry that parents are going to complain and disapprove. They worry that at the first sign of *King and King*[1] in the classroom library, parents will question a teacher's motives, competence, and professional integrity. Unhappy and critical parents raise the specter of a political stink, administrative reprisal, even the loss of a job for the teacher who intentionally addresses GSD. While there are certainly some who fit this description, the majority of parents support teachers who are trying to make school a safe and inclusive learning environment for all students and families (GLSEN, 2001). As this parent says, *the school is way behind in talking about these issues. I want my kids exposed to a variety of families and lifestyles. I want more—not fewer—conversations about this.*

And what about GLBTQI parents? They may be fewer in number but their wish for an affirmative classroom experience for their children is just as fervent as the next parent's (see *The Different Dragon* in Preschool). Remember the framework established in chapter 3? A teacher must make decisions about how to engage GSD based on (1) her understanding of gender identity development and sexual identity development in children and (2) the mission of her school. A teacher makes a decision to read *King and King* or *The Different Dragon* based on the educational mission of the school, not because a parent wants or does not want her to read that book.

The Different Dragon *in Preschool*

Our son's preschool teacher read The Different Dragon *to the class and a spontaneous discussion ensued about different types of families, including protagonist Noah's family with two moms. Several of the kids said that they wished they could have two moms too and how special that was. The kids enjoyed the story so much that they have asked for it to be read again and again. It touched us so deeply that this book was embraced by the children and teachers at our preschool. This creates a more loving world for all children, including our son.*

Structured Parent Communication as "Strategy"

Another paradigm shift is to see parents as partners and allies in the effort to move schools in an inclusive and fair direction with regard to gender and sexuality diversity. As one parent asserts, *I want more—not fewer—conversations about this.* In the same way that a structured, predictable venue for communication serves students and the class group, like Mr. Bowman's SGS (Teaching Strategy 1), regular communication from teacher to parents creates a tremendous opportunity to

1. improve communication.
2. minimize misunderstandings between school and home.
3. create partnerships among all the adults involved in "educating" students.
4. give students multiple opportunities to bridge learning between school and home.

Some teachers fear that more communication just invites trouble. **Yet asking parents to be informed and participate in these conversations with their children can only be positive for the learning process, even when kids are hearing different messages at home than the ones at school.** The reality is that students sometimes hear similar and different ideas from trusted adults in their lives. Pretending otherwise does not facilitate learning about how to live in the real world. Making this fact explicit—that important people agree and disagree about important things—allows children to grapple with contradictions and complexity. For example, it is okay, helpful even, for Brandon to hear that his father and his teacher disagree about girls who wrestle (see Opinions about the Girl Who Wrestles). Listen in.

Opinions about the Girl Who Wrestles

There has been a lot of media attention being paid lately to a local female high school student's success on the Varsity Boy's Wrestling team. Fourth graders are having a conversation about this. Scotty, who has an older brother on the team, says, "I don't think she should be allowed to wrestle boys."

Grace asks, Why not?

Scotty: Because it's too weird for guys to have to grab a girl like that.

Teacher: I think she's got a lot of courage. She's brave enough to do something that most girls don't do. And I hear she's pretty good.

Brandon: Well, my dad doesn't like it at all, and he thinks the school is not being fair to the boys on the team. Everybody only talks about the girl all the time now, not anybody else.

Teacher: Didn't she win a really big match last week?

Brandon: My dad said that was only because the boy she wrestled was so nervous about losing to a girl.

Teacher: How can your dad be sure it wasn't because she was just a better wrestler?

Brandon: Oh, he's totally sure. He used to wrestle in college.

Teacher: Hmmm. Well I guess your dad and I think differently about this. And sometimes that happens; important grown-ups in your life may not always agree with each other.

Who Has Time for This?

Even if a teacher believes talking with parents is a good idea, he worries about the extra time needed for regular communication. Consider this. The weekly blurb that is e-mailed home on Fridays does *not* have to be gracefully and thoroughly articulated (Teaching Resource 2). It is not the same as the carefully crafted monthly newsletter. At the beginning of the year, orient parents to the function of this particular piece of communication. While this weekly e-mail may include a box that pertains to special permissions and events, or reminders about proper winter clothing, the section called *What Kids Are Talking About at School* **serves a different purpose**. This is a place to let parents know about the noteworthy conversations and activities—planned and unplanned—that occurred during the week.

Teaching Resource 2

The Weekly Scoop—Mrs. Cibrowski's Second Grade

REMINDERS

- Nature Center field trip permission slips due 10/10.
- We are still collecting bottle caps of all kinds. Keep contributions coming!
- Check the Lower School Lost and Found for items that have gone astray.

ACTIVITIES

- Met with sixth grade Reading Buddies for the first time.
- Started learning songs for Thanksgiving Assembly.

WHAT KIDS ARE TALKING ABOUT

- Halloween costumes (already!)
- Gender Rules: "What sports are okay for girls/boys to play?"
- Recess negotiations in relation to the "Gender Rules."
- A student had a family pet die. The kids have been talking a lot about pets and death.

Grease the wheels now. Improving student group work and parent/teacher communication will help teachers address gender and sexuality diversity more effectively. In truth, however, most of what happens in school does not necessitate an SGS or a letter home to parents. It is the day-to-day conversations and questions that are at the center of students' lives.

> *How are babies born?*
> *Will the terrorists come back to New York?*
> *How come you don't have a dad?*
> *What happens to the body after someone dies?*

Providing parents with a specific kind of information, in a predictable context like Mrs. Cibrowski's Weekly Scoop (Teaching Strategy 2), invites parents to join an important part of the learning process (if they so choose). If this kind of communication is routine, you do not have to create a conspicuous letter home when a conversation/incident occurs that you definitely think parents should know about. When Mr. Bowman asks students to continue a SGS conversation with their parents, an important bridge between school and home is created.

> How do you currently communicate with parents?
> What would stop you from integrating something like the SGS and/or The Weekly Scoop into your approach to communication?

SECTION II
DEVELOPMENTAL TASKS, UNITS OF STUDY, GSD LESSONS

DEVELOPMENTAL TASKS OF ECEE

Early childhood and elementary education (ECEE) focuses on children exploring Self, Family, and Community. While the specifics of the ECEE curriculum may

---

Box 6.1

ECEE Units of Study

• Ocean Life	• Ecosystems	• Native American Cultures
• Animal Families	• Weather	• Great Changers Throughout
• All About Me	• Self-Portrait	History
• Seeds to Flowers	• The Self in Relation to Others	

ECEE Core Developmental Skills

• Observe	• Research	• Infer
• Record	• Read	• Question
• Listen	• Write	• Explore
• Compare	• Strategize	• Synthesize

differ from school to school, the developmental tasks and learning goals are the same (see box 6.1). The business of comprehending and organizing the world—people, animals, places, customs—is central to ECEE. Students learn to observe, compare, and contrast everything and everyone. Their natural curiosity and desire for mastery create strong receptivity for learning all they can about themselves, others, and the world around them.

In the upper grades of ECEE, students continue to study their surroundings in more complex forms such as ecosystems, history, and broader society. In addition to mastery of facts and information, students are encouraged to think critically during their explorations of systems and cultures, not only learning "what" they do, but "how" and "why" as well. The cultivation of critical thinking skills, and the ongoing development of cooperative learning and social competency skills, help students become efficacious members of their classroom and school communities.

Bias Affects Development; Development Affects Bias

Lesley Ellis is a preK–6 independent school. Teachers there have developed an award-winning antibias curriculum that takes into account "the impact of bias on the children's social and intellectual development." Learning how to identify biased perspectives and assumptions that narrow the way people see themselves and others helps students use a critical eye as they assess the way society works. The concept of a **stereotype** is one that young students can grasp and use to sharpen their observation, categorization, and critical thinking skills.

> Stereotypes keep kids from knowing each other well and discourage real thinking about differences. . . . [This] is not only a social curriculum, it's also an approach to developing critical thinking. We believe that students who are comfortable questioning social stereotypes will also question academic assumptions, read more critically, and think harder about the processes of analysis and interpretation.
>
> —Lesley Ellis School
> Arlington, Massachusetts

Cultivating the ability to distinguish between that which has been "oversimplified" and that which is naturally complex and diverse will help students see themselves and others more accurately. This applies to everything from stereotypes about sharks and Native Americans to stereotypes about "what girls can do" and who gay people really are.

Stereotype—something repeated or reproduced without variation: something conforming to a fixed or general pattern and lacking individual distinguishing marks or qualities; *especially*: a standardized mental picture held in common by members of a group and representing an oversimplified opinion, affective attitude, or uncritical judgment (as of a person, a race, an issue, or an event). (*Webster's Third New International Dictionary, Unabridged*. Merriam-Webster, 2002, http://unabridged.merriam-webster.com)

CURRICULA: "SEEING" WHAT YOU ALREADY HAVE

ECEE teachers ask, "Where and when can we address issues of gender and sexuality in our curriculum?" The answer is "everywhere" and "any time." There may indeed be a need to build some curricula specifically designed to address GSD. However, in many instances, the task is in seeing—and working with—the GSD that already exists in the standard units of study. Recall Schopenhauer's challenge back in chapter 5? *"It is not so much about to see what no one has seen before, but to think what nobody has yet thought about that which everybody sees."* **The first step is in thinking differently about what is already there.**

Given the ECEE tasks and themes, explorations of "differences" and "similarities" that pertain to race, sex, family configuration, body size, religion, gender, ability, and sexuality should be central to ECEE student inquiry. Yet because of the "sensitive" nature of certain identities, educators are cautious about focusing on each of them equally. In the examples that follow, mixed messages to students about what to see and what not to see pop up frequently.

Standard Unit of Study: FAMILY
Similarities, Differences, Assumptions, and Stereotypes

Learning about families is often a starting point for students in ECEE, and discussions of family configurations, functions, and customs continue throughout the elementary years. Examining family life naturally includes issues of gender and sexuality diversity, though sometimes it is difficult for teachers to make full use of these teaching opportunities. For example, here is an indirect approach to introducing "different kinds of families."

❖ *In Kindergarten we read Todd Parr's "It's Okay to be Different." We don't go into much detail, but we do simply mention there are many different types of families and that these different family types make us special. We make graphs of how many people live in your family and the different types of homes.*

This teacher is on the right track, yet indirect in her approach to recognizing different types of families. "Simply mentioning" the existence of that which is different from the majority norm is not sufficient. A more intentional approach is needed, such as the lesson plan based on Todd Parr's *The Family Book* that puts the "details" of different types of families at the heart of the lesson (box 6.2).

Box 6.2.   Lesson Plan

Todd Parr's *The Family Book*: Finding Similarities and Differences

Ask students to pay attention to the broad similarities and subtle differences—or the subtle similarities and broad differences—among the families in Todd Parr's *The Family Book*. Ask about types of parents, the number of family members, what everybody looks like.

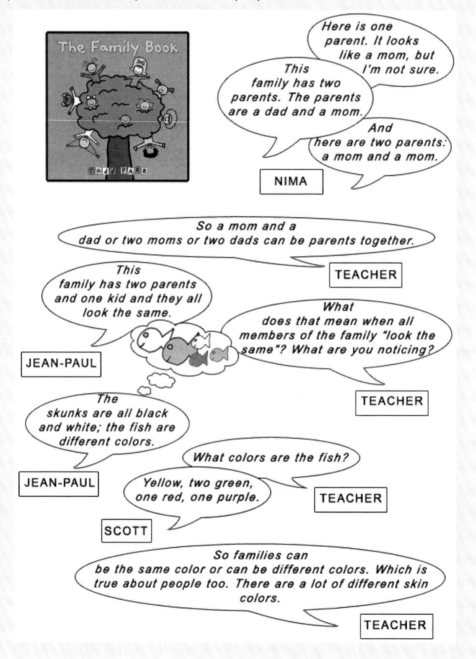

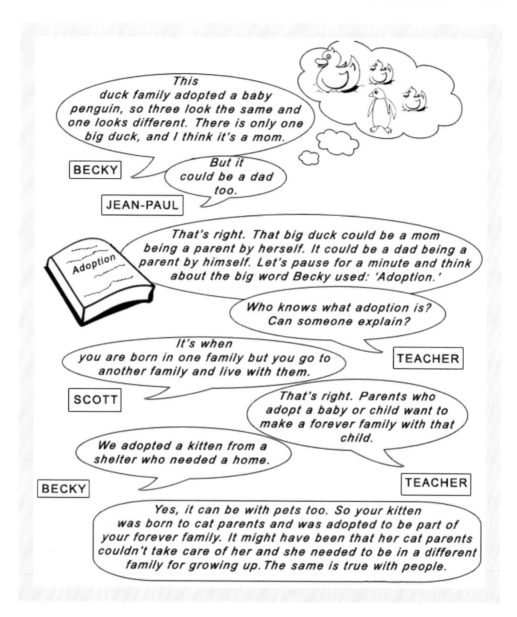

Asking students to pay attention to the details in *The Family Book* leads naturally into observations about same-sex parents, multiracial families, single parent families, and adoptive families. It is through **multiple exposures** to and discussions about these different types that students will begin to grasp the true variety of family configurations. The teacher in this scenario both listens and leads. She validates and clarifies. She will do this many, many times throughout the year, as her students gradually internalize all the ways a family can be (see Once Upon a Time).

Once Upon a Time

I have had a positive experience in my storytelling. I start all of my stories in the same way and I have to say, after the children are with me for 2 years, they don't focus on what I say at the beginning anymore. They just act like what I say is true and how it is and focus on the story now instead. "Once upon a time there was a family. And as you all know there are all different types of families. Some families have two Mommies, some families have a Grandma, some families don't have any children, some families have a Mom and Stepdad . . ." It is a good way to start a conversation with a group.

(Don't) tell unless they ask. Another approach to teaching about "differences" is based on the notion that it is better if the questions and ideas come directly from the students themselves. While this strategy certainly has pedagogical merit, it may not be an effective approach for learning that involves gender and sexuality diversity.

❖ *Today I was using the book* A Chair for My Mother *for a 2nd grade writing lesson. After I was done I took the opportunity to discuss family structures. I asked kids to tell me which characters made up the family in the story. Kids matter-of-factly stated that there was a mother, girl, and grandmother. Then as I had hoped someone asked, "Where is the father?" Kids shared their ideas. Some said, he may have died, one child explained that his parents lived in different houses because they were divorced. One child said there does not have to be a dad. I tried not to say too much but rather listen. Our conversation definitely left them thinking about different family makeups. There was some discussion about whether or not there has to be a dad. . . . I contemplated whether or not to name some other types of families, e.g., two moms, two dads . . . but I did not. I figured after I read the book* The Different Dragon *the seed will be planted and a discussion will take place. Your thoughts?*

Letting the students brainstorm, name different kinds of families, and speculate about various possibilities is pedagogically on target. By listening, the teacher makes space for the children to share what they "know." Yet, like many others, this teacher hesitates to be explicit. Teachers feel professionally protected if the issue of same-sex parents comes up organically, from the students themselves. If the teacher introduces the fact that there are GLBTQI families in the world, she might be perceived as "pushing an agenda."

Validate now. It is also pedagogically appropriate in certain instances to "plant seeds" and wait for them to sprout. However, the important question here is, *Why wait?* Knowing that GSD is not always an easy or acceptable topic to discuss, teachers should err on the side of modeling openness and directness. Certainly if there were a child in the circle who had same-sex parents, it is unlikely that the teacher would wait to validate that child's family configuration. It may be harder to recognize the importance of *all* students in the circle hearing GLBTQI families validated. This should happen regardless of whether there are GLBTQI characters in the book, and regardless of whether there is a child with gay parents sitting in the classroom circle.

Mirrors and windows.   The "mirrors and windows" metaphor, as described by Jen McClean in the epigraph at the beginning of the chapter, is fitting here. Good practices involve teaching students about the world in which they live, where GLBTQI parents are part of the diverse institution that we call "family." To teach them otherwise—by omission, in this case—is to provide a distorted view of the world. By naming two mom or two dad families as possibilities, the teacher gives permission for GLBTQI families to be discussed. Here are some possibilities for what this teacher might say

There was some discussion about whether or not there has to be a dad:

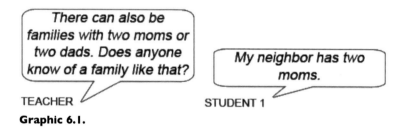

Graphic 6.1.

Or naming GLBTQI families could expose students to something new.
There was some discussion about whether or not there has to be a dad:

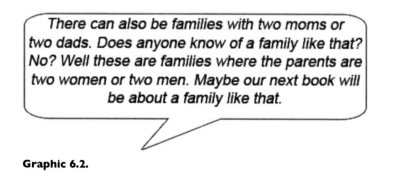

Graphic 6.2.

There are a dozen variations of this conversation. What if there is a child in the class with same-sex parents? Or in another class? Or nowhere to be found in the entire school?

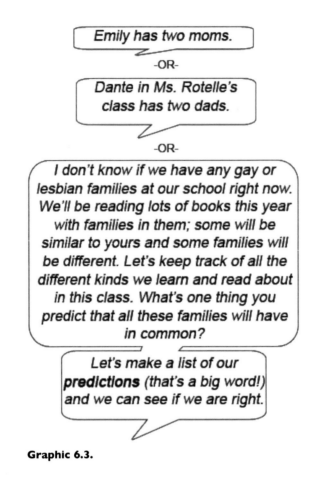

Graphic 6.3.

What Does Proactive Teaching Look Like?

The teacher who waits for the organic, spontaneous appearance of these issues forfeits the opportunity to plan ahead, to teach proactively, to model for students a readiness and willingness to talk about issues related to gender and sexuality. Teachers who invite conversation, ask questions, and create lessons quickly discover that creating a safe space and providing language allows students to talk openly and publicly about things that are **already part of their experience**.

Consider the question posed by this teacher:

❖ *We don't have any same-sex parents in our school or even that much racial diversity. How can I "naturally" introduce my students to these kinds of families?*

One obvious way to make the curriculum more diverse and inclusive is to bring different kinds of families into the classroom through literature and media. Many

ECEE classrooms create some kind of visual representation of students' families, by using drawings, photographs, collages. The montage of family images goes up on the bulletin board or in the hallway outside the classroom. Then for the rest of the term, students create illustrations of the families they come to know in books (Teaching Resource 3), and add them to the bulletin board display. Designing a "Family Collage Project" this way means that the "classroom family" keeps growing throughout the year.

Teaching Resource 3

Children's Books Featuring Diverse Families

- *We Belong Together: A Book about Adoption and Families* (multiple adoptive families)
- *And Tango Makes Three* (two penguin dads, one penguin son)
- *Ryan's Mom Is Tall* (one mom, one mum, one son)
- *Whistle for Willie* (African American mother and father, one son, one dog)
- *Ferdinand* (one mother cow, one shy bull/son)
- *I Love Saturdays y Domingos* (one bilingual girl, two sets of grandparents)
- *ABC A Family Alphabet Book* (many multiethnic, multiracial, gay and lesbian families)

Teaching Resource 4

That's a Family! : A Film for Kids about Family Diversity

That's a Family! is the first documentary in the Respect for All Project produced by Women's Educational Media (now Groundspark). The project has produced kid-friendly, age appropriate media resources for teachers and parents, with the goal of helping children understand and respect differences of all kinds. Released in 2000, *That's a Family!* features children narrating the story of their families, including those of mixed races, religions, adoptive families, divorced, same sex, and single parent. The film is an excellent teaching tool, with "chapters" that can be shown one at a time, if preferred.

The video comes with a Discussion and Teaching Guide that suggests how to integrate the film into curriculum for students of varying ages and grade levels. It includes lesson plans, activities, suggested readings and resources, and also offers advice on how to prepare for and handle challenges and questions from administrations, school boards, and/or parents. Grades 2–6.

Get more info and/or order the film at http://groundspark.org/our-films-and-campaigns/thatfamily.

Family Stereotypes

As work with the Family theme progresses through elementary grades, students will notice that indeed there are many different types of families. As they get older, however, students will also discern that popular images of family—from movies, television, and magazines—are often based on stereotypes. The challenge is to teach elementary children to unpack the heteronormative stereotype that all families have two parents—a feminine heterosexual mom and a masculine heterosexual dad—and that the parents have only gender-typical, heterosexual children.

Teaching kids to think critically about biased representations of people on one dimension (i.e., GSD) gives them the skills to understand family stereotypes related to other identities, such as race, religion, age, child bearing, and more. The lesson "Mix and Match Families" (see box 6.3) invites students to think critically about families, and the Welcoming Schools "Family Diversity Scavenger Hunt" (see Additional Resource 6.1) is an excellent teaching tool on multiple levels. In the scavenger hunt fourth and fifth grade students use their (1) research skills, (2) critical reading skills, and (3) graphing and tabulating skills to collect and organize data about the different types of families they discover in a dozen books. Then they must draw inferences about how different societies and cultures portray families and gender roles. They compare and contrast representations of families in the books and the images of families that dominant popular U.S. culture.

Happy families; strong families.   Students learn that there are conflicts in society about which families are "right" or normal or acceptable. While offering a realistic portrayal of the bias against GLBTQI families is important (e.g., *Molly's Family, Asha's Mums, In Our House*), people in marginalized groups rarely benefit from being exclusively represented as victims of prejudice or oppression.[2] Teachers must also provide a balanced view of everyday, happy GLBTQI families. Students need to understand that in spite of prejudice, people and families can thrive.

There are a number of resources that emphasize the strength and resilience of families. For example, these books are not about "gay families" per se. They are stories about counting, magical dragons, making maple syrup, and kittens.

- *Everywhere Babies*
- *1,2,3: A Family Counting Book*
- *The White Swan Express*
- *The Different Dragon*
- *Buster's Sugartime*
- *Felicia's Favorite Story*
- *Tanny's Meow*
- *The Trouble with Babies*

Box 6.3. Lesson Plan

Mix and Match Families

Make color copies of the photographs in Susan Kuklin's book *Families*. Cut out the various figures of adults and children in the book. Have groups of third graders work together at tables. Each table has a complete set of cutout figures. Ask students to combine the figures to create the sixteen families that are featured in the book. Invite students to pay attention to the "clues" they use and "assumptions" they make as they try to put the families together. Conversations will include observations about race, ethnicity, gender, sexual orientation, religion, culture, and more. Children will have a chance to examine their own assumptions and identify the truly universal elements that bind a family together.

The powerful traveling photo exhibit "In Our Family" (Teaching Resource 5) invites the entire school community to engage in learning and conversations about contemporary American families. In addition the multiple lessons, guidelines, and strategies offered by Welcoming Schools (Teaching Resource 6) means that teachers have access to a wide variety of resources for their family curricula.

Teaching Resource 5

In Our Family: Portraits of All Kinds of Families

In Our Family is a traveling photo-text exhibit from Family Diversity Projects of twenty families representing a breadth of diversity and family configurations including adoptive and foster families, divorced and stepfamilies, single parent households, multiracial families, families facing chronic illness and death, families living with mental and physical disabilities, lesbian and gay-parented families, interfaith families, multigenerational households, and immigrant families.

The exhibit, which is designed for audiences of all ages, includes positive photographic portrayals of the families, as well as candid interviews with family members. *In Our Family* challenges stereotypes and helps dismantle prejudice by celebrating and affirming differences of all kinds while promoting an inclusive and expansive vision of family life today.

Like the other traveling exhibits° from Family Diversity Projects, *In Our Family* can be brought to K–12 schools, colleges, houses of worship, libraries, conferences, community centers, and so on, and is paired with a curriculum guide complete with lesson plans and activities.

(Adapted from exhibit website, http://www.familydiv.org/inourfamily.php)

°Other exhibits from Family Diversity Projects: *Love Makes a Family: Portraits of LGBT People and Their Families; The Road to Freedom: Portraits of People with Disabilities; Nothing to Hide: Mental Illness in the Family; Of Many Colors: Portraits of Multiracial Families; Pioneering Voices: Portraits of Transgender People.* (http://www.familydiv.org)

Teaching Resource 6

Welcoming Schools Guide

Welcoming Schools is an LGBT-inclusive approach to addressing family diversity, gender stereotyping, bullying and name-calling in K–5 learning environments. Welcoming Schools provides administrators, educators and parents/guardians with the resources necessary to create learning environments in which all learners are welcomed and respected.

The program was initiated by a group of parents and educators to meet the needs of students whose family structures are not well represented or included in school environments, Welcoming Schools is also a response to educators who have asked for tools to address bias-based name-calling and bullying. Additionally, it offers a wide range of resources for school administrators and educators to support students who don't conform to gender norms.

The Welcoming Schools Guide offers tools, lessons and resources on embracing family diversity, avoiding gender stereotyping and ending bullying and name-calling. The primer version of the Guide, An Introduction to Welcoming Schools, is a 93-page resource available for download in its entirety. (http://www.welcomingschools.org/about)

Standard Unit of Study: SELF, OTHER, RELATIONSHIPS (Similarities, Differences, Assumptions, and Stereotypes)

Learning about Self and Other is another primary area of study in ECEE. Whatever the curriculum may be, there are an infinite number of moments—formal and informal—where dilemmas related to gender identity and gender expression are manifest. Crayons, hopscotch, friendships, crushes. Teachers, however, find themselves uncomfortable at times with just how much their students are observing.

> You can't spend 30 minutes teaching about the differences among plants or animals and then turn around and ignore the differences among the children themselves. That kind of dissonance stifles children's intellectual development.
>
> —First grade teacher, Lesley Ellis School

As this first grade teacher notes, asking students to be keen observers of one species, but to be selective about what they notice and name about themselves and each other, interferes with the very skills ECEE emphasizes most.

The observations that follow make clear how much students are immersed in observing, thinking and talking about these aspects of identity.

❖ *I have 2 girls who wish very vocally that they were boys. And many boys prefer to play with girls, until they can tell they aren't supposed to prefer it. I'm not sure exactly how to talk about this.*

❖ *First graders tend to be more matter-of-fact about things . . . e.g., "Oh yeah, Jane thinks she's a boy" but the bias against those who are "different" emerges quickly.*

❖ *Recently a boy in my class said, "It's kind of corny and not very effective to say, 'It's okay for boys to play with dolls or wear pink.' I fear he's right. So how do we help? Kids are so savvy and know when we're feeding them a line.*

How is it that they "know when we're feeding them a line"? Students react not only to the mixed messages about what to observe; they pick up on the discomfort and hypocrisy of adults. The "feeding of a line" often occurs when we say something simplistic to a child such as "boys can play with dolls" but do not acknowledge the complexity of the gender rules that children actually live by (see It's Not a Boy Thing).

It's Not a Boy Thing

I am the parent of 2 boys. When my oldest was 5 he was interested in my makeup and his aunties' nail polish. I have always supported his interests. My husband is not thrilled but mostly tolerant. This year, my son is in kindergarten, and has started saying things like "I can't do that/or bring that to school . . . it's not a boy thing." This breaks my heart.

Gender Rules

Discussions about Self and Other often focus on gender roles and gender rules. The question of what boys can do and what girls can do refers to acceptable color selection, wardrobe choices, and playground activities.

❖ *What you can "like" or "do" comes up constantly at this age and it is unsettling how adamant students are about what's okay for boys and what's okay for girls.*

At the same time that students are negotiating the present moment, they are also laying the groundwork for lifelong limitations or allowances based on gender. To counter this, teachers at The Little School in California designed a lesson for preschoolers that emphasizes abundant choices of what someone can like or do, with no limitations on selection (see box 6.4). Similarly the guidance team at Ethical Culture Fieldston School invited second graders to challenge their own "rules" about gender by reading and discussing *The Princess Boy*[3] (see box 6.5).

Teaching children how to identify and dismantle the gender stereotypes that limit their field of possibilities will enable them to preserve a broad, inclusive perspective on the world. They will be free to discover their own true capacities and desires, and accept the predispositions of Others.

Box 6.4.   Lesson Plan

Exploring Gender with Preschoolers

Pictures of activities or objects were posted on boards around the classroom: animals, blocks, babies, Legos, cupcakes, video games, rainbows, etc. Each child was given twenty pictures of themselves (small, xeroxed) and a glue stick. Then children were invited to go around the classroom and glue their picture on things they enjoy or like to do. At meeting, the teachers and children looked at each activity board and explored who had stuck their photo on the different choices. "We talked about what games we liked, if things were just for boys or just for girls and what to do if somebody says you can't play with something because of who you are."
Student responses:

- If someone says you can't play because you are a boy or a girl, that feels mean.
- If someone says you can't dress up, you could just put it on and keep playing.
- If they say it's not for you, you could say "you can't change my mind."

—Teachers at the Little School, San Francisco, California

Gender, jobs and stereotypes.   Depending on the age group, ask students to research and find examples of women and men, in history or current time, who defy stereotypical expectations about occupations based on gender (e.g., Amelia Earhart, Bill T. Jones). Conduct a school-wide Gender and Jobs project (see Additional Resource 6.4) or use the lesson plan from Teaching Tolerance, *Girls Can Be Plumbers* (Additional Resource 6.3) as a way to build community. Students will discover the range of jobs that the people they see every day have had during their lives. Kids benefit from learning about real people who challenge stereotypes; these role models become important reference points as students explore their own possibilities.

Active Learning

Having role models is important; children need to be able to see and interact with what is possible. At the same time, changing biased behaviors takes practice. **The work of actually changing stereotypical behaviors requires active learning**.

❖ *Conversations happen, but I don't know if the kids really internalize what they can "parrot."*

This teacher wonders how much children are really learning for themselves. In her research on the role of children in enforcing gender stereotypes, developmental psychologist Rebecca Bigler has demonstrated that **students need more than just exposure to stories that challenge these stereotypes.**

BOX 6.5. Lesson Plan

Exploring Gender with Second Graders

At Ethical Culture Fieldston School, Andrea Udoff, a psychologist, and Margot Tennenbaum, a social worker, are part of the guidance team that teachers can call on for consultation of various kinds. A second grade teacher invites them in to facilitate a discussion about gender roles, and after hearing that some children feel limited in what they can "do" as boys (e.g., cooking) or girls (e.g., rapping), Andrea and Margot decide to read *The Princess Boy* to the students.

As we begin reading, many kids are giggling but as we continue to read, the class becomes increasingly quiet. It becomes clear that the kids know it is "different" for a boy to wear dresses but they seem to feel empathy for the boy especially when his mother talks about how hurtful it is when people laugh at her son. We ask the class if they can think of things they like to do that people usually think of as something the opposite sex does. The teacher (female) starts off by saying that she enjoys football. Initially, the boys say they like sports but then one boy says he likes to dance. Other kids follow his lead and say things like, "I like to dance too."

Then the kids start to question each other. For example, when a boy identifies video games as something boys like, a girl says she likes to play video games too. This leads to a comment about the marketing of toys: A child points out that Princess Peach is in the Mario Brothers video because "that's the only way girls will play."

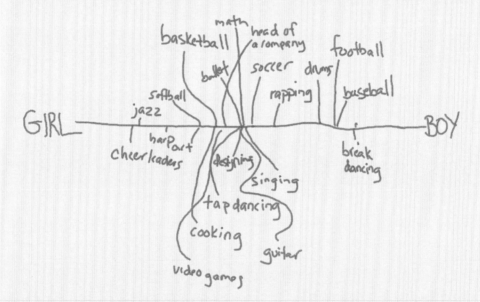

In an effort to further the discussion about what their ideas are of what boys should like or do versus what girls should like or do, we make a gender line on the Smart Board with boys at one end and girls at the other. We ask the kids to come up with hobbies, interests, and professions that they think belong on one end of the line or the other or somewhere in between. The kids come up with a lot of activities—there is some debate on things like "cooking" with one student saying that cooking is for girls because his father NEVER cooks and another child pointing out that there are men chefs.

Similarly with "design" where one child thought that this is something women do but then another child disagrees and gives the example of a man who is an architect. What's striking is how many activities are in the middle—for example, they don't hesitate for a second to say that either a girl or a boy can be a CEO (Head of Company)—so that's progress!!

The Teaching Tolerance lesson plan "Not True, Gender Doesn't Limit You" (http://www.tolerance.org/magazine/number-32-fall-2007/not-true-gender-doesnt-limit-you) is based on a study conducted by Bigler and her colleagues with 150 five- to ten-year-old students. Researchers hoped to (a) improve school climate for gender nontraditional children, (b) decrease children's gender-typed attitudes, and (c) test hypotheses linking gender identity and peer-directed gender role behaviors (Lamb, Bigler, Liben, and Green 2009).

In the experiment, the first group of students practiced using retorts to sexist or stereotyping remarks of peers, such as: *This sandbox is only for girls. Why do you have a boy's haircut? Only girls like to bake.*

This group first mastered these retorts (e.g., *Give it a rest, no group is the best!*) and then practiced using them in self-relevant skits. The second group did not learn or use the retorts but instead heard stories about other people using these retorts to confront sexist remarks.

Graphic 6.4.

Left to their own devices.   Prior to the intervention, students rarely challenged their peers' sexist remarks. Bigler and her colleagues (Lamb et al. 2009) speculate that school-age children lack readily accessible strategies to use when faced with sexist or stereotyped challenges. Their hypothesis? **Students who actively learn specific strategies (e.g., retorts) and practice using them are more likely to confront gender stereotyping and sexism**. Indeed, in this study, students in the "practice" group made significantly more challenges to sexist remarks than the "narrative" group.

> Given the need to create school climates that are supportive of students who vary in their conformity to cultural gender stereotypes, the conclusion that effective strategies for confronting sexism can be taught is an important contribution to education and suggests the potential efficacy of developing and implementing intervention programs of this kind more broadly. (Lamb et al. 2009, 377)

The study also made it clear that without some type of active intervention, students almost never challenged their classmate's sexist remarks.

Reread that last sentence. This is a *critical* finding. It challenges the notion that reading a story and inviting children's empathy and passive strategizing is sufficient in creating behavior change. Children must be taught the skills (i.e., retorts) and given opportunities to practice and apply them again and again.

Learn in groups, practice in groups.   Previous interventions aimed at changing sexist behavior among school-age children targeted *individual* beliefs rather than *group-level, public behavior* (Lamb et al. 2009). As noted earlier in the chapter, peer groups can be more effective agents of social change than adults. Studies support the notion that peer pressure and peer modeling create significant change effects over time (Salmivalli, Kaukiainen, and Voeten 2005; Killen and Stangor 2001).

However, the skills for confronting gender bias must be taught in ways that allow students to *actively* practice implementation of these new strategies. **Hearing about how other people have changed their behavior is not enough.** In the next section there are several lessons that demonstrate ways for children to learn and rehearse behaviors in a context that is entirely relevant and meaningful to them.

CREATING ACTIVE PROCESS; BUILDING GSD LESSONS

Julia Smith and Chelsea Coussens coteach a mixed-age classroom of six- and seven-year-olds at The Corlears School in New York City. In developing an explicit curriculum for social and emotional learning they have experimented with different approaches to addressing gender and sexuality diversity. First, they use drama to create a comfortable working environment for their classroom community. Students become familiar with a particular format for acting out characters, scenes, and emotions; they learn how to collaborate as "actors" and "audience" in creating different outcomes. The teachers guide the exploration and rehearsal of responses, asking "How do you think _____ was feeling?" "What could _____ have done differently?"

When given the opportunity to "tap in" and do the scene again, students practice using language that enables them to be **active agents** in creating more positive social interactions. Smith and Coussens address the topic of gender role stereotypes through this same process of acting out a scenario, with students discussing not only the experiences of the characters they are playing, but their own experiences in real life. The vitality of the exercise is palpable, as is its relevance to the lives of students in the class (box 6.6).

BOX 6.6.   Lesson Plan

Identifying Gender Stereotypes: Practicing What to Say

We began by presenting kids with a common scenario.

> *During Choice Time, four kids were sitting at the purple table coloring pictures. Ken was drawing a picture of a boy and he started to color the shirt with a pink colored pencil. Sarah started laughing and said, "Why are you using pink?! Pink is a girl color!" Jose said, "Yeah! I hate pink!" Ken stopped coloring, and put the pencil down. He crumpled up his paper and put it in the recycling bin.*

Next, we asked the children to finish the scene. We posed the questions: "Are there other people in the classroom? What do they do?" "What would you say to Ken?" "What would you say to Sarah and Jose?" With the call of "1, 2, 3 . . . action" we began the scene again. Eager shrieks of "PAUSE" rang throughout the room, and we called on students, one at a time, to enter into the scene. Some kids chose to tap in and replace the characters of Sarah or Jose, acting as advocates for Ken by stating things like "I really like pink and I know lots of other boys who do too," or "my brother is a boy and he has a pink shirt."

Other children tapped in to replace the character of Ken, deciding that he should stand strong against these comments, continue his picture, and not allow his desires to be subverted because of what the other children were saying. Still other students decided to tap in and join the scene as another kid, perhaps someone sitting at a different table, to try on the role of ally. Even though not directly involved, they elected to stand up for the idea that people should be able to choose—no matter who they are.

Afterwards, we gathered together in the meeting area to debrief, posing the questions: "Has there been a time when someone told you that you couldn't do something because you are a boy/girl?" and "Have you ever felt that you couldn't do something because you were a boy/girl, *even if someone didn't say that you couldn't?*" Instances in which kids had felt this way came pouring out of them. Children talked about clubs that were for boys or girls only, games and toys that were "boy" toys or "girl" toys. They talked about being excluded from birthday parties and other activities that were designed for boys or girls only. Some children talked about times when they had excluded someone in this way, pondering aloud whether their innocent intentions might have really hurt someone's feelings.

Something that we already had awareness about became instantly clear to us—these were issues that our kids had been wrestling with in an ongoing way, many of them in silence. Through these activities and discussions, we were creating a forum and providing language by which they could explore and express their experiences. Soon, these conversations transferred from the explicit spaces we had provided into the day-to-day fabric of our classroom life.

Gendered Reality for Boys

❖ *One of my students was called gay and said to have no penis. This is a sensitive, nonathletic child. He does not fit the stereotype of a boy his age.*

❖ *We were listening to music in class and one boy said, "I don't like this song because he sounds like a girl."*

❖ *There's a parent I can think of who addresses his son's femininity in negative ways and wishes we could help the child change. I don't even know how to begin talking to him.*

When students notice boys who are behaving in stereotypically feminine ways and say something about this, teachers are not always sure what to do. Here is a real-life scenario that allows us to explore this dilemma.

A teacher shared this story at a workshop and I now use it as a teaching example.

❖ *Second graders are listening to a read-aloud of Oliver Button Is a Sissy and Clarissa points at a boy sitting across from her in the circle. "Robby is just like Oliver!" she says excitedly.*

When I ask teachers how they would respond in this situation, most are clear about intervening on Clarissa's shouting out of turn. And they are certain about discussing the rudeness of pointing at someone. However, many are uncertain about what to do with the substance and accuracy of Clarissa's observation: Robby *is* like Oliver. He likes activities that most other boys (ostensibly) do not (e.g., painting his nails, wearing pink crocs, dressing up and putting on shows). Like Oliver, Robby is teased sometimes for "acting like a girl." Teachers ask, "What should we do? We don't want to put Robby on the spot."

First, it is important to acknowledge that Clarissa is right on task: observing, identifying, comparing, and connecting. These are the skills we want her to use in order to understand the world around her. Yet she is naming something "sensitive." Refer back to the teacher quotations at the beginning of this section, Gendered Reality for Boys. Negative reactions to femininity in boys is the standard, and here, the teacher must contend with that reality.

- All the students in the class know that Robby "acts like a girl."
- Most parents also know about Robby's behavior.
- It could be Robby's father who wants the teachers to change his son's "feminine behavior."
- Students this age certainly understand that boys have penises and girls have vaginas.
- A boy who acts like a girl might well be "said to have no penis."
- Some of these second graders have also learned to make stereotypical assumptions; *boys who are feminine are probably "gay."*

Talking about Feminine Boys

Is it okay to talk openly about feminine boys? The typical outcome of a situation like this is for the teacher to address the behavioral issues (i.e., calling out of turn, finger pointing) and perhaps to suggest that Clarissa be "more sensitive about Robby's feelings." End of conversation. What, then, is the "unintentional lesson" for this group of students? The unintentional lesson refers to the hidden instruction that teachers regularly deliver to students, knowingly and unknowingly, about who students are and what is okay to do or "be" (Howard 2009). These students learn that it is not okay to speak directly about who Robby is. The teacher models that something about this situation is uncomfortable and best not talked about directly.

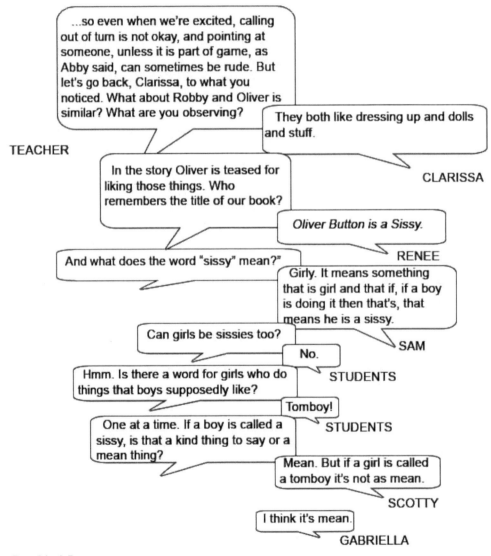

Graphic 6.5a.

I like being called a tomboy because I *am* a tomboy.

SOPHIE

I see we have some different ideas about this. I want to bring the word "stereotype" into the conversation. [Teacher picks up a placard with the word "stereoptype" on it.] We've been using the idea of stereotypes a lot lately as we try to understand some of the "rules" for society. Everybody remember what a stereotype is?

TEACHER

When you think everyone in a group will be the same just because they are in the group. Like, all girls will like pink just because, because they are girls.

RENEE

Good. We have added "stereotype" to our box of helpful words, and this week it is written up on the Word Board. Our Word Board Keeper, Josh, did a great job of writing out the definition. So. Why isn't it okay for a boy such as Oliver to like tap dancing?

Because dancing is for girls.

RENEE

I don't think dancing is just for girls. There is a boy in my jazz dance class.

ZAHRA

Yeah but only one and his sister is in the class too.

SAM

Can someone tell me who decided that dancing was only for girls? Why can't it be both for both girls and boys? Do you think there is any stereotyping going on?

Graphic 6.5b.

The teachable moment.   What might a conversation sound like if the teacher leans right into the discomfort around Robby's "sissiness"? Again, there is no one right way to approach gender and sexuality diversity in a given moment, but it can be helpful to hear examples and learn ways that language can be used. Listen in.

The conversation continues, as the students examine the stereotypes in *Oliver Button Is a Sissy* and in their own lives. One of the teaching strategies used here is putting key concepts such as *stereotype, collaborate, investigate, compromise, metaphor* on a placard. Each concept is defined and featured on the Word Board during the week it is first introduced. The placards are kept in a box, and during class

TEACHER

We have to finish up in a minute, but before we do, let's go back over a few important things. It is pretty clear that you all do not think teasing someone for what he likes to do or what she likes to do is okay. And that's good news, because as you know, at our school and in this class, that kind of teasing is against the rules and just not what we believe in.

Yet sometimes I *do* hear that kind of teasing going in this class. Including teasing Robby for what he likes to do. Not okay. Not okay to tease anyone for what she likes or he likes. So if Robby wants to play with his Polly Pocket collection, should he be teased for that?

No.

STUDENTS

Robby do you want to add anything?

I'm just saying that if there are other boys who want to play with my Polly Pockets or other stuff, they can, because it's okay with me.

ROBBY

Thank you for making that invitation, Robby.

Here is our challenge: We have to work hard to be *better friends* and *better thinkers*. And *stereotypes do not help* us with either of those. How does a stereotype get in the way of being a good friend?

Your friends should support what you like, even if there is a stereotype about it.

GABRIELLA

Can you give us an example?

If I want to play with cars and my friends tell me I shouldn't because I'm a girl, they are supporting the stereotype and not me.

GABRIELLA

Great! And how does a stereotype get in the way of being a good thinker?

(NO STUDENT RESPONSE)

Look at the definition Josh wrote up on the Word Board.

Stereotypes make things simple but they're not necessarily right or true.

SAM

So it may be simpler to say "only girls can dance" but the truth is that some boys can dance too if they want. Good job everybody!

Graphic 6.6.

discussions the teacher uses the placards at different times to illustrate "bringing in" a useful idea or action. Students who are "stuck" in a task or conflict also retrieve a word from the box if they think the concept might help them move forward.

Toward the end of the discussion, the teacher brings the focus back to Robby.

Finding a balance between speaking specifically about a particular child and drawing unwanted attention to that child is always a concern. However, providing children with the tools to speak accurately and thoughtfully about themselves and others is never a bad idea. Not talking about the gender variance everyone "sees" only moves the learning process underground where there is no opportunity to explore. Inviting children to regularly and openly challenge gender stereotypes, particularly the ones that are most relevant in their own lives, provides them with lifelong thinking and social skills.

Making the Abstract Accessible

It is also valuable to help children understand their own experience of feeling one way on the inside and being perceived differently or negatively on the outside. Smith and Coussens, the Corlears teaching team, used a mapping approach to help their students explore more deeply the effect of stereotyping and gender role expectations on the character, Oliver Button, in Tomie dePaola's *Oliver Button Is a Sissy*. These teachers found a way to help young, primarily concrete thinkers grasp a more complex, abstract concept. Theirs is an excellent example of finding creative ways to help younger students thinking critically about gender and sexuality diversity (see box 6.7).

Box 6.7. Lesson Plan

Talking about "Seeing": Mapping Oliver Button

After reading the story *Oliver Button Is a Sissy*, by Tomie dePaola, we felt strongly that there was an opportunity to go deeper in the ways that we asked our students to think about issues of gender stereotypes, and the ways in which the messages that some people receive about who they "should" be can clash with who they actually "are." We knew that we would be asking the children to talk about some deep and rather abstract concepts, but we also knew that they had experiences and understandings that would allow them to engage in the discussion if we provided an effective framework.

Because children at six and seven typically learn best through concrete examples and representations, we decided to create a "map" of Oliver Button's experience. Using a large piece of plain butcher paper as the backdrop, we cut two simple "human" figures out of construction paper. We glued one of these cutouts down to the butcher paper and attached the other cutout directly on top of the first, using a paper fastener at the top of the head to allow it to swing left and right, revealing the cutout underneath. At the top of the page, we wrote the name "Oliver Button."

During Community Meeting, we reread *Oliver Button Is a Sissy*, this time showing each page under our document camera so that it was projected onto the Smart Board for the children to see and study. After we read each page aloud, we asked the children simply, "What do we know about Oliver Button

(continued)

now?" As children would pull explicit and sometimes implicit details from the text, we recorded their words on our map.

Kids began to notice that we wrote things in different spaces, depending on the nature of what they had shared. For example, "Oliver's father calls him a sissy" was recorded on the butcher paper, outside of the cutout, with an arrow pointing towards the figure. Comments such as, "Oliver would dance and sing and pretend to be a movie star" and "No matter what, Oliver kept dancing" were recorded on the top cutout. Comments like, "He doesn't like to do things boys are 'supposed' to do," and "He felt upset that he didn't win" were recorded underneath, on the bottom cutout. Soon, the children began to interpret our schema. *"You're writing things on the bottom that are inside of Oliver!" "Things that happen to Oliver go on the outside!" "On the top is what is on the outside of Oliver, things the world can see!"*

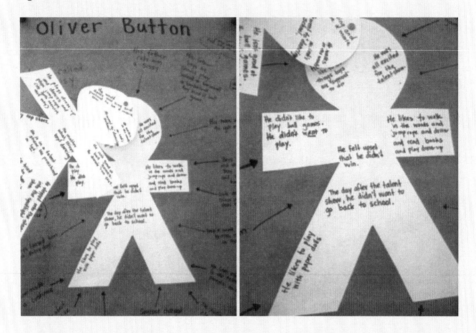

They were right, and through this lens our discussion continued about the ways in which messages from outside matched, or didn't match, with what was inside; ways in which Oliver showed his real self to the world and what things he kept inside. We were astonished by the depth of student learning. They were able to grasp concepts that loomed so large and complex in our adult minds.

To close each day together we have a meeting with special rituals attached to it such as the dimming of overhead lights, the lighting of a special lamp, forming our bodies into a large circle and the passing of a ball for each person to have a turn to speak. Each week we have a question for reflection. During the period of these Oliver activities we asked the kids "What is something that you would stand up for?" At the beginning of the week, many children talked about standing up against danger, like protecting their homes against robbers. Soon, they began to talk about standing up against bullies, standing up for people to be able to be themselves. A number of kids had Oliver Button in the front of their minds, stating that if they saw someone being teased for being different, they would stand up for that person.

It became clear that we had created a space and a language through which the kids could openly and publicly talk about things that had long been a part of their experiences. We had not taught them new ideas, but rather provided an opportunity for them to express things that had previously resided primarily inside of themselves.

Tracking GSD Stereotypes through Media Literacy

In addition to the influence of peer culture, multiple forms of media have a tremendous impact on the perpetuation and reinforcement of gender stereotyping, sexism, heterosexism, and homophobia. Directly and indirectly school-age children are exposed to such images and messages constantly, whether it is through highway billboards, music videos, weekly television, or a furniture catalog (see Teaching Resource 7). The Welcoming Schools lesson "Media Sleuths: Examining Gender Roles in Advertising" provides older elementary students with several activities, done in class with peers and at home with parents, that identify gender bias and stereotypes in their daily lives (Additional Resource 6.2).

Teaching Resource 7

Gender Stereotypes, Media Literacy, and Taking On Pottery Barn

In Newton Public Schools, as part of an antibias initiative, fourth graders learn about stereotypes and the cycles of oppression that create and reinforce them. Working within this curriculum, Robin Cooley and her students explored gender stereotypes, the study of which prompted the students to initiate a letter-writing campaign to *Pottery Barn Kids* catalog. Cooley observed that after her students analyzed the catalog, they were able to pick out instances of gender bias and stereotyping that even she hadn't noticed. Below are two of the letters the class mailed.

Dear Pottery Barn Kids,

I do not like the way you put together your catalogs because it reinforces too many stereotypes about boys and girls. For instance, in a picture of the boys' room, there are only two books and the rest of the stuff are trophies. This shows boys and girls who look at your catalog that boys should be good at sports and girls should be very smart. I am a boy and I love to read.

Dear Pottery Barn Kids,

I am writing this letter because I am mad that you have so many stereotypes in your magazine. You're making me feel uncomfortable because I'm a boy and I like pink, reading, and stuffed animals. All I saw in the boys' pages were dinosaurs and a lot of blue and sports.

Also, it's not just that your stereotypes make me mad but you're also sending messages to kids that this is what they should be. If it doesn't stop soon, then there will be a boys world and a girls world. I'd really like it if (and I bet other kids would too) you had girls playing sports stuff and boys playing with stuffed animals and dolls.

Thank you for taking the time to read this letter. I hope I made you stop and think. (Robin Coole, Beyond pink and blue, *Rethinking Schools* 18(2); Winter 2003, http://www.rethinkingschools.org/archive/18_02/pink182.shtml)

Self and Other; Romance and Relationships

Conversations about boys, girls, and gender can segue seamlessly into conversations about crushes, romance, and relationships. Teaching students how to recognize sexist and heterosexist stereotypes is a critical part of addressing gender and sexuality diversity with older elementary age children. If they have been indoctrinated in the Disney ideals (see chapter 2) where will they now turn to learn about meaningful, intimate relationships? The "tweens" (which is not a bona fide developmental stage but a marketing category) are enormously vulnerable and impressionable as they anticipate moving into puberty.

Valentine's Day, just like other major holidays, is a media event. Children and adolescents are inundated with images of heterosexual couples falling in love and being sexual together. Some schools have abandoned recognizing Valentine's Day altogether because these celebrations bring several undesirable elements into the school community: (a) an abundance of candy, (b) spotlighting popular and unpopular students, and (c) sexualized behavior. Tackling Valentine's Day head on is an opportunity, as one teacher suggests, to address "GLBT issues explicitly—not just sneak it into other topics" (see Teaching Resource 8).

Teaching Resource 8

Valentine's Day: Roses, Candy, and Critical Thinking

The school has decided to use Valentine's Day as a catalyst for addressing issues of gender and sexuality diversity in every grade. Each teacher or teaching team must prepare a grade-appropriate lesson or project or activity that will engage students in learning about different kinds of love, relationships, and family configurations.

This is an opportunity to address some of the following:

- Define/explore concepts of familial, platonic, and romantic/sexual love
- Define/explore different kinds of "love" relationships
- Define explore the concept of discrimination
- Explore history of discrimination against certain kinds of love (e.g., based on race, religion, ethnicity, sexual identity)
- Define/explore the terms gay, straight, bisexual, lesbian, queer, transgender, intersex
- Define marriage

- Explore the history of marriage in the United States for the past two hundred years
- Research current status of same-sex marriage
- Explore religious views on love and marriage
- Explore relationship between love, sexual identity, and parenting
- Research the history of Valentine's Day: when, why, and how did it become a "holiday"?
- Conduct a media literacy review of the marketing behind Valentine's Day

Each class will submit a brief description of their lesson or project, along with a poster illustration of their learning. These will be on display on the bulletin board outside the library for the month of February.

Standard Unit of Study: BioDiversity, Cultural Diversity (Similarities, Differences, Assumptions and Stereotypes)

Making Cultural Comparisons

In addition to wanting elementary children to learn about the biodiversity of flowers, birds, and ocean life, we want them to marvel at the variety of cultures in the world. These are "cultures" based on religion, nationality, ethnicity, geographic region, and more. Whether the unit of study is Ancient Greece, the Puritans, Japan, Native Americans, or Our Favorite Holidays, students learn about history, customs, food, rituals, and values that are similar to and different from their own.

Here again students are encouraged to observe and be curious about Self, Other, and World.

> ❖ *I think what is on the forefront of my mind right now is how impressionable our youngest students are and how they receive and perceive information. To cite an example, last December when discussing Hanukkah in class, a 5 year old boy from a Catholic family came home saying to his parents that he was now Jewish, and he was quite adamant about it for several weeks. The parents were uncomfortable and didn't know how to handle this and neither did I.*

What is the discomfort and concern of the preK teacher and parents when this Catholic child wants to be "Jewish" at Hanukkah time? If the boy wore a cape for several weeks and insisted on being Super-Man, would the adults involved be worried? Probably not. His behavior would be understood as the natural imagining, wondering, and trying on that is characteristic of children at this age.

Yet this religious pretending touches on an aspect of identity that, like talking about "sissies," is "sensitive." While it is possible that this boy is destined to renounce Catholicism and convert to Judaism, more likely his intrigue with the

Hanukkah rituals of lighting candles and gift giving is temporary. If the goal of the lesson is to teach children about different religions, trying one on through pretend play is a method of learning that is typical of this age group. Teachers must be conscious of the way adult worries about "sensitive" aspects of identity can impact students engaging in the developmental tasks for ECEE.

Multicultural heroes.   In different grades kids often learn about people who are acclaimed because of their positive impact on society. Kindergartners may learn a song about Rosa Parks; first graders may write poems about Martin Luther King Jr.; fifth graders may write biographies of the great changer of their choice. These units of study provide windows into particular parts of history, different parts of the world, and a variety of cultures. A social justice focus helps students see that though oppression exists in the world, people can always stand up for what is right.

It is tempting to frame conversations about prejudice in "us versus them" terms. However, the "we"-are-free-of-bias-and-"they"-are-full-of-prejudice stance leaves teachers in a bind in relation to explorations of gender and sexuality diversity. Looking at true feelings and beliefs about sex, gender, and sexuality will bring students and adults alike to their own potentially biased perspectives. As this fourth grade teacher facilitating a conversation about Arabs and terrorists attests, listening to and understanding where students are coming from means examining the origins of their prejudice without judgment.

> ❖   *I know that I feel more prepared to deal with issues as they arise, not just in terms of sexual orientation/gender identity issues, but other issues around prejudice as well. Someone said something about Arabs in relation to terrorism in a 4th grade class the other day, and I settled into it and we talked about it for a while. I think that the most important tool from that GSD workshop was the idea that first, you need to settle in to have the conversation; second, that you need to figure out where the students are coming from, i.e., ask questions, rather than tell them they're wrong. And, in the process, acknowledge their feelings and thoughts rather than make them feel bad.*

Adding to the list of great changers.   Danielle Morrison, an elementary teacher at a charter school in Brooklyn, New York, added Harvey Milk, the first openly gay elected official in the United States, to her Great Changers curriculum (see box 6.8). She discovered that her students were more than able to grasp the essence of Milk's contributions to society and also to understand the prejudice that was levied against him. In the same way that conversations about racism during Martin Luther King Jr.'s time lead to comparisons with racism today, examining the assassination of Harvey Milk brings students to discussions about today's battles over gays in the military, same-sex marriage, and bullying in schools.

The unit of study is History and Cultural Diversity. If it is okay to teach students about the Montgomery Bus Boycott, is it okay to teach about the Stonewall Riots?

BOX 6.8. Lesson Plan

One of the Great Changers: Harvey Milk

We talk about Harvey Milk as part of our conversations about nonviolent civil rights leaders and movements. In this study, which lasts about 6 weeks and eventually culminates in a social action plan and project, we spend time talking about Mohandas Gandhi, Martin Luther King, Jr., Cesar Chavez, Harvey Milk and Shirin Ebadi (a leader who is currently working for women's and children's rights in Iran). We work in this order (chronologically) and it works well this way. We spend about 3 days on Milk, using morning work, discussion at meetings, activities and homework to find out and process what he did and worked for. We also watch parts of *The Times of Harvey Milk* — obviously, these portions are selected carefully because it is not a movie made for 8 year olds, but there is a lot of actual footage of his campaigns, etc. The Candlelight March is also incredible for the kids to see.

I've used the book *The Harvey Milk Story* in a couple of different ways to complement and get this part of the study rolling. It works because there is a context to the story for the kids—of rights and fighting for rights. They are already trained to look for nonviolent ways to protest injustice. Milk becomes another example of an activist. One way I have done this is to read the book with them and talk it through as we go. I usually ask questions to tease out (1) his background, where he lived, worked, grew up, etc., (2) the kinds of injustice he saw in San Francisco, (3) the methods he used to effect change, and (4) the similarities he shared with other leaders of movements. Along with various other things, I want them to see that people can work from the inside out—becoming a part of the government or the system to make change happen. Up until Milk, they have only seen people who fought against the system from *outside* of the system.

The other way I have done this is by creating passages (2)—the first on the first two ideas up there and the second on the last two from above. I give this out in the morning when the kids arrive and they read it just like they would a passage on Chavez. It is taken almost verbatim from the book. There is nothing "special" or "different" about reading about Milk, then, and I have found that this works well, too, establishing the tone in the room from the morning on. There is a portion of the passages, like the book, that states what the terms gay/straight/lesbian and homosexual/heterosexual mean. This helps the kids who have never heard these terms before (they get smaller every year!) and they usually bring this to the discussion then.

The other interesting thing that I have noticed about these conversations—well, there are lots of interesting things really, but one is that they want to know a lot about Joe Campbell and Scott Smith. Usually I have a picture or two ready to show them. Just like I had a picture or two of Coretta Scott King for MLK, as people who supported these leaders. For Milk, though, this leads to a conversation about marriage and gay marriage. In the past, this has been something that the kids have felt really strongly about and have wanted to or actually written letters to Congress, etc. regarding gay marriage initiatives. That, then, becomes their social action project—it's really neat and organic, really comes from the kids.

—Danielle Morrison
Elementary school teacher
Brooklyn, New York

Can the fifth grade class studying Native American culture focus on gender roles, highlight two-spirit people, and then compare them to contemporary transgender identities? Will the unit on the civil rights movement include Bayard Rustin, a gay man who was a key figure in organizing the March on Washington? Rustin is often left out of the contemporary curricula for the same reason he was kept in the background of the movement itself—his sexuality.

Cultural Diversity, Social Diversity: The Health and Wellness Curriculum

Given the centrality of social development in ECEE, it is surprising how many schools do not have a comprehensive health and wellness curriculum (CHW). Most schools have discrete units of study scattered throughout the grades: third grade hygiene, fifth grade anatomy, sixth grade just-say-no-to-drugs project. The benefits of having a comprehensive health and wellness curriculum at every grade level—preK through high school—cannot be overstated.

The Charles River School (CRS) has created a developmentally appropriate and culturally relevant program of study that begins in prekindergarten and continues until students graduate in eighth grade (see box 8.1, chapter 8). This curriculum creates a natural location for learning about and conversations related to gender and sexuality diversity. Topics such as (1) respect for differences, (2) friendships, (3) conflict resolution, and (4) human diversity are studied multiple times over the years, allowing for continuity and progression as students mature in their experience of these social issues in their day-to-day lives.

Further discussion of the CRS curriculum appears in chapter 8, which focuses on comprehensive health and sexuality curricula for every grade in preK–12 schools.

Have We Neglected the Core Skills of ECEE?

Glance back at what you have read in this chapter. Consider the lessons and projects described, and identify the skills involved in completing them. While they are learning about family and self and gender and stereotypes, students are observing, comparing, recording, listening, predicting, researching, problem solving, sorting, quantifying, and more. Teachers identify "lack of time" and "no room in the curriculum" as the two biggest obstacles to addressing GSD, yet the themes and skills of ECEE are, in many ways, a perfect match for this area of learning.

ADDITIONAL RESOURCES

Additional Resource 6.1

Family Diversity Scavenger Hunt
Lesson Plan from Welcoming Schools

Suggested Grade Level: 4–5
Length of Time: Two to three sessions of 45 minutes each
Goals:

- To increase student awareness of family diversity and ways the media presents family life.
- To develop sensitivity and awareness of underrepresented or marginalized families.

Objectives:

- Students will be able to identify and describe a variety of families.
- Students will be able to identify common characteristics within all families.
- Students will understand that families have some similarities and some differences.
- Students will be able to identify which families are represented the most and the least in literature and/or the media.

Academic Standards:

- Writing: Perform short, focused research tasks that build knowledge through investigation of different aspects of a single topic.
- Reading: Integrate information from several texts on the same subject in order to write or speak about the subject knowledgeably.
- Social Studies: Provide for the study of people, places, and environments.

Educators' Notes:

There are many ways to live and form a loving, caring family. Many kinds of families are largely absent from our literature, such as families with lesbian or gay parents. This lesson offers students a chance to look through books to gather their own data on how families are represented. If students have not yet had a lesson on families, you may want to start with the "What Is a Family?" lesson, modifying it for their grade level.

Materials:

Pencils, chart paper, markers, and the two worksheets: Family Diversity Scavenger Hunt and Family Structure Graph.

Required Books:

Access to a public or school library.

Activities:

Session 1. Remind students that there are all kinds of families. Tell students that one can learn about what is important in a particular society by looking at the literature of that society. Tell them that they are going to be visiting the library and researching the kinds of families that are in the books and magazines at the library. Pass out the first worksheet: Family Diversity Scavenger Hunt.

- Tell students to find ten books that include stories or pictures of a family or families. Model how they might look through a book to discover if that book portrays a family. Brainstorm with the students about where in the library those books might be found. Encourage them also to look at picture books for younger children.
- Brainstorm some words or phrases they might use to describe the families— for example, "One mom, one dad, and two kids: a boy and a girl." Build a word/description bank on chart paper to which students can later refer.
- On the worksheet, have students record the name and author of each book and descriptions of what the family in the book looks like.

Session 2. (Can be combined with session 1.) Take students to the library and give them adequate time to research and write their results on worksheet 1. Remind students that their task is to find ten books that include a story or pictures of a family or families. They should then record the name and author of the book on worksheet 1 and describe what the family in the book looks like.

Session 3. When students return to class, have them share their results with a partner.

Pass out second worksheet: Family Structure Graph.

- Have students graph their results by coloring one square in the appropriate column for each family structure that they found. You could also make a class graph with all the information that the class has compiled.
- Ask the students what they notice when they look at their graphs. What kinds of families are shown most often? Least often? Are there any family structures that are absent? (Most likely, families headed by gay or lesbian parents will be absent.)
- Ask students how they think kids whose families are not represented might feel when they never see their families in any of the books they read.

Modifications:

- As students are researching the structures of families portrayed in the books, also have them look at what the different members of the family are doing and write it down. Discuss roles and expectations within the family, including expectations related to gender, etc.
- Research families using socioeconomic, ethnic, racial, and gender categories. Include discussion of multiracial families in your research.

Extensions:

- Have students watch different television shows. Each group can watch one channel on a given night so as not to encourage too much television. Conduct this research in the same way you conducted the library research project. Put the students in small groups. Pass out the Family Diversity Scavenger Hunt and Family Structure Graph. Ask students to brainstorm about the shows they see on television and fill out a new graph for the families represented on those shows.
- Have students compare biographies of one famous LGBT person and one famous non-LGBT person. Some questions to ask: Do the two biographies offer equal amounts of information about the subjects' partners or family members? Are there differences in the ways LGBT people and non-LGBT people are described in terms of their personal lives, love, marriage, family, etc.?
- Invite members of a variety of underrepresented families to your class to talk about their families.

Assessment and Evaluation:

- As a class, brainstorm what students have learned about families and the way the media or children's literature portrays families.
- Or they can complete a class KWL (I Know, I Wonder, I Learned) chart before and after this activity.

Additional Resource 6.2

Media Sleuths: Examining Gender Roles in Advertising
Welcoming Schools Guide (www.welcomingschools.org)

Suggested Grade Level: 4–5
Length of Time: Two 35- to 45-minute sessions and one homework assignment
Goal:

- To develop students' critical thinking skills about gender stereotyping

Objectives:

- To talk about the concept of gender roles
- To identify stereotypical and nonstereotypical gender roles through exploring media

Academic Standards:

- Writing: Gather information from experience as well as print and digital resources, take simple notes on sources, and sort evidence into provided categories.
- Speaking and Listening: Paraphrase the key information or ideas presented graphically, visually, orally, or multimodally.
- Social Studies: Provide for the study of people, places, and environments.

Educators' Notes:

Students will have an opportunity to identify and discuss what is traditional or stereotypical male and female behavior. It is important that students have had a discussion or lesson based on the ideas in the Human Being Lesson specifically, that all human beings have many things in common and that stereotypes only describe some individuals and characteristics in that group.

A stereotype is a generalization applying certain, usually negative or limiting, characteristics to a group of people or an individual based on restricted or incomplete knowledge or experience. Stereotypes are not accurate. They cause people to prejudge individuals and groups. They limit people. There are many gender stereotypes in our culture that are not true of the boys and girls we teach. We need to help them realize that it is okay to be true to themselves.

The in-class activity is active and prompts many conversations about gender as students look through magazines and catalogs in small groups and notice what men, women, boys, and girls are doing. It is also interesting to discover what is being marketed to males versus females, revealing the prescriptive power of advertising. Catalogs advertising and selling products for children are very good for this activity, as are mainstream magazines.

This lesson provides an opportunity for students to develop tools for identifying stereotypes in television advertising. It involves a homework assignment that can be done most easily on a weekend. The homework is a great opportunity to engage parents in critically watching television with their children. Students can watch television with a parent or guardian and talk about what assumptions the advertisers are making about boys and girls.

Materials:

Paper, pencil, a collection of magazines and catalogs, chart paper, markers, tape or glue stick, television at home, TV Log Worksheet.

Activities:

Prepare large chart papers: one titled "MALES," one titled "FEMALES," and one untitled (in case there are images that need a third category). As the class discussion progresses you may decide to include subcategories such as "active" and "passive, "indoor" and "outdoor," "moving" and "still," "appropriately dressed" and "inappropriately dressed."

Activity 1. Begin the lesson by asking your students to write a list of five to ten of their favorite activities, their favorite color(s), and what they hope to do or be when they grow up.

Divide the class into small groups. Give each small group five or six magazines and catalogs. Direct the students to cut out pictures of people doing things like working, reading, driving, playing, and so on. Spend about 15 minutes searching for images.

When each group has cut out a dozen images from advertisements, have them put each picture on the chart paper in the MALE and FEMALE categories. Have the class generate a list of descriptive words that characterize what they see in the pictures in each category.

Ask the class if they have any observations about the photos themselves.

- What do these photos/images say about the behavior, likes and dislikes, etc. of men and women and boys and girls?
- What are the females doing? Where are they pictured? Are they active? Are they in powerful positions? What colors are chosen in the ads targeted at females?
- What are the males doing? Where are they pictured? Are they active? Are they in powerful positions? What colors are chosen in ads targeted at males?

Then, have students review the lists they made about themselves. Hold a discussion about whether the images they found in magazines accurately reflect their reality. What is true and not true, and what's missing?

Ask students how they feel about this. If the representations do not reflect their reality, then should something be done to change it? If so, what could be done?

Modification:

Have students make an ad using magazine pictures or photos and their own text to advertise a product they use or a cause they are interested in such as prevention of cruelty to animals or recycling or healthy living.

Activity 2. Collect the lists that students made of things they like to do, favorite colors and hopes for the future. Have students work in mixed-sex groups to make posters titled:

- "OUR CLASS LIKES TO . . ."
- "OUR FAVORITE COLORS ARE . . ."
- "IN THE FUTURE WE WANT TO BE . . ."

Activity 3. Homework—Students should take home the TV Log Worksheet. Have students watch two cartoons or other children's shows on commercial television and fill in their log sheets. (Some students may not have a television. Make alternate arrangements for them to complete the homework assignment, such as with another student or at a grandparent's house.)

In class—Tally the results by category on a large piece of chart paper.

- How many ads are directed at girls?
- How many ads are directed at boys?
- How many ads are directed at both?

Then, list what the "boy" ads were selling, what the "girl" ads were selling, and what the "both" ads were selling.

Have a discussion:

- Do the "boy" ads imply that only boys should be interested in these things?
- Do the "girl" ads imply that only girls should be interested in these things?
- What category of things do advertisers believe should be for everybody? Are there more or fewer items in this category?

Ask the students the same questions they were asked about the magazine and catalog images.

- What do the ads say about the behavior or likes and dislikes of boys and girls?
- What topics do the editors think boys are interested in? Girls?
- What are the girls doing? How are they portrayed? Are they active? Are they in powerful positions? What colors are chosen in the ads targeted at girls?
- What are the boys doing? How are they portrayed? Are they active? Are they in powerful positions? What colors are chosen in ads targeted at boys?

Extensions:

- This lesson can be adapted to look at stereotyped images based on race. Students could also look at both race and gender stereotypes together.
- Ask students to seek out images that break traditional and stereotypical expectations and share them with the class or in small groups.

Assessment and Evaluation:

- Ongoing teacher observation of how students are making choices and whether or not they accept student choices outside of gender expectations.

Additional Resource 6.3

Girls Can Be Plumbers?
Teaching Tolerance (www.teachingtolerance.org)

This activity helps early-grade students begin to think about gender roles, stereotypes, and career choices.

Grade Level: K–5
Subjects: Social Studies, Science, and Health
Time: One class period

Supplies Needed:
"School Workers" display (made in advance, see steps 1 and 2, below)

Procedure:
This activity strengthens the school community while helping young students begin to explore stereotyping as it relates to careers and gender.

1. Prior to the activity, tell adults on campus that you need their assistance to help students get to know school employees and to help them explore examples of gender diversity in career roles. Ask the adults to provide you with a recent photo and a brief list of their previous jobs, accompanied by a one-sentence job description.

2. Use the photographs to create a "School Workers" display, with photographs in one column, and a list of previous jobs (with the one-sentence description) in a second column. Identify each photograph with a number. Identify each job with a letter.

3. Review the display with your students. Challenge students to match the former jobs to the people. Students can talk to each other and share their assumptions openly. Once they have an idea, they can raise their hand and share their guess. Facilitate the matching exercise, recording the letter of the correct job match by the name. Allow 15 to 20 minutes to match all the adults correctly. Now the real lesson begins.

4. Explain that they are going to discuss the matching game and explore the different ideas about how gender (whether you are a boy or girl) affects beliefs about career, or work, choices and options.

5. Ask the students if any of the matches surprised them and why. Gender stereotyping and prejudicial statements about appearance will probably surface. Statements like, "But she is a girl and she parked cars?" or "I thought only boys were police officers."

6. After the discussion, encourage students to "think aloud" and teach the class what they learned during the activity. Not only will students learn more about their school community, but also they will begin to question attitudes about gender stereotypes and sexism.

Additional Resource 6.4

K–6 Project
Gender and Jobs: A Project for Elementary Students

Give students at every grade level, K–6, the task of sorting jobs by gender identity. Occupations from Electrician to Baker to Lifeguard to Dentist are printed on index cards, and students are asked first to define the tasks of the job. What skills do you need to be a _____? Then students put the jobs that are "best" for women in one pile and the jobs that are "best" for men in another pile. In their deliberations, how often are their decisions based on the actual tasks of the job? At what age will a student ask, "Can we assign a job to both women *and* men?" Once they recognize the limitation imposed by stereotypical gender expectations, how many students will advocate for putting *every* job in both piles?

Collect the results from each classroom and analyze. Ask students themselves to predict the outcomes. Will there be significant differences between older and younger student perspectives? Between girls and boys? What conclusions can be drawn from the data? How might students display and share their findings?

NOTES

1. Children's book by Linda de Haan about a prince who must find a princess but would rather choose another prince.

2. Chapter 7 examines the impact of "victim discourse" on GLBTQI adolescents.

3. Cheryl Kilodavis's children's book about a four-year-old boy who enjoys "girl" things like jewelry, sparkles, and the color pink.

GSD IN MIDDLE AND HIGH SCHOOL EDUCATION

Development, Safety, and Curriculum

Whether or not we are aware of it, when educators work with adolescents in school spaces, we are engaging the interplay of intellect, feelings, behaviors, and bodies—both ours and our students—which makes it a complex understanding. Perhaps the most effective way to understand what is at stake in these interactions is to view them as manifestations of identity . . . our work in schools is identity work.

—Nakkula and Toshalis (2006, 17–18)

I assert my identity, but it is often expressed to me that people think I am a "freak," and that my gender and sexuality are "phases." My gender exploration is taken as a joke but it's not a joke to me.

—High school student

This chapter (1) explores the developmental realities of middle school (MS) and high school (HS) students, (2) calls attention to the particular experience of GLBTQI students in relation to safety at school, and (3) highlights a curriculum integration approach that promotes contextualized learning about GSD. Models of curriculum integration projects, one for sixth through ninth grade and one for ninth through twelfth grade, are offered, though many of the teaching strategies in this chapter can be used with other pedagogical approaches as well.

SECTION I
DEVELOPMENTAL CONSIDERATIONS

WHO ARE MIDDLE SCHOOL STUDENTS?

❖ *I don't know how I am supposed to get my middle school kids to talk about these issues in a serious manner. They just don't seem ready for that.*

❖ *The social issues come up all the time with 7th, 8th and 9th graders. There is a lot of stereotyping, name-calling and cruelty. I deal with these issues every day.*

❖ *Student comfort in discussing these issues, in a classroom setting, varies greatly. Some students close up. Others giggle and joke. Some get agitated. They have a multitude of experiences, feelings, emotions, biases, fears and ideas about sexuality. It is a broad topic. Also, it requires me to take time to really think about my own experiences and views before engaging them in discussion. It takes a lot of reflection and preparation time.*

It is a special breed of educator who willingly signs up to teach middle school.[1] The developmental variability among ten- to fifteen-year-old girls and boys is hard to fathom at times. The homeroom teacher looks out at a classroom full of bodies in various stages of prepubescent, pubescent, and pubertal development. He wonders, "How can these kids all be the same age and look so different?" Voices are changing—or not, hips and breasts are filling out—or not, kids are growing taller—or staying short. The question of *who is where* in terms of physiological, psychological, cognitive, and social maturity hovers in the air and does not dissipate, even as students leave MS and head off to HS.

The National Middle School Association (NMSA) recognizes the imperative for middle school learning to reflect the complex world in which students live.

> Every day, millions of diverse, rapidly changing 10–15-year-olds make critical and complex life choices and form attitudes, values, and dispositions that will direct their behavior as adults. They deserve an education that will enhance their healthy growth as lifelong learners, ethical and democratic citizens, and increasingly competent, self-sufficient individuals who are optimistic about the future and prepared to succeed in our ever-changing world. (Position paper of National Middle School Association, *This We Believe: Keys to Educating Young Adolescents*, NMSA 2010)

Teachers must juggle the reality that some students are in the thick of deciding what to actually "do" with their more gendered and sexually mature bodies, while others are spectating from a distance. In spite of these developmental differences, it is a mistake to equate the *onset of puberty* with *readiness to learn* about gender identity and sexual identity. **All MS students are ready to explore the way these aspects of identity affect their experience in the world, regardless of where they are in their own pubertal development.**

Students enter MS with quite a bit of "learning" about GSD already in hand, and it may, as this teacher observes, seem "automatic, an attitude that doesn't even have to be spoken."

> ❖ *How can we address the issue that middle school boys who enjoy the arts— music, singing, dance, drama (less) are perceived as gay? It seems automatic, an attitude that doesn't even have to be spoken. Is homophobia already engrained in kids this age? (grown-ups too!)*

When I conduct workshops with students this age, they politely but firmly tell me: *We've already made up our minds about these issues. We're not going to change them now just because you're here to do a program on gender and sexuality. No offense, but we know this stuff already.* There is a stubborn quality to their rejection of new information that might compete with the "stuff" they already know. They're sure that they're sure, yet a little poking around reveals that they do not all share the *same* certainties.

> ➢ *My school is very open-minded and accepting, especially compared to other schools. We are taught not to discriminate and about the negative power of stereotypes.*
> ➢ *I am well informed about these issues, but I think my school is relatively ignorant, given the number of people who use "gay" as an insult.*
> ➢ *I honestly think it's not a big deal. Only teachers and a few kids care about it at all.*
> ➢ *What we learn in Health is **not** helpful.*
> ➢ *Thank God we have a GSA. It's the one place I can be myself.*

There are several factors that contribute to some early adolescents demonstrating a kind of ethical, cognitive, and emotional rigidity regarding complex issues of social identity (Levy-Warren 1996). Kids this age are imagining and/or experimenting with these evolving parts of themselves much of the time, and they may find too much ambiguity and contradiction scary. As middle schoolers prepare to embark on their pubertal journey of physiological, psychological, cognitive, and social disruption, they want to have some solid "truths" to hold onto, even if those truths are false (e.g., *Boys who sing and dance aren't athletic so they must be gay*) or inflexible (e.g., *Boys need to act like boys and girls need to act like girls, otherwise I won't know who to ask to the dance*).

As they mature, most middle schoolers will demonstrate increasing adaptability in thinking and behavior. During early adolescence, however, they need structure, information, and the patience of adults around them, as they insist they "know it all" in one moment and then forget their backpack at school the next. Their being prone to giggling, clowning, and rigid thinking should not be equated with lack of readiness to participate in learning about GSD. "The Story of What One Eighth Grader Can Do" is an important reminder of just how much is possible.

The Story of What One Eighth Grader Can Do

You might think that starting a GSA in one little school would have no effect on the wider world. And you might think that an eighth grader's decision to join or not would be easy. But I have learned better. Any decision that requires standing up for your beliefs and associating yourself with a controversial cause is a difficult one. And any step that helps educate people peacefully and works towards justice is an effective one. Just wrestling with my own concerns, and then standing up for what I think is right, is an effective step, because it helps other kids do the same thing. We learned this term that Gandhi's non-violent movement eventually affected millions of people around the world. If my actions can prompt even one other young person involved in personal conflict to make the right decision, it will be worth it.

—Sofia Riva, eighth grade student, Rhode Island

How often do you believe/assume that middle school students are not "ready" for complex understanding of social issues involving GSD? What is your assumption based on?

Are there other sophisticated concepts and complex topics that you present, regardless of whether the students seem "ready"? What makes GSD different?

WHO ARE HIGH SCHOOL STUDENTS?

High school serves as the major socializing institution of modern youth. It is the place where adolescents (ostensibly) grow into young adults and eventually graduate into the "real world" of work, financial responsibility, and mature relationships. High school students' coming of age is measured by milestones like learning to drive, getting a job, applying to college, enlisting in the army. In addition to these tangible rites of passage, fourteen- to eighteen-year-olds are also exploring and clarifying various aspects of identity, and using their advanced skills to interpret the world in more complex ways. The certainties of childhood—*I'm going to grow up to be a major league baseball player*—give way to new, more realistic possibilities.

This process of identity exploration, clarification, and ultimately, consolidation, is at work all the time (Nakkula and Toshalis 2006; Levy-Warren 1996). Adolescents' activities, relationships, and behaviors all serve a developmental purpose, and many students this age struggle with the wish to be their "own person" and, at the same time, belong to an identifiable group. The tension between (1) asserting oneself and (2) conforming to group norms is often played out in the realm of gender identity and sexual identity. Coming of age as a potentially sexually active person raises the stakes around personal decision making and group affiliation:

- *How do I want to be known as a female? Male? Trans?*
- *How and who do I want to be in the world as a sexually mature young woman?*
- *As a sexually mature young man?*
- *As a sexually mature queer person?*
- *What kinds of intimate relationships do I want to have? What is the role of sex in those relationships?*
- *How do I want my friends and my group to see me?*

As this hockey cartoon suggests, one's group identification, at least in stereotypical terms, may not necessarily match up with one's emerging gender or sexual identity. We do not tend to think of male high school hockey players as being gay, though surely some are. It is important to remember that some adolescents must negotiate emerging aspects of identity that do not line up with heteronormative

"Good game." "Good game." "Nice game." "Good game."
"I'm in love with you." "Good game." "Nice game."

Graphic 7.1.
© New Yorker

expectations. There is also a kind of reverse stereotyping for those who do not conform to "queer expectations." Those whose manner, appearance, and behavior do not meet GLBTQI stereotypes can also be questioned: *But you don't look gay. You don't act like you're gay* (Epstein 1997).

Gender and Sexual Identity Development

> By early adolescence . . . scripts have been so thoroughly presented and practiced that they have come to define what it means to be male and female within particular settings. In essence, the players are lost to the play itself. Their roles are so thoroughly scripted that modifying or breaking out of them takes extraordinary acts of insight and courage. (Nakkula and Toshalis 2006, 100)

In the adolescent's search for authenticity in her expressions of Self, the impact of a dozen years of gender and sexuality "development" and "socialization" are now in full view. As Nakkula and Toshalis (2006) suggest, questioning and reckoning with the "scripts" of gender and sexuality they have been following all their lives is a major task for many adolescents. For example, a script might go like this: you are the only girl in a family of many boys and you are expected to be feminine, a real "girl," one who likes dresses and dolls and makeup. Everyone wants you to be different from your brothers; they assume you will be different by virtue of your biological sex. Many of your caregivers delight in buying girl clothes and girl toys. When you turn out to be a tomboy, there is plenty of disappointment and redirection. When you hit puberty, the fear that you might be a lesbian becomes palpable, so you work very hard to follow the script and date boys like all your friends do.

> What was your own "script" for gender and sexuality growing up? Was your script a good fit for who you are? Have you stayed with or changed your script since adolescence?

Relational Learning

A vital part of "teaching" adolescents about GSD (or anything related to personal values) is *relational*. Experienced, talented educators who work with this age group know that without some kind of personal, authentic connection with students, the learning process is greatly diminished. If a teacher is asking students to engage in *transformational learning*, in addition to *informational learning* (see chapter 5), there must be a relational context in which this can happen. There must be a willingness by both student *and* teacher to take risks.

> In fact, the adults who take risks in their work with youth are better positioned to influence youth risk taking than those who do not. As school-based profes-

sionals try to encourage students to defend a victim from bullying, step outside the de facto dress code dictated by their peers, voice an unpopular opinion or raise their hand in class despite being shy, they are most likely to be heard by the youth they are attempting to influence if they have practiced taking the same risks in faculty meetings! (Nakkula and Toshalis 2006, 55)

Reread that quotation! How many times have you exhorted your students in just this way, urging them to stand up, take a risk, brave nonconformity? (Especially if you happen to be reading Emerson and Thoreau at the time.) Walking in the shoes of an adolescent means experiencing firsthand the vulnerability involved when you behave according to personal values and those values clash with the status quo.

Even the most relationally gifted high school teachers are uncertain about engaging students in conversations when it comes to the personal world of gender and sexuality.

- ❖ *I don't know how to approach a kid whom I perceive to be experiencing gender confusion/sexuality issues but does not recognize the same issues in him/herself. Don't really want to broach something they haven't confronted (at least consciously) themselves yet.*
- ❖ *How do you separate the physical sexual acts from sexual orientation/identity in discussing the issue? I'm okay with talking about one but not the other.*
- ❖ *I don't even feel comfortable addressing the way straight teens are so "sexualized." I can't imagine adding the sexuality of gay teens to the mix.*
- ❖ *I continue to be concerned that those students in the middle of the spectrum/continuum may be emboldened to "experiment" and find themselves "choosing" homosexuality. So why fear this? Because it is a tougher row to hoe than as a heterosexual.*

In elementary school, teachers worry about exposing "innocent children" to matters related to sexuality. In middle and high school, teachers are concerned about engaging the emerging sexuality of adolescents directly, because acknowledging the sexual behavior of students can be uncomfortable. In addition, most sexual behavior is also against school rules. ***Why would I want to promote students "learning about" something we don't want them doing at school?!***

Whose Job Is This?

Parents struggle with viewing their "child" as a sexual person; teachers avoid viewing their students as sexual beings and/or sexually active people. If all the important adults in students' lives avoid the reality of adolescent sexuality, then students are on their own in trying to understand and meet these emotional, psychological, relational, and physical needs. This internal and highly individual search is influenced at every turn by external forces such as peers, media, marketers, religious doctrine, and celebrity "role models." What is typically offered in schools are rules about what *not* to do sexually, and information about the *dangers* of sexual behavior (e.g., sexually transmitted diseases, unwanted pregnancies).

School missions everywhere charge teachers with the task of "supporting the healthy development" of their students, yet in spite of this mandate, educators continue to struggle with how to explicitly nurture the healthy development of gender and sexual identity, a developmental process that is at the *heart* of adolescence. Providing opportunities for students to make meaning of their gender and sexuality is central to the task of supporting healthy development and, as such, very much in keeping with school mission. (Chapter 8 focuses on comprehensive sexuality education for students of every age.)

> Who taught you about gender and sexuality when you were growing up? What role did your parents have? Your teachers? Your school?
>
> How does your own experience shape your attitudes now about who should participate in educating teens about GSD?

SECTION II
"SAFETY" FOR GLBTQI STUDENTS AT SCHOOL

> It is an absolute travesty of our educational system when students fear for their safety at school, worry about being bullied, or suffer discrimination and taunts because of their ethnicity, religion, sexual orientation, disability, or a host of other reasons.
>
> —Arne Duncan (2010), Secretary of Education

Gender identity development (GID) and sexual identity development (SID) are relevant concerns for *all* MS and HS students. Yet there are realities to confront and considerations to be made in promoting and supporting healthy GID and SID for GLBTQI students in particular. This section provides a critical window into the fundamental lack of safety that GLBTQI students—or those perceived to be—experience at school.

With gender identity and sexual identity development at the center of adolescence, where does that leave GLBTQI students? As these student comments make clear, schools vary widely in their safety for students who are "different."

> ➤ *We have a lot of ally teachers . . . and some gay/lesbian teachers. . . . But we also have a lot of "haters" and uninformed teachers.*

> ➤ *My school is fantastically open. A "safe place" for students from all walks of life. I wish everyone could have the opportunity that I have.*

In so many important ways GLBTQI students are no different from their straight peers; they care about belonging, exploring relationships, and finding their place in the world (Savin-Williams 2005, Campos 2005). GLBTQI students want to play on teams, join clubs, discover a creative niche or personal passion. However, in many instances, talking about GLBTQI students' experiences in school is first—out of necessity—a conversation about **safety**.

Educators and parents understand that in the twenty-first century "safety in schools" is not always a given. Secretary of Education Duncan tells us as much. The impact of drugs, gangs, poverty, inadequate funding, racism, urban decay, and more pose grave risks in schools across the country (Pollock 2008). This section describes the particular experience of "danger" that many GLBTQI students have at school. While many educators have at least a general sense of the way nonheteronormative students are at risk for being "bullied," most do not understand the specifics, the totality, and the full impact of this kind of physical, sexual, and psychological fear (see diagram 7.1).

THE SPECTRUM OF SCHOOL SAFETY

Violence

GLBTQI students experience safety on a continuum. Safety is multidimensional; it is multidetermined; it is not always easy to quantify. The GSO Spectrum of safety at school (diagram 7.1) is more illustrative than definitive. In different schools in different districts in different parts of the country, the ordering of items on the scale might change. Or there may be particular activities or issues omitted from the spectrum. What matters is that schools recognize how many elements of "safety" exist for GLBTQI students and those perceived to be GLBTQI.

Overt physical violence against GLBTQI students is visible, and as such, should be easy to identify and rectify. When Jamie Nabozny sued his Wisconsin school district in 1995 he exposed the profound negligence of teachers and school officials who time after time, over the course of several years, did not intervene to protect him from homophobic harassment. He was physically beaten up, subjected to a mock rape, and urinated on. Nabozny ultimately won his suit, and his case is the subject of a recent documentary that serves as a teaching tool for schools (see Bullied).

Bullied: A Student, a School, and a Case That Made History

In 2010, Teaching Tolerance released a documentary about Jamie Nabozny, a victim of antigay bullying at his Wisconsin high school in the 1990s, and his

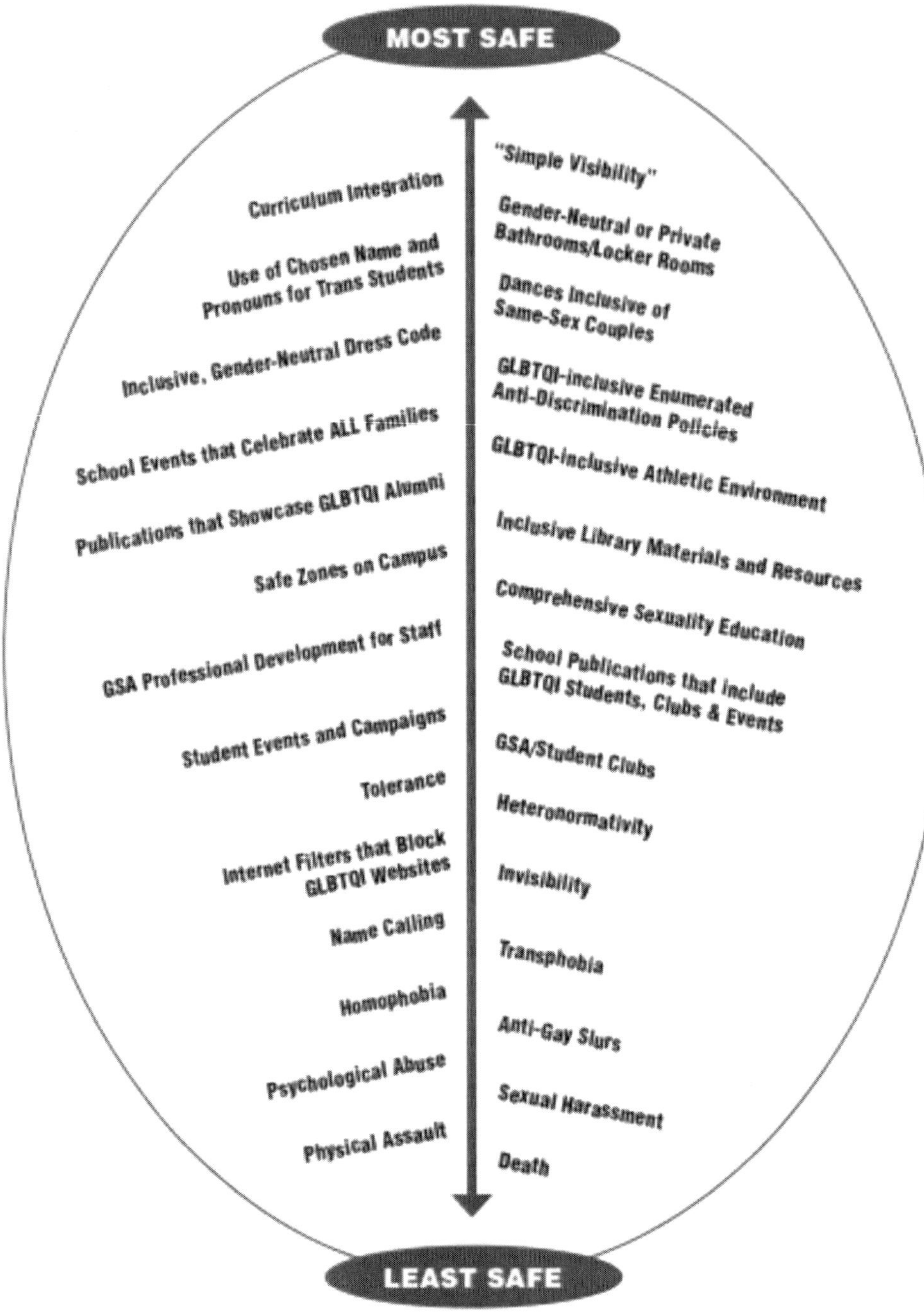

MOST SAFE

"Simple Visibility"

Curriculum Integration

Gender-Neutral or Private
Bathrooms/Locker Rooms

Use of Chosen Name and
Pronouns for Trans Students

Dances Inclusive of
Same-Sex Couples

Inclusive, Gender-Neutral Dress Code

GLBTQI-inclusive Enumerated
Anti-Discrimination Policies

School Events that Celebrate ALL Families

GLBTQI-inclusive Athletic Environment

Publications that Showcase GLBTQI Alumni

Inclusive Library Materials and Resources

Safe Zones on Campus

Comprehensive Sexuality Education

GSA Professional Development for Staff

School Publications that Include
GLBTQI Students, Clubs & Events

Student Events and Campaigns

GSA/Student Clubs

Tolerance

Heteronormativity

Internet Filters that Block
GLBTQI Websites

Invisibility

Name Calling

Transphobia

Homophobia

Anti-Gay Slurs

Psychological Abuse

Sexual Harassment

Physical Assault

Death

LEAST SAFE

Diagram 7.1. The GSD Spectrum of Safety at School
© 2011 Jennifer Bryan and Sebastian Mitchell Barr.

lawsuit against the school district for failing to protect him from such harassment. The documentary comes with a two-part viewer's guide for teachers and students. Part One, "Using *Bullied* in the Classroom," includes lesson plans and discussion tips. Part Two, "Using *Bullied* in Your School and District," includes legal information and guides for using the film in professional development. Order free copies of the film at www.tolerance.org/bullied.

The Nabozny case was decided over eighteen years ago, yet currently there are still many instances where repeated acts of physical and sexual violence against students go unaddressed. The ubiquity of this kind of harassment and a number of gay teen suicides in the fall of 2010 prompted author and syndicated columnist Dan Savage to create a YouTube video with his partner Terry to offer a message of hope and reassurance to bullied LGBT students.

Their "It Gets Better" video sparked a grassroots effort that, within six months, had generated over 25,000 videos and attracted over 40 million viewers. The "It Gets Better Project" was created "to show young LGBT people the levels of happiness, potential, and positivity their lives will reach—if they can just get through their teen years." The project assures LGBT teens that they are not alone "and it WILL get better" (www.itgetsbetter.org).

Stop and think about this project for a minute. Celebrities, authors, artists, military personnel, and politicians, along with average citizens of every age, race, class, and religion, have posted messages about life getting better if students "can just get through their teen years."

Even the president of the United States has a video that acknowledges the torment of GLBTQI kids and teens in America's schools and assures them life will improve if they can just make it through high school. In addition to promising that things will get better, President Obama says,

> with time you're going to see that your differences are a source of pride and a source of strength. You'll look back on the struggles you've faced with compassion and wisdom. And that's not just going to serve you, but it will help you get involved and make this country a better place (http://www.whitehouse.gov/it-gets-better-transcript).

This is a remarkable admission of systemic failure in America's middle and high schools by the leader of the United States. He concedes that for GLBTQI students, chronic harassment in school is something to be endured. He reassures them that if they can survive, life will get better and will likely prompt civic engagement when they get older. What kind of solace do these words provide for the student who is terrified of going to school? (See What Lack of Safety Can Look Like and Feel Like in School) Does the It Gets Better campaign give hope to parents about the day-to-day circumstances of their bullied teen?

What Lack of Safety Can Look Like and Feel Like in School

I just know that it hurt a lot to hear those words on a daily basis. People calling me queer, fag, homo. . . . Yes I'm gay but at the same time I'm not this horrible person that they think I am. When I was walking down the hallway, I'd have things thrown at me. I'd be kicked, punched, spit on, tripped.

Somehow, part of me always knew that I didn't deserve what was happening to me. But after enough time and enough harassment, you start wondering, what did I do to deserve this and what is wrong with me?

I went home and felt completely helpless. When you're in 7th grade, it's an eternity until you're going to graduate high school and be able to leave. And I was going to be stuck with these kids for all of that time. And there was no way that I could face going to school every day for my junior high and high school career. And I ended up going into my bathroom taking a whole bunch of pills and going to sleep, hoping that I would not wake up again because I did not want to go back to school.

—Jaime Nabozny, excerpt from the film *Bullied*
(Teaching Tolerance 2010)

Obstacles to Safety

Even though antibullying campaigns have been adopted in many school districts across the country in the past twenty years, these programs and initiatives typically do not *explicitly* address the kind of abuse that Jamie Nabozny endured, nor do they address the homophobia *behind* that abuse. Because these school-based initiatives do not enumerate gender identity/expression and sexual orientation as protected categories, they continue to fail in providing fundamental safety for GLBTQI students.

How hard can it be to protect students from this kind of abuse? Why not just make these bullying programs more inclusive? Because there is a fundamental conflict that impedes basic school safety for GLBTQI students:

1. Any *effective* policies related to student conduct must explicitly enumerate and repudiate antigay harassment in order to protect GLBTQI students.
2. Moral conservatives[2] reject this approach as unnecessary and view it as an attempt to influence young people's attitudes toward homosexuality in general.

Here's the ideological bind: if you are going to stop abuse in schools, you have to acknowledge in some measure that discriminating against GLBTQI people is *wrong*. Moral conservatives worry that this message may lead some students to conclude that GLBTQI people should not be discriminated against in school, or anywhere else for that matter. While most moral conservatives do not want to see gay kids being physically abused in schools, they also do not want the message

Box 7.1. Two Neighboring Districts; Two Different Policies

The Minneapolis school board voted unanimously in January 2011 to pass a resolution mandating increased LGBT antibullying efforts and LGBT-inclusive curriculums in all public schools. The resolution requires that the district offer educational material and yearly trainings on LGBT student safety for all staff, from administrators to bus drivers. Additionally, the sexual health curriculums within these schools must include LGBT issues, and each school must offer an elective course in LGBT history. The board has received a great deal of praise from across the state for their LGBT supportive policies (Birkey 2011). "Not all other districts are doing this work," notes Superintendent Bernadeia Johnson. "When we are out at the Pride Parade, when you talk to our youth, we hear how proud they are that they have a district that acknowledges them and cares about their safety" (Birkey 2011).

In contrast, the Anoka-Hennepin School District (30 minutes from Minneapolis) at present faces a lawsuit due to its inaction in protecting nonheterosexual students. The district has a "neutrality policy," which forbids teachers from discussing nonheterosexual issues. In 2011 Southern Poverty Law Center (SPLC) and the National Center for Lesbian Rights (NCLR) took legal action, arguing that the school district has allowed a culture of antigay harassment to persist, and as a result, gay students are being harassed. The SPLC asked that the victims of antigay bullying in the district be compensated and that the district revoke their "neutrality policy." As of August 2011, the school board was opposed to reconsidering the neutrality policy (Weber 2011).

that "gay is okay" to be an outcome of any school-based policy (Kumashiro 2008; Macgillivray 2004).

Here is an example of two Minnesota districts only 30 minutes apart that have pursued opposing courses of action in relation to this fundamental conflict over policy enumeration. As discussed elsewhere in this book, "neutrality" in relation to GSD is a pedagogical and philosophical impossibility, though school districts continue to base policy on this flawed foundation (see box 7.1).

Suicide

The "neutrality policy" adopted by Anoka-Hennepin School District represents an attempt to placate both sides of the *is-gay-okay-or-not?* conflict. Teachers are required to remain "neutral" on discussions of sexual orientation, so "for example, [they] won't advocate for or against gay and lesbian issues in the classroom" (Weber 2011). The policy has come under intense scrutiny since seven students in the district killed themselves in 2009/2010. One of the seven, ninth grader Justin Aaberg, was known to be the victim of chronic antigay harassment at school, and two others are suspected of being targeted as well (Weber 2011). Investigations into these deaths resulted in the current lawsuit against Anoka-Hennepin.

Homicide

What else can happen when students are chronically and systematically abused at school? In addition to taking their own lives, they may also be driven to kill other people. In the wake of multiple school shootings, the U.S. Secret Service and the Department of Education issued a report in 2002 on the *Implications for the Prevention of School Attacks in the United States*. The study revealed that many attackers felt persecuted by others prior to the attack, and even though none of the attackers in the 2002 study identified as gay, some of the harassment they endured was homophobic.

It is important to recognize the ruthless quality of this kind of harassment. "Attackers described being bullied in terms that suggested that these experiences approached torment . . . behaviors that, if they occurred in the workplace, likely would meet legal definitions of harassment and/or assault" (Vossekuil et al. 2002, 35–36). This comparison to workplace standards is a brutal reality check for school administrators who believe that "implicitness" or "neutrality" are appropriate policy positions. How can school communities condone, permit, or fail to intervene on behaviors that "torment" students and would be considered a criminal elsewhere? In their attempt to placate opponents of effective enumerated safety policies, some school communities create environments that are literally life-threatening for all students (and school personnel) who could be targets or bystanders in these kind of attacks.

Harassment

There are harassing behaviors that fall short of physical violence yet still amplify a hostile environment. A GLBTQI student—or one who is perceived to be—can be targeted by vandalism, graffiti, cyber bullying, verbal insults, social ostracism, and more. In addition, the use of antigay language and homophobic slurs also contribute to an antagonistic environment, whether students using that language have a specific target in mind or not. And climate surveys reveal time and again how frequent the use of such language is in schools across the country (Kosciw et al. 2010). Chapter 9 examines fully what behaviors constitute "bullying" and/or "harassment" and the implications for related policies and programs (Meyer 2009).

Classroom responsibility. While this type of harassment rarely occurs in the classroom, the classroom is one of the few places where a productive, teacher-facilitated conversation about gender and sexuality based harassment can occur. As one teacher notes, *I'm certain the lack of an active and open discussion of gender and sexuality has had a negative impact on students. We can be caring teachers and still not be creating a safe space.* Students need to have conversations with teachers about GSD in order to examine the attitudes behind this type of violence. Students need to hear from teachers, not only as spokespersons for "what the rules are," but as human beings who want to change the climate at school. That type of change often happens one conversation, one class period, one assignment at a time.

How might you use your classroom to address these issues of basic safety for all students in school? What kind of conversation can you have with your classes that gets beyond "bullying is wrong"? (See resources in chapter 9)

MOVING BEYOND PHYSICAL SAFETY

Clearly, there is plenty of work to do in order to prevent GLBTQI students from being harassed or harmed. Yet establishing basic physical safety alone will not suffice for the healthy intellectual, emotional, and social development of GLBTQI students. *Unqualified safety* takes more than the absence of harassment. The GLBTQI student can only feel truly safe when she is

1. seen and recognized as herself.
2. treated like other adolescents her age.

Being recognized and being treated like other adolescents enables GLBTQI students to experience the same successes, disappointments, embarrassments, trials, and accomplishments that their peers do. "Feeling safe" is not a guarantee of happiness; safety creates the opportunity to experience the world of school with two feet on the ground, come what may.

The safety that comes from "being seen" sounds easy enough, yet the invisibility/visibility conundrum is difficult for GLBTQI students and teachers alike to navigate (see chapter 10 for further discussion of invisibility, simple visibility, and surplus visibility). According to Judith Butler, "In order to act, one must be seen." The bind for GLBTQI students is that often they must *act* in order to *be seen*. They must *come out* in order to be fully known, yet coming out can be, for some adolescents, a complex, fraught process. Educators need to create a school environment where GLBTQI students can be seen and affirmed *before*, *during*, and *after* they are aware of, and/or claim a sexual and/or gender identity (see The Story of the Librarian Who Created a Safe Space). Remember that even if GLBTQI students do not "come out" during MS and HS—and plenty do not—they are still the beneficiaries of an explicitly inclusive educational environment, as are all students.

The Story of the Librarian Who Created a Safe Space

Early in my career as the School's librarian I became aware (in the context of lots of professional discussion about making sure diversity is represented in the collections) that a lot of people did not think of Sexuality as part of that diversity. Racial Diversity and Gender issues were evident. GLBTQI issues were not recognized. I began to realize the enormous power of the Library to be a resource when a student wrote an anonymous essay about going to his library and look-ing at the "sex books." The student wrote that no one ever signed out the book (back in the days when one signed circulation cards), but he was heartened that they had been moved . . . that "someone was reading them." That was an A-ha moment for the author (he was not alone) and it was an A-ha moment for me: the students saw the library as a resource for books (and other things) on topics having to deal with sexuality.

—Walter DeMelle, librarian

Tolerance

❖ *While teaching students to be tolerant is not inherently bad, it is a signifi-cantly lesser goal than the transformations I aspire to (Gonzales 2010, 79).*

Tolerance is certainly an improvement over harassment, yet GLBTQI students who feel they are being "endured" rather than genuinely accepted do not feel safe psychologically. Accomplishing the developmental tasks of adolescence means experimenting with ideas, personas, and interests. Adolescent students take risks socially and academically in order to find out more about themselves and others. Being "tolerated" leaves the GLBTQI teen in a precarious position, where healthy risk-taking may draw unwanted attention to an already vulnerable condition. While HS student David is ready to explore his attraction to boys, it is not safe for him to venture forth, as his presence at school is merely tolerated (see The E-mail from David).

As a Puerto Rican in a predominantly white boarding school David is visible and "seen" but not in a way that makes him feel known or accepted. His some-what feminine bearing is conspicuous in a school environment that values rugged, athletic masculinity. There are no overt acts of harassment directed at David, yet comments, attitudes, and innuendos make it clear about what and who is valued in this community. David is acutely aware that, on multiple dimensions (e.g., race, class, gender expression, sexual orientation, hometown), he does not belong to the fraternity of this private school.

The E-mail from David

I'm a Puerto Rican from the Bronx and I've always know something was differ-ent about me. Which is why I've e-mailed you this lengthy letter. I've probably known that I'm either gay or bisexual since like the sixth grade. I have never had any experience with any sex but I just know. I think I lean towards the pronomi-nal homosexual side but I don't know. Being here really sucks for me. I have yet to talk to anyone at the school about this and so I've been keeping it to myself for a while. I have told a few friends that go to other schools and are in college and

From: "David ▮▮▮▮▮ ▮ ▮▮▮▮▮▮▮▮▮▮▮▮ ▮ ▮▮▮ ▮▮▮ ▮▮▮▮
Date: April 17, 2004 12:01:55 AM EDT
To: jbryan@jenniferbryanphd.com

Dr. Bryan,
    I just really want to thank you once again for today presentation at
▮▮▮▮▮▮▮. It was very informative and I think and hope that it sparked
something. If you don't know already, ▮▮▮▮▮▮▮▮ is not the best setting
for GLBTQ people. The ignorance about that and other issues of diversity
are usually just brushed under the carpet. I've been here three years
already and have seen little difference in the attitude of the the
students and faculty towards these issues. For the first time in the last
couple of weeks there has been actual talk about these issues and
personally I find it very pleasing. I'm a Puerto Rican from the Bronx and
it hasn't been easy for me. In addition I've always know something was
different about me. Which is why I've e-mailed you this length letter.
I've probably known that I'm either gay or bisexual since like the sixth
grade. I have never has any experience with any sex but i just know. i
think i lean towards the pronominal homosexual side but i don't know.
Being here really sucks for me. I have yet to talk to anyone at the school
about this and so I've been keeping it to myself for a while. I have told
a few friends that go to other schools and are in college and they have
all been females which is hard because I've never talked to another male.
i believe that many of the students already suspect that i am gay but none
have ever said anything(to my face). The jokes made and the things said
really get to me sometimes but there little i can say with out people come
out right back towards me with things i don't want to hear. Growing up i
was always ridiculed and taunted by my peers. i kind of got used to it and
then coming here no one really said anything but i always felt like i was
being watched or talked about. i still do. its such a burden because now
at this point in my life i think I'm ready to experiment with males but i
don't know how or where and i have no one to ask. so i guess the reason
for all of this was to ask if you had any suggestions or reference books
or anything that would help me.

        thanks, David
as you know no one knows about this so i think you understand my situation
my e-mail is ▮▮▮▮▮▮▮▮▮▮▮▮▮▮▮▮▮▮▮▮▮▮▮

Graphic 7.2.

they have all been females which is hard because I've never talked to another
male. I believe that many of the students already suspect that I am gay but none
have ever said anything (to my face). The jokes made and the things said really
get to me sometimes but there little I can say without people coming right back
towards me with things I don't want to hear. Growing up I was always ridiculed
and taunted by my peers. I kind of got used to it and then coming here no one
really said anything but I always felt like I was being watched or talked about. I
still do. It's such a burden because now at this point in my life I think I'm ready

to experiment with males but I don't know how or where and I have no one to
ask. So I guess the reason for all of this was to ask if you had any suggestions or
reference books or anything that would help me.
    Thanks, David

The Reality of Multiple Identities

As noted in the introduction, this book does not, for the most part, address the critical intersections of multiple aspects of identity. When gender and sexuality intersect with race, religion, nationality, class, geography, and so on the influence on development and identity can be profound (Misawa 2010; Blackburn and Smith 2010; Blackburn and McCready 2009; Kumashiro 2002). In these lines, the poet and activist Pat Parker captures the tension of intersectionality.[3]

> If I could take all my parts with me when I go somewhere, and not have to say to one of them, "No, you stay home tonight, you won't be welcome," because I'm going to an all-white party where I can be gay but not Black. Or I'm going to a Black poetry reading, and half the poets are anti-homosexual, or thousands of situations where something of what I am cannot come with me. The day all the different parts of me can come along, we would have what I would call a revolution. (Parker 1999)

There is tremendous diversity *within* the GLBTQI population in relation to these other sociocultural identifiers. David's experience of himself as "other" on multiple dimensions speaks to his unique challenge of developing a "healthy identity" in this school environment. In its 2009 report the National Education Association (NEA) offers multiple examples of such intersections of identity (see box 7.2).

As Kumashiro notes, "Activism will always create its own margin . . . ; when we fail to acknowledge and grapple with that, are we allowing those margins to exist? Are we actually sanctioning them?" (Kumashiro 2008). Multiple identities are the current reality now for many GLBTQI members of any school community. Yet until we make better progress in our basic understanding and acceptance of GSD, grappling with the complexity of intersectionality will remain at the margins. Fortunately there are scholars and researchers who are committed to addressing intersectionality and highlighting its centrality in conversations about diversity (Blackburn and Smith 2010; Blackburn and McCready 2009).

Identities and Essentialism

While illustrative of intersectionality, the NEA's list of scenarios in box 7.2 runs the risk of making stereotypical generalizations about the various groups portrayed. One Latino household may enforce traditional gender roles, another may not.

BOX 7.2. Intersections of GLBTQI Identity and _____.

From the National Education Association 2009
Report on the Status of Gay, Lesbian, Bisexual and Transgender People in Education:
Stepping Out of the Closet, Into the Light

- An African American parent or guardian rejects homosexuality as against her community and religious values.
- A GLBT community center is located in an affluent, White neighborhood, away from predominantly ethnic minority neighborhoods.
- A student of color does not feel comfortable joining a predominantly White GSA at school.
- The church, synagogue, temple, or mosque that a student and her family attend preaches against homosexuality.
- An Asian American parent or guardian rejects a GLBT son or daughter because GLBT people "do not exist in our culture."
- GLBT services and materials do not exist in languages other than English.
- A Latino household rejects boys who are not masculine or girls who are not feminine as against cultural "norms."

(Kim, Sheridan, and Holcomb 2009, 11)

There may be some students of color who *are* comfortable joining the mostly white GSA, and so forth. **Thus while some trends in attitudes and behaviors exist, cultures and identities are dynamic, interactive, and changeable**.

For example, Renée DePalma shares that "one Muslim father said, at a planning meeting at his son's primary school, that the point was not whether teaching about GSD coincided with his cultural and religious beliefs. He wanted his son to be prepared to live in a pluralistic democracy" (2011, personal communication). Similarly, the teacher in a Catholic girls school counters the common assumption that "all Catholics are antigay" by describing the way the faith on which her school is founded serves as the primary reference point in their social justice and ally work (see Safety in a Catholic School).

Safety in a Catholic School

As a school founded by a religious order with a faith-based mission, we have struggled to understand how to best approach gender and sexuality diversity. On the one hand, we are stewards of our faith tradition which has very clear moral teachings about sexuality and expressions of sexual love, and we do instruct our students about these teachings in our religious education classes. On the other hand, we are stewards of our faith tradition which has very clear teachings about human dignity and solidarity, that every person (including homosexual persons) are made in the image and likeness of God and "must be accepted with respect, compassion and sensitivity" and "every sign of unjust discrimination in their regard should be avoided."

How do we live out our school mission with regard to gender and sexuality diversity? Perhaps the most effective format we use to address issues of gender and sexuality diversity in our Catholic context is the use of narrative storytelling or panel discussions. This format helps to break down barriers of misunderstanding. When someone tells a story from the "I-perspective," it can help move the conversation beyond moral assessments and judgments. Those assessments and judgments might still be there for the listener, but the speaker who tells his or her story offers the opportunity for the listener to empathize, to step into another pair of shoes, to experience the world from a different perspective, if only for a moment.

*For example, about four years ago, we held an all staff retreat during which gay and lesbian faculty shared their stories of marginalization based on their sexual orientation. The goal of the year was "To Create Unity through Diversity" and their stories helped move us out of the fear of openly discussing sexual orientation in a faith-based school and moved us into an active conversation about how to listen to diverse voices, **because** we are in a faith-based school.*

Largely inspired by the social justice interests of our students, we have extended the conversation about gender and sexuality diversity to our students, using the narrative storytelling format. We have tried to facilitate developmentally appropriate forums where students share their stories and listen to others' stories about their experience of being LGBTQ, with an emphasis on creating a safe climate for all students devoid of bullying and humiliation.

Diversity initiatives that explicitly discuss gender and sexuality diversity, such as the annual Ally Week and Day of Silence, become an exercise of allyship and solidarity. It is clear to us that Jesus is a profound model of allyship—Fully God, Jesus became human to be in solidarity with humanity; fully human, Jesus stood with the marginalized, the outsider, the sinner and invited all to His table.

—Teacher, Sacred Heart School for Girls

Heteronormativity as a Blinder

In many cases being "seen" can only occur when the heteronormativity of the school environment is recognized and challenged. Consider the experience of this transgender student.

> ➤ *I attend an all-girls school, but I'm an FTM. I don't bring it up much at all, but it gets miserable when every class begins with "Settle down, ladies."*

When this teacher begins her class with "Settle down, ladies," she does not "see" her transgender student. The teacher knows this student is physically in the classroom, but she has not yet considered a way to include the trans student in the salutation at the beginning of the period. GLBTQI students experience moments like this, "a moment of psychic disequilibrium" dozens of times every day. They do not feel seen; they do not feel they even exist (Rich 1986).

How readily do you "see" your GLBTQI students? Are there ways you could more explicitly include them in the social and academic exchanges in your classroom, on your athletic team, and in student club settings?

Does your language acknowledge—and thereby possibly invite—nonhetero-normative identities, perspectives, and attitudes? Remember that GLBTQI individuals listen for inclusive language all the time as a "clue" about whether they are welcome.

The safety that comes with treating GLBTQI students like any other adolescents means creating an environment that allows them to explore

- themselves
- friendships
- behaviors
- styles
- interests
- intimacies

with the same awkwardness and finesse of their peers. Straight kids have their gendered, social and sexual behaviors "supervised," related to, and regulated frequently by adults in schools. Teachers discuss cultural and social issues associated with dating and relationships, offering teens advice or an adult perspective on current trends (e.g., *friends with benefits, is oral sex really sex? is rap degrading to women?*). Remember, GLBTQI students need limit-setting and adult wisdom just as much as their straight peers. Consider the examples in Equal Opportunity Limit-Setting (diagram 7.2).

In order to treat GLBTQI students "like all adolescents" there must be safe, equitable, and inviting social opportunities. Yet, in many ways, the social curriculum is harder to change than the academic, as it is directly tied to popular cultural norms outside of the school. Activities such as a pep rally, the talent show, and senior prom are visible manifestations of the culture and climate of the school. Entertainment icons and sports heroes are the role models of choice for many adolescents. Some of these "stars" send an inclusive message in relation to GSD (e.g., Lady Gaga); many do not (e.g., Chris Brown).

SCHOOL SPORTS RULE

In most private and public schools, athletics serve as the primary showcase for talent, school spirit, and success. Certainly students who garner academic prizes are recognized too, but the "community" does not typically rally around a math competition the way it does a play-off basketball game. Becoming All-State champions or winning a division, these successes earn banners that hang from the ceiling of

Diagram 7.2.   Equal Opportunity Limit-Setting

the gym, maybe even a road sign on the local interstate. As Stuart Biegel reminds us, "not only does sports cast a giant shadow on the day-to-day interactions and mindsets of people in educational settings, but in many places it is the single most important factor in the school's climate and is located at the very center of a school's culture" (Biegel 2010, 51).

Unfortunately, modeling in relation to gender and sexuality at the professional and college sports level is almost exclusively heteronormative. In addition several prominent sports figures were "caught" during 2011 making homophobic remarks during games. After the videotape of NBA All-Star Kobe Bryant calling a referee a "fucking faggot" hit the airwaves, Bryant explained that the comment should not be taken literally. "My actions were out of frustration during the heat of the game, period," he said. "The words expressed do not reflect my feelings towards the gay and lesbian communities and were not meant to offend anyone" (Rhoden 2011). Joakim Noah, star center of the Chicago Bulls, was seen a month later, hurling the same slur at a heckling fan during a nationally televised play-off game; he too apologized and denied any disrespect to gays (Abrams 2011).

The example being set here is clear. *I mean "faggot" as a despicable thing to say in the moment but I don't really hate gays.* Students who use "That's so gay" to describe something or someone as stupid or lame also deny any intention of "putting down gays." Bryant and Noah model a self-serving disconnect between using slurs and taking responsibility for what the slurs mean to all people. In addition, it is hard to distinguish between those stars who use antigay slurs but "don't mean them" and those who use them and own the intent, like former NBA player Tim Hardaway: "You know, I hate gay people, so I let it be known. I don't like gay people and I don't like to be around gay people. I am homophobic. I don't like it. It shouldn't be in the world or in the United States" ("Retired" 2007).

Coaching Strategy?

Using homophobic and sexist language as a motivational tool is also a time-honored coaching strategy. Telling male athletes that they are "playing like a bunch of girls," or "look like pussies out there" ostensibly motivates players to work harder, run harder, hit harder. Performances that are perceived as "less than" are equated with being female or gay; male athletes are humiliated by such comparisons and strive to avoid them. Players hear coaches use these pejoratives and subsequently adopt this language themselves. *You better sprint after that ball you faggot, or else we'll all be doing laps.*

Traditions and School Spirit

With athletes, coaches, cheerleaders, and parents of the "star" players being among some of the most admired figures in the community at the local level, any suggestion that their antigay behavior or heteronormative attitudes should change is likely to be met with resistance and rationalization. Blackburn and Smith (2010) offer a case example, where students at one school paint misogynistic and homophobic messages about their athletic rivals on a big rock. This public display is part of a long-standing tradition; during "spirit week" athletes and cheerleaders gear up for the big game by offending the opposing high school.

While the messages are clearly offensive, the behavior is understood only as students expressing "school spirit." Everyone seems to accept that this student behavior is not intended to demean anyone other than the rival team. So even though the put-down is at the expense of real people in the community, it should not matter because it is just students showing support for their athletes. Anyone who questions the language and the method of expressing school spirit is seen as not supporting the team, not supporting the school, making a big deal out of something that "everyone else" sees as harmless. The challenge, once again, is to consider "what nobody has yet thought about that which everybody sees" (Schopenhauer; see chapter 5).

So when women and gays *are* offended by being used as a motivational whip by coaches or *do* feel degraded when homophobic slurs are used in the service of "school spirit," their protests can be met with incredulity and outrage (see The Fictional Account of the True Story of the Cancelled Pep Rally Skit). Their oversensitivity becomes the problem; their demands for respect and equity are seen as self-serving acts of political correctness.

The Fictional Account of the True Story of the Cancelled Pep Rally Skit

It's time for the big football game of the season, with the Wildcats of Clearview High School facing the Panthers of Westridge High in the play-offs. Everyone is anticipating the Friday afternoon pep rally. There is lots of energy going into the show, particularly the traditional skit where seniors on the Wildcat's football team dress as Panthers cheerleaders and stuff balloons in their shirts. They dance around stage with their big faux boobs, act vampy, and then perform a few awkward cartwheels that reveal the colorful boxer shorts beneath their skirts.

Team moms have stepped in to make skirts big enough for the boys; they have searched far and wide for wigs, pom-poms, and megaphones in the correct shade of green. The boys have been practicing all week in the halls and courtyard. The girls' cheerleading squad has been helping them with their routine. The school is abuzz with anticipation.

Then a few teachers and students complain about the skit. It reinforces negative gender stereotypes, *they say.* It's demeaning to girls and women. *At the last minute, the administrator in charge of the pep rally cancels the skit. The parents are outraged, especially the moms backstage who are working hard to help with costume changes.* Who complained? *they wonder.* How could anyone think that these boys were trying to hurt somebody's feelings? The biggest issue has been helping the football players get up the nerve to make fun of themselves by putting on the costumes!

A not-so-subtle campaign to discredit those who objected to the skit quickly begins. One teacher is described as a "feminist" and a "leftist." After all she had even suggested one year that homecoming be held at a girls' field hockey game instead of at a football game. One of the students who objected is president of the Diversity Club and rumored to be gay. Parents decry the "political correctness" of the school and wonder what ever happened to common sense. Everyone is upset, taking sides, pointing fingers. People write letters to the editor of the local paper, lamenting the demise of "good-natured fun." And the Wildcats, of course, get clobbered in the play-off game.

As the traditional pep rally skit demonstrates, the "rightness" of heteronormativity is reinforced, in part, because for so many, it has "always been that way." Prowess in sports is associated with masculinity. Successful male athletes are masculine and assumed to be straight. Masculinity in female athletes, on the other hand, is associated with lesbianism. Girls can be admired for competing aggressively, as long as they assert their femininity and straightness at the same time (*It Takes a Team!* training video[4]).

Ways to Change the Game

The depth and breadth of misogyny and homophobic influences in school sports can appear overwhelming. Fortunately there are new resources aimed at shifting the attitudes that permeate school sports. The need to transform the culture of school-based athletics has inspired GLSEN to create an initiative called Changing the Game (see Teaching Resouce I). The goal of the project is to support K–12 schools in creating and sustaining athletic and physical education programs that are welcoming to all students regardless of sexual orientation or gender identity/expression (sports.glsen.org). When athletes, coaches, P.E. teachers, and fans become messengers of respectful inclusion, and when they actively challenge long-standing stereotypes and assumptions about student athletes, school becomes a much safer place for *all* students. Respect for those who are GLBTQI in the domain of athletics sends a loud message: *"inclusion" at this school really does mean everyone.*

The Changing the Game initiative provides an opportunity for coaches and P.E. instructors to expand their considerable influence on school climate and culture. If enough coaches, teams, schools, districts, and divisions adopt this program, it could be the beginning of a much-needed cultural shift in middle and high school communities across the country. In addition, learning an inclusive approach to participating in and supporting team sports has become another component of the time-honored goal of "preparing for college." Efforts to create just and equitable programs are well under way at the college level. The NCAA Executive Committee adopted a comprehensive statement in 2010 to frame its inclusion work:

> As a core value, the NCAA believes in and is committed to diversity, inclusion and gender equity among its student-athletes, coaches and administrators. We seek to establish and maintain an inclusive culture that fosters equitable participation for student-athletes and career opportunities for coaches and administrators from diverse backgrounds. Diversity and inclusion improve the learning environment for all student-athletes and enhance excellence within the Association.
>
> The NCAA will provide or enable programming and education, which sustains foundations of a diverse and inclusive culture across dimensions of diversity including, but not limited to age, race, sex, class, national origin, creed,

educational background, disability, gender expression, geographical location, income, marital status, parental status, sexual orientation and work experiences. (NCAA Executive Committee, 2010, NCAA Inclusion Initiative, http://www.ncaa .org/wps/wcm/connect/ncaa/ncaa/about+the+ncaa/diversity+and+inclusion/ gender+equity+and+title+ix/lgbtq+resources)

In addition, the National Center for Lesbian Rights (NCLR), which is known for its work across the gender and sexuality diversity spectrum, and *It Takes a Team!* (a LGBT initiative from Women's Sports Foundation) released a report urging high school and college athletic associations to adopt standard policies that provide transgender student-athletes fair and equal opportunity to participate in team sports (Griffin and Carroll). The report offers

- explanations about transgender identities and background information regarding transgender students and their importance related to athletics.
- "practical recommendations for including transgender student athletes" that include guidelines about facilities, media, and other less-foreseen challenges.
- "best practices recommendations for implementing transgender student athlete inclusion policies," with sections specifically for Athletic Administrators, Coaches, Student Athletes (nontransgender), Parents (of both transgender and nontransgender student athletes), and Media/PR Staff.

Definitions, legal rights/protections, and additional resources on transgender issues are included (http://www.nclrights.org/site/DocServer/TransgenderStudent AthleteReport.pdf?docID=7901).

> Most school teams are organized by sex. In your role as a coach, how do you address issues of GSD? What distinguishes boys' teams from girls' teams at your school? Is there parity between boys/girls teams in terms of resources (e.g., field time, funds for gear, paid coaching staff)?
>
> Have you ever coached an openly gay player? Is yours a team that GLBTQI students would feel comfortable playing on? What changes might you make in coaching style and/or player expectations that would create an GSD-inclusive athletic environment?

Teaching Resource I: Changing the Game

The GLSEN Sports Project launched in early 2011 with the mission of "assisting K–12 schools in creating and maintaining an athletic and physical education climate that is based on the core principles of respect, safety and equal access for all, regardless of sexual orientation or gender identity/expression." The project is intended to expand opportunities for school-based education about gender and sexuality for the hundreds of thousands of youth who participate in team sports every year in schools across the country. The project website offers resources for athletes, coaches, athletic directors, parents, and administrative teams, as well as video and photo campaigns. (*Source*: http://sports.glsen.org)

THE SOCIAL CURRICULUM

Only students with a particular set of skills can participate on school teams, but social rituals such as attending the prom, having a picture in the yearbook, and marching in graduation are purportedly for everyone. Most rituals of this kind are based on heteronormative ideals. The emphasis for girls is on looking pretty and hot for prom, and looking beautiful, even elegant, for graduation. Boys are handsome in jackets, ties, and tuxedos. Heterosexual pairing is reinforced by the "tradition" of boys inviting girls to be their dates for the prom. A guy asking a girl if she wants to dance is still considered a privilege and responsibility of male heterosexual court-ship. Students sometimes march into the graduation ceremony in boy/girl pairs.

Heterosexuality is not the problem here. It is the absence of any *additional* representations of genders, sexualities, or pairings that denies the existence of non-heteronormative students (see The Story of Missing Out). Remember: in order to act, one must be seen. In addition, it helps to have visible GLBTQI adults in the school community who model a range of possibilities for students. However, since GLBTQI adults are often in a similar struggle for inclusion, they may be model-ing limitations (e.g., remaining closeted) as well as possibilities (see chapter 10 for further discussion of GLBTQI educators).

The Story of Missing Out

I came out as liking girls when I was in high school. My concern with coming out actually wasn't one of safety or discomfort. Although my school was socially conservative, its climate was also one of respect and I never feared harassment because of my sexual orientation. For me, the downside of coming out—of living as a girl who didn't want to date boys—was that I knew I would no longer fit into the social landscape of my school and community. While never being out-right homophobic, the school's social events left no room for non-heterosexual students or couples.

School dances were the obvious example here. While some students went in groups, there was still a lot of ritual and excitement surrounding "dates"—the asking of dates, showing up early and getting pictures in front of the house, buy-ing corsages or boutonnières, etc. And this was for heterosexual couples; even non-romantic pairings were always boy-girl. I remember specifically the Sadie Hawkins dance, for which "the girl asked the guy"—not the girl asked the person she wanted to go with. I ended up asking a guy friend of mine. And eventually, I just stopped going to dances.

Looking back, what is hardest for me is that, at the time I never even thought, hey I should be able to take a girl to this dance. It was so obvious to me that non-heterosexual couples didn't belong at those dances that I had just accepted that my relationships didn't belong in that sort of social world as a girl attracted to girls. There was no place for me in the mainstream.

And truthfully, I regret missing the dances and not being my girlfriend's cotillion escort, and avoiding pep rallies and football games (which were also somehow centered around heterosexual pairings). I missed out on a huge part of the social education that my peers enjoyed.

—S. Barr

While individual GLBTQI students in different schools across the country have been successful in fighting their way into these social rites of passage (see The Girl Who Wore a Tux to the Prom and The Trans Prom Queen), their victories are newsworthy exceptions to the prevailing norms. If GLBTQI students are to have a chance of being treated just like any other adolescent, then schools must create a social environment that explicitly includes them *and* challenges heteronormativity, challenges traditions that "have always been that way."

The Girl Who Wore a Tux to the Prom

St. Francis High School, a Catholic school in Sacramento, California, drew national attention in 2011 when administrators told student Jade Goodwin-Carter that she could not wear a tuxedo to her senior prom. Goodwin-Carter, a lesbian, believed that the administration's reaction was related to their discomfort with homosexuality and nontraditional gender roles. The school's president denies that the decision had anything to do with sexual orientation. After public outcry and a follow-up meeting with Jade, the school changed their mind and allowed her to wear her tuxedo (Monacelli 2011).

The Trans Prom Queen

In May 2011, Andii Viveros, a young trans woman, was crowned prom queen at McFatter High School, a technical school in southern Florida. Her name was featured on the ballot and received the most student votes out of fifteen runners. "It's a big stepping stone," Viveros said. "People can see it's finally OK to be who you are and do what you want no matter how different you are" (Stanglin 2011). Around the country, a small but growing number of high schools are seeing transgender students being nominated for homecoming and prom court. The first reported transgender prom queen was Crystal Vero, a Fresno, California, high school student in 2007.

The Benefits of Participation

As stated in earlier chapters, the benefits of coming out for GLBTQI students outweigh potential negative consequences (Kosciw et al. 2010, 50–51). One of those benefits is having an opportunity to participate as a full human being in the social life of the school. If social events are welcoming and inclusive, it is likely that more GLBTQI students will feel safe coming out. If more students are out at school, being GLBTQI becomes less conspicuous and less isolating. With more expansive parameters of acceptability, *all* students will feel less pressured to meet singular and narrow ideals in terms of gender and sexuality.

> How GLBTQI inclusive is the social curriculum at your school? Are there gender-neutral activities or events?

SECTION III
CURRICULUM INTEGRATION

> Teaching the "basic curriculum," by most definitions of the term, perpetuates the status quo of socially constructed gender and sexual identity hierarchies in that they teach the biology and technology of heterosexual relations without expanding outward toward a fuller array of the sexual realities existing in a given classroom. (Nakkula and Toshalis 2006, 190)

What is the place of gender and sexuality diversity in the standard academic curriculum? A vexing question. Consider the perspectives of these three teachers:

❖ *We have a responsibility to "unlearn" and recognize misinformation about gender, race, religion and sexual orientation. We need to seek out and provide more accurate information and adjust accordingly. Without this, behavior will not change.*

❖ *Where and when am I supposed to find time for this? I believe preparing my students for the AP exam is much more relevant to the job I was hired to do than spending class time discussing personal matters.*

❖ *For my students to feel at home, it is not enough simply to fail to perpetuate discrimination. I need to enlarge the culture of my classroom.*

Each of these educators has strong pedagogical priorities and a clear commitment to student education. All three raise important concerns. Until those who shape curricula for MS and HS fully address this quandary, teachers will continue to be divided about who should teach what to whom and when in relation to gender and sexuality.

In addition, students will continue to receive inadequate information and be denied opportunities to critically examine the social, legal, historical, political, religious, literary, scientific, and ethical dimensions of GSD in the world. Clearly the complexity, ubiquity, and interrelatedness of gender and sexuality cannot be sufficiently addressed in a single subject (e.g., English) or in a single class (e.g., health). What follows is one method of instruction that can work between, among, and across disciplines, and successfully engage students in learning about GSD.

CURRICULUM INTEGRATION FUNDAMENTALS

The **curriculum integration**[5] approach is one option for engaging students in relevant examinations of GSD. The primary characteristics of curriculum integration (CI) are

- Using knowledge, perspectives, methods of inquiry, and critical thinking skills from more than one discipline to create a deeper understanding of the subject at hand (Hinde 2005).
- Capitalizing on the interdependence of (1) emotional, (2) social, and (3) intellectual "learning."
- Emphasizing teacher-student planning, and selecting themes, topics, and projects that are meaningful and relevant to adolescent students (Brown 2006).
- Involving students in (1) identifying, (2) building projects around, and (3) assessing mastery of relevant core competencies.

Inviting adolescents to relate *personally* to classroom content is a long-standing strategy for increasing student engagement. CI is based on students selecting themes, designing projects, and connecting the course material in some measure to their own personal needs and interests. In addition, they assume responsibility for linking project tasks (e.g., researching, writing, presenting) to required core competencies.

Effectiveness and Standardized Testing

Is a methodology that strays from a single-subject, content-driven focus compatible with the current standards-based method of evaluating school efficacy? This question perpetuates a false dichotomy between these two approaches.

Knowledge of the various disciplines is fundamental to effective interdisciplinary teaching. Therefore, teaching "subject content" separately should not be abandoned in favor of integration, nor should integration be set aside in efforts to teach individual subjects separately. A balance between the two strategies is necessary because both are effective means of increasing student achievement (Hinde 2005, 107).

Teachers may be concerned about standardized test preparation yet some research indicates that students educated using the CI approach do as well, if not better, than those in a conventional, departmentalized program (NMSA 2002; Vars and Beane 2000).

What About the AP?

The teacher quoted at the beginning of this section is concerned that inviting "personal matters" into the classroom will interfere with academic preparation for Advanced Placement exams. Yet, as former GLBTQ student Stephanie Gentry-Fernandez shares, it can be impossible to achieve academically when one's life is in personal turmoil.

> *Although I have always been an honors student and took all honors and AP classes, my grades definitely suffered whenever I had a bad night or had fought recently. Needless to say, I simply did not care about school on the days I was tired. How would knowing the subjunctive form of French verbs help me in life when I wasn't even sure if I was welcomed back to my parents' house that night?*
>
> —Stephanie Gentry-Fernandez, former student, Chicago Public Schools
> (quoted in Kim, Sheridan, and Holcomb 2009, 24)

Students need *both* academic preparation *and* opportunities for personal and emotional growth in the classroom, not just one or the other. CI rests on the belief that these aims are not at cross-purposes but rather mutually reinforcing.

Students can be held accountable for learning content and developing relevant skills, while making the learning personal at the same time. For example, in "A Poem by the Boy Who Loved to Sing," this seventh grader addresses the project theme of Gender Stereotypes intellectually, personally, emotionally, and socially. He fulfills the academic requirement and, at the same time, he explores a complicated, highly personal dilemma. Clearly he benefits from the different aspects of "learning" involved in this work.

A Poem by the Boy Who Loved to Sing

"Learning to Love Singing"
Because it's hard
And I would always tell myself not to:
Be like the other guys, and pretend you hate it
Because I love to do it,
I know that people will make fun of me,

Telling me that I shouldn't
Or I Can't,
Or it's not a "guy" thing
Because when I sing, I am somewhere else,
I enjoy it, more than I ever thought I would,
I forget about everything that's going on, and I just sing
And while the last couple notes of the song come out of my mouth,
The song is over,
And it's back to hiding
What I love to do.

—Ping Promrat, seventh grade student

Keep in mind that you do not have to adopt the CI approach in total in order to make use of certain CI components or strategies. **If you are educator who is not inclined to fully adopt this method, read on anyway.** "Teachers should consider integration as another pedagogical tool and not as an end in itself" (Hinde 2005, 107). Some of the most important principles presented here can be adapted to more conventional approaches to classroom instruction.

Where to Begin

Using the CI approach does not necessarily require a complete revamping of your current curriculum. The curriculum integration: gender and sexuality diversity (CIGSD) worksheet (see diagram 7.3) allows you to assess what you are already teaching in terms of how it relates to GSD. This assessment provides data about ways you already address GSD (and might not even know it!) and where/what you might add. You can assess your curriculum in this way at any time: before the school year begins, between semesters, in response to issues/ideas that have come up in class.

Using your mission statement as the central reference point helps you determine how GSD relates not only to content and competency goals, but to your overarching educational mission as well. For example, the religion teacher consistently links the content and objectives of her eighth grade religious studies class to the religious traditions on which the school is founded (see diagram 7.4). One might wrongly assume that the mission of a Catholic school would preclude engaging in broad conversations and considerations of GSD. This teacher helps her students engage scripture and GSD as a means of "exploring questions of personal integrity, ethical decision-making, and social justice."

Teachers in different disciplines who want to collaborate on CI projects can use CIGSD to compare teaching and competency goals. For example, students might investigate gender bias from scientific, historical and literary perspectives. The

Integrating Gender and Sexuality Diversity Issues Across Grade Level and Subject Matter

Grade _____ Subject(s) _____

> **Your School Mission Here**

1. In what ways do you already address issues of GENDER (identity, roles, expression) in your curriculum?

2. In what ways do you already address issues of SEXUALITY (identity, orientation, behavior) in your curriculum?

3. What materials (books, videos, workbooks, posters) do you already make use of in your classroom?

4. What are your primary pedagogical goals with the particular lessons or curricula you use? (list each "lesson" and relevant goals: providing factual information; teaching research skills; comparing/contrasting groups in a historical context; fostering empathy; multicultural competence etc.)

5. How might you integrate GSD into your existing curricula?

6. What additional lessons or goals do you need to incorporate into your curriculum in order to engage with GSD?

7. What materials and resources would help you implement these pedagogical goals?

Diagram 7.3.

Integrating Gender and Sexuality Diversity Issues Across Grade Level and Subject Matter

Grade _8_   Subject(s) _Religious Studies_

1. In what ways do you already address issues of GENDER (identity, roles, expression) in your curriculum?

We also discuss gender of God as expressed in Genesis 1: 26-27: Then God said: "Let us make man in our image, after our likeness. Let them have dominion over the fish of the sea, the birds of the air, and the cattle, and over all the wild animals and all the creatures that crawl on the ground." God created man in his image; in the divine image he created him; male and female he created them. This passage emphasizes that all human beings, both male and female (not just male) are created in the image and likeness of God, in the divine image. It also infers that maleness and femaleness (not just maleness) are part of the identity of God (in order for humans to be created as such, in God's likeness).

2. In what ways do you already address issues of SEXUALITY (identity, orientation, behavior) in your curriculum?

In our section on sexuality, much of our discussion is placed in the context of decision-making and moral decision-making. We don't approach sexual orientation as a decision that a person makes so much as an aspect of that person's identity. We use the moral framework about chastity provided by our religious tradition as a guide in the discussion about sexuality. It is part of our obligation to present this framework. At the same time, we allow students to think critically about this framework and whether it speaks to all experiences, including those in same-sex relationships. For example, we ask students to research church teaching and to become fluent in this. At the same time we ask them to research an alternative point of view and to be an articulate advocate of that view. They are required to present both of these views to the class. Finally, they are asked to write a position paper stating their own viewpoint regarding the issue and turn it in to the teacher. It is in this position paper that they are asked to grapple with any gaps that they might experience between what the church teaches and what they believe to be morally correct with regard to sexuality, orientation and behavior.

3. What materials (books, videos, workbooks, posters) do you already make use of in your classroom?

We are limited here and would like some better resources. Most religious education materials address GSD as a "difficult issue" and we spend a lot of class time deconstructing and reframing those resources.

During Ally Week we approached the concept of Jesus as Ally. We used scriptural images and passages that emphasized the table fellowship of Jesus and His efforts to be inclusive as a model of solidarity and anti-bias.

Diagram 7.4.

biology, history, and English teachers use the CIGSD assessment tool as a starting point in identifying ways to overlap, link, and supplement their course goals, learning objectives, and materials.

What About Content?

Whether you are teaching percentages, masculine forms of Spanish pronouns, genetics, or Greek history, the links to GSD are there if you want to pursue them. In truth there are very few subjects that do not relate to gender and sexuality in some way. CI themes can be drawn from

- Existing subject curriculum (e.g., Middle Ages, myths and legends, technology, poetry)
- Major social issues (e.g., environment, poverty, prejudice)
- Personal concerns of students (e.g., who am I?, getting along with others)
- Process concepts (e.g., cycles, systems)
- Appealing topics (e.g., love, inventions, movies)

Again, your CIGSD assessment will reveal natural areas for GSD integration or enhancement.

If We Integrate, Will They Listen?

Teachers often wonder what students are actually paying attention to in a given class or subject. It can be frustrating to discover that the "content" of a lesson has eluded them completely, yet they do remember what they had for lunch the period before (see The Story of the Dangling Modifier). However, when the conversation is about gender and sexuality, most students pay attention. After all, these issues are highly pertinent to the developmental experience they are right smack in the middle of.

They may remember the science behind gender bias more effectively when it becomes part of understanding their own narrative. Analyzing the role of gender in relation to technology or political science may affect career choices and professional aspirations. Interviewing adults of various genders about their own employment and professional history allows students to "see" possibilities. Integrating GSD into any lesson or project instantly establishes "relevance" for adolescents.

The Story of the Dangling Modifier

One of the problems with teaching is that it's hard to know when you are good. How do you know when you've been successful? Here's a typical example, one from last year. Seniors had just gotten back drafts of papers with my corrections. I asked if they had any questions, any questions at all. A girl, Emma, raised her hand eagerly. "I've never understood what a dangling modifier is," she complained. I leapt upon this opportunity as if I were a starving coyote. After almost twenty years of teaching, I knew dangling modifiers cold. I spontaneously composed witty sentences to write on the board; I was clear and made the explanation simple, but simultaneously revealed the subtle and logical beauty of English grammar. I did this in six minutes flat. I brushed chalk from my hands and smiled. "Does that answer your question, Emma?" Emma jerked her head up. I repeated, "Does that answer your question?" "Oh, I don't know," she said. "I wasn't listening."

—Mary Burchenal, English Department Chair, Brookline High School
(Excerpted from her speech "Re-Imagining Success" upon acceptance of the
Caverly Committee Award: Exceptional Achievement and
Contributions to the Public Schools of Brookline, Massachusetts)

CURRICULUM INTEGRATION: PROJECT MODELS

A comprehensive review of all the ways GSD can be integrated into existing or new curricula is worthy of an entire book. Here are two examples of the CI approach that are designed to model a range of possibilities. Hopefully they will inspire application of GSD curriculum integration in your own subject area. Read through the project. Assess its various components, as well as the project as a whole. Look for links to materials, themes, and competency goals that already exist in your curriculum. The GSD-related learning opportunities that exist in this model are reviewed at the end of the project outline.

Curriculum Integration, Model One

Middle School Project:
"Watch What You Read! Books, Students, Censorship"

Efforts to protect children and young adults have brought the censorship debate into school and public libraries throughout the country. Parents and school boards have subjected children's literature to the closest scrutiny, with the frequent result of challenging concepts, words, and illustrations. Successful objections have resulted in the removal of books from classrooms, library shelves, and reading lists. In other districts, schools have imposed limitations on access by placing books in restricted areas available only to children with parental approval.

—Censored: Wielding the Red Pen—"Through the Eyes of a Child"
University of Virginia Library, Special Collections[6]

I.   **Overview:** Throughout the school year, eighth grade students will read a series of classic, age-appropriate books that have a history of being banned. In addition to studying and completing assignments based on individual texts, students will examine the causes and consequences of censorship. Students will be responsible for conducting research, writing personal and persuasive essays, collaborating in groups, and presenting material orally and visually on the theme of Books, Students, Censorship.

II.   **Core Standards:**[7]

    A. **Reading:** The emphasis is on text complexity and the growth of comprehension. What students read and how they read it matters. Over the course of the year, students will be challenged to create more connections between texts and among ideas.

    B. **Writing:** The emphasis is on responding to reading and researching ideas. Students will be required to write in (1) narrative, (2) explanatory, and (3) persuasive styles.

    C. **Speaking and Listening:** The emphasis is on flexible communication and collaboration in the class as a whole and in small groups. The oral communication and interpersonal skills involved in small group work helps students (a) express and listen to ideas, (b) integrate information, (c) evaluate what they hear, and (d) synthesize data from a range of sources.

III.   **Central Questions:**

    A. What role does censorship of books play in American society?

    B. In particular, what is the (intended) impact of preventing students from reading certain books?

    C. Have the types of books censored changed in the past fifty years?

    D. Is there any merit to banning books?

IV. **Warm-ups:**

    A. **Word Search/Brainstorm (Individual Task)**

        1. Search the words "ban" and "censor." Record definitions, synonyms, antonyms, related words.

        2. Brainstorm[8] all the issues you think might cause a book to be banned. (Graphic 7.3)

    B. **Book Cover Collage (Small Group Activity)**

        1. Examine the banned book covers and try to guess when the books were published. Place them in chronological order. Identify the clues and cues you used to guess the date of publication.

        2. Create a collage of the banned book covers. (Note: book covers included in this miniproject are not all on the class reading list, yet they have all been banned at one time.)

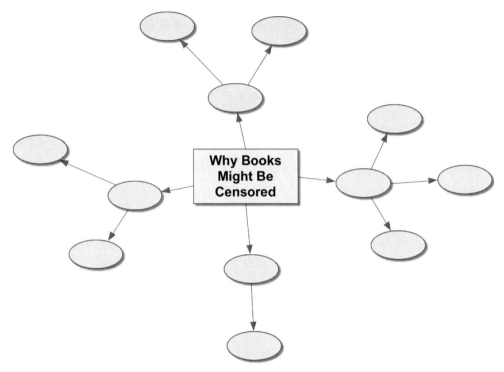

Graphic 7.3.

   C. Quick Writes (Individual Activity)
     1. View another small group's collage and jot down your impressions (thoughts, feelings, observations, associations, questions).
     2. Repeat until you have viewed three different collages.
     3. Make a list of the titles that intrigue you and spark curiosity about the cause for censorship.
   D. Share Quick Write (Pairs)
     1. Share your quick writes with a partner. Take turns reading and listening.
   E. What I Know/Want to Know/Learned (Whole Class)
     Materials: Index cards of different colors and sizes and a large piece of poster board or classroom wall. Using index cards allows for flexibility in adding and modifying the diagram over time as more books are read and/or new questions and ideas emerge.
     • As a class, begin to create a KWL diagram to track knowledge, questions, and learning. (Graphic 7.4)
  V. Related (Social Studies): First Amendment Review
     Understanding the First Amendment is critical to the study of banned books (Graphic 7.5). Researching the First Amendment could be part of a Social Studies lesson that is linked to the Language Arts banned book project.

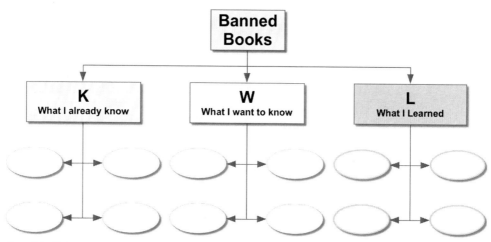

Graphic 7.4.

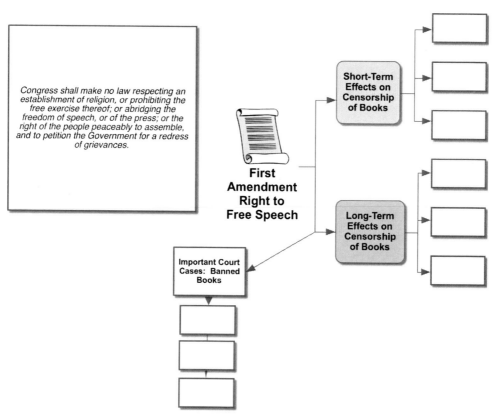

Graphic 7.5.

VI.   **Related (Science):** The Scopes Trial

   A. Researching the Scopes Trial in Science class will allow students to learn about another form of school-based censorship. The 1925 Scopes Trial is an important reference point in the "science versus religion" debate; students will also discover that the controversy over the teaching of "evolution versus creationism" in high school Biology classes is alive and well in the twenty-first century.

   B. Students watch the film *Inherit The Wind* and write a response paper (questions provided) that is turned in for both Science and English class.

VII. **Activities (Individual and Group)**
   Reading List:

   Annie on My Mind, Nancy Garden
   Raisin in the Sun, Lorraine Hansberry
   Catcher in the Rye, J.D. Salinger
   To Kill a Mockingbird, Harper Lee
   The Misfits, James Howe
   The Lord of the Flies, William Golding
   Anne Frank: The Diary of a Young Girl, Anne Frank

   For each of these seven books students are responsible for completing the activities listed below. Due dates for activities will be posted on the board in class. Small groups (SG) will meet periodically to share information and responses. SGs will also brainstorm ideas for the Group Presentation at the end of the term.

   A. **Preview Activity:** "Questions before Answers"

   Creating interest and stimulating curiosity *before* beginning to read the assigned text enhances comprehension and engagement.

   1. Before reading the book, use your Personal Journal to write a list of questions you have about the story, the author, and/or the topic. If you have heard about the book before, use that information to generate additional questions.

   2. Repeat this process at the beginning of each new chapter. Use the Chapter Summary Graphic Organizer (CSGO) to keep track of and describe the major/minor characters, setting, and plot thus far (Graphic 7.6). Identify the most important facts, ideas, symbols, metaphors. NB: There will be weekly quizzes on this material. Completing the CSGO will help you prepare!

   3. What questions do you have at this particular point in the story? What or who are you most curious about? Do you have predictions? Write these on the CSGO too.

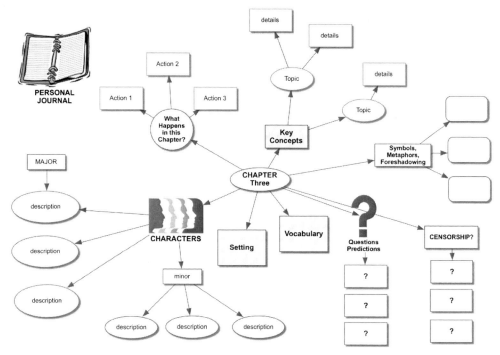

Graphic 7.6.

B. Reading Activities: Active Reading; Selective Highlighting

1. Students read with pencil or highlighter in hand, noting vocabulary words, important ideas, significant quotations, descriptions, material that may be related to censorship. Effective highlighting (reviewed in class) will make chapter summaries and journaling easier.

C. Writing Activities: Personal Journal (PJ)—Entries for each chapter

1. The PJ is a place to record your own experiences, ideas, feelings in relationship to what you are reading in the book. There may be characters with whom you identify or ideas with which you disagree. This is the place to respond personally and thoughtfully to the material. NB: Journals turned in on Fridays, returned on Mondays, unless directed otherwise.

D. Research Activity: Censorship Interview

1. When the class is finished reading a book, one small group will conduct a censorship interview about that book. (Interview questions will be generated by the whole class at the beginning of the term.) The goal is to gather information about (1) student, faculty, and family member familiarity with the text, (2) awareness

of censorship issues, (3) opinions about whether or not the book should be banned in schools.

2. At the end of the year, we will analyze the data from all the censorship surveys and create a visual representation of findings to be posted in the central hallway by the main office.

VIII. Compare and Contrast Reasons for Censorship (Small Group)

Each small group (SG) is assigned two books to compare/contrast in relationship to censorship (Graphic 7.7). Each SG will give a 5-minute presentation on the observations made and conclusions drawn via the Compare/Contrast task.

IX. Individual Essay

Use the Persuasive Essay guidelines to write your paper (separate handout; review in class). It is important to

- present your argument clearly.
- use facts from multiple sources to support your opinion.
- offer a convincing rationale.
- address opposing points of view.
- conclude by summarizing your thesis and underscoring relevance of topic.

A list of paper topics will be provided. You may select a different topic; however, you *must* okay the topic with me before you start the paper.

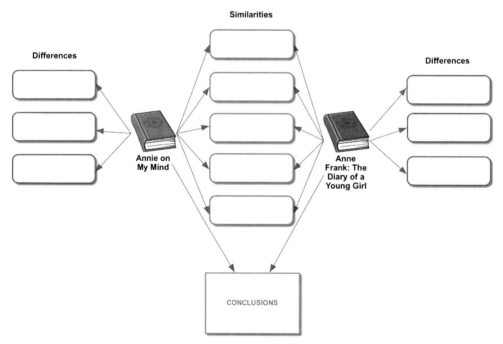

Graphic 7.7.

X. Group Project

As a group you are responsible for presenting your learning in relation to the central questions of the Books, Students, Censorship project. Presentations will be 10–12 minutes long. Your presentation should *not* summarize the texts! Present your learning as a means of supporting the conclusion(s) you have made about the banning of books in school. You must also provide a written summary of the presentation.

Your presentation will be evaluated in terms of

- Coherence
- Organization
- Effective use of medium
- Quantity and quality of "learning" presented
- Integration of ideas, themes, materials from variety of sources
- Equal participation of all members of the group
- Creativity

XI. Going Further

A. Students write a newspaper-style editorial about the recent banning of children's books that depict Gender and Sexuality Diversity themes. Select one of the books below and

- research the history of the book being banned.
- explain the rationale behind the censorship.
- present an argument that either supports or refutes the banning of the book.

And Tango Makes Three, Justin Richardson

King and King, Linda De Haan

Luv Ya Bunches, Lauren Myracle

Gender and Sexuality Diversity Learning

Discussions about censorship revolve around fundamental questions: What is threatening about this story? What makes this book dangerous? What will happen if children and adolescents read these books? As Barbara Miner notes in her article "Reading, Writing and Censorship: When Good Books Can Get Schools in Trouble," appraising the function and legitimacy of censorship requires the critical thinking skills we want students to learn.

> If certain books are avoided because they are controversial, how does that undercut what should be one of the central purposes of education—to help students learn to critically evaluate and make informed decisions about controversial issues so they can become full participants in this country's civic and political life? (Miner 1998)

Students need the tools to evaluate controversies that lead to the suppression of literature, art, or political dissent.

How does the Watch What You Read! Books, Students, Censorship project create learning opportunities related to GSD? In each of these books the main characters struggle with forming, claiming, rejecting, and integrating essential aspects of identity. Gender and sexuality are central to that struggle, and to understand Liza in *Annie on My Mind* or Anne Frank in her diary is to bear witness to their coming of age as girls, as young women, and as sexual people. Joe Bunch, a gay eighth grader, is painfully attuned to bias against those who are "different." He and his friends seek acceptance in *The Misfits*, while the boys on the island in *Lord of the Flies* grapple with masculine identity and use scapegoating as a primitive means of survival.

Exploring the arguments for banning these works of literature leads students directly into the social and cultural fray:

- Adolescent sexuality is a threat to propriety.
- Gender role expectations must be adhered to.
- GLBTQI identities are not well understood.
- Racial conflicts are inevitably incendiary.

The notion that students should not read and learn about these "truths" is fraught with adult anxiety and misgivings. Keeping students in the dark about themselves (the main characters in most of these books are adolescents) and about the (bio) diversity of the human species is a flawed attempt at "protecting" them. Banning books promotes ignorance and prejudice over knowledge and acceptance.

The struggle for acceptance and the search for self are at the heart of these narratives, and it is this same heart center that grabs the attention of most middle school students. They understand about searching; they relate to fears of rejection. The adolescent who is prodded to "be himself," understands that self-definition and self-determination are not always that easy to achieve. Many of these titles are already on MS reading lists. Thoughtful, in-depth discussions about these books and their authors must include careful considerations of gender and sexuality.

Curriculum Integration, Model Two

High School Project:
"Seventy-Seven Cents to the Dollar: Women and Jobs"

Because of its complexity, understanding gender requires careful study. Ironically, though gender identity development is central to adolescence, it is only studied toward the end of that period, if at all, and only by the select few who attend college and are exposed to feminist theory in one form or another. Yet middle and high school language arts classes—not to mention math, science and history—are replete with gender dramas that would allow for critical discussion on this topic. But who would hold that discussion? And how far would they take it? (Nakkula and Toshalis 2006, 113–14)

I. **Overview:** Using national and local newspapers, students will examine the theme of Women and Jobs. By reading various forms of newspaper-based information (e.g., articles, editorials, letters to the editor) over various sections (e.g., National news, Local news, Sports, Business, Entertainment, Obituaries) students will be able to compare and contrast (1) news formats, (2) sources, and (3) content related to women and employment. Students will be responsible for (a) research, (b) writing, (c) group collaboration, and (d) oral presentations on assigned and chosen topics related to the theme of Women and Jobs.

II. **Core Standards:**
The new core standards aim to prepare students for college level work. In this Women and Jobs project students (1) summarize and analyze informational texts, (2) create broad interpretations based on multiple sources of data, and (3) present findings orally, visually, and in writing.

III. **Central Questions:**
   A. Over the past fifty years and at present, how did/does gender impact the role of women in the world of work?
   B. What incidents and outcomes reflect the unique experience of women being "on the job" in the United States between 1961 and 2011?
   C. What are the differences and similarities in National versus Local news coverage of these issues?
   D. How do the different formats and sections of a newspaper influence the presentation and impact of "news" in this subject area?

IV. **Warm-ups:**
   A. **Finding Out about Newspapers (Group Task)**
      1. Identify the different sections and writing formats typically found in national and local newspapers.
      2. Define key characteristics and functions of each format.
   B. **Quick Write (Individual Task)**
      1. Jot down your ideas quickly in response to words read out loud (e.g., *woman, job, gender, career, advancement, bias, salary, awards*)
      2. "I want to know (select eight things) about women and jobs."
   C. **Share Quick Writes (In Pairs from Small Group)**
V. **Read Obituary of Jean Bartik Together as a Class**
   A. Students complete the Text-to-Self, Text-to-Text, Text-to-World handout 10 (TS/TT/TW).
   B. As a class, complete a KWL chart based on the Bartik obituary. (Graphic 7.8)

Box 7.4.

Jean Bartik, Software Pioneer, Dies at 86
by Steve Lohr

Jean Jennings Bartik, one of the first computer programmers and a pioneering forerunner in a technology that came to be known as software, died on March 23 at a nursing home in Poughkeepsie, N.Y. She was 86.

The cause was congestive heart disease, her son, Timothy Bartik, said.

Ms. Bartik was the last surviving member of the group of women who programmed the Eniac, or Electronic Numerical Integrator and Computer, which is credited as the first all-electronic digital computer.

The Eniac, designed to calculate the firing trajectories for artillery shells, turned out to be a historic demonstration project. It was completed in 1946, too late for use in World War II, but was a milestone in the evolution of modern computing.

When the Eniac was shown off at the University of Pennsylvania in February 1946, it generated headlines in newspapers across the country. But the attention was all on the men and the machine. The women were not even introduced at the event.

"For years, we celebrated the people who built it, not the people who programmed it," said David Alan Grier, a technology historian at George Washington University and a senior vice president of the IEEE Computer Society.

The oversight has been somewhat redressed in recent years, and Ms. Bartik, in particular, received professional recognition as a result. Ms. Bartik and Frances Elizabeth Holberton, who died in 2001, were the lead programmers among the small team of women who worked on the Eniac.

In 2009, Ms. Bartik received a Pioneer Award from the IEEE Computer Society, and in 2008 she was named a fellow by the Computer History Museum in Mountain View, Calif.

The Eniac women were wartime recruits with math skills, whose job was initially described as plugging in wires to "set up the machine." But converting the math analysis into a process that made sense to the machine, so that a calculation could flow through the electronic circuitry to completion, proved to be a daunting challenge.

"These women, being the first to enter this new territory, were the first to encounter the whole question of programming," said Paul E. Ceruzzi, a computer historian at the Smithsonian Institution. "And they met the challenge."

Betty Jean Jennings was born on Dec. 27, 1924, in rural Missouri, the sixth of seven children in a farm family whose parents valued education, said her son. She attended Northwest Missouri State Teachers College, now Northwest Missouri State University, majoring in math.

Her faculty adviser saw an advertisement in a math journal in 1945 that said the Army was recruiting math graduates for a wartime project in Philadelphia. She applied, was accepted and told to come quickly. She got on the next train, according to her son. "She wanted adventure, and she got it," he said.

In Philadelphia, while working on the Eniac, she dropped the use of the first name Betty, which she never liked, her son said. And down the hall at the University of Pennsylvania, she met William Bartik, an engineer working on another Pentagon project. They were married in 1946. (They divorced in 1968.)

After the war, Ms. Bartik joined the Eniac designers, John Presper Eckert and John W. Mauchly, in their effort to develop the Univac, an early commercial computer, which was introduced in 1951. While at the Eckert-Mauchly Computer Corporation—acquired by Remington Rand in 1950—Ms. Bartik worked on hardware and software for both the Binac, a small computer made for Northrop Aircraft, and the general purpose Univac.

Ms. Bartik called working with the Eckert-Mauchly team on the Eniac and later the Univac a "technical Camelot," a tight-knit group advancing the frontiers of computing.

"This was the most exciting time in her life," said Kathy Kleiman, a technology policy lawyer who has been making a documentary film about the women who programmed Eniac.

Ms. Bartik left the computer industry in 1951 to raise her three children and returned to it in 1967. After holding a series of jobs in programming, training and technical publishing, she was laid off in 1985 as she was nearing 61 and could not find another job in the industry.

"There's a lot of age discrimination, then and now, and I see it in my research," said Mr. Bartik, a labor economist.

For the next 25 years Ms. Bartik was a real estate agent in New Jersey.
*   Besides her son, of Kalamazoo, Mich., Ms. Bartik is survived by two daughters, Mary Williams of Long Beach, Calif., and Jane Bartik of Poughkeepsie.*

Source: Steve Lohr. Jean Bartik, software pioneer, dies at 86. *New York Times,* April 7, 2011, http://www.nytimes.com/2011/04/08/business/08bartik.html

VI. Find Articles (Group Task)
   A. Each small group (SG) is assigned a decade.
   B. Choose a single edition of a national paper and a local paper to review.
   C. Select articles related to topic of "Women and Jobs" from the papers.
   D. Assign one article/letter/obituary/editorial from the national and one from the local paper to each member of the group.
   E. By reading the title and briefly skimming the article, generate three or four questions about each piece of informational text (see Graphic 7.9).

VII. Read Articles (Individual Task)
   A. Members read assigned articles, one from national and one from local paper individually.
   B. Collect vocabulary and define words.
   C. Complete a TS/TT/TW handout and a KWL chart for each article.
   D. Members present articles to small group, using Q/A graphic.

Example: Articles Related to Women and Jobes

From the *New York Times* April 7, 2011
Article: *At Yale, Sharper Look at Treatment of Women*

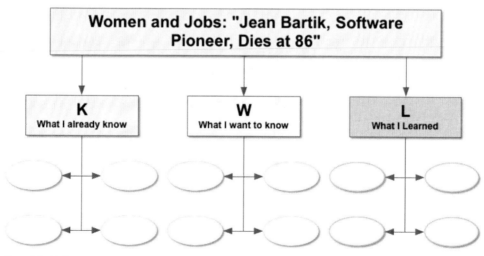

Graphic 7.8.

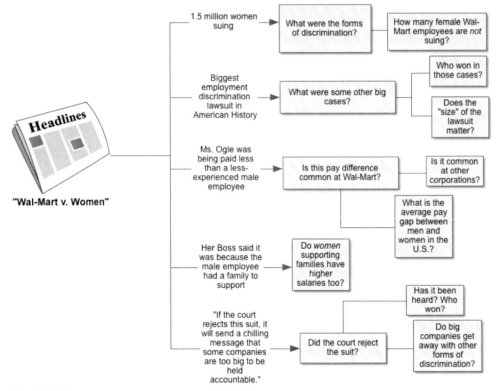

Graphic 7.9.

Letters to the Editor: *The Doctor Is In . . . or Maybe She Isn't*
Editorial: *Wal-Mart v. Women*
Obituary: *Jean Bartik*
NY/Region: *A 45-Year-Old Apprentice, Holding Her Own*
Metro: *Prostitutes' Disappearances Noticed Only When First Bodies Were Found*
Sports: *After Long Fight for Inclusion, Women's Ski Jumping Gains Olympic Status*
Home: *A New Cottage in New Orleans with Katrina Patina*
Styles: *As Days Grow Longer, So Do Hems*

VIII. Compare and Contrast Articles (Pairs in Group)
   A. Working in pairs, select two articles to compare/contrast. Comparisons should be about formats of text (e.g., opinion vs. article) and about content (e.g., power, ingenuity).
   B. Complete Compare/Contrast worksheet.
   C. Pairs present findings to group.
IX. Mid-project Review (Group Task)
   A. Review all the work done to date in group.
   B. Pool vocabulary and definitions to create master list.

    C. Use the TS/TT/TW handouts, KWL charts, and Q/A Graphic to identify themes, trends, and patterns that have emerged.

    D. Create a visual representation of these themes, trends, patterns.

    E. Choose a paper topic based on these themes.

    F. Preview group presentation ideas.

X.   **Individual Essay**

Use the Persuasive Essay guidelines to write your paper. It is important to (1) present your argument clearly, (2) use facts from multiple sources to support your opinion, (3) offer a convincing rationale, (4) address opposing points of view, and (5) conclude by summarizing argument and underscoring relevance of topic.

XI.   **Group Project**

As a group you are responsible for presenting your learning in relation to the central questions of the Women and Jobs project. You can "present" in any manner you wish: traditional PowerPoint, fishbowl discussion, skit(s) involving the women studied, panel discussion, video interviews, etc. Your presentation will be evaluated in terms of

- Coherence
- Organization
- Effective use of medium
- Creativity
- Quantity and quality of "learning" presented
- Integration of ideas, themes, materials from variety of sources
- Equal participation of all members of the group

XII. **Going Further**

    A. Invite students to write a letter to the editor of a national or local newspaper to share their learnings from the Women and Jobs project.

    B. Invite students to write a letter to one of the women they studied during the project to share their learning and ask questions.

    C. Invite students to write a letter to a future employer about the impact of the Women and Jobs project on their views of "work" and their career ambitions.

XIII. Going Further; Staying Local

    ❖ *We have two plaques in our lobby—one containing Summa Cum Laude recipients (senior with highest GPA), and the other containing school presidents—elected by the student body. The first, almost all girls. The second, almost all boys—going back 20 years or more. Neither position necessarily represents the heart and soul of the school, but they're celebrated on these public plaques. I would love to get to a place where girls who wished to, could lead in school culture in ways that are public, acknowledged, respected—where girls could be funny regularly.*

Students can engage this "local" manifestation of a "gender and jobs" conundrum and apply their learning from the project to analyze this pattern at the school. The class then shares their learning in a public forum (school assembly; parents night; school committee; trustee weekend) via a mixed media presentation that may include video, music, interviews, photography.

Gender and Sexuality Diversity Learning

In the epigraph at the beginning of the "Seventy-Seven Cents to the Dollar: Women and Jobs" project Nakkula and Toshalis (2006) assert that the typical high school curriculum is replete with "gender dramas" worthy of critical study. The obstacle to engaging issues of GSD is not "the curriculum" per se. Which teacher will pursue this course of study? How far will he take the inquiry? Imagine the protests of the male students: *Why aren't we studying men and jobs too? Why are we only looking at women?* Sound familiar? *Why are we spending so much time learning about black people? Why are we reading all these books about gays?*

In fact the "Women and Jobs" focus includes all manner of questions about how men and women have operated in the workforce for over fifty years. In the same way that studying people of color is also a study of the dominant white race, any inquiry about gender and sexuality "includes" all genders and sexualities. The challenge is to make the inclusion and exclusion explicit. Critical inquiry in the Women and Jobs project uncovers the dynamics of power that are as relevant in students' lives today as they were yesterday. Students are invited to understand and actively participate in the still-unfolding history of women's search for equity in the workplace.

From the outset, the project demonstrates the ubiquity of "gender" as a topic; students have no difficulty finding relevant informational texts in every section of the newspaper, any day of the week, any month, any year. The obituary of Jean Bartik sets the stage for understanding the ways women's contributions to science, technology, medicine, athletics, and so on have been made invisible throughout history. When students think about "computers" today, it is unlikely that they have ever heard of Jean Bartik or Alan Turing—Bartik because of her gender and Turing because of his sexuality.

The "Going Further; Staying Local" option brings GSD right into the current school community. Looking at local gender dynamics is rarely an easy course of inquiry. In the same way that GLBTQI adults serve as role models of possibilities and struggles, women in schools model their own gender and power battles, however implicit or explicit they may be. When students begin thinking critically about these issues, adults must too. A teacher quoted at the beginning of section 1 in this chapter identifies the challenge: *It requires me to take time to really think about my own experiences and views before engaging [students] in discussion. It takes a lot of reflection and preparation time.*

Identify the biggest obstacles to integrating GSD explicitly into your classroom/discipline/division. What concepts or strategies from this chapter could you apply that would help integrate GSD into your curriculum?

NOTES

1. Middle school is broadly defined here to include any combination of sixth, seventh, and eighth grade.

2. In his in-depth study of one school district's battle over enumeration and inclusion, Macgillivray (2004) uses the term "morally conservative" to describe those who oppose adopting a nondiscrimination policy that includes sexual orientation. I use the term similarly here.

3. Intersectionality is a theory that challenges the classical conceptualizations of oppression within society, such as homophobia, racism, and sexism. These forms of oppression do not act independently of one another; instead they create a system of oppression that reflects the "intersection" of multiple forms of discrimination (Knudsen 2005).

4. This video is part of the It Takes a Team! Educational Kit, available here at http://www.womenssportsfoundation.org/home/advocate/know-your-rights/coach-and-athletic-director-resources/about-itat.

5. A comprehensive review of CI is not possible here. See James A. Beane. Curriculum integration: Designing the core of a democratic education (New York: Teachers College Press, 1997).

6. http://www2.lib.virginia.edu/exhibits/censored/child.html.

7. See Common Core State Standards for English Language Arts and Literacy in History/Social Studies, Science, and Technical Subjects, at http://www.corestandards.org/assets/CCSSI_ELA%20Standards.pdf.

8. There are many different graphic organizers available online. Some of these images in this chapter were created using Inspiration, at http://www.inspiration.com/Inspiration.

9. See Common Core State Standards for English Language Arts and Literacy in History/Social Studies, Science, and Technical Subjects, at http://www.corestandards.org/assets/CCSSI_ELA%20Standards.pdf.

10. http://www.nytimes.com/learning/teachers/studentactivity/ConnectingToWorld.pdf.

8

COMPREHENSIVE HEALTH AND SEXUALITY EDUCATION

Providing Foundations for GSD Literacy

After all, as a culture we virtually worship knowledge about practically every other aspect of human existence. Truly, all we really need to do to bring sexuality education into the 21st Century is decide to apply the same standards to learning about sexuality—Knowledge is good! Knowledge is the cornerstone of responsibility! Knowledge is the key to a fulfilling life!—as we do all others.

—Deborah Roffman, Sexuality Educator, the Park School

❖ *Sexuality, in general, is a topic that should be part of the curriculum at every grade, but it is not. We still have the "puberty talk" once each year and a unit about "the body." That's pretty much all we do.*
➢ *We talk about it for one health class, and that's about it.*

Curricula and programs related to health and sexuality go by many different names and vary widely in their scope and depth. This chapter emphasizes curricula that provide students of every age with comprehensive health and wellness education (CHW) and/or comprehensive sexuality education (CSE). Health and sexuality education is central to supporting healthy identity development in children and adolescents. As sexuality educator and author Deborah Roffman[1] contends, "Knowledge is the cornerstone of responsibility," and providing preK–12 students with CHW and CSE gives them an abundance of ways to "grow up" responsibly (Roffman 2001).

Comprehensive Health and Wellness

In its use here CHW refers to curricula in early childhood and elementary education (ECEE) that teach students about topics such as (a) safety, (b) friendships, (c) hygiene, (d) communication skills, (e) conflict resolution, and (e) human diversity, including gender and sexuality diversity (GSD). It makes sense developmentally to begin this education with our very youngest children; daily they are immersed in tasks that promote physical, emotional, and social well-being. These topics and tasks are typically imbedded in the preschool and elementary social curriculum, as well as in standard units of classroom study (see chapter 6).

It is also possible to create a freestanding CHW curriculum, such as the one offered by Charles River School in Dover, Massachusetts (see box 8.1). The Health and Wellness program is self-contained but not isolated from the rest of the curriculum. For example, talking about "sameness and difference" can be applied to a unit on Animal Families and continued in conversations about human families. Exploring gender stereotypes becomes part of the Native American Cultures unit, and the study of Martin Luther King Jr. serves as the catalyst for discussions about human diversity and conflict resolution. Integrating CHW with other areas of study is good pedagogy; it allows students to establish a broad foundation from which to understand Self, Other, and the World.

Comprehensive Sexuality Education

Comprehensive sexuality education educates students about all matters relating to sexuality and its expression. In addition to reproductive anatomy and birth control methods, CSE also covers topics such as intimate relationships, gender roles, social pressure to be sexually active, media literacy, personal and sexual safety, communication skills, and values clarification. Schools that offer CHW and/or CSE are well positioned to address GSD in all its forms, in a context that includes informational and transformational opportunities for learning.

Teaching ABCs; Teaching the Birds and the Bees

If you are a preschool teacher, it is not unusual to field questions such as these: *Why do boys have a penis and girls don't? Where do babies come from? Why does Sylvia have two moms? Why does Sydney act like a girl when he is a boy?* (see The Story of the School Photo). While some teachers feel steady and comfortable answering such inquiries, many do not. As suggested in other parts of this book, teachers have not been authorized or adequately trained to engage students in matter-of-fact learning about GSD.

Box 8.1.   Charles River School, Dover, MA: PreK–8 Health and Wellness Curriculum

Prekindergarten
- Respect for Oneself and Others
- Families
- Awareness of Feelings
- Taking Care of Your Body
- Hygiene
- School Safety
- Medicines and Safe Use
- Personal Safety Skills
- How We Grow

Kindergarten
- Friendship
- Expressing Feelings
- Differences
- Manners
- Individual Development
- Personal Hygiene
- Loss, Emotions
- Personal Safety Skills
- School Safety
- Conflict Resolution

First Grade
- Self-Esteem
- Communication Skills
- Conflict Resolution
- Developing Individual Responsibility
- Families
- Physical Anatomy
- Nutrition
- Hygiene
- Managing Physical Aggression
- Personal Safety Issues
- Emergency Procedures

Second Grade
- Self-Esteem
- Understanding and Respecting Differences
- Social Competency
- Conflict Resolution
- Personal Differences in Development
- Hygiene
- Communication Skills

Third Grade
- Conflict Resolution
- Respecting Differences
- Family Diversity
- Gender Stereotypes
- Positive Leadership

Fourth Grade
- Human Diversity
- Diversity of Families
- Teasing, Put-downs
- Stereotypes and Prejudice
- Health and Fitness
- Group Skills
- Death, Loss, Grief
- Personal Safety
- Decision Making and Peer Pressure
- Conflict Resolution
- Positive Leadership

Fifth Grade
- Relationships
- Friendships
- Family Diversity
- Social Competency
- Positive Leadership
- Aging, Death
- Reproduction
- Peer Pressure and Decision-making Strategies

Sixth Grade
- Friendships, Peer Pressure, Decision Making
- Patterns of Abuse, Harassment
- Homophobia
- Human Body Systems
- Internal Organs
- Gender Differences and Bias
- Alcohol and Other Drugs

Seventh/Eighth Grade
- Emotional Well-Being throughout Adolescence
- Communication with Peers, Building Peer Support Systems
- Sexual Harassment/Bullying
- Nutrition
- First Aid
- Eating Disorders/Body Image
- Sexually Transmitted Diseases
- Human Sexuality
- Chemical Dependency and Resources for Help
- Personal Body Safety and Abuse
- Media Literacy
- Internet Safety
- Knowing Self and Others
- Leadership

❖ *After 20 years of teaching I am finally comfortable initiating and navigating conversations with my preschoolers about dressing up in whatever clothes they wish, exploring what it's like to play someone of a different gender, gender roles, acceptance of difference, etc. They are some of the richest and most validating conversations I have as a teacher.*

As this teacher observes, it took a long time to feel at ease with this aspect of her teaching. Most ECEE teachers do not enter the profession thinking about the day when a student calls out loudly during circle, "Is it true that if you don't have a penis then you're not a boy?!"

The Story of the School Photo

It was second grade, and Sydney was already fairly depressed and her hair was pretty long and shaggy for a boy. This drove her teacher crazy. During school photos that year, they were offering girls a flower to hold for the photo, but boys didn't get anything. Sydney asked the photographer if she could hold the flower for her photo, and the photographer was willing, but her teacher freaked out. She said that Sydney's parents would never want to pay for that kind of photo and it would be a waste of money. Sydney was heartbroken and also somewhat angry at the double standard. (Parents had never been informed of any flower option of course, or I would have said something.) In the end the photographer offered to take the normal "boy" pictures and add an additional free photo of Sydney with the flower. Guess which picture she is actually smiling in?

—Mother of a transgender elementary student

Teaching MS and HS; (Still) Teaching the Birds and the Bees

Similarly in middle school (MS) and high school (HS) everyone counts on the health teacher—if the school is lucky enough to have one—to provide all the information students need about "sex" and answer all questions about "sex." Faculty are relieved that it is the health teacher who must contend with describing sexually transmitted diseases, explaining premature ejaculation, and conducting a condom demonstration with a banana. *You couldn't pay me to teach that stuff*, most educators say. Only the steady school nurse can handle the details about what actually goes on in "health class."

Misperceptions about the content of comprehensive sexuality education are epic, and unfortunately there is a whole lot less going on in the realm of CSE than legend would have it. First, the number of schools without any CSE at all is startling. Second, many of the programs that do exist are spotty and incomplete. Third, most subject teachers know very little about the (a) content, (b) purpose, and (c) value of whatever CSE *is* in place.

❖ *I think they get the "plumbing talk" in 5th grade.*
❖ *I think some group comes in and does a presentation about drugs for the 8th graders.*
❖ *We had several 9th grade girls get pregnant last year and now there's a program of some kind.*
❖ *I don't really know what the students are taught, but I know there was a big uproar last year about the school nurse providing condoms.*

Classroom teachers not only need to be knowledgeable about the content and role of CSE in the overall curriculum but they also need to advocate for its existence.

Health class is often perceived as "soft" in terms of academic significance; it is typically one of the first items on the budgetary chopping block when cuts are in store. Yet if you consider the major developmental tasks of adolescents, Spanish 3 or Ceramics 1 are the truly optional courses. *Every* student has to "take" (i.e., participate in) gender identity development and sexual identity development. Where should they get the knowledge and context they need in order to succeed in this domain?

Not Just about "Sex"

A credible CSE program is about far more than just sexual behavior, though preventing that ninth grader's unwanted pregnancy is a worthwhile achievement all by itself. In the same way that GSD represents a broad framework for understanding gender and sexuality, CSE addresses the multiple variables that are part of healthy social, emotional, physical, and sexual development. Look back at the mission statements in chapter 3. Goals related to healthy socioemotional development of the whole child are featured prominently.

Thus weighing the "academic substance" of Health against AP Physics is a flawed comparison. Students need intellectual *and* relational skills to succeed in the world. They need to be smart intellectually and socially in order to make good decisions. Helping students shape a value system in school that guides their relationships and sexual behaviors out in the world makes sense.

It also makes sense that CHW and CSE are closely linked to effective engagement with gender and sexuality diversity. The focus and framework of health and sexuality education overlap with the developmental necessity and pedagogical rationale for addressing GSD with preK–12 students. Knowledge in the realm of gender and sexuality is a powerful tool for students who must navigate the complex and contradictory world of work and love. If we expect them to make good decisions, then we must provide a variety of opportunities where they can learn "the facts" and, more importantly, clarify the values that will guide their behavior.

THE POLITICS OF CSE

Recognizing the need for sexuality education for our children and youth has evolved over several decades. The **Sexuality Information and Education Council of the U.S.** (SIECUS) formed in 1964 as an educational resource for professionals, parents, and the public, and SIECUS continues to be a major source of information, educational resources, and policy positions today (www.siecus. org). While there has been general agreement over the past several decades that students should receive education about sexuality, there has never been any consensus about what, exactly, should be taught (Walters and Hayes 2007).

Is Knowledge Good?

Promotion of healthy identity development, *support* for inclusive learning communities, and *prevention* of harassment in relation to GSD are best accomplished through education—not litigation. However, there are legal and political factors that can support or hinder a proactive approach to CHW and CSE in school districts across the country. While private schools are not subject to local, state, and federal mandates to the same degree, they must reckon with parents and trustees who may or may not support a proactive approach for teaching students about sexual and relational health.

Major political and religious differences have led to substantial government involvement in the debate about CSE. Federal funding for CSE and related programs dictates the "content" of a given sexuality education curriculum. A **comprehensive** approach to sexuality education has been proven **effective** in delaying students' initiation of sex, reducing the number of sexual partners, and increasing the use of effective birth control methods (SIECUS 2009b; Boonstra 2009; Trenholm et al. 2007; American Psychological Association 2005). The **abstinence-only-until-marriage** approach has been proven **ineffective** (SIECUS 2009a; Kirby 2007).

Even though President George W. Bush mandated scientifically proven methods as part of his No Child Left Behind legislation, his administration chose to ignore the results of multiple longitudinal studies that proved the abstinence-only-until-marriage approach ineffective. However, abstinence-only was then, and is now, more politically acceptable to conservatives who emphasize the "moral values" behind a no-sex-until-marriage stance. When asked about the lack of supporting scientific evidence for the abstinence approach, a Bush spokesperson said at the time, "Values trumps data" (Wingert 2002).

Failed and biased.   In addition to being ineffective in helping students abstain from heterosexual intercourse, the abstinence-only approach creates a negative, inadequate, and frequently hostile learning environment for those students who do not conform to heteronormative expectations.

❖ *Our sex education class basically expects you to be straight and gender conforming. We even have a "marriage appreciation" segment. We are required to take a semester of health/sex education. I feel very much left out of the curriculum because I do not fit the gender or sexuality boundaries set by my school.*

As this student attests, the abstinence-only curriculum presumes the heterosexuality of all students, and depicts boys and girls as having stereotypical gender expression, inhabiting traditional gender roles, and embodying mainstream gender identity. Marriage between one man and one woman serves as the central organizing construct for abstinence-only programs (SIECUS 2009a), leaving GLBTQI students with no healthy models to emulate and inadequate information about their sexual health needs (Elia and Eliason 2010).

Failed, biased, still funded.   Currently the Obama administration has made funding for CSE available through Personal Responsibility Education Program (PREP) funding (Additional Resource 8.1). However, 250 million federal dollars have also been committed to funding the abstinence-only curriculum over the course of FY2010–2014. That means that 50 million dollars a year will be spent on a program that the American Medical Association, the American Academy of Pediatrics, the Society of Adolescent Medicine, the American Public Health Association, and the American Psychological Association have deemed ineffective and unethical (Boonstra 2009).

CSE includes abstinence.   Lawmakers who object to CSE are usually concerned that conservative moral and/or religious values will not be reflected in the curriculum. It is worth noting that the most effective form of CSE *includes* abstinence-only principles and provides students with information about *all* options for pursuing healthy relationships, including abstention (SIECUS 2009b; Boonstra 2009). **Many people—politicians, parents, teachers, and students alike—do not understand that abstinence is an acceptable approach to maintaining sexual health. It just cannot be the only approach.**

The Role of Parents

It is also true that schools engaged in CSE are looking to *partner* with parents, recognizing that children and adolescents need multiple opportunities to clarify their values in relation to gender and sexuality. As this typical letter home to parents indicates, CSE programs do not seek to override parental instruction (see

Letter from School to Parents). They seek to promote child and adolescent health by having adults at school *and* at home get involved.

Letter from School to Parents: Partners in Sexuality Education and Values

This letter provides information about the upcoming program in Wellness class but it also encourages parents to talk to their children at home: "This would be an excellent time for you to discuss and reinforce your own values regarding these issues with your daughter or son." The deference to parental values is clear. In addition, many schools like this one give parents the right to remove their child from these particular class sessions. The hope is, however, that parents will discuss their concerns with the teacher before doing so and understand exactly what they are opting out of. As suggested earlier, there are many misperceptions about what CSE is and is not. Every parent should know what the CSE curriculum is in order to make an informed decision.

SEXUAL HEALTH OF ALL CHILDREN AND ADOLESCENTS

Start at the Beginning

One of the biggest obstacles to successful sexuality education is starting it too late. The idea that adolescence is the time to *begin* talking with students about "sex" and "identity" and "relationships" goes against everything we know about human identity development (see chapter 1). The foundational learning that occurs in preK–8 is critical in supporting and guiding children as they develop these aspects of themselves. Anecdotal and scientific evidence throughout this book point to how early GID and SID begin.

The Story of What a Four-Year-Old Can Know

The first time I knew I was a man, I was 21 years old. The first time I even heard of transgender men, I was 18, and it was in a documentary on one of the expensive cable stations I was fortunate to have.

I had a great education. My parents spent a boatload to send me to some of the best schools in my area. I came out with a strong knowledge set in almost everything—and I could have told you a lot about chromosomes and genetics and hormones and sex organs. I even knew about the act of sex itself and about sexual attraction and what happens to our bodies at puberty. But nothing in my 14 years of pre-college education even touched on the fact that a person could be a man without having been born with a Y chromosome.

 PUBLIC SCHOOLS

Telephone

FAX

SCHOOL COMMITTEE

SUPERINTENDENT

BUSINESS MANAGER

Date: 4/27/11

Dear Parent/Guardian:

During the next few weeks, the Wellness classes at ▮▮▮▮▮▮ High School will be studying a unit on Healthy Dating Relationships and Sexual Responsibility. This unit will provide the student with basic information about healthy relationships, warning signs of potentially abusive relationships, sexual decision-making, abstinence, assertive responses, reproductive anatomy, birth control, sexually transmitted diseases, and other related topics.

This would be an excellent time for you to discuss and reinforce your own values regarding these issues with your daughter or son. It is hoped that this unit will help to supplement the education given at home.

Although parents/guardians may request that their child does not participate in this program, we recommend that you first contact me to discuss your concerns and to learn more about the curriculum.

Sincerely yours,

Director of Health Services

Graphics 8.1.

I was introduced to the concept on TV, and all I saw were people who had been very butch (not me) and very depressed (also not me) when they were living as women. It wasn't until I took queer studies in college and met real trans men that I started to understand what it actually meant to be transgender. And once I understood what it meant, I almost immediately understood that that was who I was.

When I was four, I said I was "a boy on the inside." If someone had verbalized to me as a child, as a middle schooler, as a high schooler even, that there was such a thing as gender diversity and that our genetics didn't dictate every aspect of sex and gender, I (and my parents) would have known I was male a decade ago, and I could have transitioned before puberty. I could have started my life as it should be 10 years earlier.

—Sebastian Barr

Consider "The Story of What a Four-Year-Old Can Know." It echoes the experience of Sydney in "The Story of the School Photo." In terms of gender and sexuality, we must shift the educational paradigm to match the developmental reality of our youngest students. In this regard, SIECUS is a tremendous resource, modeling ways to talk to students at every age about issues that range from gender roles to sexuality and religion (see examples below).

Gender Roles:
Cultures teach what it means to be a man or a woman.
Developmental Messages Appropriate for Children Ages 5–8

- Girls and boys have many similarities and a few differences.
- Some people may expect or demand that boys and girls behave in certain ways, but this is beginning to change.
- Both women and men can be involved and caring parents.
- Boys and girls can do the same chores at home.
- Men and women are capable of doing almost all the same jobs.
- Some men and women may be told that certain jobs and tasks are only for women or only for men, but this is beginning to change.

Sexuality and Religion:
Religions' views about sexuality affect people's sexual attitudes and behaviors
Developmental Messages Appropriate for Preadolescents Ages 12–15

- All world religions have views about sexuality and its place in the human experience.
- Some religions have more liberal and moderate views on sexuality, while others are more conservative.
- One's religious values can play an important role in sexual decision making.
- When people's values about sexuality differ from those taught by their religion, they may experience conflict

(Guidelines for Comprehensive Sexuality Education, K–12, 3rd ed., http://www.siecus.org/_data/global/images/guidelines.pdf ©2004 SIECUS)

Same Topic, Different "Facts"

SIECUS guidelines are based on cognitive and emotional readiness. The key concepts, regardless of their complexity, are meant to be discussed with students in every age group (see diagram 8.1, SIECUS Guidelines for Comprehensive Sexuality Education). The educational goals of SIECUS line up with many of the pedagogical goals outlined in preK–12 school missions (see chapter 3). Educating and preparing students for their own healthy development, plus creating a greater understanding of others in an increasingly diverse global society are goals that SIECUS *and* school communities share.

Preparing For Puberty

There is very little about the process of human development that is exclusively linear, yet our narratives often suggest that one thing follows neatly after the next. There are many "steps" taken and building blocks established on the road to puberty. Think of development as gradual "assembly" and consider the car (read: student) in diagram 8.2. The tires of the car are constructed over time.

- **Tire One:** ECEE students learn about respect, families, feelings, friendships, and differences.
- **Tire Two:** Middle elementary grades focus on individual development, conflict resolution, communication, stereotyping, and various forms of human diversity.
- **Tire Three:** Fifth and sixth graders study human anatomy, engage in inquiries about different cultures, and grapple with historical and contemporary forms of prejudice.
- **Tire Four:** Middle school students address puberty, emotions, drugs, alcohol, peer pressure, homophobia, and skills for building healthy intimate relationships.

When elementary schools provide this type of CHW, students then have foundational concepts and relational skills in hand when it is time to engage in the more mature elements of CSE. There is no set dividing line between CHW and CSE; conversations about healthy sexuality occur well before and well after students actually engage in any sexual behavior. This incremental and developmental approach **provides curricular and pedagogical continuity** for students through preschool, elementary, middle, and high school.

Invest in good tires.   The "tires" on the car are essential; driving around without adequate support is dangerous. The study of math begins with preschoolers learning their "numbers" and ends with seniors taking calculus. Would we wait until high school to begin teaching students to count? Yet some adults still maintain that education about healthy identity, sexuality, and relationships should not begin until adolescence. Essentially they support waiting until there is gas (hormones!) in the car and the student is driving away before starting Driver's Ed.

SIECUS Guidelines for Comprehensive Sexuality Education: K-12

In 2004, Sexuality Instruction and Education Council of the United States (SIECUS) released the Third Edition of its Guidelines For Comprehensive Sexuality Education: Kindergarten through 12th Grade. These guidelines were developed by a national task force of leading educators, health professionals and advocacy organizations to provide schools with age-appropriate goals, topics, and approaches for sexuality education. SIECUS identifies six Key Concepts: (1) Human Development, (2) Relationships, (3) Personal Skills, (4) Sexual Behavior, (5) Sexual Health, (6) Society and Culture. Each concept has specific topics of instruction, and within each topic, essential messages are organized by developmental age group. (Abridged examples below)

Human Development: Sexual Orientation

Grades Pre-K – 2
(ages 5-8)

- Human beings can love people of the same gender and people of another gender.
- People deserve respect regardless of who they are attracted to.
- Making fun of people by calling them gay (e.g. "homo," "fag," "queer") is disrespectful and hurtful.

Grades 3 – 6
(ages 9-12)

- Sexual Orientation refers to a person's physical and/or romantic attraction to an individual of the same and/or different gender.
- Sexual orientation is just one part of who a person is.
- People of all sexual orientations can have relationships that are equally fulfilling.

Grades 7 – 9
(ages 12-15)

- Gay, lesbian, bisexual, and heterosexual people come from all countries, cultures, races, ethnicities, socio-economic backgrounds, and religions.
- Understanding one's sexual orientation can be an evolving process.
- Teenagers who have questions about their sexual orientation should consult a trusted and knowledgeable adult.

Grades 10 – 12
(ages 15-18)

- Sexual orientation is determined by a combination of a person's attractions, fantasies, and sexual behaviors.
- The understanding and identification of one's sexual orientation may change over the course of his/her lifetime.
- Civil rights for gay men and lesbian women are being debated in many states and communities across the United States.

Diagram 8.1.

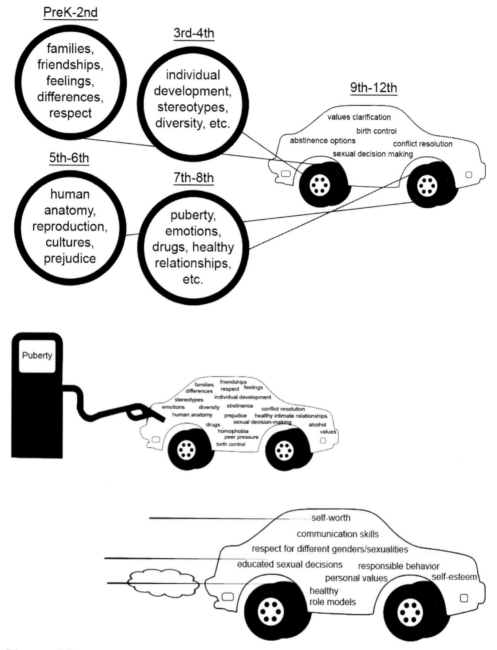

Diagram 8.2.

Ideally by the time puberty occurs, the car not only has a sturdy foundation of knowledge but is also full of valuable critical thinking and relational skills. In order to continue healthy gender identity development (GID) and sexual identity development (SID) students need accurate information and the capacity to contend with competing value systems (e.g., parental, popular, religious) as they became sexually active. **The substance of CSE is as much about the *meaning* of being sexual as a person and a citizen as it is about sexual behavior itself.**

Ambivalence about Adolescent Sexuality

Even when we acknowledge that our teens could benefit from CSE, our ambivalence about adolescent sexuality clouds our judgment about what *kind* of education they really need in order to develop healthy, respectful, and satisfying intimate relationships. Parents and educators often insist that teens are too young to know about sex and fear that giving them accurate information about sexuality might prove dangerous. Our failure to recognize that "knowledge is the cornerstone of responsible behavior" (Roffman 2001) results in students not having the necessary information, context, and practice (e.g., decision making, values clarification, conflict resolution) to make healthy decisions.

As a result, students may be taught the "facts" about sex and drugs during four 30-minute classes over the course of a single semester during one or two of their MS and HS years. Addressing the facts without addressing the relational component is like presenting art students with a palette full of different colors but never talking about what painting with these colors actually means and looks like. And the concern about providing students with "too much information" is no longer viable in the age of the Internet. It is deeply disturbing to think about the "information" that is now a mere mouse click away for any student who has access to a computer.

Media Literacy

Media literacy must be a central feature of contemporary CHW and CSE. The question is not *whether* students should have the information; the question is *where* do we want them to get the information and *how* do we want them to interpret that information. The unregulated Internet serves up everything from sexuality education materials offered by reputable organizations to graphic pornography and images of sexual exploitation. It is a chaotic mishmash of "information," with search engines listing the website for a reliable source right next to a link for free porn.

It is clear that media literacy is now relevant for children and adolescents of every age. Recent studies indicate that small children are more likely to navigate a computer mouse and play computer games than tie their own shoes or ride a bike ("Forget" 2010). In Additional Resource 6.2 (chapter 6), the Welcoming Schools "Media Sleuths" lesson invites elementary students to assess the way gender and gender roles are portrayed in the media. The essence of the lesson is not to find the "correct sites" about gender; the purpose is to teach kids how to think about and critique the multiple, everyday images of gender that they encounter. Similarly "I Heard It 'Round the Internet: A Lesson Plan from The Media Awareness Network" teaches students how to conduct research on the sprawling Internet, while learning about "the myths and realities of sexuality and contraception."

Teaching Resource I
I Heard It 'Round the Internet:
A Lesson Plan from the Media Awareness Network

The Media Awareness Network offers a multidisciplinary lesson plan for grades 6–9, teaching students how to conduct research on the Internet, while simultaneously teaching them about the myths and realities of *sexuality* and *contraception*.

1. Teachers have the students discuss their sources of information—the most popular source will likely be the Internet.
2. Teachers and students discuss the fallbacks of Internet research.
3. Teacher provides tips and rules of online researching (handout, Media Awareness Network) and "myth busting."
4. Teachers give each student "Myths and Facts about Teens and Sex" (handout, Media Awareness Networks), which includes items such as:
   a. There is a cure for AIDS.
   b. You cannot buy condoms if you are under eighteen years of age.
   c. It is unhealthy for men to go without sex for long periods of time.
   d. Birth control pills do not prevent STIs.
5. Students first privately mark each statement as true or false and then use their new Internet search skills to confirm the answers with a group. (Adapted from www.media-awareness.com. All materials at www.media-awareness.ca/english/resources/educational/lessons/elementary/internet/sex_health_ed.cfm.)

The CSE and GSD Link

It makes sense that schools with comprehensive sexuality education are well positioned to include supportive GSD education. CSE includes information about all sexual and gender identities, which in turn points to the unique experiences of GLBTQI youth in schools. Chapter 7 outlines the need for greater understanding of these students, both in terms of "facts" and "feelings" and CSE creates much needed opportunities for learning. In addition, there are now many thoughtful, accessible, free resources for integrating GLBTQI into or as a complement to CSE. The five resources shared here are a small sample of what is available.

GLBTQI Lesson Plans

1. Human Rights Resource Center: **Lesbian, Gay, Bisexual, and Transgender Rights as Human Rights**

   A series of nine lesson plans focusing on LGBT rights, intended to further the discussion beyond civil and political rights.

   Curriculum examples:

   a. *Are Gay Rights "Special"? What Does the Declaration of Universal Human Rights Say?*

   b. *What Must Be Done to Achieve Equality?*

   c. *Youth Dealing with Homophobia*

   (http://www1.umn.edu/humanrts/edumat/hreduseries/TB3/toc.html)

2. Advocates for Youth: **The Nuts and Bolts: Lesson Plans for Building Allies for GLBTQ Youth**

   A series of twelve chronological lesson plans, with the ultimate goal of getting students involved in social justice for GBLTQ people.

   Examples from the curriculum:

   a. *Who Am I?*

   b. *Q&A on Sexual Orientation and Gender Identity*

   c. *What Can I Do to Create a Safe Space?*

   (http://www.advocatesforyouth.org/publications/608#lessonplans)

3. Advocates for Youth: **Miscellaneous Lesson Plans: Sexual Orientation & Gender Identity and Discrimination & Stereotypes**

   In addition to their comprehensive social justice curriculum, Advocates for Youth also has a collection of miscellaneous lesson plans that focus more on education and less on activism.

   Curriculum examples:

   a. *Gender Roles and Relationships*

   b. *A-B-C-Diversity*

   c. *Media Messages and Stereotypes*

   d. *Nontraditional Workers' Panel*

   (http://www.advocatesforyouth.org/sexual-orientation-and-gender-identity-lessons; http://www.advocatesforyouth.org/discrimination-and-stereotypes-lessons)

4. Seattle / King County School District: **Family Life and Sexual Health (FLASH)**

   A comprehensive sexuality education course that is GLBTQI-inclusive and addresses GSD specifically in a number of lessons.

   Curriculum examples:

   a. *Gender Stereotypes*

   b. *Healthy Relationships*

   c. *Lesbian, Gay, Bisexual and Transgender Youth*

   d. *Sex: Myths, Facts, Feelings & Values*

5. Looking for more? Safe Schools Coalition has a regularly updated list of GLBTQI lesson plans and resources for elementary, middle, and high school educators. (http://www.safeschoolscoalition.org/RG-lessonplans.html)

The Link between CSE and Harassment Policy

There is a critical connection between comprehensive sexuality education and an effective Gender and Sexuality Harassment Policy (GSHP). First, CSE provides a foundation of knowledge about gender and sexuality that enables students to fully comprehend *what* the Gender and Sexuality Harassment Policy actually says and means. It is not safe to assume that students are literate in this regard. Second, without elaboration and meaningful context, some students are not likely to understand *why* such a policy is vital to creating a safe community for all students, staff, and parents.

In the next chapter you will find an abundance of policies and programs and laws that relate to GSD. Unfortunately much of the information is framed in the "negative." For instance there are laws *against* harassment, policies about what *cannot* be said in school, arguments about what constitutes *inappropriate* behavior, etc. **Comprehensive health and wellness and comprehensive sexuality education provide opportunities to promote that which is healthy—rather than remediate that which is negative—about love, relationships, sexuality, and responsibility.** Helping students learn "what to do" is more effective than punishing them for unwanted behavior.

CHW and CSE help students grow in ways that are vital to their search for community, partnership, family, and their place in the world. Recall that "educational mission" serves as a primary framework in all school endeavors (see chapter 3). Consider these examples.

- *Academic community dedicated to nurturing mind, body, and soul*
- *To prepare students for socially responsible, values based leadership in a culturally and religiously diverse world*
- *That he/she will be informed, prepared and capable of assuming full responsibility for making his/her own decisions*
- *Promote the full development of mind, body, and spirit*

We want children and adolescents to grow into socially competent and responsible adults. It is difficult to imagine fully accomplishing these goals without CHW and CSE as part of the school program.

ADDITIONAL RESOURCES

Additional Resource 8.1

Sexuality Education Funding Sources: PREP and Title V

Personal Responsibility Education Program (PREP) is a federal funding stream for comprehensive sexuality education. Created in 2010 through health care reform legislation, PREP marks the first time government funds have been available to programs that go beyond abstinence-only education. Programs supported by PREP are required to provide information on both abstinence and contraception for the prevention of unintended pregnancy and sexually transmitted infections, including HIV/AIDS, emphasizing both abstinence and contraceptive use. Programs must also address certain "adulthood preparation" topics: (a) healthy relationships, (b) adolescent development, (c) financial literacy, (d) educational and career success, and (e) healthy life skills.

Programs supported by the Title V grant must teach abstinence to the exclusion of other sexual health and prevention methods. These programs cannot contradict the federal definition for "abstinence education," which specifies, in part, that "a mutually faithful monogamous relationship in the context of marriage is the expected standard of all human sexual activity." It also states that "sexual activity outside the context of marriage is likely to have harmful psychological and physical effects" (SIECUS 2010).

Currently, states have the option to apply for PREP funds, for Title V abstinence-only-until-marriage program funds, or both. Forty-seven states, the District of Columbia, and two U.S. territories applied for grants in 2010. Of those, forty-three states, D.C., and the two territories applied for PREP grants, and thirty applied for Title V abstinence-only grants. Sixteen states applied solely for the PREP funding (SIECUS 2010).

NOTES

1. *Sex & Sensibility: The Thinking Parent's Guide to Talking Sense about Sex*: A new paradigm for talking honestly about sex and sexuality with our children.

LEADERSHIP, POLICIES, AND PROGRAMS

Supporting GSD Education at Schools
(Not For Administrators Only!)

Polls show that the public's stance against same-sex marriage is softening, and education about gay issues has expanded dramatically in recent years around the country, but experts suggest that the battle over what should and should not be part of public school curriculums has just begun.

—Gerry Shih, "Clashes Pit Parents vs. Gay-Friendly Curriculums in Schools," *New York Times*, 2011

As long as these attitudes and behaviors go unchallenged, then schools will continue to be sites where youths are harassed out of an education.

—Elizabeth Meyer, *Gender, Bullying, and Harassment*

The previous three chapters offer an abundance of curricular material and identify effective approaches for teaching GSD. Yet without administrative support that fully authorizes the implementation of GSD-related education, classroom teachers are on their own. In addition, leadership that fosters the development of antibias policies and programs can and must come from students and parents as well. If a school community strives to be truly inclusive of all, multiple acts of leadership across constituencies are essential in order to accomplish that goal.

School **policies** provide *curricular structure*, such as requiring certain content areas or academic courses. Policies can also establish *behavioral expectations*, such as a dress code for students or an antibullying code of conduct. Official **programs** like No Name-Calling Week (p. 299) reflect *educational values* and often invite community-wide participation. This chapter examines policies and programs that support the effort to effectively and appropriately integrate gender and sexuality diversity into the life of a school.

SECTION I
THE CHALLENGE OF EFFECTIVE LEADERSHIP

Progress on problems is the measure of leadership; leaders mobilize people to face problems, and communities make progress on problems because leaders challenge and help them do so. If something goes wrong, the fault lies with both leaders and the community.

—Ronald Heifetz, *Leadership without Easy Answers*

WHO'S IN CHARGE?

The search for consistent leadership in relation to gender and sexuality diversity programming in the United States reveals multiple "authorities" providing contradictory and inconsistent messages. Though certain federal laws have been applied in court cases in order to protect students' rights, there are no national guidelines that specifically address GSD in preK–12 schools. The absence of federal guidelines is compounded by an abundance of contradictory state laws. This often leaves superintendents, principals, heads, local school boards, and trustees to establish policy and provide direction themselves.

Consider the number of constituents with a hat in the educational ring.

- ❖ *I don't envy the administrators who must logistically make this school welcome transgender students.*
- ☐ *I support antibullying efforts but I don't support having books about transsexuals in my daughter's kindergarten class.*
- ➤ *I'm cool with the trans kid using the boys' bathroom. It doesn't bother me.*

Parents, accreditation reviewers, students, state legislatures, teachers, staff, alumni, and donors—to name a few—all have a vested interest in influencing a school's position in relation to GSD. Conflicts among these constituents are inevitable, and attempts to forge new paradigms are often met with misunderstanding and hostility. Indeed, contending with "conflicts" becomes a central part of the work (DePalma and Atkinson 2010b).

Competing Value Perspectives: A Working Example

Consider this example. A school district is poised to implement a sexuality education curriculum and these are the realities:

1. A group of parents supports comprehensive sexuality education for their children.

2. Another group of parents demands that their children be allowed to "opt out" of such classes.
3. There is financial pressure to qualify for federal funds that support sexuality education, but this particular state has applied for a grant that supports the "abstinence-only" approach—which has repeatedly been proven ineffective (see chapter 8).
4. Some parents and a local pediatric practice have voiced concerns about a rise in the number of middle and high school girls performing oral sex on boys.[1]
5. A gay high school student in a nearby town recently won a lawsuit against his school district for not protecting him from chronic verbal and physical harassment.[2]
6. There will be a transgender child enrolling in fourth grade in the fall.

In the previous chapter we learned about the importance of comprehensive sexuality education (CSE) in relation to GSD education. As you can see in this example, different people want different outcomes. Based on personal and professional values, adults in the community are divided about the place of CSE in the curriculum. The health (e.g., STD's) and safety (e.g., chronic harassment) of students are at stake, and federal funding in this case is tied to an approach that will not address either of these immediate problems. What should the district do?

Conflict as a Path to Success?

Ron Heifetz studies and teaches leadership at Harvard's Kennedy School of Government, and he tells us "the inclusion of competing value perspectives may be essential to adaptive success" (1998, 23). What kind of leadership will facilitate "adaptive success" in this sexuality education example? With so many forces to contend with, how can school administrators chart a path that leads not to mere appeasement but to substantive progress? It is difficult to shift from the leader-should-put-out-the-fire-as-quickly-as-possible mind-set to one that calls for more collective responsibility for the fire itself.

Heifetz (1994) endorses the leader who "mobilizes people to face problems" (15). This leader does not create a solution and then convince people to follow her. Effective leaders, in this approach, challenge and help people tackle problems; "success" is measured by the amount and quality of progress made in solving these problems. One key element of this approach is recognizing that anybody in the system can provide leadership, and that, in fact, a variety of skills and abilities are required to effectively address complex problems that arise from GSD education. Conceptualizing leadership as an *activity* performed by *multiple people* in multiple positions dramatically increases the likelihood of success (Heifetz 1998).

Who Should "Solve" the Problem?

In the sexuality education example, the leader (e.g., superintendent, principal) should charge all the vested parties with the task of reaching a solution. The group of stakeholders must contend with their competing value perspectives and create an approach and plan that (1) upholds the stated mission of the school (see chapter 3) and (2) reflects the concerns of the community. The educational leaders help structure the process and provide support to all parties who seek to work together, using the school's mission as the central reference point.

This approach of delegation and support might produce a variety of outcomes, such as

- Alternative funding for comprehensive sexuality education (rather than abstinence only) is secured via Planned Parenthood, the Centers for Disease Control (CDC), and a local community health organization.
- Parents retain the right to prohibit their child from participating in these classes but only after they have reviewed the curriculum and signed off.
- A coalition of local agencies and businesses partner with the local chapter of Parents and Friends of Lesbians and Gays (PFLAG) to sponsor an educational series for parents entitled: "Your Children, My Children: Keeping Schools Safe for All Our Children."
- A working committee of board members, parents, teachers, attend a free conference to learn more about CSE teaching materials and resources.[3]
- Various local religious leaders come together and agree to deliver a coordinated message of (1) compassion and respect for all children and families, and (2) condemnation of harassment of any kind against any person.

This coalition-building strategy is strongly endorsed by experts on effective leadership. It is also endorsed by numerous state boards of education (e.g., California State Board of Education) and social justice advocacy groups (e.g., Advocates for Youth).

Leadership as an Activity

In a single school community gender and sexuality diversity affects administrators, teachers, staff, students, and parents. Ideally, solutions to problems, and advancement in educational efforts related to GSD, come from all of these constituencies. Leadership is an activity that any member of the community can engage in; the level of passion and energy the leader(s) has for—or against—a particular change will influence the outcome.

Increasing teacher "influence" has been shown to have a positive impact on school improvement (Mayrowetz et al. 2007), and working collaboratively and sharing responsibilities supports the strategy of creating a professional learning community (see chapter 5). Yet the **designated leader** has to be willing to relinquish some decision-making power to truly support a **distributed leadership** model (Wahlstrom and Louis 2008). It comes as no surprise that this is not always easy for superintendents, principals, and heads of school to do.

Changes in perceptions, attitudes, and behaviors related to GSD take a lot of work. This is not the kind of "work" that can be accomplished by a single leader at the "top."

> One thing is clear in today's schools, however, that although the system is designed as a hierarchical model where the responsibility for ensuring quality education rests at the "top" of the organization, there is increasing recognition everywhere that there is a need for more leadership from more people to get needed work done. (Leithwood and Mascall 2007, 461–62 as cited in Wahlstrom and Louis 2008)

There may be concern that involving multiple leaders and distributing responsibilities will actually impede progress (i.e., too many cooks in the kitchen) rather than facilitate it. The truth is that in order to be successful in implementing GSD curricula, policies, and programs, there must be leadership from every corner of the community (see diagram 9.1).

The school community is represented by the circle in diagram 9.1. The circle has a permeable boundary that allows external actions, events, identities, and attitudes to influence what happens "inside" the community. Thus there is the interplay among different constituencies within the school that are influenced to some degree by elements outside the school. The working example that follows involves the formation of a Gay Straight Alliance (GSA) and illustrates the dynamics of leadership and influence.

Working Example: Forming a GSA

1. The state legislature is deeply involved in a debate about same-sex marriage.
2. A recent bullying incident at a nearby high school has been labeled a hate crime and three students are set to be charged with assault.
3. Students in this school want to form a Gay Straight Alliance, and they take their request to a teacher.
   > *Will you be our advisor?*
4. Students approach the administration.
   > *We'd like to form a student club, a GSA, and we have someone to be our advisor. What do we need to do to get approval?*
5. A parent comes forward, raises concern about the appropriateness of a GSA.
   > ☐ *Why do we need a club like this in middle school? This doesn't seem like appropriate school business.*

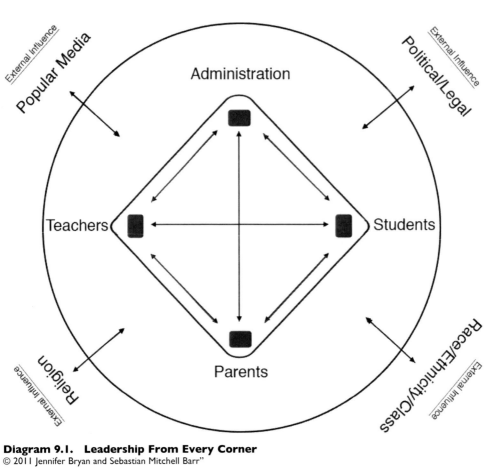

Diagram 9.1. Leadership From Every Corner
© 2011 Jennifer Bryan and Sebastian Mitchell Barr"

6. Many teachers are fully behind the students' desire to create a GSA.
   ❖ *These kids want to do something positive for the school and need our sup-port. A club like this is important in creating safety and sending a message.*
7. A group of parents rally behind the students; a lawyer (who is a parent) re-minds the district of their legal obligation to permit the club to form.
   ☐ *If you have other students clubs at school, you must allow this one too.*
8. The administration decides . . . ?

What does the administration decide? You might expect the "authority" to ren-der an opinion: *Yes, students may move forward*, or *No, students may not move forward with starting a GSA*. Instead, the administration can exercise leadership by creating a structured process that invites those with "competing value perspec-tives" to work out a solution.

   1. Establish a working group to conduct research on GSAs in other districts.
   2. Sponsor forums for open dialogue among students, teachers, and parents.

3. Make use of resources and guidance from organizations like GLSEN.
4. Create a democratic process that invites participation and teaches students (and adults) how to advocate for change, appropriately, respectfully, and effectively.
5. Encourage students to attend a legislative session, perhaps even speak to lawmakers.

The leadership helps those involved to address this shared problem. If the process of reaching a decision is inclusive and fair, stakeholders are more likely to accept the outcome (Macgillivray 2004). And the process itself becomes a valuable learning experience.

What's the Point?

In the midst of all of this researching, participating, and negotiating, it is easy to forget "the point." What exactly is the educational opportunity being pursued by all this activity around the Gay Straight Alliance? "The Surprising Story of an Eighth Grader Starting a GSA" reminds us of the depth and breadth of learning that happens when students must think critically about and engage personally with GSD. Whether it is the first graders having an "aha!" about "what's on the inside" versus "what's on the outside of Oliver Button" (see chapter 6) or this eighth grader confronting her own discomfort with being an ally, students benefit tremendously from such lessons. And the benefits continue, long after the students have left the classroom.

The Surprising Story of an Eighth Grader Starting a GSA

A few months ago, one of my favorite teachers asked if I would be interested in starting a Gay Straight Alliance in the eighth grade. He felt I would make a good student leader. From one point of view, I have no reason to be involved with this cause. I'm not gay, and I don't have gay parents. On the other hand, two of my closest friends come from families with two moms and this same teacher, whom I greatly respect, is a gay dad. I feel strongly that LGBT people should enjoy the same rights as everyone else, and I've always been outspoken about this when we've discussed the issue in class. To me, it's just an issue of basic fairness and respect. I may not be gay, but I do have a stake in making my school, my country and my world a safer, more just place for everyone. In eighth grade, we study the civil rights movement, which based itself on Gandhi's legacy of non-violent protest, and gay rights feels like my generation's civil rights battle.

At first I was flattered by my teacher's trust in me and was eager to start work. The next day I talked to my friends from gay families. They quickly agreed to help out, and soon two other girls joined as well. Word began spreading through the grade more quickly than I had imagined. Soon I was urged to talk to some boys whom I didn't know very well. Suddenly, although I was ashamed to admit it, I started having second thoughts. What were people thinking about me now that I was involved in creating a GSA? Were they making assumptions about me, or my sexuality?

Help came in the form of another friend who confessed that she worried what people thought, too. Part of my load lifted. I wasn't the only one struggling. With her help, and the example of my teacher, I gathered my courage, talked to the male classmates and was gratified with the answer that they would attend the next meeting, and would bring a couple of friends.

—Sofia Riva, eighth grade student

Leadership from the Top

Where exactly is the "top"? There are many tiers of "authority" in the educational decision-making system, and section II of this chapter highlights various sources of power that create policy. The top can be a board member, a district supervisor, or a principal. Each "administrator" or decision maker has an important role in supporting or impeding change.

❖ *The overall tone that is set by the administration matters a lot. There needs to be a unified adult voice about acceptance and a willingness to respond to student behavior that is intolerant.*

❖ *You have to find a way to get the administration to embrace GSD issues as relevant.*

❖ *Recently, our Head of School wrote a supportive letter to the Board of Trustees and the whole community outlining why we, as a school, will continue to champion actions towards a more equitable world around LGBT issues.*

Without administrative support from the top, achieving lasting change in policy or programs is much more difficult. It does not mean that reform is impossible, but lacking "official" support means a much longer, less efficient, and more contentious process.

Chapter 5 highlights the importance of *transformational learning* for educators involved in professional development work. The same emphasis on the "qualitative shift [that] occurs in *how a person actively interprets, organizes, understands, and makes sense of his or her experience*" applies to leaders as well (Drago-Severson 2009, 11). Without a willingness to address the underlying systemic patterns that contribute to problems, it is unlikely that meaningful changes in policy, programs, and behavior will occur (Evans 2001).

However, shifting away from popular, accepted paradigms for addressing GSD is a risk for leaders of all stripes. For example, popular approaches to school-based bullying offer leaders streamlined, conventional courses of intervention for this problem. (Further exploration of bullying and harassment policies appears later in this chapter.) However, implementing a "bullying program" is not necessarily the most effective intervention (DePalma and Atkinson 2010). Making the shift from seeing antigay bullying as a specific problem, to understanding it as a "systemic, institutional manifestation of cultural bias" (1670), **requires leadership that challenges the accepted interpretation of bullying**. In this case, the transformational leader comprehends bullying behaviors differently (i.e., systemic rather than specific), and as a result, proposes a different course of action (e.g., addressing school climate and providing education about GSD).

Styles of Leadership

Transformational leadership, as exercised by this headmistress, is not always a singular act but rather a steady position that allows change to happen at "new levels" over time.

> ❖ *Our headmistress's support has also been instrumental in pushing forward this conversation to new levels. She is at once respectful of Church tradition and respectful of the diverse students, families, staff and faculty who make up our community. She does not discriminate in the hiring or admissions process against staff, faculty, students or their families based on their sex, gender expression, gender identity or sexual orientation.*

The entire community of this school is aware of the headmistress's stance. She leads by example, and as a result, nurtures the GSD learning process in a slow, unwavering manner over time.

Internal and external influences. The catalyst for leadership activity can be influenced by an *internal* event. For instance, in response to the increasing variety of family configurations in the community, the Parent Diversity Committee sponsors a family diversity photo exhibit at the school (see In Our Family, chapter 6). The catalyst can also be *external* influences like a local gay-related suicide that generates a lot of media attention (Peet 2010). In both cases teachers need to be prepared to facilitate "learning" about these issues, and often, teachers do not feel prepared.

> ❖ *Our middle school head wanted teachers to discuss the recent suicide at a college following his sexuality being revealed via internet. We teachers felt that, although it is an important subject, we feel inadequately prepared to discuss some of the issues that would come up in such a discussion, in an educated and sensitive manner. Clearly, we do not know where we stand, and would have a hard time modeling enlightened thinking on this subject for our students. Also, many of us felt our students were too young for such a discussion.*

As this teacher suggests, until there is an opportunity for teachers themselves to prepare, they are not in a position to do the good work necessary with students. When real-life events make their way into the classroom discourse, like this highly publicized gay student suicide, **we cannot expect teachers to feel pedagogically equipped just by virtue of their being educators.**

Leaders must mobilize and access resources in either case, whether there is time for professional preparation (e.g., family photo exhibit) or not (e.g., teen suicide). For example, after the suicide of sixth grade student Carl Hoover Walker in spring 2009, the Gay, Lesbian, Bisexual and Transgender Youth Support Project, a Program of Healthcare of Southeastern Massachusetts, offered free training, strategic planning, and technical assistance to Massachusetts schools. These resources were designed to support teachers who did not feel adequately prepared to lead discussions about GSD-related suicide "in an educated and sensitive manner." Yet, despite these resources being offered for free and on site, only a small percentage of administrators in districts across the state requested this assistance. *How come?* What gets in the way?

OBSTACLES TO LEADERSHIP: WHO OR WHAT GETS IN THE WAY?

Here teachers identify some of the many obstacles to leadership in relation to GSD education.

* ❖ *Upper administration, especially older persons with more antiquated ideas of "what the kids are ready for," are an obstacle.*
* ❖ *Lack of time is a fundamental obstacle. As a teaching/learning community, we have too many such matters to track with our kids. Unless a "cause" has an influential "champion," not much happens.*
* ❖ *Because of our financial situation there is absolutely no money to support the kind of programs we need to fully address the needs in this area.*
* ❖ *My school is a Catholic boys school, and our teachers are uneducated as to how they can appropriately discuss issues of gender and sexuality diversity and remain within the teachings of the Catholic Church. Because it is something the church is so outspoken about, teachers often feel scared to broach the topic with students.*
* ❖ *I have very little tolerance for the roadblock of "religion" which frankly is the major obstacle to our addressing GLBTQ issues more directly and effectively.*

Whether is it a lack of funding, negative publicity, misinformation, overburdened teachers, apathetic students, or parental protest, the forces working against progress in this domain are numerous and unavoidable. This is the reality: whoever offers the necessary leadership in relation to GSD should never expect it to be easy.

DISRUPTING THE STATUS QUO

Even with free funding, expert trainers at the ready, on-site support and consultation, the majority of administrators in the state of Massachusetts did not use these resources to educate and support their communities after the Carl Walker suicide. One can imagine the reasons why they did not.

- ❖ *Spring is a busy time at school. There is so much to be done before the end of the term. You cannot ask teachers to take on one more thing at this time of year.*
- ❖ *There are a mandated number of professional days for teachers and there is no contractual agreement for an additional meeting.*
- ❖ *These are not issues in our school. Maybe in Springfield there is this kind of bullying and harassment, but not in our community.*
- ☐ *What happened to the young boy in Springfield was a tragedy but I don't think that warrants conversations with elementary students in our district. They are too young to even understand what "gay" means.*

Administrators would have had to disrupt the status quo in order to make room for this GSD education: interrupt "school business," interfere with community denial, challenge the assumption that elementary students are "too young" to understand why Carl Walker killed himself.

Those who "lead" have to expect and prepare for the inevitable roadblocks and setbacks; cultural change rarely happens without plenty of trials and tribulations.

> To lead is to live dangerously because when leadership counts, when you lead people through difficult change, you challenge what people hold dear—their daily habits, tools, loyalties, and ways of thinking—with nothing more to offer perhaps than a possibility. Moreover, leadership often means exceeding the authority you are given to tackle the challenge at hand. People push back when you disturb the personal and institutional equilibrium they know. (Heifetz and Linsky 2002, 2)

"The Story of the GSA Advisor Who Challenged the Board of Trustees" is a powerful example; one teacher challenges the leadership several rungs up the hierarchical ladder, perhaps "exceeding her authority," as Heifetz and Linsky describe. There is no predicting the outcome; trailblazers, torchbearers, and a high school teacher who feels compelled to speak out never possess guarantees.

The Story of the GSA Advisor
Who Challenged the Board of Trustees

[Excerpted from a letter written in response to the board's decision to prevent the GSA from meeting on school grounds. The school rents its space from the Catholic Church.]

If the Board is basing its objection to housing a GSA on the grounds that it might be offensive to the Catholic Church, I invite you to consider evidence that the church may not actually take issue with our commitment to embracing diversity and protecting our students. Take, for example, the growing list of private Catholic colleges and universities that proudly feature LGBTQ groups as an aspect of campus life. Tolerance and acceptance are alive and well, at, among other places, Loyola University, Georgetown University, Albertus Magnus College, University of Notre Dame, Holy Cross, and Boston College. It strikes me as strange that (our school) would assume the worst of the Church—and of the potential for a broader interpretation of the terms of our lease—in the face of this kind of precedent.

As far as the Board's objection to publicizing the AIDS Walk, I strongly urge you to reconsider that as well. In 1987, over 20 years ago, the United States Catholic Conference approved a publication called The Many Faces of AIDS: A Global Response. From this publication:

"As members of the Church and society, we have a responsibility to stand in solidarity with and reach out with compassion and understanding to those exposed to or experiencing this disease. We must provide spiritual and pastoral care as well as medical and social services for them and support for their families and friends."

I am truly shocked that (our school) would agree to minimize its support of this important cause because of an anticipated negative reaction from the Diocese, especially when there is ample precedent for the Church's support of people living with HIV and AIDS.

—High school GSA advisor

WHAT HELPS LEADERS LEAD?

Clarity of Purpose

Though it is not always easy to achieve or maintain, *clarity of purpose* is a major asset for leaders. Distractions, obfuscations, and detours are commonplace; remembering the goal you are pursuing and why you are pursuing it increases the likelihood of successfully staying the course. More importantly, "change" that is being sought as **part of fulfilling the school's stated mission** has pedagogical and philosophical legitimacy, as illustrated in "The Story of the GLBTQ Bulletin Board." This echoes the essence of chapter 3: actualizing educational mission should be the impetus and foundation for all actions related to gender and sexuality diversity in the preK–12 setting.

The Story of the GLBTQ Bulletin Board

During Gay and Lesbian History Month, the ethics teacher at one elementary school created a bulletin board display that depicted an array of notable GLBTQ authors, politicians, performers, scholars, and activists. This is the same board the teacher used for a similar kind of display during Black History Month. There were photos of Barney Frank, Martina Navratilova, Bessie Smith, and Keith Haring.

A parent complained to a board member. The parent found the display highly inappropriate for a preK–5 school. He found it too conspicuous and blatant. He questioned the display's academic integrity, suggesting it represented political correctness rather than something of educational value.

The board member then shared these complaints with the principal of the lower school and asked for his input. Here is how George Burns, principal of Fieldston Lower School, responded:

What is the problem with sharing this? Did the parent find it perfectly all right to highlight famous African-Americans, but now finds it objectionable to mention another group that has suffered and continues to suffer all kinds of bias? Is the parent concerned that we are bringing up the topic of sex (which we are not)? I guess my answer would be that it is an important part of the school's mission to recognize and embrace all kinds of diversity, and to help children and adults think about how to create a more inclusive society. What better way for kids to embrace inclusiveness than to understand the contributions that many groups have made to our world, and to have them realize that many of the people whose work they are aware of are/were homosexuals, in addition to being talented, productive and wonderful people?

Managing Change

Number five on Principal Mike McCarthy's list of "Ten Big Ideas of School Leadership" (Additional Resource 9.1) is **"Find time to think during the day."**

> They pay me to worry. It's OK to stare at the wall and think about how to manage change. I have 70 people who work at King. Even the most centered has three bad days each school year. Multiply that by 70 people and that's 210 bad days, which is more than the 180 school days in a year. So, me, I am never going to have a good day—just get over it.

McCarthy is the principal of Helen King Middle School in Portland, Maine, and was named Middle School Principal of the Year in 2010. His endorsement of staring at the wall and thinking about how to "manage change" underscores the ever-present challenge of maintaining clarity and then determining the best course of action.

While "Ten Big Ideas of School Leadership" (Additional Resource 9.1) offers a straight-up dose of wisdom and practicality, big idea number nine may be the most controversial: **"Consensus is overrated."**

> Twenty percent of people will be against anything. When you realize this, you avoid compromising what really should be done because you stop watering things down. If you always try to reach consensus, you are being led by the 20 percent. (McCarthy and Baron 2010)

At first glance, this may seem like a jaded perspective. After all, if everyone is in agreement about which course of action to pursue, then conflicts will be minimized. It should be possible for reasonable people to agree on what's best for kids, right?

McCarthy is articulating a fundamental truth about democracy. The decision-making process must be fair, but consensus is not a mandated outcome. Collaboration and concession are valid components of the democratic process. Yet in spite of cooperative efforts, the nay-saying twenty percent may remain unrelenting in their opposition to genuine change in schools. The "watering down" that McCarthy refers to occurs when appeasement of the minority voice trumps upholding core educational values. In order to truly pursue the mission of the school, leaders must have a realistic perspective on the "twenty percent of people [who] will be against anything."

WHAT TO REMEMBER: SECTION I

Effective Leadership

1. Multiple acts of leadership across constituencies are needed to address GSD effectively in schools.
2. Schools benefit from having specific policies and programs that address curriculum and student behavior in relation to GSD.
3. Engaging competing value perspectives can be essential in the pursuit of "adaptive success."
4. Designated, shared, and delegated leadership are important components of the change process in schools.
5. "Leadership from Every Corner" is one model of leadership that involves the whole community, including administration, students, teachers, and parents, as well as external influences (e.g., media, religion).
6. Designated leaders (e.g., administration) must mobilize resources that allow others to engage in problem solving.

7. Obstacles to leadership in the GSD domain include practical concerns (e.g., lack of time, funding) yet there are also risks for those who lead in opposition to the status quo.

8. Clarity of purpose, taking time to think, and keeping "consensus" in perspective all support effective leadership.

SECTION II
POLICIES AND PHILOSOPHIES

Investigating the nature of heteronormativity illustrates that anti-bullying policy is not enough, as reactive responses in the form of post-hoc punishment schemes and "Zero Tolerance" policies do little to address the sociocultural nature of discrimination and oppression. (DePalma and Atkinson 2010)

GOVERNMENT POLICIES RELATED TO GSD

The three branches of government significantly impact school policies related to gender and sexuality diversity. However, there is little consistency and uniformity in the dictates issued by each branch. The most recent school climate survey reveals that, in spite of the current hodgepodge of policies related to student safety, schools remain a hostile environment for students who identify as or are perceived as GLBTQI (box 9.2).

Safety of LGBT-Identified Students in Middle and High School

1. 84.6 percent of LGBT students reported being verbally harassed, 40.1 percent reported being physically harassed, and 18.8 percent reported being physically assaulted at school in the past year because of their *sexual orientation*.

2. 63.7 percent of LGBT students reported being verbally harassed, 27.2 percent reported being physically harassed, and 12.5 percent reported being physically assaulted at school in the past year because of their *gender expression*.

3. 72.4 percent heard homophobic remarks, such as "faggot" or "dyke," frequently or often at school.

4. Nearly two-thirds (61.1 percent) of students reported that they felt unsafe in school because of their sexual orientation, and more than a third (39.9 percent) felt unsafe because of their gender expression.

5. 29.1 percent of LGBT students missed a class at least once and 30.0 percent missed at least one day of school in the past month because of safety

concerns, compared to only 8.0 percent and 6.7 percent, respectively, of a national sample of secondary school students.

6. The reported grade point average of students who were more frequently harassed because of their sexual orientation or gender expression was almost half a grade lower than for students who were harassed less often (2.7 vs. 3.1).

7. Increased levels of victimization were related to increased levels of depression and anxiety and decreased levels of self-esteem.

8. Being "out" at school had negative and positive repercussions for LGBT students. Outness was related to higher levels of victimization, but also to higher levels of psychological well-being and a greater sense of belongingness at school. (GLSEN 2009 National Climate Survey of 7,261 LGBTQ middle and high school students; Kosciw et al. 2010).

These statistics from GLSEN paint a grim portrait of MS and HS life for nonheteronormative students. The need for coherent, overlapping, and effective government policies is indisputable.

Legislative Influence

Federal policy.   At the federal level, Congress has not yet passed a bill that directly addresses school safety for GLBTQI students or those perceived to be GLBTQI. However, in 2011, a bipartisan group of sponsors reintroduced the Safe Schools Improvement Act (SSIA) in the Senate. This act would amend the Elementary and Secondary Education Act and require schools and districts receiving federal funds to adopt policies that (1) specifically prohibit bullying and harassment and (2) specifically include sexual orientation and gender identity as protected categories. As a means of measuring effectiveness, the SSIA would also require that states report data on school-related bullying and harassment to the Department of Education, who would then provide a biannual report to Congress.

State policies.   State legislatures across the country offer guidelines for educational policy in relation to GSD in the form of (1) bills (proposed legislation), (2) acts (adopted legislation), (3) statutes (law enacted by legislature), and (4) policies (viewpoints or interpretations that may or may not involve specific legislation).[4] As illustrated in box 9.1, legislative mandates vary widely from state to state, indicating that geographical location has a significant impact on the level of safety students are likely to experience at school.

So if you are a student in the state of California, you will study GLBT people in your social studies class. Conversely, if you are a student in the state of Tennessee you are not likely to be exposed to "any instruction or material that discusses sexual orientation other than heterosexuality." As of this writing the Tennessee "Don't Say Gay" bill has been approved by the Senate, is being considered in the House,

Box 9.1. State Legislation That Addresses Gender and Sexuality Diversity in PreK–12

- In February 2011, Montana's State House passed a bill (HB 456) that requires parental permission for students to attend classes, assemblies, "organized school functions," and "instruction of any type" that involves " human sexual education, human sexuality issues, or information regarding sexual acts" in K–12 public schools.
- A proposed New Hampshire bill (House Bill 370) sought to edit the antibullying law that passed in 2010. HB 370 would have *removed* the list of characteristics and identities protected from bullying, which includes sexual orientation, gender identity, and gender expression. In April 2011, the bill passed the House but was quickly killed in the Senate.
- In February 2011, two Tennessee state senators introduced a bill (Senate Bill 49/House Bill 229) that would prohibit public elementary and middle schools from "providing any instruction or material that discusses sexual orientation other than heterosexuality." In May, the bill passed the Senate largely along party lines with all no votes from Democrats; it will likely have a hearing in the House in 2012.
- In June 2009, Maine's Human Rights Commission ruled that the Orono School Department discriminated against a male-to-female transgender student by forcing her to use a single-stall faculty bathroom instead of the girls' bathroom. This set a precedent for Maine schools that they must allow transgender students to use the bathrooms of the gender with which they identify.
- In July 2011, California legislature passed a law that adds lesbian, gay, bisexual, and transgender people to the list of groups that schools must include in social studies lessons. This list already includes people with disabilities, African Americans, women, Mexican Americans, European Americans, Asian Americans, American Indians, entrepreneurs, and labor. The new law also prohibits lessons that present GLBT people adversely. A week after it passed, the governor signed the bill into law, making California the first state to require this type of LGBT-inclusive curriculum.

and, if passed, is likely to be signed into law by the governor (Terkel 2011). States' rights are a cherished aspect of democracy in the United States, yet it is clear that the laws in some states actually foster a hostile school climate for students. These state laws violate certain executive mandates and judicial rulings. Thus, in these cases, students must then turn to other branches of government for protection.

Executive Influence

The executive branch offers extensive educational guidelines of all kinds through the Department of Education (DOE). The Office of Civil Rights (OCR), in particular, advises state departments of education and local school districts on issues related to harassment and bullying. A Dear Colleague Letter[5] distributed in October 2010 by the OCR that specifically relates to GSD does the following:

- Clarifies the relationship between bullying and discriminatory harassment under the civil rights laws enforced by the Department of Education's (DOE) Office for Civil Rights (OCR).
- Explains how student misconduct that falls under an *antibullying policy* may also trigger responsibilities under one or more of the *antidiscrimination statutes* enforced by OCR.

- Reminds schools that failure to recognize discriminatory harassment when addressing student misconduct may lead to inadequate or inappropriate responses that fail to remedy violations of students' civil rights.
- Discusses racial and national origin harassment, sexual harassment, gender-based harassment, and disability harassment and illustrates how a school should respond in each case (see Additional Resource 9.2 for complete summary).

Through the Dear Colleague Letter (DCL), the Department of Education offers a comprehensive review that provides educators with concrete examples of what harassment and bullying look like in school—including those related to sexuality and gender. The DCL also spells out what the appropriate response should be. In addition it alerts schools to the fact that **addressing student misconduct via the school's antibullying policy may not be sufficient.** Some misconduct also falls under one or more of the *federal* antidiscrimination laws enforced by the Office of Civil Rights. For example:

> It can be sex discrimination if students are harassed either for exhibiting what is perceived as stereotypical characteristics for their sex, or for failing to conform to stereotypical notions of masculinity and femininity. Title IX also prohibits sexual harassment and gender-based harassment of all students; regardless of the actual or perceived sexual orientation or gender identity of the harasser or target. (U.S. Department of Education, 2010a)

This is essentially an admission by the DOE that antibullying policies alone do not provide sufficient civil rights protection for all students.

Based on these legal stipulations it would appear that **the majority of school districts in the United States are not in compliance with this government policy**. Take a moment to look at the summary in Additional Resource 9.2. Basically if a school knows—or should know—that harassment has occurred, "a school must take prompt and effective steps reasonably calculated to end the harassment, eliminate any hostile environment, and prevent its recurrence" (United States Department of Education, 2010a).

Now consider the disconnect between what climate surveys tell us about the chronically high levels of GSD hostility in schools and the Department of Education's mandate to "eliminate any hostile environment" in schools. How do we understand this gap between reality and the mandate? This gap is what prompted Dan Savage's "It Gets Better" campaign (see chapter 7). When you have politicians, including the president of the United States, religious leaders, social justice activists, military personnel, and hundreds of MS and HS students across the country imploring those students who are chronically harassed at school to hang in there until "it gets better," something is fundamentally wrong with the system.

> **Box 9.2. Judicial Rulings Related to Gender and Sexuality Education in PreK–12**
>
> - In 2009, the Alameda Unified School District (AUSD) in California approved a curriculum addressing diversity, bullying, respect, and acceptance, which had an annual 45-minute lesson focusing on LGBT issues for students in kindergarten through fifth grade. A group of parents protested and sued the school district for making these lessons mandatory for students. Though the Alameda Superior Court judge ruled in favor of the school district and its mandatory LGBT lessons, AUSD ultimately dropped the curriculum.
> - In 2008, the U.S. Court of Appeals for the First Circuit upheld a ruling rejecting four Lexington, Massachusetts, parents' claim that curricula including LGBT-related books violated free exercise rights. The court found that the end goal of such curricula was not "indoctrination," as the lawsuit stated, but tolerance, and added that "public schools are not obliged to shield individual students from ideas which potentially are religiously offensive" (Associated Press 2008).
> - In 2006, the student group Straights and Gays for Equality (SAGE) sued the Osseo Area Schools in Minnesota after being denied access to the school's PA system, yearbook, and other forms of communication and publicity. SAGE's lawsuit alleged that the district was in violation of the Equal Access Act, which states that if a public school provides forums and facilities to one student group, it may not prohibit other groups from using the same resources. The 8th Circuit court ruled in favor of SAGE, setting a precedent for the rights of GLBTQI extracurricular clubs.
> - In *Theno v. Tonganoxie Unified School District*, the plaintiff sued his school district for failing to uphold their legal obligation to protect him from bullying on the basis of his perceived gender and sexual orientation. The court used Title IX and its prohibition of gender-based harassment to find that the student had been a victim of sex discrimination, ruling that gender stereotyping is a "method of proving actionable harassment under Title IX." In 2005 the plaintiff was awarded $440,000.

Judicial Rulings

Some battles about GSD education are fought in the state house but several precedent-setting cases have been ruled on in courts of law (see box 9.2). Students and student organizations that have faced discrimination and harassment because of their actual or perceived sexual orientation and gender identity have won in court using three different federal laws.

- **Title IX:** sexual harassment, gender harassment.
- **Equal Access Act:** Requires that public schools offer fair opportunities for students to form student-led extracurricular groups, regardless of their religious, political, and philosophical meanings.
- **Equal Protection Clause** of the Fourteenth Amendment guarantees equal application of the law to all people.

Because the bias against GLBTQI persons is still prevalent in so many schools across the country, it is likely that there will be an increasing number of cases brought before the courts in the years ahead. This is one more indicator of inadequate compliance with DOE directives; students must go to court to fight for fair and equal treatment in school.

School Boards: All Politics Are Local

❖ *We have an antiharassment policy that has been tested and challenged and upheld and reinforced. We have a nondiscrimination policy in place in the district. Teachers are free to be out. These policies are actually working.*

Both public and independent schools are most directly and immediately beholden to their boards. Federal and state mandates are relevant only to the extent that the "local authority" takes them in to account while making and enforcing school policy.

> The goal of refocusing policy development strategies is to achieve policies that are driven by the district's vision, direction, and goals for student learning and achievement; and closing the achievement gap. Compliance/accountability with legal mandates is not enough. ("Strategies" 2010)

Because of the contradictions between federal and individual state guidelines, local authorities must create policies that serve the vision and mission of the district, and **address the reality of day-to-day school life in the present.** Recognizing that "legal mandates" are insufficient means school boards must provide local, community-based leadership in relation to GSD.

Public Schools

Many districts already have designated leadership to address issues of equity and justice.[6] For example, the director of Institutional Equity and Multicultural Education oversees policies and programs that can and should include GSD. Some districts use Governance Teams made up of staff, parents, and students to address a range of policy issues (Macgillivray 2004). Leadership on the local level can, in many instances, be accomplished by prompting those already in positions of responsibility to take on matters related to GSD. However, as the examples in box 9.3 illustrate, local authorities can move in both positive and negative directions as they create GSD policy.

Same-sex parents, their children, and school policy. The experience of students with same-sex parents provides a compelling example of the need for "local" authority and clarity in creating school policy. In 2006 the American Academy of Pediatrics (AAP) commissioned a multiagency (e.g., government, medical, research) study to examine the legal, financial, and psychosocial health of children with gay parents (Pawelski et al. 2006). AAP's vested interest in this issue is based on the fact that children's health and well-being are protected by their own legal rights *and* the rights of their parents. Because the federal government does not recognize same-sex marriage, and because state legislatures continue to battle

Box 9.3. Local Policies Related to Gender and Sexuality Diversity in PreK–12

- The West Chester, Pennsylvania, school board has maintained support for an optional relationship and abstinence program, in spite of concerns expressed by parents and students that the curriculum is ineffective. The RealEd4U program is a series of health and human sexuality presentations for middle schoolers, run by Amnion, a faith-based, abstinence-only-until-marriage organization. RealEd4U is the only sexuality education option for students until tenth grade. Healthy relationships are presented exclusively in the context of heterosexual pairings and marriage.
- In February 2011, Flour Bluff Intermediate School District in Corpus Christi, Texas, shut down all extracurricular clubs in an attempt to legally prevent students from starting a Gay Straight Alliance. The Equal Access Act (a federal law) requires that public schools offer "fair opportunities for students to form student-led extracurricular groups, regardless of their religious, political, and philosophical meanings."
- A group of parents have been fighting the Vallejo City Unified School District since its introduction of their Respect For All curriculum, an antibullying program that includes two films about gender and sexuality diversity, *That's a Family*, directed toward elementary school students, and *Straight-laced*, intended for adolescents. In December of 2010, the school board voted 4-1 to retain the program, and the superintendent recommended retention of the curriculum again in April of 2011.
- In 2009, the Anoka-Hennepin school district, Minnesota's largest, adopted a policy dubbed "the neutrality policy," which prevents teachers from talking about sexual orientation. This policy was challenged publicly in 2010 after anti-LGBT bullying played a role in at least four of the nine "local" student suicides that occurred in just one year, and has come under fire again in 2011 as parents challenge the school board to control the bullying that has persisted. As of August 2011, the policy remains in place. The U.S. Department of Education's Office of Civil Rights and the U.S. Justice Department announced an investigation into "incidents involving harassment and bullying" in the district to determine if there have been ongoing violations of civil rights law. The district also faces private lawsuits from the ACLU and NCLR (see box 7.1).

over the legitimacy of GLBTQI families (Additional Resource 9.5), committed same-sex couples do not have the rights, benefits, and protections afforded to married heterosexual couples. Therefore, **their children also have fewer protections**.

As a result of their investigation, AAP determined that the general public—including many pediatricians—is unaware of the breadth and depth of vulnerability experienced by children with same-sex parents. When school boards and districts fail to provide adequate rights and protections to students with gay parents, they perpetuate the legal, financial, and psychosocial discrimination these children already experience at the state and federal level. **Schools have a responsibility to work with the reality of a student's actual family and not the socially or legally approved definition of family** (Powell et al. 2010).

What is in the way of creating a favorable educational climate for all students? Systemic discrimination—conscious or unconscious—against nonheteronormativity is at the heart of much school-based bias and harassment. Only comprehensive and consistent preK–12 GSD education for teachers, students, and parents alike will foster a shift in this deeply ingrained prejudice. The good news is that the "shift" is possible (see Model, next section).

GSD Equitable District Policy

School districts *can* fully address the needs of those students, teachers, and families who represent a range of genders and sexualities. The Lesbian, Gay, Bisexual, Transgender, Transsexual, Two-Spirit, Questioning policy from the Vancouver School Board (VSB) serves as a comprehensive, explicit directive that addresses

- Leadership
- Counseling and Student Support
- Anti-Harassment
- Curriculum Learning Resources
- Staff Development, In-Service and Professional Development
- School-Community Involvement
- Employment Equity

The VSB also claims responsibility for ensuring that schools uphold each component of the policy. Creating this kind of policy does not ensure implementation and enforcement. However, it does provide a clear map for navigating the discreet and interrelated aspects of school life that are affected by GSD.

Model: The Vancouver School Board Lesbian, Gay, Bisexual, Transgender, Transsexual, Two-Spirit, Questioning Policy

"The Board will provide a safe environment, free from harassment and discrimination, while also promoting pro-active strategies and guidelines to ensure that lesbian, gay, transgender, transsexual, two-spirit, bisexual and questioning students, employees and families are welcomed and included in all aspects of education and school life and treated with respect and dignity. The purpose of this policy is to define appropriate behaviours and actions in order to prevent discrimination and harassment through greater awareness of and responsiveness to their deleterious effects. This policy is also drafted to ensure that homophobic complaints are taken seriously and dealt with expeditiously and effectively through consistently applied policy and procedures. The policy will also raise awareness and improve understanding of the lives of people who identify themselves on the basis of sexual orientation or gender identity. By valuing diversity and respecting differences, students and staff act in accordance with the Vancouver district's social responsibility initiative." (See Additional Resource 9.3 for full policy statement.)

Independent Schools

Independent schools are also overseen by a school board, typically known as the Board of Trustees (BOT). The trustees work most directly in collaboration with the head of school and are charged with a range of far-reaching steward-ship responsibilities (see Additional Resource 9.7). Changes in school mission, or changes in the *interpretation* of school mission, are typically reviewed and voted on by the board. When the head of school is looked to by the school community for leadership and guidance in relation to GSD, she must confer with the board before making major "operational" changes. However, the influence of the BOT varies from school to school and even from board to board at the same school over time.

Important BOT work is often done via committees, and there is typically a committee devoted to diversity, multicultural education, cultural competence or the like. This committee is often charged with looking at mission, philosophy, and policy that affect the religious, racial, and socioeconomic equity of the school. For example, the Gordon School Statement on Inclusivity was written by a task force of faculty, trustees, parents, and administrators. Working with a recommendation from an accreditation team, the task force created this statement to more clearly reflect and incorporate core principles related to diversity.

Model: The Gordon School Statement on Inclusivity

> *Gordon proudly honors each individual within its community. The school respects the customs, traditions, values and perspectives of individuals of different gender, race, religion, socioeconomic status, family configuration, sexual orientation, ethnicity, ability and age. The faculty actively teaches students to confidently consider multiple perspectives, examine and express their own beliefs and respond respectfully to the ideas and beliefs of others. To the greatest extent possible, Gordon takes steps to ensure equal and equitable participation for all members of the school community.*
>
> *Gordon's emphasis on inclusivity, an evolving process, is essential to its mission to prepare students for active citizenship in the world.*
>
> —Gordon School, East Providence, Rhode Island

Elaborating and specifying core principles of "diversity" is similar to enumerating antidiscrimination policies in order to clarify exactly who is protected by them. Gordon's statement makes clear what "honoring each individual within its community" really means. In the same way, the Board Committee on Cultural Competence at Brookwood School "drafted a list of beliefs relating to cultural competence that have been long supported by the school but had not yet been expressly articulated" (see Additional Resource 9.4). The document was approved by the full board and then introduced to faculty and community. Articulation and specificity of this kind clarifies what the school's mission (e.g., "respecting diversity") is meant to look like in actual practice.

As important as the philosophy or policy itself is, the process by which such values are clarified is highly salient. Consider the two policy changes below:

❖ *We recently changed our lower school uniform for girls to include pants (instead of a jumper only).*

❖ *A significant policy which permits same sex couples to live in dormitory housing has had a profound effect.*

Small groups of people working hard together over time grappled with big questions in order to affect these policy changes. *Is there a reason we shouldn't let girls wear pants to school? What makes a straight couple acceptable as dorm parents but not a gay couple? What message are we sending with this policy? What best reflects our values as a school: changing the policy or keeping it the same?* In essence this small group process represents transformational learning, achieved on behalf of further transformational learning that will be done by the rest of the community (i.e., faculty, parents, students, alums).

What Can One School Do?

Regardless of governmental and accreditation oversight, individual schools (public and private) still have a meaningful degree of autonomy. They can enact short- and long-term policies such as this one.

❖ *In the last two years we have adopted a school-wide diversity statement, which includes specifically gender and orientation as "individual characteristics" worthy of respect.*

This "local intervention" is designed to educate this particular community, and as a result, improve the climate for *all* students, families, and teachers, not just those who identify as GLBTQI. Similarly, individual schools and individual teachers do not need legislative or school board approval to participate in No Name-Calling Week (see section IV). Local or individual school efforts of this kind foster "community," which, in turn, counteracts the negative climate in which bullying thrives.

Philosophy as Policy

At the individual school level, the clear articulation of rules and behavioral expectations is an essential component of policy. However, as noted earlier in this section, policies can also be understood as *viewpoints* or *interpretations*, not just rules and laws. The challenge is to find a balance between "having a rule for everything" on the one hand, and uneven, inconsistent guidelines on the other. In chapter 3, school mission and educational values are identified as essential guideposts in the search for positive, effective approaches to GSD. In taking the time to consider, create, revise, and commit their *philosophies* about GSD to paper, schools provide a foundational reference point for all community members.

The Ethical Culture Fieldston School's (ECFS) "Health and Human Sexuality Education Philosophy Statement" is a perfect example of "philosophy as policy." The importance of this type of explicitness is well understood by any educator who has needed "something in writing" to support his content and/or pedagogy. When a student asks, *Why is this important to learn?* or a parent asks, *Why are you sponsoring this program?* there may not be an exact or ready answer in the school handbook. **But philosophy that is thoughtfully laid out and made known is often where the best "answers" to such questions can be found.**

Model: ECFS Health and Human Sexuality Education Philosophy Statement

> *As a progressive school, we view the teaching of health and human sexuality as fundamental to our educational mission. We are committed to nurturing the whole child, which includes the personal, emotional, social and physical aspects of development. From the earliest grades through high school, we help our students understand and value the healthy growth and development of their bodies, identities, and relationships.*
>
> *We see health as the promotion of wellness and safety in all areas of life and assume a broad definition of sexuality that encompasses not only our physical selves, but also our gender and the diverse ways we experience and express ourselves and relate to one another. We believe that the school and parents complement each other in giving children the knowledge and skills they need to make informed, responsible, and ethical decisions about their physical well-being, their personal and social choices, and their sexual health as they grow and mature.*
>
> *When taught in a developmentally appropriate way, children at every age learn that they have the freedom to ask questions, to be themselves, and to rely on the adults in their lives to be sensitive and supportive. Drawing on this foundation of open dialogue and instruction, children acquire clear and accurate information and develop an understanding of their own values and attitudes about health and sexuality, as well as a deep appreciation for the diversity of individual expression, identity, and family.*
>
> —Ethical Culture Fieldston School, New York

WHAT TO REMEMBER: SECTION II

Policies and Philosophies

1. The legislative, executive, and judicial branches of government impact school policies related to GSD.

2. In spite of various laws, mandates, and court rulings, school safety for GLBTQI students continues to be a chronic problem in schools across the United States.

3. Because individual states have vastly different laws related to GSD, where a student lives (e.g., California vs. Tennessee) has a huge impact on school safety. Certain state laws actually increase the likelihood of a hostile school climate.

4. The Department of Education's Office of Civil Rights specifically addresses the relationship between antibullying policies and civil rights laws that protect students. Climate surveys suggest that the majority of schools in the United States are not in compliance with the OCR directives.

5. Students who have been chronically harassed at school have won court rulings based on Title IX, Equal Access Act, and Equal Protection Clause.

6. Local school boards have the power to influence district policy in relation to GSD.

7. The Board of Trustees in independent schools has a role in shaping programs, policies, and philosophies in relation to GSD. Thus, board education in the GSD domain is critical.

8. Putting pedagogical philosophies in writing is another way to create broad support for GSD programming and curriculum.

SECTION III
CREATING AND IMPLEMENTING POLICIES

To challenge moral conservatives' worldview about the superiority of heterosexuality is to challenge their worldviews of what it means to be a man or a woman, a husband or a wife, a family, a Christian, even a human.

—Ian Macgillivray, *Sexual Orientation and School Policy*

GUIDELINES FOR CREATING SUCCESSFUL POLICIES

The good news is that the guidelines for creating successful policy at the local and district level are plentiful and accessible. Scholars (Meyer 2009), state boards of education (California), social justice advocacy groups (Advocates for Youth), health organizations (Planned Parenthood), and educational advocacy organizations (GLSEN; Human Rights Campaign's Welcoming Schools) all provide protocols and strategies for advancing the safety, health, and inclusion of all students in preK–12 schools. So road maps are available. Understanding all those who are on the journey together, however, is as important as having good directions.

The Importance of Understanding the Players

Ian Macgillivray's book *Sexual Orientation and School Policy: A Practical Guide for Teachers, Administrators, and Community Activists* addresses a critical component of effecting school change in this domain. In addition to offering comprehensive strategies for (1) creating GLBTQI inclusive policies, and (2) implementing GLBTQI inclusive policies, Macgillivray (2004) examines the underlying motivations of those who support and those who object to this type of change. The depth and objectivity of his exploration offers critical insight into the all-to-familiar image of "two groups [that] continue to talk past each other" (112), unable to collaborate.

If district policy supports the idea that "it's okay to be gay," moral conservatives[7] fear that their own valuing of heterosexuality and traditional gender roles will be undermined. They do not want gay kids to be harassed, but they do not believe GLBTQI students need explicit policies for protection. "'There shouldn't be special policies for gay students because they should be treated as everyone else is, with respect'" (118). Supporters of enumerated GLBTQI policies are quick to label nonsupporters as narrow-minded bigots. Supporters also tend to emphasize the goal of student safety alone and minimize their desire to do anything more than stop antigay harassment. In truth, they *do* want to change hearts and minds; they *do* want the message and curriculum at school to support the acceptability of being GLBTQI.

First Amendment rights. Macgillivray contends that the value of the First Amendment right to free speech is its equal application to all parties. Consequently, no student or parent ought to be discriminated against for expressing her beliefs about religion *or* about gender and sexuality. Thus, establishing a culture of "safety and respect" in schools means respecting other's *rights* to an opinion, not necessarily respecting *the opinion itself*. If the discourse is respectful, all parties have a right to be heard. Change becomes possible when people feel understood—rather than vilified.

Teachers Caught in the Crossfire

Creating a safe and democratic culture in schools, and a safe and democratic process for making school policy, can be an exacting and painful experience. The battle between advocates and opponents of GLBTQI policies can leave teachers caught right in the middle.

> On the one hand they want to create a safe classroom for all of their students, and they certainly want to foster in their students democratic ideals regarding the proper treatment of others; on the other hand, they need to respect the rights and wishes of all students and their families who hold differing opinions

about what a safe and welcoming classroom environment entails. (Macgillivray 2004, 138)

For many teachers, the explicit recognition, inclusion, and support of GLBTQI people is not only a profound shift in policy but also in their own way of understanding the world. This contributes to their uncertainty about "where to stand" in relation to the ongoing policy battle.

Teachers caught in this bind must have opportunities to

- review current policy and weigh it against actual experience.
- understand proposed policy changes and what those changes will actually look like daily in school.
- explore the impact of the policy change on their professional and personal beliefs.
- identify strategies and tools for new policy implementation.

Without these professional development policy review and personal values clarification opportunities (see chapter 5), teachers will continue to feel disempowered and "caught in the middle" of a fight they did not choose.

GENDER AND SEXUALITY HARASSMENT POLICY

A detailed, comprehensive, and exhaustive gender and sexuality harassment policy (GSHP) differs from a standard antibullying policy in critical ways, and every preK–12 school community needs to understand these differences. Sexism, heterosexism, and homophobia operate at an institutional level, and as such, they are not always readily discernable. Typically schools are institutions that, consciously or unconsciously, reinforce heteronormative expectations (see chapter 2), which further obscures the elements that contribute to a hostile environment (Meyer 2011; Meyer 2009).

Therefore, harassment related to gender and sexuality must first be clearly defined before it can then be actively monitored (Gruber and Finneran 2008).

> ❖ *I wish the student code of conduct explicitly categorized bias incidents and hate-based harassment as violations instead of implicitly including them under "bullying."*

As this teacher suggests, codes of conduct must be explicit about what behaviors are and are not sanctioned in the school community.

Bullying vs. Harassment

There are important differences between what we call *bullying* and what we call *harassment*. **Bullying** is intentional injurious behavior toward another individual. **Harassment** is bias-based behavior that can have a negative impact on both the individual *and* the environment. Thus, harassment does *not* have to be targeted at an individual. Bullying and harassment clearly overlap; the key distinction is that the bully intends to do harm, whereas those who engage in biased behavior may or may not be intentionally creating a hostile climate for others (Meyer 2009).

A simple example of this? Students who claim that their use of "that's so gay" is not meant to be hurtful or homophobic. *We don't mean anything by it. We're not talking about actual people. It's just a word that means "lame" or "stupid."* In fact, these students may truly not intend to create a hostile climate, but that can be the impact of their behavior nonetheless. Similarly male peers who use the word "faggot" primarily to put each other down direct the insult at each other, not at an individual they actually think is gay. Regardless of intention or target, using the term "faggot" to label unacceptable male behavior contributes to a hostile environment for other people.

Different Types of Harassment

Schools must identify and describe different types of harassment in order for their gender and sexuality harassment policy (GSHP) to be effective. Meyer (2009; 2011) highlights three primary categories:

- **(Hetero) Sexual Harassment**—verbal and behavioral hostility of a sexual nature intended to degrade and objectify girls/women primarily; however, men and GLBTQI people can also be sexually harassed.
- **Sexual Orientation Harassment**—any behavior, hidden or obvious, that reinforces negative attitudes toward gay, lesbian, bisexual, or queer people.
- **Harassment for Gender Nonconformity**—any behavior, hidden or obvious, that reinforces negative attitudes toward those who do not express masculinity and/or femininity according to traditional cultural expectations.

Creating policy in this area requires the education of all community members, students, teachers, and parents alike. Everyone needs to know the specific behaviors and language, *in a school-based context,* that are prohibited.

For example, a general ban on name-calling does not address the sexism involved when female students are called "bitch" or "baby" or "ho" by some males who consider this a cultural norm, not a form of harassment. Similarly, the mandate of "treat others with respect" is vague. A group of students who repeatedly question a genderqueer peer about what s/he is going to wear to the senior dance may consider this "teasing" behavior, whereas the student may experience it as harassment.

The GSHP must not only identify to whom the policy applies; it must also provide examples of the harassing behaviors that are prohibited. Dominant, popular imagery of adolescent culture makes challenging heteronormativity, sexism, misogyny, homophobia, and transphobia no small task. **Educators may assume that students have a solid understanding of what "appropriate" and "inappropriate" behavior should look like in school; the truth is, many do not.** The behaviors glorified in music videos, reality shows, movies, and advertisements portray women as sexual objects (or sexual predators) dominated by men who use violence and degradation to meet their own sexual and psychological needs. How exactly would students know that these attitudes and behaviors are not appropriate at school?

The Rules at School

School personnel are not going to eradicate vulgar lyrics or pornographic music videos. However, administrators and teachers do have the authority to **educate students about what conduct is acceptable at school**. And because the line between what is appropriate or inappropriate in social media has become entirely blurred, schools may struggle to combat considerably lowered standards that represent the "new normal."

Here is an example from a female administrator.

> ❖ *A freshman girl revealed several incidents of sexual harassment from a number of freshmen boys. In the discussion with the administration about the event (the student withdrew from school before official charges could be brought forth), an administrator said that, "We need to be careful when we use the term 'sexual harassment.' As adults 'sexual harassment' has a distinct definition, but some of this is just regular boy/girl stuff."*

Perhaps this male administrator is right, that in this case the serious language of sexual harassment is being erroneously applied to "regular boy/girl stuff." Yet what constitutes "regular boy/girl stuff" today is probably different from when these administrators were adolescents.

Kedrick Griffin spends his time meeting with groups of boys in District of Columbia schools to talk about masculinity; he finds that teenage boys feel entitled to harassing behavior and attitudes (Hess 2010).

> ➢ *From where I come from, you holler at a girl.*
> ➢ *A girl can't be too upset when a guy is paying attention to her.*
> ➢ *It depends on the type of girl and whether she has respect for herself.*
> ➢ *Some girls will say, stop. But they like it, for real.*

> ➤ *If she's wearing short shorts, booty shorts, short skirt, with the thong show-*
> *ing, she wants it. Can't blame it on the boy. She knows what she's doing.*

Kedrick helps students challenge the cultural messages of hypermasculinity and aggression. He asserts that being fun, nice, caring, and respectful does not make a boy less of a man. But he is up against formidable cultural forces that broadcast the opposite message.

More Than Just Changing the Words

It is clear that for many schools, updating or revising harassment policy will require more than just changing the language in an existing statement. A realistic review of GSHP means (1) taking a hard look at the current sexualized climate in which students are growing up and (2) actively countering it at the schoolhouse door. The American Psychological Association's Task Force on the Sexualization of Girls reports (Zurbriggen et al. 2007) that both girls and boys are sexualized when

- a person's value comes only from his or her sexual appeal or behavior, to the exclusion of other characteristics;
- a person is held to a standard that equates physical attractiveness (narrowly defined) with being sexy;
- a person is sexually objectified—that is, made into a thing for other's sexual use, rather than seen as a person with the capacity for independent action and decision making; and/or
- sexuality is inappropriately imposed upon a person.[8]

Boys do not benefit from pejorative stereotypes of males any more than girls benefit from being objectified. As discussed in chapters 7 and 8, students must be taught media literacy so they can deconstruct the overt and covert messages about acceptable interpersonal and community behavior. However, the behavioral and philosophical bottom line must be explicated in the school's GSHP. Why? Because adults who work in the school system are left to contend with this enormous cultural problem on a daily basis in the school setting. The kids-should-know-better approach is a passive, ineffective defense against the pornographic "new normal" in which children and adolescents are currently being socialized (*Sexy, Inc.*).

EDUCATION + PROGRAMS + POLICIES

The links between gender and sexuality diversity education, comprehensive sexuality education, and gender and sexuality harassment policy are unmistakable. Each program/policy reinforces fundamental components of the school mission.

Without the essential academic, social, behavioral, and attitudinal guidelines these programs and policies provide, it seems unlikely that educational institutions will be able to achieve their stated goals:

- Create a safe, welcoming effective and innovative learning environment . . . that supports civility, respect and academic achievement. (Dallas, TX)
- Maintain safe and orderly school environments for all students and employees . . . and promote a culture of mutual trust and respect. (Santa Barbara, CA)
- Reinforce mutual respect as the foundation of our School community. . . . Respect for others leads us to serve them and to embrace diverse peoples and cultures. (Charlotte, NC)
- Cultivate respect for diversity and engender habits of moral and ethical leadership and a sense of responsibility to the broader community. (Baltimore, MD)

The chronicity of harassment in schools, the harm it perpetuates, and the degree of disruption it causes should be reasons enough to advocate and support GSD education, CSE, and CSHP. Yet it is the positive outcomes—such as mutual respect, ethical leadership, and community responsibility—that can and should provide the inspiration to tackle this problem head on.

WHAT TO REMEMBER: SECTION III

Creating and Implementing Policy

1. Guidelines for creating successful GSD policy at the local and district levels are plentiful.
2. All sides of the GSD debate have First Amendment rights to express their opinions.
3. Teachers are often caught in the middle of the debate, wanting to respect parents who have different points of view and also wanting to provide students with good practices.
4. The establishment and implementation of a comprehensive gender and sexuality harassment policy is a critical component in supporting GSD education and creating safety in schools.
5. There are different types of GSD harassment: (a) (Hetero)Sexual Harassment, (b) Sexual Orientation Harassment, and (c) Harassment for Gender Nonconformity.
6. Instruction about appropriate/inappropriate conduct at school must be proactive and specific. Given the increasingly sexualized culture students are growing up in, they do not automatically know what appropriate behavior looks like.

7. Gender and sexuality diversity education, comprehensive sexuality education, and gender and sexuality harassment policy work together to create a safe learning and social environment for all students.

SECTION IV
PROGRAMS THAT SUPPORT GENDER AND SEXUALITY DIVERSITY EDUCATION

There are dozens of successful student and community-based programs that support gender and sexuality diversity education. This section of the chapter highlights programs that are accessible, affordable (most of them are free), and time-tested. Some resources focus on curriculum, some feature national campaigns that address bullying, and some constitute special school-wide projects and exhibits.

Diversity Council's Spark Curriculum

In 1996 the Diversity Council of Rochester, Minnesota, developed the Spark Curriculum as a comprehensive K–12 program dedicated to prejudice-reduction. The program consists of yearly workshops at every grade level; as students progress through their education, they begin with basic concepts such as "same & different" and move to more challenging discussions of discrimination and respect in areas such as disability, race, body size, social class, gender identity, sexual orientation, and religion. The Diversity Council lists the goals of these workshops as (1) increasing knowledge, (2) building empathy and self-esteem, and (3) developing critical thinking skills. Research has shown these steps to be critical factors in reducing prejudice among children. Over the past fifteen years Spark has gone from an initial group of three hundred students to now reaching nearly eighteen thousand K–12 students each year. (See Additional Resource 9.6 for the curriculum overview.)

No Name-Calling Week

James Howe's *The Misfits* tells the story of four middle school students who run for student office on a campaign to eliminate name-calling of all kinds. This novel is the inspiration behind No Name-Calling Week (NNCW). The NNCW Coalition consists of over forty national partner organizations, and schools all across the country participate in this annual event. Aimed at grades K–12, the project seeks to focus national attention on the problem of name-calling in schools. NNCW provides students and educators with the tools and inspiration to launch an ongoing dialogue about ways to eliminate name-calling in their communities.

A guide to organizing a school-wide No Name-Calling Week, including tips on getting administrative support and encouraging participation from all members of the school community, is available for download. Additionally, there is a 27-minute video that focuses on name-calling in grades 5–8, accompanied by a Teacher Resource Book (www.nonamecallingweek.org).

Gay Straight Alliance

Gay Straight Alliances (GSA) are student clubs that work to make schools safer and more supportive of students of all sexualities, gender identities, and expressions. The first GSA was formed in 1988, and by 2008 over four thousand clubs were registered with the Gay, Lesbian and Straight Education Network (GLSEN). Having a GSA at school correlates with GLBTQ students or those perceived to be GLBTQ, feeling safer. Additionally, faculty, administrators, and staff are perceived to be more supportive at schools with a GSA (Kosciw et al. 2010). GLSEN provides a comprehensive guide for starting a GSA (see Jump-Start Guide).

GLSEN's Jump-Start Guide for Building and Activating a Gay Straight Alliance

GLSEN, the Gay, Lesbian and Straight Education Network, offers a comprehensive resource for new and already established Gay Straight Alliances and similar clubs. The guide takes students through the process of (a) establishing or reestablishing their group, (b) identifying their mission and goals, and (c) assessing their school's climate. Jump-Start offers seasoned advice along with creative activities designed to "bring fresh and creative energy" to the club.

1. **Building and Activating Your GSA or Similar Student Club**
   - 10 Steps Toward Starting a GSA or Similar Student Club
   - Advice from Student Club Leaders and Faculty Advisors
   - Creating a Mission Statement
   - Finding New Members for Your GSA
   - Identifying Anti-LGBT Biases at Your School
   - School Climate Outlines and Surveys
2. **Tips and Tools for Organizing an Action Campaign**
   - Using Your Mission Statement and Climate Survey to Strategize
   - Framing Your Message
   - Creating an Action Plan
3. **Strategies for Training Teachers**
   - Planning a Teacher Training
   - What Can Teachers Do?
4. **Understanding Direct-Action Organizing**
   - Introduction to Organizing
   - Movements in History
   - Sample Strategy Chart

5. **Examining Power, Privilege and Oppression**
   - What Does "Anti-Oppression" Mean?
   - Exploring Identity and Identity Shields; Exploring Power and Privilege
   - Being an Ally
6. **Creating Youth-Adult Partnerships**
   - What Is a Partnership?
   - Exploring Ageism and Adultism
   - Why We Work with Adults
7. **Making Your Student Club Trans-Inclusive**
   - What Is Transgender?
   - Learning the Language
   - Exploring Transphobia and Genderism
   - The Pronoun Game
8. **Evaluation, Continuation, Celebration**
   - Assessing Your Group's Work
   - Looking Forward, Looking Back

The Jump-Start Guide is available from GLSEN as PDFs of individual sections (http://www.glsen.org/cgi-bin/iowa/all/news/record/2226.html).

Ally Week

GLSEN sponsors an annual Ally Week in October, a five-day event and campaign "to identify, support and celebrate allies against anti-LGBT language, bullying and harassment in America's schools" (Ally Week FAQs, www.allyweek.org). Most participating schools encourage students and educators to sign the Ally Pledge: *I believe all students, regardless of sexual orientation or gender identity/expression, deserve to feel safe and supported. That means I pledge to: 1) Not use anti-LGBT language and slurs; 2) Intervene, if I safely can, in situations where other students are being harassed; and 3) Support efforts to end bullying and harassment.*

More information, suggestions, free resources, and materials are available at www.allyweek.org.

Day of Silence

The Day of Silence is the largest student-led action to date aimed at creating safer schools for all, regardless of sexual orientation, gender identity, or gender expression. This is a national event in which students take a vow of silence to raise awareness of anti-LGBT harassment and discrimination, and to draw attention to the way LGBT students often feel invisible and silenced in the school setting. GLSEN sponsors the annual event; as of 2008, over eight thousand schools had participated. Free downloadable organizing manual, stickers, posters, and "speaking cards" that help participants communicate while maintaining their vow of silence are all available at www.dayofsilence.org.

Gay and Lesbian History Month (Black History Month; Women's History Month)

Important figures in history who belong to marginalized groups have often had their presence in, and contributions to, society overlooked. Black History Month has roots that go as far back as the 1920s,[9] and Congress officially recognized Women's History Month in 1981.[10] Designating certain months for the study and celebration of cultural minorities is an acknowledged method of attempting to create equity in both contemporary and historical representation.

GLBT History Month is not a federally recognized entity and only a handful of government officials have publicly endorsed October as GLBT History Month. Advocacy organizations such the Gay and Lesbian Alliance Against Defamation, Human Rights Campaign, and National Gay and Lesbian Task Force have endorsed this form of recognition, and in 1995 the National Education Association (NEA) passed an amendment supporting Gay and Lesbian History Month. The NEA endorsement speaks to the need for this aspect of history to be taught in preK–12 schools.

Lesbian, Gay, Bisexual, and Transgender History Month resources. In 2006, Equality Forum started a program that recognizes one notable LGBT person each day of the month in October. Thirty-one icons who represent politics, the arts, fashion, law, and science are honored with a video, bio, bibliography, downloadable images, and educational resources. Here is the list of the 2011 icons.

> Kye Allums, Athlete °° John Ashbery, Poet °° Alison Bechdel, Cartoonist °° John Berry, Government Official °° Dustin Lance Black, Screenwriter/Director °° Keith Boykin, Political Commentator °° Rita Mae Brown, Author °° Dan Choi, Veteran °° Aaron Copland, Composer °° Alan Cumming, Actor °° Denise Eger, Rabbi °° Lady Gaga, Singer °° Michael Guest, Ambassador °° Neil Patrick Harris, Actor °° Daniel Hernandez Jr., Student and Media Hero °° Langston Hughes, Poet °° Frida Kahlo, Artist °° David Kato, Ugandan Activist °° Michael Kirby, Former Australian Supreme Court Justice °° Victoria Kolakowski, Judge °° Dave Kopay, Athlete °° Ricky Martin, Singer °° Amélie Mauresmo, Athlete °° Constance McMillen, Activist °° Ryan Murphy, TV Writer/Director/Producer °° Dan Savage, Journalist °° Amanda Simpson, Government Official °° Wanda Sykes, Actor and Comedian °° Lilli Vincenz, Activist °° Virginia Woolf, Author

Equality Forum offers special features for students and provides all materials free. Additionally, the previous 155 Icons (2006–2010) are archived on the site (www.lgbthistorymonth.com).

ADDITIONAL RESOURCES

Additional Resource 9.1

Ten Big Ideas of School Leadership

Mike McCarthy, is the principal at Helen King Middle School in Portland and Maine's 2010 Middle School Principal of the Year

Here are ten ideas I have learned in the 30 years since I became a principal:

1. **Your School Must Be for All Kids 100 Percent of the Time**

   If you start making decisions based on avoiding conflict, the students lose. This is what sustained me through one of my most difficult decisions. I asked the school district to let our school health center offer birth control after four girls became pregnant in one semester. For this group of kids, the health center at King was their primary health care provider. Although we offer birth control to our students, we are not the birth control school; we are the school that cares about all of its kids. This decision was the right one, and it cemented for all time the central values of King.

2. **Create a Vision, Write It Down, and Start Implementing It**

   Don't put your vision in your drawer and hope for the best. Every decision must be aligned with that vision. The whole organization is watching when you make a decision, so consistency is crucial.

3. **It's the People, Stupid**

   The secret of managing is to keep the guys who hate you away from those who are still undecided. (That's adapted from Casey Stengel.) Hire people who support your vision, who are bright, and who like kids.

4. **Paddles in the Water**

   In Outward Bound, you learn that when you are navigating dangerous rapids in a raft, the only way to succeed is for everyone in the boat to sit out on the edge and paddle really hard, even though everyone would rather be sitting in the center, where it's safer. At King, in times of crisis, everyone responds with paddles in the water.

5. **Find Time to Think during the Day**

   They pay me to worry. It's OK to stare at the wall and think about how to manage change. I have 70 people who work at King. Even the most centered has three bad days each school year. Multiply that by 70 people and that's 210 bad days, which is more than the 180 school days in a year. So, me, I am never going to have a good day—just get over it.

6. **Take Responsibility for the Good and the Bad**

   If the problems in your school or organization lie below you and the solutions lie above you, then you have rendered yourself irrelevant. The genius of school lies within the school. The solutions to problems are almost always right in front of you.

7. **You Have the Ultimate Responsibility**

   Have very clear expectations. Make sure people have the knowledge, resources, and time to accomplish what you expect. This shows respect. As much as possible, give people the autonomy to manage their own work, budget, time, and curriculum. Autonomy is the goal, though you still have to inspect.

8. **Have a Bias for Yes**

   When my son was little, I was going through a lot of turmoil at King, and I did not feel like doing much of anything when I got home. One day, I just decided that whatever he wanted to do, I would do—play ball, eat ice cream, and so on. I realized the power of yes. It changed our relationship. The only progress you will ever make involves risk: Ideas that teachers have may seem a little unsafe and crazy. Try to think, "How can I make this request into a yes?"

9. **Consensus Is Overrated**

   Twenty percent of people will be against anything. When you realize this, you avoid compromising what really should be done because you stop watering things down. If you always try to reach consensus, you are being led by the 20 percent.

10. **Large Change Needs to Be Done Quickly**

    If you wait too long to make changes to a school culture, you have already sanctioned mediocre behavior because you're allowing it. That's when change is hard, and you begin making bad deals. (Reprinted with permission from McCarthy and Baron 2010)

Additional Resource 9.2

Department of Education, Office of Civil Rights: Background, Summary, and Fast Facts on Harassment and Bullying (October 2010)*

What are the possible effects of student-on-student harassment and bullying?

- Lowered academic achievement and aspirations
- Increased anxiety
- Loss of self-esteem and confidence
- Depression and post-traumatic stress
- General deterioration in physical health

- Self-harm and suicidal thinking
- Feelings of alienation in the school environment, such as fear of other children
- Absenteeism from school

What does the Dear Colleague Letter (DCL) do?

- Clarifies the relationship between bullying and discriminatory harassment under the civil rights laws enforced by the Department of Education's (ED) Office for Civil Rights (OCR).
- Explains how student misconduct that falls under an anti-bullying policy also may trigger responsibilities under one or more of the anti-discrimination statutes enforced by OCR.
- Reminds schools that failure to recognize discriminatory harassment when addressing student misconduct may lead to inadequate or inappropriate responses that fail to remedy violations of students' civil rights. Colleges and universities have the same obligations under the anti-discrimination statues as elementary and secondary schools.
- Discusses racial and national origin harassment, sexual harassment, gender-based harassment, and disability harassment and illustrates how a school should respond in each case.

Why is ED issuing the DCL? ED is issuing the DCL to clarify the relationship between bullying and discriminatory harassment, and to remind schools that by limiting their responses to specific application of an anti-bullying or other disciplinary policy, they may fail to properly consider whether the student misconduct also results in discrimination in violation of students' federal civil rights.

What are the anti-discrimination statues that the Office for Civil Rights enforces?

- Title VI of the Civil Rights Act of 1964, which prohibits discrimination on the basis of race, color, or national origin.
- Title IX of the Education Amendments of 1972, which prohibits discrimination on the basis of sex.
- Section 504 of the Rehabilitation Act of 1973 and Title II of the Americans with Disabilities Act of 1990, which prohibits discrimination on the basis of disability.
- (The OCR also enforces the Age Discrimination Act of 1975 and the Boy Scouts of America Equal Access Act. The DCL does not address these statutes.)

What are a school's obligations under these anti-discrimination statutes?

- Once a school knows or reasonably should know of possible student-on-student harassment, it must take immediate and appropriate action to investigate or otherwise determine what occurred. If harassment has occurred, a school must take prompt and effective steps reasonably calculated to end the harassment, eliminate any hostile environment, and prevent its recurrence. These duties are a school's responsibility even if a) the misconduct is also covered by an anti-bullying policy and b) regardless of whether the student makes a complaint, asks the school to take action, or identifies the harassment as a form of discrimination.

How can I get help from OCR?   OCR offers technical assistance to help schools achieve voluntary compliance with the civil rights laws it enforces and works with schools to develop creative approaches to preventing and addressing discrimination. A school should contact the OCR enforcement office serving its jurisdiction for technical assistance. For contact information, please visit ED's website at http://wdcrobcolp01.ed.gov/CFAPPS/OCR/contactus.cfm.

A complaint of discrimination can be filed by anyone who believes that a school that receives Federal financial assistance has discriminated against someone on the basis of race, color, national origin, sex, disability, or age. The person or organization filing the complaint need not be a victim of the alleged discrimination, but may complain on behalf of another person or group. Information about how to file a complaint with OCR is at http://www2.ed.gov/about/offices/list/ocr/complaintintro.html or by contacting OCR's Customer Service Team at 1-800-421-3481.

* This summary accompanied the DCL on the subject of Bullying and Harassment, issued by ED and OCR, http://www2.ed.gov/about/offices/list/ocr/letters/colleague-201010.pdf.

Additional Resource 9.3

Vancouver School Board Lesbian, Gay, Bisexual, Transgender, Transsexual, Two-Spirit, Questioning Policy (February 2004)

Intent   The Board of School Trustees (the "Board") is committed to establishing and maintaining a safe and positive learning environment for all students and employees including those who identify as lesbian, gay, bisexual, transgender, transsexual, two-spirit, or who are questioning their sexual orientation or gender identity. These students and employees, as all students and employees, have the right to learn and work in an environment free of discrimination and harassment. The letter and spirit of the Canadian Charter of Rights and Freedoms, the B. C. Human Rights Acts and the Collective Agreements shall be carefully observed, enforced, and supported, so that all members of the school community may work together in an atmosphere of respect and tolerance for individual differences. Specifically, the Board will not tolerate hate crimes, harassment or discrimination, and will vigorously enforce policy and regulations dealing with such matters.

The Board will provide a safe environment, free from harassment and discrimination, while also promoting pro-active strategies and guidelines to ensure that lesbian, gay, transgender, transsexual, two-spirit, bisexual and questioning students, employees and families are welcomed and included in all aspects of education and school life and treated with respect and dignity. The purpose of this policy is to define appropriate behaviours and actions in order to prevent discrimination and harassment through greater awareness of and responsiveness to their deleterious effects. This policy is also drafted to ensure that homophobic complaints are taken seriously and dealt with expeditiously and effectively through consistently applied policy and procedures. The policy will also raise awareness and improve understanding of the lives of people who identify themselves on the basis of sexual orientation or gender identity. By valuing diversity and respecting differences, students and staff act in accordance with the Vancouver district's social responsibility initiative.

Leadership The Vancouver School Board shall ensure that all staff will be able to identify individual discriminatory attitudes and behaviours, as well as work to eliminate the systemic inequities and barriers to learning for students who identify themselves on the basis of sexual orientation or gender identity and demonstrate accountability for their removal so that all students are treated with fairness and respect. All administrators, teachers, counselors, and staff and student leaders will communicate the board's position to their employees, staff and students. In the course of their leadership roles, they will commit to listen to lesbian, gay, transgender, transsexual, two-spirit, bisexual and questioning youth and their designated support groups and take concrete actions to make schools more welcoming and safer places for these students.

The Board shall consult with the LGBTTQ Advisory Committee to ensure that policy directions, priorities and implementation of programs and services are consistent with this LGBTTQ policy.

Counselling and Student Support The Vancouver School Board is committed to maintaining a safe learning and working environment which actively provides counselling and support to students who identify themselves on the basis of sexual orientation or gender identity. All counsellors provided by the board shall be educated in the knowledge and skills required to deal with LGBTTQ issues with students. Counsellors will be informed and familiar with all policies with respect to human rights, anti-homophobia, hate literature, discrimination and harassment, and will alert their school community to these policies. Counsellors will be sensitive to lesbian, gay, transgender, transsexual, two-spirit, bisexual and questioning students as well as students from LGBTT-headed families.

Elementary and secondary schools are encouraged to appoint a staff person to be a safe contact for students who identify themselves on the basis of sexual orientation or gender identity. School administrators should inform students and other staff about the location and availability of this contact person. Schools are encouraged in their goal planning to advocate for students who identify themselves on the basis of sexual orientation or gender identity and those who are questioning their gender identity.

Where students request and where staff are willing to volunteer their time, Gay/Straight Alliance clubs (GSAs) will be encouraged at secondary schools in the district.

Anti-Harassment Homophobic harassment is demeaning treatment to all students, students' parents or guardians, and employees regardless of their sexual orientation. Harassment based on gender identities is also demeaning to all students and employees. These forms of harassment and discrimination are prohibited under the B.C. Human Rights Code.

Any language or behaviour that deliberately degrades, denigrates, labels, stereotypes, incites hatred, prejudice, discrimination, harassment towards students or employees on the basis of their real or perceived sexual orientation or gender identification will not be tolerated. Schools will be encouraged to specifically include the prohibition of such language and behaviour in their student codes of conduct. Please refer to the "General Anti-Harassment VSB Policy."

Curriculum Learning Resources Anti-Homophobia Education strives to identify and change educational practices, policies, and procedures that promote homophobia, as well as the homophobic attitudes and behaviours that underlie and reinforce such policies and practices. Anti-homophobia education provides knowledge, skills, and strategies for educators to examine such discrimination critically in order to understand its origin and to recognize and challenge it.

The Board is committed to enabling all lesbian, gay, transgender, transsexual, two-spirit, bisexual and questioning students to see themselves and their lives positively reflected in the curriculum. Resources should be chosen or updated in order to promote critical thinking and include materials that accurately reflect the range of Canada's LGBTTQ communities. Keeping in mind the multi-cultural aspect of the district, as many of the above resources as possible should be available in different languages and in formats easily accessible to ESL students.

Staff Development, In-Service and Professional Development The Vancouver School Board is committed to ongoing staff development in anti-homophobia education and sexual orientation equity for trustees and Board staff, and will assist them to acquire the knowledge, skills, attitudes and behaviours to identify and eliminate homophobic practices. The Board will provide in-service training for teaching and support staff in anti-homophobia methodologies to enable them to deliver an inclusive curriculum. The Board will also provide in-service training for employees to deal effectively and confidently with issues of homophobia, heterosexism and gender identity and support initiatives that foster dialogue to create understanding and respect for diversity.

School-Community Involvement   The Vancouver School Board is committed to ongoing, constructive and open dialogue with lesbian, gay, bisexual and transgender communities and other communities who identify themselves on the basis of sexual orientation or gender identity to increase co-operation and collaboration among home, school and the community.

The Board will work to create partnerships that ensure effective participation in the education process by representative and inclusive organizations and LGBTTQ communities that are committed to the mission of the VSB. (To enable students to reach their intellectual, social, aesthetic and physical potential in challenging and stimulating settings which reflect the worth of each individual and promote mutual respect, co-operation, and social responsibility.)

The Board will encourage parent advisory councils to reflect the diversity of the District. The Vancouver School Board will acknowledge through its communication to students, staff, and the community that some children live in LGBTT-headed families and need to be positively recognized and included as such. Any information to students and parents on anti-homophobia, anti-discrimination and sexual orientation equity needs to be translated into the languages spoken in the home. Parent Advisory Councils and students will be encouraged to engage in dialogue with openly identified LGBTTQ youth and their organizations.

Employment Equity   The Board of School Trustees (the "Board") believes in equitable treatment for all individuals regardless of race, colour, ancestry, ethnic origin, religion, socio-economic status, gender, sexual orientation, gender identity, physical or mental ability, or political beliefs. The letter and spirit of the Canadian Charter of Rights and Freedoms, the B. C. Human Rights Acts and the VSB/VTF Collective Agreement shall be carefully observed, enforced, and supported, so that all members of the school community may work together in an atmosphere of respect and tolerance for individual differences.

The Board will ensure that the confidentiality of the sexual orientation and gender identity of staff will be protected. Employees who are out as lesbian, gay, bisexual, transgender, or transitioning to another gender will be given the support they require to do their work in a safe and respectful environment.

Additional Resource 9.4

Model: Multicultural Competence: Philosophy as "Policy"

The Brookwood School Board of Trustees recognizes the importance of developing a student body competent to negotiate a world that is made up of peoples of different races, cultures, backgrounds, belief systems and orientations. Towards this end, the Board Committee on Cultural Competence drafted a list of beliefs relating to cultural competence that have been long supported by the school but had not yet been expressly articulated. This list was unanimously endorsed by the Board and was received with overwhelming enthusiasm by our faculty. We hope this list will serve to clarify for both current and prospective parents our commitment to cultivating cultural competence. We believe

- Students' membership in their immediate communities, as well as their competence and confidence as global citizens, will be significantly enhanced by virtue of a global consciousness and a broad cultural awareness.
- Students will be better prepared to solve problems, simple and grand, when their empathetic imaginations have been enlarged by exposure to and consideration of the culturally and ecologically rich world that surrounds and contains them.
- In the importance of a school culture that values inquiry and inspires students to consider multiple perspectives to push past what otherwise gets taken at face value.
- Encounters with diversity and appreciation for differences within the Brookwood classroom, faculty and curriculum are essential to the development of cultural competence.
- Our students' experience with differences will develop an enhanced self-awareness, and a fuller understanding and respect for those who practice, believe and live differently.
- Our experiences with diversity can sometimes pose challenges, but with a spirit of exploration and respect, these experiences will cultivate a sense of global citizenship and a greater appreciation for the common humanity that binds us.
- The development of cultural competence is essential for success in a global environment and in our pursuit "to graduate academically accomplished students of conscience, character and compassion".

—Brookwood School, preK–8, Manchester, Massachusetts

Additional Resource 9.5

Marriage and Partnership Rights in the United States

States That Issue Marriage Licenses to Same-Sex Couples

- Massachusetts (2004)
- Connecticut (2008)

- Iowa (2009)
- Vermont (2009)
- District of Columbia (2010)
- New Hampshire (2010)
- New York (2011)

States That Provide at Least Partial Spousal Rights to Same-Sex Couples through Domestic Partnership or Civil Unions

- California (1999)*
- Maine (2004)
- Washington (2007)
- New Jersey (2007)
- Oregon (2008)
- Colorado (2009)
- Nevada (2009)
- Wisconsin (2009)
- Illinois (2011)
- Hawaii (2012)

States That Recognize Out-of-State Same-Sex Marriages

- California (2009)*
- Rhode Island (2007)**
- New York (2008)
- Maryland (2010)

* Same-sex marriages that took place between June 16, 2008, and November 4, 2008, are legally recognized by California. The state also recognizes all out-of-state same-sex marriages that took place in that time period.

** The Rhode Island Attorney General issued an advisory opinion declaring that the state can recognize out-of-state same-sex marriages, but later that year the Rhode Island Supreme Court refused to grant a divorce to a same-sex couple legally married in Massachusetts.

Additional Resource 9.6

Diversity Council's Spark Curriculum

The Spark workshops are a series of 13 age-appropriate programs that focus on increasing knowledge, building empathy and self-esteem, and developing critical thinking skills for K–12 students. Research has shown these four steps to be critical factors in reducing prejudice among children.

Kindergarten: Same & Different   This workshop introduces students to the concept that a person can be the same as them and different from them at the same time. Activities focus on some of the things that make people the same or different and demonstrate that differences can be wonderful and exciting.

Grade 1: We Are All Unique!   This workshop focuses on the concept of individual uniqueness. Activities concentrate on the uniqueness of the students and the diversity in their classroom.

Grade 2: Disability Awareness   This workshop aims to show students that people with disabilities may be different on the outside, but they are the same on the inside. It also gives students a chance to experience some of the challenges that people with disabilities may face.

Grade 3: My Banana   Students get to know an individual banana in an activity illustrating that once you get to know someone, they are no longer just "one of the bunch." Students come to recognize that all people are unique individuals, and getting to know them breaks down stereotypes.

Grade 4: A Class Divided   Students watch a video about Jane Elliot's Brown Eyes, Blue Eyes experiment, in which she divided her class by eye color and allowed them to experience prejudice and discrimination from both sides. An activity with an apple shows how teasing and discrimination bruise the inside even when they don't show on the outside. Students are encouraged to think of ways to counteract this form of discrimination.

Grade 5: What Would You Do?   In a hidden camera experiment from *20/20*, a group of white teenagers vandalizes a car in broad daylight. Later, the experiment is repeated with a group of black teenagers. The different responses from witnesses are truly eye opening as students discover that racism is still a reality in modern America. A game of "Diversity Jeopardy" reinforces the message.

Grade 6: Our Minnesota Heritage   *NorthStar* is a film that tells the stories of Minnesota's black pioneers. Students watch two of the segments, learning about Minnesota's diverse heritage and the power of the individual to stand up against prejudice.

Grade 7: Bullying   In another hidden camera experiment from *20/20*, young actors are paid to bully each other in public. Students watch to see how passersby will respond and explore what they can do to stand up against bullying. The film is followed by a game of "Who Wants to Be a Millionaire" to reinforce what was learned.

Grade 8: Sizism and Body Image   In the opening exercise, students are shown pictures of four people, similar in every way except for body size and shape. They are asked to guess which person is most active, most popular, most influential. This activity and others open students' eyes to the many stereotypes associated with body size and to the profound prejudice and discrimination against those who do not measure up to our society's "ideal" body size.

High School Instead of presenting a set curriculum for each grade level, in high school we work with schools to provide customized workshops that are relevant to their current needs. We conduct a needs assessment at each high school, gathering input from teachers, administrators, and students. We select from a menu of films, activities, and discussion guides to create workshops for each grade level addressing the areas of greatest need. And we train select teachers and staff members to lead continuing discussions as issues arise throughout the school year. Workshops will be based on five critical subject areas: *Race, Gender & sexual orientation, Socioeconomic status, Disability,* and *Religion.* (http://www.diversity council.org/curriculum.shtml)

Additional Resource 9.7

An Outline of Board Operations (from the NAIS Trustees' Guide)

- **Keeping the Mission of the School**
  - Each trustee is expected to be a visible advocate for the mission of the school and for the board's policy decisions, whether or not such positions are popular with all constituencies.
- **Developing and Reviewing Policy**
  - Internal institutional policies are set by the board to ensure that a school's operations are conducted appropriately. The administration then develops operational policies and procedures that implement broad policies and puts them into practice.
- **Planning Strategically (Why Do It)**
  - The board periodically undertakes a strategic planning process that stems from the board-approved mission statement.
- **Planning Strategically (The Process)**
  1. Planning to plan.
  2. Gathering information about and assessing the environment.
     a. External information gathering.
     b. Internal information gathering.
  3. Developing the strategic plan's mission, vision, values, and goals.
  4. Developing action plans and more detailed yearly operational plans.
  5. Generating buy-in with scenario testing.
  6. Approving the plan.
  7. Celebrating and communicating the plan (mission, vision, and goals) to all school constituencies.
  8. Implementing the plan.

- **Ensuring Financial Stability**
  - The board approves the annual budget based on operational needs, the strategic plan's priorities, and financial forecasts for the next three to five years.
- **Fund Raising for the School**
  - Once trustees have committed to a personal contribution, they need to participate in raising funds from others.
- **Selecting New Trustees**
  - The committee needs to be sure that the qualifications and qualities of new trustees further the work of the board, the strategic plan, and the school's mission. Diversity in all of its manifestations should be encouraged and celebrated.
- **Orienting New Trustees**
  - The committee on trustees, in partnership with the board chair and head . . . should plan a formal board orientation for new trustees each year.
- **Developing the Board**
  - If the board evaluates the performance of the head, it is only appropriate that the board also evaluate the performance of the chair and the board itself, including the actions it takes regarding annual professional development about independent school governance.
- **Serving as Community Ambassadors**
  - Trustees, along with the head and other administrators, can play an important role in community relations, whether by meeting with neighborhood associations or by speaking to zoning boards.

More information is available at the NAIS website: http://www.nais.org/trustees/index.cfm?ItemNumber=150843&sn.ItemNumber=150899.

NOTES

1. See Robert Murray Thomas, *Sex and the American Teenager: Seeing through the Myths and Confronting the Issues*, 2009.

2. See *Theno v. Tonganoxie Unified School District* (http://ks.findacase.com/research/wfrmDoc Viewer.aspx/xq/fac.20050624_0000335.DKS.htm/qx).

3. *Adolescent Sexual Health: Looking Ahead with 20-20* held in 2011 was a free, two-day conference in Fargo, North Dakota, for teachers, counselors, clinicians, and school board members interested in providing effective sexual health programs for adolescents.

4. http://govpubs.lib.umn.edu/guides.

5. The DOE releases Dear Colleague Letters (DCL) to address current issues facing schools and to remind schools of their legal obligations. The full text of this DCL is available at http://www2 .ed.gov/about/offices/list/ocr/letters/colleague-201010.pdf.

6. Examples: (1) Office of Cultural Diversity and Student Achievement, Ladue School District, MO, http://beta.ladue.k12.mo.us/district/content/our-district/diversity.shtml; (2) Office of Diversity Affairs, Puyallup School District, WA, http://www.puyallup.k12.wa.us/ourdistrict/diversity; (3) Diversity Oversight Committee, Methacton School District, PA, www.methacton.org/6880101211105027710/site/default.asp; (4) Task Force on Diversity and Equity, Burlington, VT, http://www.bsdvt.org/diversity/taskforce.

7. Defined by Macgillivray (2004) as those concerned that "public schools, with a liberal and secular agenda, would usurp their parental authority to instill in their children their antigay beliefs" (17).

8. Report of the APA Task Force on the Sexualization of Girls: Executive Summary (www.apa.org/pi/women/programs/girls/report.aspx).

9. http://www.asalh.org/blackhistorymonthorigins.html.

10. http://www.infoplease.com/spot/womensintro1.html.

10

PERSONAL AND PROFESSIONAL IDENTITY IN GSD EDUCATION

Teaching as a "Whole Person"

Unlike many professions, teaching is always done at the dangerous intersection of personal and public life . . . we try to connect ourselves, as well as our subjects, with our students . . . we make ourselves, as well as our subjects, vulnerable to indifference, judgment, ridicule.

—Parker Palmer, *The Courage to Teach:*
Exploring the Inner Landscape of a Teacher's Life

Nine chapters in this book are devoted to what adults need to know and need to do in order to make school a safe, productive environment for "the whole child." This includes attending to the complex ways in which children experience gender and sexuality in their everyday lives at school. This last chapter focuses on the adults in the school community, who they are and who they are allowed to be as "whole" educators, staff, and parents in relation to gender and sexuality diversity (GSD). These adults also experience GSD in their everyday lives, and they are challenged to work well not only with their students but with each other.

The question of whether it is okay for a teacher to be GLBTQI and to be "out" in his professional role is, in some ways, more complex than any of the questions about how to best serve nonheteronormative students. Trying to untangle the concerns, misperceptions, and incomprehension that are at the core of the should-educators-come-out debate has made this the most difficult chapter of the book to write. I have learned in school consultations many times over that how the adults in an educational community understand and treat each other in relation to GSD can be the most divisive, painful issue of all. It can also be the most healing.

Some of you may come to this chapter wondering why there should be any question at all about whether it is okay for GLBTQI teachers to be out. Chapter 5 emphasized the importance of teacher's "use of self" and the value of modeling authenticity. How can a teacher be authentic without bringing her whole self to the job? Yet some of you continue to experience the "outness" of GLBTQI colleagues as problematic, as unprofessional, as being motivated by "politics" rather than by a wish for personal and professional integration.

Whatever your opinion may be, don't skip this chapter. Throughout the book you have been offered different frameworks for understanding gender and sexuality diversity; you have been encouraged to change how you "see" and think about the commonplace. The same is true here, and a fresh perspective might just lead to improved relationships with colleagues and a more supportive work environment all around. As you read the stories featured in this chapter, I invite you to think critically about what it means to teach with your whole self, what it means for you and what it means for anyone who dares to teach.

SECTION I
TEACHER IDENTITY DEVELOPMENT:
WHERE PROFESSIONAL AND PERSONAL MEET

WE TEACH WHO WE ARE

Educator Parker Palmer speaks and writes extensively about *knowing, teaching, and learning*, with a particular emphasis on the importance of teachers' inner lives. Connectedness—to one's work, students, colleagues, and one's self—is central to the enterprise of education. "We teach who we are" (2007, 2), Palmer suggests, and who one is as a **person** is, ideally, integrated with who one is as an **educator**. However, Palmer also acknowledges that the intersection of personal and public life can be "dangerous" for teachers, who are exposed daily to the critique of others. Teachers, coaches, administrators, and counselors take the stage every day, opening themselves up repeatedly to the joy of success and the sting of failure.

Identity and Integrity

Not only do educators teach who they are but "good teaching comes from the identity and integrity of the teacher" (Palmer 2007, 13). This makes "who you are" a major instructional asset for teachers. **Who you are** (i.e., identity) and **how you conduct yourself** (i.e., integrity) serve as fundamental pedagogical conduits for teaching and learning. Think about this for a moment. It means that in some measure, the educator's age, sex, race, marital status, physical ability, gender, religion, ethnicity, and sexuality are potentially vital components for her teaching.

For example, a teacher's age may be a reference point in learning about certain parts of history. *What was it like during Vietnam, Mr. Schwinn?* An African American calculus teacher uses her own race and gender as reference points in discussing opportunities for women of color in the fields of math and engineering. *Because of my race and gender, there weren't a lot people encouraging me to focus on math during high school or college.* A teacher who uses a wheelchair helps children in his elementary classroom broaden their understanding of (dis)ability. *Many people look at my wheelchair and immediately think of what I can't do. I think about what I can do.* The students whose teacher has a spouse expecting a baby are excited. *Has your wife had the baby yet?! Have you picked out a name!?*

Adapting to New Elements

So personal identity, history, and experience become part of a teacher's professional identity (Akkerman and Meijer 2011), and balancing the personal and professional is a career-long task. In addition, educators must change with the times and adapt to "new elements" that impact teaching and teacher identity (Geijsel and Meijer 2005, 425), from technology advances to increased racial and ethnic diversity, to high stakes testing. The greater emphasis on gender and sexuality diversity (GSD) as an educational matter is another new element that demands (re)"configuration" of teacher identity in order to adjust.

Exactly Who Gets to Teach Who They Are?

❖ *Shouldn't there be a policy or a protocol for gay teachers who want to come out? It seems like something that should be consistent.*

❖ *I find it hard to believe that any faculty member would feel discriminated against. I have no sense that that is happening on campus.*

❖ *I am not out at work as transgender, but I am identified by most people with sight as gender variant. I am not out because I am not yet ready to defend myself, particularly without the protection to be certain my job would not be at stake.*

The debate about whether GLBTQI teachers can or should come out begins with the following question. If *identity* and *integrity* are the building blocks of professional excellence for educators (Palmer 2007), how can any teacher, coach, or counselor function effectively if he is implicitly or explicitly asked not to bring a complete identity to his work? Seems impossible. Yet when GLBTQI educators "teach who they are" and model authenticity, this somehow raises concerns about "personal agendas" and unprofessional behavior.

Consider something as basic as a teacher introducing herself to a class. We expect teachers to introduce themselves to the students they work with; we expect teachers will present themselves as real people doing an important job. The two stories that follow illustrate the dilemmas for GLBTQI educators, one beginner (The Story of My First Introduction) and one veteran (The Story of Making Introductions for the Hundredth Time) in this very basic task.

The Story of My First Introduction

Introducing myself seemed like a natural and necessary part of our first class in my 4th grade teaching placement. When I asked my lead teacher about what kinds of things to share with the students, she said, "Just tell them a little bit about who you are, what you like to do, hobbies, that sort of thing." As a lesbian I had so many questions running through my head. All of a sudden I had a huge awareness of my sexual orientation and whether or not I would be perceived as an "other." What if the kids thought I was straight? Would this matter? What if they found out later on that I am gay? What message would I be sending? What "incidental learning" would I be promoting about whether or not it's okay to be gay, let alone okay to be a gay teacher? I am a teacher and whether I like it or not I am a role model, but I wondered what role I was supposed to be modeling when I introduced myself to my students.

In my Master's Program for the Art of Teaching at the Elementary Level, I didn't really receive any explicit training about what is and is not appropriate to talk about in the classroom in this area. I had only my own preconceived notions of what was or was not "professional." I wasn't sure what to do with my internal dialogues. I further didn't know how the issues changed depending on what grade level I taught.

In my second placement in a sixth grade class my teacher mentioned his wife frequently, which is technically talking about sexual orientation although not explicitly labeling it as such. I don't think a straight teacher would say, "Hello class. My name is Ms. Jones and I am straight." Yet, would it be inappropriate for me to label my sexual orientation so the students wouldn't assume I'm straight? What if I were married and wanted to mention my wife in the exact same vein that he mentioned his wife? How is that not the same thing? Yet it did not feel the same.

—Kathleen Boucher, MAT

The Story of Making Introductions for the One Hundredth Time

Every year the student leaders are invited back to campus before the official start of school, and we do a two-day training that helps them prepare for their responsibilities as dormitory proctors. This is the opening meeting of all residential faculty, administrators and student proctors. My colleague introduces herself: I'm Mrs. Scott and that handsome man over there is my husband, Mr. Scott. We live on the first floor of Baker. *Her husband offers a sheepish grin and raises his hand. Mrs. Scott talks about her role and responsibilities in relation to dormitory life, and then another faculty member begins to introduce himself.* I'm Mr. Gregory and this gorgeous woman standing next to me is my wife, Mrs. Delaney-Gregory. *Plenty of smiles and laughter from students and teachers alike. More talk about roles and responsibilities, but what really has everyone's attention is the clever playing off of Mrs. Scott's original witty remark. A young, new male faculty member:* I'm Mr. Shinner and I wish I had a gorgeous wife but I don't. *Lots of laughter. I smile too but it is a fake smile.*

I am a lesbian who is out in this medium-sized boarding school community, but I have maintained a fairly low profile at school over the years in relation to my sexuality. I find myself increasingly uneasy about what I will say in my introduction to this group. Will I mention my female partner who does not work or live at the school?

I'm Mr. Stevens and I'm secretly the love child of these two. *He gestures to a married couple who have already introduced themselves. A whoop of laughter. There is another lesbian faculty member standing across from me who is also out and single and has a child. What's she going to say?* A male teacher says, I'm Mr. Conklin, and we have a very special relationship. *He gestures to a young single male teacher. The joking insinuation that these two guys are a gay couple is a huge hit with the students and most of the teachers. I lock eyes with a friend across the circle, and I see her pull back a bit from the laughter.*

The majority of my straight colleagues seem oblivious to the "norms" being established here through the guise of humor. What message are we giving to this group of student leaders? I wonder what this is like for a gay kid; there must be at least one or two sitting in this group of 35 students.

Now I'm in a bind. When it is my turn to introduce myself, if I don't keep the joke going, I will be the conspicuous party-pooper who didn't play along. Will I make a "straight" joke that is likely to draw nervous laughter from just a few? It feels unsafe to come out in any manner. I have taught here for twelve years and it only takes an instant like this one to make me feel like I don't really belong.

—Faculty member and dorm parent
Boarding school grades 9–12

HETERONORMATIVITY AND PROFESSIONALISM

In both these stories, the teacher struggles with what is professionally appropriate and what feels personally comfortable. In Kathleen's case, the lack of critical inquiry or invitation for personal reflection about GSD in her teaching program means she must figure out on her own how to handle this personal/professional dilemma. Even with her peers in the teaching program cohort, Kathleen experiences her very self as "disruptive" of the heteronormative majority. And in her teaching placement, she does not know how to broach the subject, even with a senior teacher she guesses would be open.

Kathleen identifies another dilemma. Intellectually she knows she is supposed to be a "role model" for her students, yet wonders what role she is supposed to model when she introduces herself to the class. As a result Kathleen questions whether being true to her identity, and maintaining her integrity by being honest, is "professional" or not. She wonders if it is possible for GLBTQI teachers to be role models. Nobody has ever suggested to her that they could be or should be.

For the seasoned boarding school faculty member this is yet one more experience of how dominant the heteronormative paradigm is and how complicated and never-ending "coming out" can be. The double standard is clear: heteronormative sharing and joking is acceptable and comfortable; GLBTQI "disclosure" will be conspicuous and perhaps "inappropriate." Though a member of the school community for more than a decade, this teacher feels alienated in a meeting that is meant to bring students and dorm parents together at the beginning of the year. She feels as if her colleagues have forgotten who is in the room (i.e., teachers who are gay), and as important, who might be in the room (students who are GLBTQI; students who have GLBTQI parents or family members).

SECTION II
THE VISIBILITY DILEMMA

INVISIBILITY; SIMPLE VISIBILITY; SURPLUS VISIBILITY

> In our research, teachers sometimes described gay colleagues as "a big presence," "in-your-face," or "larger than life." This reminds us of Patai's notion of surplus visibility: One may either be invisible or exaggerated, but it is very difficult to simply be a gay or lesbian teacher. (DePalma and Atkinson 2009, 878)

How does a lesbian teacher wanting to introduce herself to students become a flashpoint for behavior that is perceived, by some, as inappropriate and unprofessional? There are several factors at work here. Shifting the coming out debate to a more productive dialogue requires thinking critically about all that is bound up in this particular "intersection" of the public and personal. As DePalma and Atkinson observe, it is "difficult to simply *be* a gay or lesbian teacher" (emphasis mine), and Patai's (1991) construct of **simple visibility** helps us understand this phenomenon in a more sophisticated manner.

First, what is it that makes that gay colleague "larger than life"? (See epigraph, this section.) What are the behaviors that people experience as "in-your-face"?

Locating the problem of excessiveness in gay teachers is a simplistic, ill-considered way to frame the issue. In the most fundamental sense, this generalization lacks validity. GLBTQI people come with the same array of relational styles and personality traits that straight people do: boisterous, shy, even-keeled, cheerful, demur, gregarious, humorless, obnoxious, amiable, boring.

Yet, despite the inevitable (bio)diversity of personas, this stereotype of the out-sized gay teacher persists. Patai offers an explanation.

> [There is a] shift that occurs in public perceptions as traditionally powerless and marginalized groups challenge the expectation that they should be invisible and silent. For those who long have been in positions of dominance, any space that minorities occupy appears excessive and the voices they raise sound loud and offensive. (Patai 1991)

When a marginalized, previously invisible GLBTQI teacher speaks, the mere act of speaking, joining, or making oneself known can be experienced by others as "excessive." The teacher must remain invisible or risk offending others with her **surplus visibility** (see The Difference One Principal Can Make). This "invisible/too visible" bind is one that many GLBTQI educators and parents (and students, for that matter) experience every day in the preK–12 setting.

Racial minorities have experienced a similar bind, particularly during the decades of protracted school integration. The mere presence of black students in predominantly white schools creates surplus visibility; the difference in skin color alone highlights their minority status. Historically, the majority "tolerates" the minority as long the minority remains invisible.

The Difference One Principal Can Make

Before I transferred to a different school as part of a mentoring program, I sent my new principal a copy of an essay I had written that had been published in a collection called We Teach Them All. *The essay detailed my journey of twenty years as a lesbian teacher. I was proud of my writing and wanted her to know I was a lesbian. I got no response. When we met a week later to talk about policies and procedure, I asked her if she had received the essay. She looked uncomfortable, and then said, "Some parents will have a really hard time with this. They might even withdraw their kids from your class. You should be careful." I thought of my former principal who knew my partner, who supported me wholeheartedly and who helped me on my journey away from fear towards pride. From my new administrator I had wanted affirmation, but instead I got censorship. As a consequence I entered my new position feeling unsupported which I'm certain affected my teaching and mentoring.*

—Nancy Allen, elementary and middle school teacher; 38 years

Reactions to Surplus Visibility

How do heteronormative teachers experience the surplus visibility of GLBTQI colleagues? Some, like this teacher, suggest that gay educators who make an "issue" of GSD are creating problems for themselves.

❖ *Don't make an issue of something that isn't there. People are a lot more open than you think if you live and let live, and let them do the same. When you push something into their face, they back off and become distant. If you can show them just how similar you are before you try and educate them, they will listen a lot better and are more willing to believe you, because you have more credit with them.*

According to this advice, the GLBTQI educator needs to demonstrate similarity with the majority before daring to speak of herself as being part of a minority. If the GLBTQI teacher takes the discreet I'm-just-like-you approach, she will have more credibility. This echoes the suggestion that a gay teacher should prove himself to be a "good teacher" before coming out.

Here is another example of the discreet approach. The head of an all girls' school ordered the removal of Gay Straight Alliance (GSA) posters from the main bulletin board on the day that prospective students and their parents were to revisit the campus. Her rationale? *We need to get these families here and let them get to know our community first. Then we can educate them about these issues.* She tried to reassure members of the GSA that she was not ashamed of them but rather trying to prevent them from being "misunderstood." Not surprisingly the students felt deeply betrayed by the head's behavior.

Truthfully, **you do not even have to actually be GLBTQI to elicit criticism for being "in-your-face."** As long as your engagement with GSD is seen as excessive, you risk being questioned, as straight middle school teacher Jill Smith describes here.

Up until my work with the GSA, no one had been troubled by the way I defined civil rights. How is it that my work now had an agenda, yet when teaching *To Kill a Mocking Bird* or Elie Wiesel's *Night*, no one ever said, "She's always talking about Blacks and Jews"? (Smith 2010, 119)

The backlash against being a visible supporter of GSD equity is real, as this straight high school teacher's account of "Teaching the Spectrum Whatever the Consequences" attests. Even in *this* book, a significant subset of teachers who contributed material asked to remain anonymous because they feared negative reactions.

Teaching the Spectrum, Whatever the Consequences

After a student life class on sexuality, the head of school called me in to let me know that a parent had called to express his outrage that I had referenced the

Kinsey Scale and that, according to him, I had suggested that all students "try anal sex." I was horrified for a number of reasons. I thought the Kinsey scale was a useful way to introduce the idea of a spectrum of sexuality. I wanted to be sure my students understood that sexuality exists on a continuum and as a straight teacher, I wanted to be sure to offer an inclusive view of non-heterosexualities. I had included anal sex in the list of different types of sex. The only thing I was advocating was information.

I had to meet with the father. I was worried about the meeting, but I had already decided that I would not apologize for anything. He and I ended up talking for a long time about many things. Ultimately it became clear that this parent had a lot of questions and he was actually using our conversation to an-swer those questions. Before he left, he reached over the table and asked me, Is homosexuality nature or nurture? *My response:* Does it matter? It is someone's life and it should be respected, honored and accepted.

—High school life skills teacher

THE SAFETY OF INVISIBILITY

Sometimes the backlash prompts those who are experienced as too visible to re-treat back into the **invisibility** of marginalization; "It is safer to go one's own way, quietly, without calling attention to oneself" (Patai 1991). The result is that the powerless often contribute to their own invisibility, as was the case for the lesbian teacher who did not feel safe calling attention to herself during faculty introduc-tions at the dorm proctor meeting. In "The Fear of Telling the Truth," Julia Hol-linger describes a similar experience of self-imposed invisibility, while working at a therapeutic boarding school.

The Fear of Telling the Truth

At 21 I was put in charge of counseling a group of kids at a boarding school for those who hadn't been "successful" elsewhere. These were kids whose parents were abusive, or just plain neglectful, kids who'd already experienced way more than I had of drugs, sex and violence. And yet my only fear that summer was that they would find out I was gay. The school had five key words it lived by—one was truth. Every time we met as a small group or as a school, the focus was on telling the truth, because it would set you free. Kids were seriously punished if they lied about anything. I supported, believed in this idea. I saw it work. Yet I lied all summer. I never told anyone that I was gay. I am so sorry for them and me that this fear kept me from being the visible, important and unique role model I could have been.

—Julia Hollinger, teacher and instructional coach
Leadership Public Schools, Richmond, California

VISIBILITY AND THE COMING OUT PROBLEM

It appears then that the only way for GLBTQI educators to fight invisibility is to "come out." Yet "coming out" is problematic and not just because it is often perceived by others as professionally imprudent. The concept of coming out is misleading; it suggests a singular, unambiguous event. In truth the process of coming out is uneven. It fluctuates and must be repeated multiple times. Because heterosexuality is assumed, GLBTQI people have to come out over and over again throughout their lives. Recall the New Diagram of Sex and Gender in chapter 2 (diagram 2.1). Which locations on the five continuums necessitate "coming out" and which do not?

1. Historically *coming out* has been applied only to homosexual or bisexual identities. Now it is also used by some to reference a range of sexualities (e.g., *I am polyamorous*) and gender identities (e.g., *I am genderqueer*). The categories of people who "need" to "come out" continues to grow.
2. *Coming out* is a term applied only to nonheteronormative identities. A female teacher who talks about her husband and children is not seen as coming out as straight. Straight people do not need to come out because heterosexuality is assumed. "Traditionally" gendered people do not need to come out because they fulfill standard gender expectations.
3. Heteronormative teachers come out all the time just by virtue of being themselves. This is the essence of **simple visibility**—the option of just "being" oneself.
4. *Coming out* is another binary option whereby one's sexual or gender identity is either openly declared or deliberately kept hidden (Rasmussen 2004). There is no allowance for a continuum of "outness" or visibility.
5. *Coming out* suggests a singular, universal action. Significant contextual factors affect coming out, such as
   a. whom you come out to or not (e.g., out to colleagues, not to students)
   b. where you come out or don't (out at school, not out at church)
   c. when you come out (e.g., not out before becoming a parent, now totally out)
   This variability is not conveyed in the static connotations of the construct.
6. *Coming out* implies that teachers (a) know what identity to come out as and (b) the identity will be "familiar, uncomplicated and definable" (Shlasko 2005). For example, those who identify as genderqueer may present as androgynous (or not) and use gender-neutral pronouns. In most school communities, genderqueer is *not* a "familiar, uncomplicated and definable" identity, and there may not be a ready taxonomy to accommodate this identity or others (see Do We Have a Gender Neutral Title?).

Do We Have a Gender Neutral Title?

Slowly over the next few decades the culture of the school changed. It has taken hard work and patience, but now in 2011 there is not a single teacher who would tolerate a student's derogatory comments about being gay. More importantly issues of gender and sexual orientation are present throughout the curriculum, and are the topic of parent presentations and classroom conversations.

There is still a lot of work to be done. I recently hired a teacher who identifies as queer and does not identify with a single gender. We are faced with a dilemma as to what title this person should have. Our formality of using Mr./Mrs./Ms. does not offer a gender non-specific option. So the work continues. I have confidence that as an institution we will do the right thing, and I know that it is the straight teachers and administrators who need to lead the way.

—Elizabeth Uhry MacCurrach, Head of Lower School
Shore Country Day School

7. "Coming out" is seen as a personal choice, which overlooks the fact that some people are—accurately or inaccurately—"read" as gay or "read" as straight or "read" as female, regardless of any statement they might actually make about their sexuality or gender (Rasmussen 2004). The experience of coming out for a transgender or intersex person entails many variations on this theme of being read one way and identifying as another (Barr 2011).

8. Teachers who realize they are transgender, plan to live in their affirmed gender, and share that information with others can be understood as coming out: *You know me as Mr. Forrest and I am transitioning to Ms. Forrest.* Or the parent of a transgender child may or may not "come out" about her child (see When a Parent Comes Out about Her Child).

When a Parent Comes Out about Her Child

Working as a counselor in an independent, private K–12 school when my son (an alum) came out as transgender (female-to-male), presented me with several challenges. Our family joked that as he "came out of the closet," we "went into the closet" . . . especially at our workplaces.

I was not embarrassed or ashamed. Actually, I was quite proud of my young adult child's courage and self-awareness. I just knew I needed to control how our family's new story was told. The mother in me needed to protect those I love from potential hurt. The counselor in me knew how distorted gossip among colleagues and parents could become. Rumor and misinformation would likely make life stressful for me and my family, and could potentially affect my ability to remain a respected, effective leader in the community.

Few people, educators included, have been educated about the "T" in LGBTQ issues. It became clear to me that I would be educating people every time I shared our news. My conservative school already struggled with uncomfortable

conversations and disagreements about race and politics. So, providing this in-
formation in a calm and deliberate manner seemed the only way to go.

People's reactions and responses have been interesting . . . more accepting
than anticipated. Everyone has been kind and some have treated me with extra
doses of compassion as they seem to compare what I've "been through" to a par-
ent coping with their child's drug addiction or incarceration. It is clearly difficult
for most to understand.

This experience has highlighted for me how those in the field of Education still
have so far to go in teaching people about differences. How can educators teach
and model what they, themselves, are still struggling to understand?

—Kathy Barr, LCSW

9. A transgender person who is already living successfully in his true gender
   may or may not choose to reveal that history: *I was assigned female at birth*
   and transitioned to my true gender (male) when I was 17.
10. Similarly, someone who is intersex may or may not choose to share that fact:
    I was born intersex, was assigned a female gender and identify as intersex.

The Crux of the Dilemma

These ten characteristics (and there are more) of "coming out" make clear that
the language of expressing and the process of sharing gender and sexuality have
not caught up with the diversity of gender and sexual identities that people actually embody. **Coming out is only required for those who represent certain**
points on the biodiversity spectrum of sex, gender, and sexuality, namely,
those that are not heteronormative. (See diagram 2.2.) The consequences of
this are clear: more often than not, "coming out" leads to "surplus visibility." By
doing nothing more than bringing a whole self to the professional role of teacher,
GLBTQI educators can be experienced as "excessive" and too visible.

So what about *identity* and *integrity* as cornerstones of excellent teaching? Are
GLBTQI educators not supposed to teach with the whole self? For these teachers,
"identity" is suddenly a liability rather than an asset, and if you are forbidden from
accessing all of who you are, the use of self as a pedagogical tool (see chapter 5)
is no longer an option. This personal and professional bind for GLBTQI teachers
is painful and untenable, and the loss for individuals and school communities is
immense (see Can I Tell Them That I'm Married?; see Can I Tell Them We're
Expecting a Baby?)

Can I Tell Them That I'm Married?

I am out as a teacher to my coworkers and administration. I tell my 2nd graders
I live with "partner's name." Several children have understood that I am a les-

bian. However, I am unsure what to say when they ask if I am married. I am (we live in MA) but I know not all families in our district support gay marriage, or want their children exposed to these kinds of conversations. I feel it is important for me to at least acknowledge my partner, in the hopes that they will someday "get it." I am not comfortable outing myself literally to 2nd graders.

—Elementary teacher, Massachusetts

Can I Tell Them We're Expecting a Baby?

When my spouse and I were expecting our first child there was immense controversy within my small independent school administration as to whether or not I was permitted to share this news with my students and their families. I was not going to be physically pregnant—my partner was—and there was concern that having an "openly lesbian mother" on staff might negatively impact reenrollment. I was taking an unpaid "family leave" in the fall, and after many, many conversations, the administration agreed that this information could be shared.

Yet by this point the happiest news of my life had already been soured and transformed into an unfortunate liability for the school.

Sixteen years later my experience in administrative meetings in public schools across New England indicates that little has changed. There continue to be lengthy debates about gay teachers sharing typical life events with students and families. Though administrators now all agree that it is a teacher's right to do so, most school leaders still feel this type of sharing isn't prudent, that it will generate backlash from the community.

—Elizabeth Slade, principal
New View Montessori Consultancy

School personnel continue to debate the appropriateness or inappropriateness of a teacher coming out. An administrator asks whether it is advisable for a gay teacher to chaperone the ski trip. A district policy requires "neutrality" in relation to GSD. Though couched in rationales such as "separating personal and professional interests" or "keeping politics out of the classroom," the central question on the table is this: *Can an educator be GLBTQI and be simply visible?*

SECTION III
GLBTQI EDUCATORS AND SIMPLE VISIBILITY

TEACHING WITH THE WHOLE SELF (PERMISSION GRANTED)

It is okay for educators to be GLBTQI and be "out" at school. More than okay, because these teachers are enormous assets to any educational community committed to

(1) upholding values such as honesty, integrity, and personal responsibility, (2) learning about gender and sexuality diversity, and (3) creating an inclusive, safe learning environment for all. Simply visible GLBTQI teachers shift what can be an intellectual debate about a "difficult issue" or "district policy" to conversations about and among real people in the community.

> ❖ *I have never had a negative experience coming out to a child or, indeed, responding to a child's questions about sex. Being unflappable is my greatest tool. I am frequently approached and given opportunities to have genuine conversations with students because they know I will give them reliable information.*

This out teacher has "genuine conversations with students" because they are drawn to her candor. She models authenticity, and students are grateful that she is available to them in this way.

BACK TO VALENTINES AND INTRODUCTIONS

Consider the multiple benefits for students of every age who have the opportunity to know, work with, and learn from GLBTQI teachers. Remember the valentine scenario in chapter 5? What if the teacher in the valentine scenario is gay? Here is how it might go.

There is still plenty of work and learning ahead for these third graders and their teacher, but the opportunity to grapple with the sexism and homophobia that is affecting the climate of the class is made richer by the gay teacher's presence, authenticity, and availability.

While teaching candidate Kathleen Boucher did not come out when she first introduced herself to her sixth grade students (see The Story of My First Introduction), she designed a lesson plan that contextualized her coming out later in the term. Using a regular forum for sharing and writing called "What Matters," Kathleen provided her students with a window into her experience of being lesbian, among her many other identities (see Sharing "What Matters"). Then she invited the students to reflect on their own "multiple identities." Reading the response of one sixth grade student (see Response to "What Matters") reflects the sophisticated and heartfelt learning the lesson inspired.

(An Excerpt from) Sharing "What Matters"

I honestly didn't know how people would perceive me if I had a lesbian label. And I still don't know, although as I reflect more about myself and what is important to me, I realize the value of being true to myself and not hiding who I am. Being true to myself means being out, which also enables me to stand up for gay

Graphic 10.1.

rights. If I were to stay "in the closet" then I'd be benefitting from the hard work of previous generations without making it better for subsequent generations. Yes, there are many parts to who I am. I am a woman, an athlete, a lover of sociology, a friend, a daughter, a sister, a teacher, a person who enjoys listening to stories and asking questions, a person whose morals have firm Irish Catholic roots, a lesbian, and so much more. Do I present all of these identities all at once? No. But there is a lot to me, and I don't want to be judged for any of my identities.

—Kathleen Boucher, MAT

Response to "What Matters"

Courage. That is one of the words that will forever come to my mind when I hear your name. What a brave person you are to have come as far as you have. I hope if I ever experience something that I know is meant to be, that is a secret or something I find shocking and maybe even the slightest bit shameful for whatever reason, that I can accept it.

If you could not guess, I was incredibly moved and honored by what you said to our class. I know we live in a progressive town but that does not change that it could be hard to say what you did. I imagine talking about your sexuality with your students could feel uncomfortable. You handled it with ease and grace. I could almost feel a breath of relief and happiness when you finished. I would feel so proud to do what you did. Thank you so much for sharing something so personal and important to a mere, idiotic sixth grader such as myself. I will probably never forget what you did today. In the most wonderful of ways.

—Sixth grade student

Role Models for Adolescents

Out faculty offer modeling and support for GLBTQI adolescent students that can be profound. As David Martinez reflects on his own experience as a high school student, he recalls never once encountering an out and open LGBTQI teacher (see Modeling Now What I Didn't Have Then). He is determined to provide modeling for his own students today. And Julia Hollinger recognizes the benefits of professional and personal integration for herself, as well as the enormous impact of modeling "courage and power to a young person trying to make sense of themselves in this world" (see The Power of Integration).

Modeling Now What I Didn't Have Then

As a young and emerging educator I often withdrew from my true self and instead entered a mode of "covering" or "hiding" my gender and sexuality. It took me back to my junior high and high school years when I learned to hone what I called my "gay survival skills." I forced a deeper, more masculine voice when speaking to parents who could be hostile against a softer spoken man, I made sure not to mention my weekend away with my boyfriend to a possibly unsupportive coworker, and brushed off questions and comments from my students about a picture with my "girlfriend" (it was actually my sister).

After some time I realized how unhappy I was. I did not want to enter my professional career in the closet. It had taken years to finally break loose from the social confines of my adolescent years and I had no desire to retreat back. More importantly I recognized that I was now in a powerful position as a teacher. Looking back at my time "hiding" in school I had never once encountered an out and open LGBTQI teacher. The one adult who kept me going was a close high school advisor and confidant who once said to me, "David, it's okay to be you!"

My purpose as an educator is to equip students with the knowledge and skills to become independent, compassionate and productive members of our global society. To do this requires an open and honest inclusion of the LGBTQI community within my curriculum, my interactions with my students, and my interactions with the greater school community. Luckily I have had the support of my school.

My students have read and discussed stories that incorporate same-sex parents; I have openly discussed with my coworkers and family the trials and tribulations of dating men and my desire to one day start a family. In my own small way these actions are my attempt to showcase that the LGBTQI community is just as unique, special and acceptable as any other community. I want to show students, parents, staff and administrators that I am a proud and open gay male. I do this to redeem that scared boy who once believed the closet was his only option. In no way am I attempting to serve as an ambassador for the gay community, but instead I do this for those students who one day might find themselves looking for that one person to tell them, "It's okay to be you!"

—David Martinez, elementary teacher, California

The Power of Integration

Suddenly, I was the out teacher. And it was incredible to be able to integrate my full, private self with my public, teaching self. And with this shift I started to see a shift in the depth of connection with my students and in their respect for and appreciation for me.

Of course, what this meant to my gay students is beyond words. So many of them hung around my class room, or came to the Gay Straight Alliance, but were far from comfortable being out, or didn't even know it or trust it at the time. But I know now that these students got something from me, and I am relieved and proud that I demonstrated courage and power to a young person trying to make sense of themselves in this world.

—Julia Hollinger, teacher and instructional coach
Leadership Public Schools, Richmond, California

Resources for Colleagues and Parents

Openly GLBTQI educators can also provide unique resources to faculty, staff, and the community as a whole. While no member of a minority group wants to bear the burden of being "the expert," consultation and collaboration among colleagues is crucial in creating a learning community that feels safe (see Helping a Colleague; Finding My Voice). Though parents are often assumed to be critical and unsupportive of GSD efforts, there are many parents who are looking for guidance and support themselves, as they do their best to parent a nonheteronormative child (see Boys with Long Hair).

Helping a Colleague; Finding My Voice

As a high school guidance counselor who was "out" to the faculty and many students, I was approached by an English teacher who wanted to discuss an "ugly" incident in one of her ninth grade literature classes. She was doing a lesson on Tennessee Williams and mentioned to the class that he was gay. Some students began laughing and making homophobic comments. "I was horrified and embarrassed, but didn't know what to say or do," she told me. She probably wasn't the only teacher who had faced such a predicament, and I felt that as a school counselor, my task was to assist the staff and help students begin a conversation about sexual orientation in a nonthreatening and inviting manner. I came to the teacher's class and gave a "lesson" on sexual orientation and attitudes toward the GLBT community.

It was not easy. As a gay man I partly resented having to be the "identified expert" on an area that all counselors should have been sensitive to.

This event forced me to examine my own reluctance to discussing this issue before I had been approached by the classroom teacher. Previous to the visit by the classroom teacher, I participated in the silence by the adults in the building when it came to homophobic comments made by students, and unfortunately by some faculty as well. The classroom incident allowed me to help a colleague and prompted me to be more vocal myself.

—Mike Koski, former guidance counselor, New York City

Boys with Long Hair

I have three boys and when the first one wanted to grow his hair while he was in preschool, I was nothing if not tickled. I put the shaggy bangs into a paintbrush style ponytail and thought him very cute. One teacher did not think him cute. She raised her eyebrows. Within her earshot, if someone referred to him as a girl, I said—maybe a little loudly—"He's a boy who likes long hair. Boys can have long hair and girls can have short hair."

His hair grew. Then his brothers' hair grew. We got very comfortable with the idea that these were boys—with long hair. Turns out my third son also liked long hair. One of his kindergarten classmates stopped me practically every morning at drop-off all fall. He would say to me, "She looks like a girl with that long hair." He would be smiling. I'd reply, "He has long hair, but you know he's a boy." It was almost a ritual, a way to connect—the boy's a boy although he doesn't look just like all the boys. Eventually, the classmate moved on to other topics with me.

Over the years, what I've learned is this: you can make that statement about how "boys can choose long hair." It's not a one-time statement, though; it's an ongoing conversation and like most things, it can take a while to sink in. I have been so grateful to an out queer teacher at my sons' school because he has helped educate kids and parents and other teachers about the wide, wide variety of ways that boys and girls can express themselves, well beyond the length of their hair. It would have been much more difficult for this small elementary school community to welcome our family without his support.

—Elementary school parent

A word of caution. The stories featured in this chapter obviously support the premise of the book, yet it would be a mistake to expect ideal outcomes from every GLBTQI teacher. As in any group, there are those who err in the most human of ways, using poor judgment, maintaining poor boundaries, meeting adult rather than student needs. GLBTQI educators who transgress in these ways are likely to have those transgressions attributed more often to their sexuality, rather than poor judgment personality problems or mental illness. The bottom line is this: GLBTQI teachers are no better or worse than any other teachers in terms of professional propriety.

SECTION IV
THE ROLE OF NOT-GLBTQI EDUCATORS

If you are a not-GLBTQI, garden variety, GSD-supportive, heteronormative teacher, this section is about you. You are difficult to categorize, since you come in all sizes, ages, colors, political affiliations, religious dominations, geographies, and cultures. In the same way that using the GLBTQI acronym is expedient at best, calling you "straight" or "heteronormative" tells us more about what you are not, than who you actually are. And truthfully, in many ways you are the most important person in this whole story.

Calling you a "straight ally" is also problematic because allies "fight" an "enemy," and working to accept the biodiversity of gender and sexuality should not be construed as a war ("ally" as a verb is okay but that doesn't really help with the issue of how to label you). When words are limiting, I turn to metaphor, and I have found a particular metaphor that is useful when trying to describe ALL members of the school community as being both similar and unique at the same time. Let me explain.

Whether I am conducting a workshop at a large educational conference or consulting with an individual school or district, I begin by defining the concept of Gender and Sexuality Diversity (GSD). Participants are initially skeptical about the need for another acronym, yet they instantly appreciate the broadness of the GSD construct. They agree that gender and sexuality are essential aspects of human identity, and they understand that the conversation needs to be about all of us, not just a subgroup. Yet when I emphasize the concept of *bio*diversity, it often feels as though people don't readily connect to what I am trying to describe.

So I show a slide of finches. Did you know there are literally hundreds of different types of finches? The slide features dark red and grass-green birds, tawny birds that sport a pattern of black speckles on the wings, and smaller birds, with black and white stripes around the neck, along with burnt-orange cheeks and bright red beaks. Even within a single species—the Zebra Finch for example—there are numerous variations. In all their brilliant colors and unique patterns, the Chestnut Flanked White Finch (aka the Black Eyed Finch), the Florida Fancy, the Dominant Silver Finch, and the Orange Breasted each belong to the Zebra Finch family. These birds are truly a marvel to look at.

Then I inform participants that often the sex of fledglings is indeterminate in the nest. Sometimes you cannot even determine the sex of an adult finch until you hear its song. Not all finches mate at the same age or in the same environment. *Within just one species of this bird*, color, size, song, habitat, and mating behavior vary. So too with human beings. We are all part of the same species yet differ in many important ways, including in our gender and sexuality. I tell the educators in the room, *Think of yourself as a finch. Each of you is a finch. Each of your students is a finch. Parents are finches. We are all finches, similar and yet predictably different. We marvel at the biodiversity of the orchid or the shark or the finch. Yet when it comes to gender and sexuality in human beings, suddenly the inevitable diversity and variations seem threatening. We want only two kinds of finches, maybe three. The rest are problematic.*

The diversity that is so apparent and beautiful in the finch slide offers a playful, accessible frame of reference in the conversation about GSD. I tell participants that if they lose their way while navigating gender and sexuality, they should just remember the finches. Remember the idea that everyone is meant to be a particular kind of finch, and different kinds of finches belong to the same family. So, in truth, I think of you—the not-GLBTQI, garden-variety, GSD-supportive, heteronormative teacher—as a particular kind of finch. Or several different kinds of finches that have the not-GLBTQI trait in common.

The Work of Finches Like You

Here are some accounts of the critical work that finches like you do. You recognize, as Elizabeth MacCurrach does, that a gay colleague is at risk in ways you are not when addressing prejudice in the classroom (see But You're Not Gay). Students are puzzled by this straight teacher confronting them and challenging their use of "gay" as a put-down. They imagine that only someone with a vested interest—such as being gay herself (e.g., a Black Eyed Finch perhaps)—would intervene so strongly.

"But You're Not Gay . . ."

I remember working with a group of twelve and thirteen year olds and one of the boys called another boy's pink shirt "gay." I assumed other teachers in the school would likely have ignored the comment or at most asked the boys to pay attention or stop goofing around without addressing the true issue. That would have been the safe way to respond at the time, but I didn't want it to be OK to make derogatory statements about gay people in my classroom.

I muddled through an explanation of why I felt it wasn't OK to use "gay" as a put down. The kids looked at me curiously and one of them said something like, "but you're not gay are you? You have a husband." That was a pivotal moment for me because it suddenly became crystal clear. As a straight person I could talk about this issue with the students without putting myself at great risk, where my gay colleagues could not.

—Elizabeth Uhry MacCurrach, Head of Lower School
Shore Country Day School

Teachers who reckon with the privilege and power afforded to heteronormative finches are then able to model conscious support of those nonheteronormative and/or GLBTQI finches who are less privileged. In his work as a camp counselor, Chris Overtree teaches and models that there are many ways to be a boy (see Many Ways to Be a Man). Not all male finches are the same, nor do they need to be. Chris teaches these boys that *"however you choose to [be male], you are okay, you are special, you are loved."*

Many Ways to Be a Man

As a teenager, I felt a passion for civil rights, and the Civil Rights Movement was something I learned enough about in school to form my attitudes about basic human fairness and respect for the dignity of others. Perhaps more important, I believed that activism was essential to attaining and protecting equal rights. It was not enough to be silently supportive.

But silent was exactly how I was when it came to sexual orientation, something that just never came up in my school or home community. In high school, any pondering I might have done about the issue was purely hypothetical since no one in my school was openly gay or lesbian. The topic came up more often when I attended college, and activities like "gay jeans day" forced me to wonder why I was comfortable being silent about homophobia as a straight person, but not comfortable being silent about racism as a white person.

When my best friend struggled to come out to me in college, it took less than a second to realize the impact my silence had been having on him. I learned in that brief moment that being an advocate is as simple as loving someone, and I never wanted to be in the position of being silent again. My work at an all boys' summer camp—whose long-standing motto is "There are many ways to be a man"—has provided multiple opportunities for embracing the uniqueness of every boy. Being a man means lots of things, and however you choose to do it, you are okay, you are special, you are loved.

—Christopher Overtree, PhD

When you as a heteronormative teacher no longer assume heterosexuality in your students, colleagues, or parents, you make room for finches of every color and song to be seen and to feel welcome. By changing her assumptions, Sara Deveaux creates a spacious learning environment, as she commits to ensuring that all her students "can see themselves in what they are studying, reading, presenting and researching" (see No More Assumptions). When Sarinda Wilson tends to the power of language as an integral part of her classroom, she models respect for and inclusion of the many ways that finches can "be" and the different ways that finches can "love" (see Tending to Language and More).

No More Assumptions

Over the years I have been frustrated that school continues to be a place where such an integral part of student identity typically remains hidden. That has prompted me to work on ways to change my teaching both inside and outside of the classroom to be inclusive of all sexual orientations.

I do not assume heterosexuality in anyone, not in the athlete, not in the actor, not in the volunteer, not in the musician, and not in anyone else who may or may not fit in our world's crisp and clean categories. One of the most important goals I have when planning the school year is to make sure that all of my students are represented, that they can see themselves in what they are studying, reading, presenting and researching. Students' skits, for example, may have a gay couple, perhaps talking about something in their own life or dealing with a child. Students might read an article about the difficulties of a gay couple trying to adopt in certain European countries. In general, when referring to relationships, I try to avoid the assumption that we are talking about "a girlfriend and a boyfriend" or a "husband and wife," instead referring to "the couple" or "the partners." All students, particularly those who are typically underrepresented, need to feel visible and validated.

—Sara Deveaux, high school modern language teacher

Tending to Language and More

My children have always known that love and affection can extend not from one kind of person to another but simply from one caring person to another, and that all forms of care and partnership are acceptable to us. I ensure that this open-mindedness is fostered in my classroom as well.

I haven't had difficult experiences with students around gender and sexual orientation, only random opportunities to guide and correct students' language on occasion. I don't believe in letting slurs slither by because "kids will be kids."

It's because they're adolescents learning together that they need reminders about the power of language, jest and gesture.

In the beginning language classroom, gender initially takes on a mechanical form that my students don't necessarily think about until they begin the practice of listening and imitating language. Why might an elbow be masculine and a shoulder feminine? Aha, because they simply ARE. In the same way that individual human beings are who they are.

—Sarinda Parsons Wilson, instructor in French

Colleagues Building Community

Consider the role of heteronormative teachers in the following scenario (see The Story of Ms. Freedman, Her Students, and Her Colleagues).

The Story of Ms. Freedman, Her Students, and Her Colleagues

My wife and I are teachers at the same school. She teaches middle school, I teach elementary. One day as we passed each other in the hall, a second grade student asked if she was my sister. "She's my wife," I said. As we continued up the staircase, that student and a few others asked more questions: "You are married?!"

"Yes," I replied.

"You are married to a girl?"

"Yes," I replied.

"Can two girls be married?" "Yes," I replied again. The students accepted my answers and moved on, asking about what we were doing after lunch. Until we got upstairs. There was a big commotion in the coat closet, and a teacher walked outside to hear a few students arguing about Ms. Freedman being gay and being married to a woman.

"Don't call her that," one student said, though she knew I was.

"My brother says gay means disgusting," said another.

"Not Ms. Freedman. She's not disgusting."

With a few amazingly supportive colleagues, we talked about the word "gay," and what it means with all of our students and many of their families. Talk about a teachable moment! I am lucky to be in a supportive environment where I did not have to face this conversation alone, or as a source of conflict.

—Jessica Freedman, second grade teacher, New York City

As the students argue about whether Ms. Freedman is gay and whether or not that is okay, her not-GLBTQI, garden-variety, heteronormative colleagues step in. They step in and have a conversation with the students about the word "gay," a conversation that would be impossible for Ms. Freedman to facilitate on her own.

How might this scene unfold if her colleagues had not stepped in for the teachable moment? In all likelihood, the big commotion in the coat closet would have been handled as a "behavioral commotion." *Alright everyone, that's enough loud talking. Put your coats away and let's get into our seats.* Or a well-meaning teacher might intervene on the use of "gay" as a bad word that should not be used at school. *I am hearing some language that I am not comfortable with. We need to treat each other with respect.* What happens instead is these colleagues work together to support one another and to help these students with their understandable confusion: *How can our beloved Ms. Freedman be gay if gay is "disgusting"?*

All the goals related to gender and sexuality diversity education that have been laid out in this book are far more likely to be accomplished if the adults in schools can understand, respect, and support one another regardless of gender identity and sexuality. How colleagues treat each other is at the heart of creating an inclusive, productive, educational environment, and as Jessica Friedman notes, it is her good fortune to work in just such a community. Thoughtful conversations such as the one prompted by the coat closet commotion absolutely contribute to community building and positive educational outcomes, for students, teachers, and parents alike.

SAME AND DIFFERENT: THE ESSENCE OF OUR DIVERSITY

There is psychic safety in the homogenization of our culture. Drive through a strip mall in towns across the United States and we find the familiar golden arches, the reliable Dunkin' Donuts, Walmart, Staples, Starbucks, Petco. The familiar is at once reassuring and also disconcerting. We're in Nebraska; why does this stretch of route 1 look like New Jersey?! On many dimensions we as a society are wrestling with our ambivalence and ignorance about our essential "biodiversity," whether we are talking about animal species, plant life, food sources, habitats, or GSD.

So while many schools may work as part of their mission toward "tolerance" or "acceptance" of those whose gender or sexuality are outside the heteronormative majority, a deeper philosophical and practical aim is to understand, value, and integrate GSD as part of the diverse essence of our species and the truth of who lives in our school communities. We are not all the same, nor are we meant to be.

Teachers, developmental experts, and parents have known for years the dangers and hypocrisy of the "do as I say, not as I do" approach to teaching children about the world. Kids are expert at learning from the spoken and unspoken, the explicit and implicit, the conscious and the unconscious. This book demonstrates many times over that students are learning about gender and sexuality from the adults in their lives all the time, as much—if not more—by what these adults do than by what these adults say. When it comes to valuing the diversity of our communities and modeling respect for all our differences, no one holds positions of greater influence than parents and teachers.

Hopefully you have come away from these pages appreciating the centrality of GSD in preK–12 school life. With this greater awareness, and with some of the many tools and resources offered here, I am confident that you will find ways to help all members of a school community understand the inherent diversity of gender and sexuality. You can start by modeling that understanding yourself. True, there is still much work to be done to make schools safe and inclusive for people of all genders and sexualities. Yet if given adequate support, there is no one better suited to tackle this inescapable challenge than you—our teachers.

REFERENCES

CHAPTER I

American Psychological Association. 2005. *Lesbian & gay parenting.* http://www.apa.org/pi/lgbt/resources/parenting.aspx.

Blakemore, Judith E. Owen, Sheri A. Berenbaum, and Lynn S. Liben. 2009. *Gender development.* New York: Psychology Press.

Boylan, Jennifer Finney. 2003. *She's not there: A life in two genders.* New York: Broadway Books.

Bradley, Harriet. 2007. *Gender.* Boston: Policy Press.

Brill, Stephanie, and Rachel Pepper. 2008. *The transgender child: A handbook for families and professionals.* San Francisco: Cleis Press.

Cathcart, Rebecca. 2008. Boy's killing labeled a hate crime, stuns a town. *New York Times* (February 23, 2008), http://www.nytimes.com/2008/02/23/us/23oxnard.html.

Children's Hospital Boston. *Gender management service clinic.* 2010.

Clarey, Christopher. 2010. As Semenya returns, so do questions. *New York Times* (August 22), http://www.nytimes.com/2010/08/23/sports/23iht-TRACK.html.

———. 2009. Gender test after a gold-medal finish. *New York Times* (August 20), http://www.nytimes.com/2009/08/20/sports/20runner.html.

Colapinto, John. 2001. *As nature made him: The boy who was raised as a girl.* 2nd ed. New York: Perennial.

Davies, Douglas. 2004. *Child Development: A practitioner's guide*, 2nd ed. New York: Guilford Press.

Denizet-Lewis, Benoit. 2009. Coming out in middle school. *New York Times Magazine* (September 27).

Dreger, Alice. 2011. Redefining the sexes in unequal terms. *New York Times* (April 23), http://www.nytimes.com/2011/04/24/sports/24testosterone.html.

Farrell, Kathleen, Nisha Gupta, and Mary Queen, eds. 2005. *Interrupting heteronormativity: Lesbian, gay, bisexual, and transgender pedagogy and responsible teaching at Syracuse University.* Syracuse, NY: Graduate School of Syracuse University.

Fausto-Sterling, Anne. 2000. *Sexing the body: Gender politics and the construction of sexuality*. New York: Basic Books.

Garcia, Ana Maria, and Graciela Slesaransky-Poe. 2010. The heteronormative classroom: Questioning and liberating policies. *The Teacher Educator* 45(4): 244–56.

Gathorne-Harty, Jonathan. 1998. *Sex, the measure of all things: A life of Alfred C. Kinsey*. Bloomington: Indiana University Press.

Greytak, Emily A., Joseph G. Kosciw, and Elizabeth M. Diaz. 2009. *Harsh realities: The experience of transgender youth in our nation's schools*. Gay, Lesbian and Straight Education Network.

Hayes, David M., and Andrew S. Walters. 2007. Teaching about sexuality: Balancing contradictory social messages with professional standards. *American Journal of Sexuality Education* 2(2): 27–49.

Is it a boy or a girl? A Discovery Channel documentary on the medical management of children with ambiguous sex anatomy. 2000. Directed by Phyllis Ward. Great Falls, VA: Discovery Channel. Cable broadcast, March 26.

Karkazis, Katrina. 2008. *Fixing sex: Intersex, medical authority, and lived experience*. Durham, NC: Duke University Press.

Kendler, K. S., L. M. Thornton, S. E. Gilman, and R. C. Kessler. 2000. Sexual orientation in a U.S. sample of twin and nontwin sibling pairs. *American Journal of Psychiatry* 157: 1843–46.

Kinsey, Alfred C., Wardell Pomeroy, and Clyde E. Martin. 1948. *Sexual behavior in the human male*. Bloomington: Indiana University Press.

Kinsey, Alfred C., Wardell Pomeroy, Clyde E. Martin, and Paul H. Gebhard. 1953. *Sexual behavior in the human female*. Bloomington: Indiana University Press.

Lamb, Sharon, and Lyn Mikel Brown. 2007. *Packaging girlhood: Saving our daughters from marketers' schemes*. New York: St. Martin's Press.

Lamb, Sharon, Lyn Mikel Brown, and Mark Tappan. 2009. *Packaging boyhood: Saving our sons from superheroes, slackers and other media stereotypes*. New York: St. Martin's Press.

LeVay, Simon, and Sharon M. Valente. 2002. *Human sexuality*. Sunderland, MA: Sinauer Associates, Inc. Publishers.

Masters, William, Virginia E. Johnson, and Robert C. Kolodny. 1997. *Human Sexuality*, 5th ed. Boston: Allyn & Bacon.

Meyer, Elizabeth J. 2010. *Gender and sexual diversity in schools*. Dordrecht: Springer.

Middle sexes: Redefining he and she. 2008. Directed by Antony Thomas. New York: HBO Home Video. DVD.

Nehm, Ross H., and Rebecca Young. 2008. "Sex hormones" in secondary school biology textbooks. *Science & Education* 17 (April): 1175–90.

Oster, M. M. 2008. Saying one thing and doing another: The paradox of best practices and sex education. *American Journal of Sexuality Education* 3(2): 117–48.

Rosenthal, Elisabeth. 2005. For fruit flies, gene shift tilts sexual orientation. *New York Times* (June 3), http://www.nytimes.com/2005/06/03/science/03cell.html.

Rosin, Hanna. 2008. A boy's life. *The Atlantic* (November), http://www.theatlantic.com/magazine/archive/2008/11/a-boy-apos-s-life/7059/.

Ruble, Diane N., Lisa J. Taylor, Lisa Cyphers, Faith K. Reulich, Leah E. Lurye, and Patrick E. Shrout. 2007. The role of gender constancy in early gender development. *Child Development* 78(4) (July/August): 1121–36.

Saillant, Catherine. 2011. Gay student's slaying carefully planned, prosecutor tells jurors. *L.A. NOW* (July 5), http://latimesblogs.latimes.com/lanow/2011/07/brandon-mcinerney-planned-and-carried-out-execution-of-gay-classmate.html.

Sexy, inc.: Our children under influence. 2007. Directed by Sophie Bissonnette. National Film Board of Canada. Streamed from http://www.nfb.ca/film/sexy_inc/download.

SIECUS. 2010. Sexuality education Q&A. http://www.siecus.org/index.cfm?fuseaction=page.viewpage &pageid=521&grandparentID=477&parentID=514#Q7.

Trachtenberg, Robert. 2005. *When I knew.* New York: Regan Books.

Trautner, Hanns M., Diane N. Ruble, Lisa Cyphers, Barbara Kirsten, Regina Behrendt, and Petra Hartmann. 2005. Rigidity and flexibility of gender stereotypes in childhood: Developmental or differential? *Infant and Child Development* 14: 365–81.

Two Spirits. 2009. Directed by Lydia Nibley. Los Angeles: Say Yes Quickly Productions. DVD.

Vasey, Paul L., and Nancy H. Bartlett. 2007. What can the Samoan "Fa'afafine" teach us about the Western concept of gender identity disorder in childhood? *Perspectives in Biology and Medicine* 50(4) (Autumn): 481–90.

Wilbourn, Makeba Parramore, and Daniel W. Kee. 2010. Henry the nurse is a doctor too: Implicitly examining children's gender stereotypes for male and female occupational roles. *Sex Roles* 62 (April): 670–83.

CHAPTER 2

Blaise, Mindy. 2009. "What a girl wants, what a girl needs": Responding to sex, gender, and sexuality in the early childhood classroom. *Journal of Research in Childhood Education* 23(4): 450–60.

DePalma, Renee, and Elizabeth Atkinson, eds. 2009. *Interrogating heteronormativity in primary schools: The No Outsiders Project.* Sterling, VA: Trentham Books.

———, eds. 2010. *Undoing homophobia in primary schools: The No Outsiders Project.* Sterling, VA: Trentham Books.

Fausto-Sterling, Anne. 2000. *Sexing the body: Gender politics and the construction of sexuality.* New York: Basic Books.

Ferran, Lee. 2010. "My son is gay" mommy speaks out on web controversy. *ABC News* (November 5), http://abcnews.go.com/GMA/son-gay-mommy-blog-ignites-controversy/story?id=12066925.

Greytak, Emily A., Joseph G. Kosciw, and Elizabeth M. Diaz. 2009. *Harsh realities: The experience of transgender youth in our nation's schools.* Gay, Lesbian and Straight Education Network.

Jennet, Mark. 2010. In Renee DePalma and Elizabeth Atkinson, eds. *Invisible boundaries: Addressing sexualities equality in children's worlds.* Sterling, VA: Trentham Books.

Kosciw, Joseph G., and Elizabeth M. Diaz. 2008. *Involved, invisible, ignored: The experiences of lesbian, gay, bisexual, and transgender parents and their children in our nation's K–12 schools.* New York: GLSEN.

Kosciw, Joseph G., Emily A. Greytak, Elizabeth M. Diaz, and Mark J. Bartkiewicz. 2010. *2009 National School Climate Survey: The experiences of lesbian, gay, bisexual and transgender youth in our nation's schools.* New York: GLSEN.

Martin, Karin A., and Emily Kazyak. 2009. Hetero-romantic love and heterosexiness in children's G-rated films. *Gender and Society* 23(3) (June): 315–36.

Meyer, Elizabeth J. 2007. "But I'm not gay": What straight teachers need to know about queer theory. *Queering straight teachers: Discourse and identity in education.* Nelson M. Rodriguez and William F. Pinar, eds. New York: Peter Lang.

Myers, Kristen, and Laura Raymond. 2010. Elementary school girls and heteronormativity: The girl project. *Gender & Society* 24(2) (April): 167–88.

Orenstein, Peggy. 2011. *Cinderella ate my daughter: Dispatches from the front lines of the new girlie-girl culture.* New York: Harper Collins.

Rich, Adrienne. 1994. *Blood, bread, and poetry.* New York: W.W. Norton.

Roughgarden, Joan. 2004. *Evolution's rainbow: Diversity, gender, and sexuality in nature and people.* Berkeley: University of California Press.

Schwyzer, Hugo. 2011. Men and the sexualization of young girls. *The Good Men Project* (February 9, 2011), http://goodmenproject.com/ethics-values/men-and-the-sexualization-of-young-girls/.

Wohlwend, Karen. 2009. Damsels in discourse: Girls consuming and producing identity texts through Disney princess play. *Reading Research Quarterly* 44(1).

CHAPTER 3

Asher, N. 2007. Made in the (multicultural) U.S.A.: Unpacking tensions of race, culture, gender, and sexuality in education. *Educational Researcher* 36(2): 65–73.

Birden, Susan. 2005. *Rethinking sexual identity in education.* Lanham, MD: Rowman & Littlefield Education.

Bronski, Michael. 2011. *A queer history of the United States: Revisioning American history.* Boston: Beacon Press.

D'Emilio, John. 2002. *The world turned: Essays on gay history, politics, and culture.* Durham, NC: Duke University Press.

DePalma, Renee, and Elizabeth Atkinson, eds. 2010. *Undoing homophobia in primary schools: The No Outsiders Project.* Sterling, VA: Trentham Books.

Jennings, Todd, and Ian K. Macgillivray. 2011. A content analysis of lesbian, gay, bisexual, and transgender topics in multicultural education textbooks. *Teaching Education* 22(1): 39–62.

Kim, Robert, David Sheridan, and Sabrina Holcomb. 2009. *A report on the status of gay, lesbian, bisexual and transgender people in education: Stepping out of the closet, into the light.* National Education Association. http://www.nea.org/assets/docs/glbtstatus09.pdf.

Kosciw, J. G., E. M. Diaz, and E. A. Greytak. 2008. *2007 National School Climate Survey: The experiences of lesbian, gay, bisexual and transgender youth in our nation's schools.* New York: GLSEN.

Kosciw, Joseph G., Emily A. Greytak, Elizabeth M. Diaz, and Mark J. Bartkiewicz. 2010. *2009 National School Climate Survey: The experiences of lesbian, gay, bisexual and transgender youth in our nation's schools.* New York: GLSEN.

Kumashiro, Kevin K. 2002. *Troubling education: "Queer" activism and anti-oppressive pedagogy.* New York: Routledge.

———. 2008. GLBT issues today—the framing of the GLBT movement, education, and politics. Speech given at NEA 2008 Summit. As cited in Kim, Sheridan, and Holcomb (2009).

Meyer, Elizabeth J. 2010. *Gender and sexual diversity in schools.* Dordrecht: Springer.

NEASC. 2007. http://www.neasc.org/.

Nussbaum, Martha Craven. 2003. *Cultivating humanity: A classical defense of reform in liberal education,* 7th printing. c.f. 1st edition, 1997. Cambridge, MA: Harvard University Press.

Out of the past: The struggle for say and lesbian rights in America. 1998. Directed by Jeffrey Dupre. Arlington, VA: Public Broadcasting Service.

Pollock, Mica. 2008. *Everyday antiracism: Getting real about race in school.* New York: The New Press.

Principles of good practice: Equity and justice. 2004. National Association of Independent Schools. http://www.nais.org/about/seriesdoc.cfm?ItemNumber=146283&sn.ItemNumber=146810.

CHAPTER 4

American Library Association. 2007. Top ten most frequently challenged books of 2006. http://www .ala.org/ala/issuesadvocacy/banned/frequentlychallenged/21stcenturychallenged/2006/index.cfm.

———. 2008. Top ten most frequently challenged books of 2007. http://www.ala.org/ala/issues advocacy/banned/frequentlychallenged/21stcenturychallenged/2007/index.cfm.

———. 2009. Top ten most frequently challenged books of 2008. http://www.ala.org/ala/issues advocacy/banned/frequentlychallenged/21stcenturychallenged/2008/index.cfm.

———. 2010. Top ten most frequently challenged books of 2009. http://www.ala.org/ala/issues advocacy/banned/frequentlychallenged/21stcenturychallenged/2009/index.cfm.

Attempts to remove children's book on male penguin couple parenting chick continue: "And Tango Makes Three" tops ALA's 2008 top ten list of most frequently challenged books. 2009. American Library Association (April 16), http://www.ala.org/ala/newspresscenter/news/pressreleases2009/april2009/nlw08bbtopten.cfm.

Becker, Ron. 2006. *Gay TV and straight America.* Piscataway, NJ: Rutgers University Press.

Bos, Henny, and Nanette Gartrell. 2010. Adolescents of the USA National Lesbian Family Study: Can family characteristics counteract the negative effects of stigmatization? *Family Process* 49(4): 559–72.

Bronski, Michael. 2011. *A queer history of the United States: Revisioning American history.* Boston: Beacon Press.

Campos, David. 2005. *Understanding gay and lesbian youth: Lessons for straight school teachers, counselors, and administrators.* Lanham, MD: Rowman & Littlefield Education.

Clark, Stephen J. 2006. Gay priests and other bogeymen. *Journal of Homosexuality* 51(4): 1–13.

Ebbets, John. 2010. Local United Way shuns discriminatory policies: Letter to the editor. *Daily Hampshire Gazette* (December).

Ehrensaft, Diane. *Mommies, daddies, donors, surrogates: Answering tough questions and building strong families.* New York: Guilford Press.

Geijsel, Femke, and Frans Meijers. 2005. Identity learning: The core process of educational change. *Educational Studies* 31(4) (December): 419–30.

Himmelstein, Kathryn E. W., and Hannah Bruckner. 2011. Criminal-justice and school sanctions against nonheterosexual youth: A national longitudinal study. *Pediatrics* 127(1) (January): 49–57.

Hubbard, Jeremy. 2010. Fifth gay teen suicide in three weeks sparks debate: As mourners were honoring Tyler Clementi, news came of a fifth suicide. *ABC News* (October 3), http://abc.go.com/US/gay-teen-suicide-sparks-debate/story?id=11788128.

Kosciw, J. G., E. M. Diaz, and E. A. Greytak. 2008. *2007 National School Climate Survey: The experiences of lesbian, gay, bisexual and transgender youth in our nation's schools.* New York: GLSEN.

Kosciw, Joseph G., Emily A. Greytak, Elizabeth M. Diaz, and Mark J. Bartkiewicz. 2010. *2009 National School Climate Survey: The experiences of lesbian, gay, bisexual and transgender youth in our nation's schools.* New York: GLSEN.

Mundy, Liza. 2008. *Everything conceivable: How the science of assisted reproduction is changing our world.* New York: Anchor.

Nakkula, Michael J., and Eric Toshalis. 2008. *Understanding youth: Adolescent development for educators,* 2nd printing. c.f. 1st printing, 2006. Cambridge, MA: Harvard University Press.

Pascoe, C. J. 2007. *Dude you're a fag: Masculinity and sexuality in high school.* Berkeley: University of California Press.

Patterson, Charlotte. 2009. Children of lesbian and gay parents: Psychology, law and policy. *American Psychologist* 64(8) (November): 727–36.

Schulz, Charles. 1987. Charles Schulz interview: An interview with America's most enduring contemporary cartoonist by Rick Marschall and Gary Groth. *Nemo* 31: 5–24.

Tomboys! Feisty girls and spirited women. 2004. Directed by Julie Akeret and Christian McEwen. New York: Women Make Movies.

CHAPTER 5

Butler, Judith. 1994. Gender as performance: An interview with Judith Butler by P. Osborne and L. Segal. *Radical Philosophy* 23(3) (Summer): 66–71.

———. 2006. Response. *British Journal of Sociology of Education* 27(4): 529–34.

Drago-Severson, Eleanor. 2009. *Leading adult learning: Supporting adult development in our schools.* Thousand Oaks, CA: Corwin.

DuFour, R. 2007. Professional learning communities: A bandwagon, an idea. *Middle School Journal* 39(1): 4–8.

Intrator, Sam M. 2006. Beginning teachers and the emotional drama of the classroom. *Journal of Teacher Education* 57(3): 232–39.

Kegan, Robert. 1982. *The evolving self: Problem and process in human development.* Cambridge, MA: Harvard University Press.

Kegan, Robert, and Lisa Lahey. 2002. Inner conflicts, inner strengths: An interview with Robert Kegan and Lisa Lahey by Dennis Sparks. *Journal of Staff Development* 23(2): 66–71.

Palmer, Parker. 2007. *The Courage to Teach Guide for Reflection and Renewal, 10th Anniversary Edition.* San Francisco: Jossey-Bass. Kindle Edition.

Rasmussen, Mary Lou. 2004. The problem of coming out. *Theory Into Practice* 43(2).

Schlasko, G. D. 2005. Queer (v) pedagogy. *Equity and Excellence in Education* 38: 123–34.

Schopenhauer, Arthur. Attributed.

CHAPTER 6

DePalma, Renee, and Elizabeth Atkinson, eds. 2010. *Undoing homophobia in primary schools: The No Outsiders Project.* Sterling, VA: Trentham Books.

Farson, Richard, and Ralph Keyes. 2003. *The innovation paradox: The success of failure, the failure of success.* New York: Free Press.

GLSEN. 2001. 4 out of 5 parents say "yes" to protecting LGBT students. Press release. (December 4), http://www.glsen.org/cgi-bin/iowa/all/news/record/872.html.

Killen, M., and C. Stangor. 2001. Children's social reasoning about inclusion and exclusion in gender and race peer group contexts. *Child Development* 72: 174–86.

Lamb, Lindsay M., Rebecca S. Bigler, Lynn S. Liben, and Vanessa A. Green. 2009. Teaching children to confront peers' sexist remarks: Implications for theories of gender development and educational practice. *Sex Roles* 61: 361–82.

Salmivalli, C., A. Kaukiainen, and M. Voeten. 2005. Anti-bullying intervention: Implementation and outcome. *British Journal of Educational Psychology* 75: 465–87.

CHAPTER 7

Abrams, Jonathan. 2011. Noah fined $50,000 for antigay slur. *New York Times* (May 23), http://www.nytimes.com/2011/05/24/sports/basketball/bulls-noah-apologizes-for-using-antigay-slur.html?scp=1&sq=noah%20joakim&st=cse.

Biegel, Stuart. 2010. *The right to be out: Sexual orientation and gender identity in America's public schools.* Minneapolis: University of Minnesota Press.

Birkey, Andy. 2011. Minneapolis school board passes stringent anti-gay bullying, pro-LGBT curriculum. *Minnesota Independent* (January 13), http://minnesotaindependent.com/76262/minneapolis-school-board-passes-stringent-anti-gay-bullying-pro-lgbt-curriculum.

Blackburn, Mollie V., and Lance T. McCready. 2009. Voices of queer youth in urban schools: Possibilities and limitations. *Theory Into Practice* 48(3): 222–30.

Blackburn, Mollie V., and Jill M. Smith. 2010. Moving beyond the inclusion of LGBT-themed literature in English language arts classrooms: Interrogating heteronormativity and exploring intersectionality. *Journal of Adolescent & Adult Literacy* 53(8): 625–34.

Brown, Dave F. 2006. It's the curriculum, stupid: There's something wrong with it. *Phi Delta Kappan* 87(10): 777–83.

Campos, David. 2005. *Understanding gay and lesbian youth: Lessons for straight school teachers, counselors, and administrators.* Lanham, MD: Rowman & Littlefield Education.

Duncan, Arne. 2010. The myths about bullying: Secretary Arne Duncan's remarks at the Bullying Prevention Summit. August 11. http://www.ed.gov/news/speeches/myths-about-bullying-secretary-arne-duncans-remarks-bullying-prevention-summit.

Epstein, Debbie. 1997. Boyz' own stories: Masculinities and sexualities in schools. *Gender & Education* 9(1) (March): 105–15.

Gonzales, Jason. 2010. Risk and threat in critical inquiry: Vacancies, violations, and vacuums. *Acting Out! Combating Homophobia Through Teacher Activism*, eds. Mollie V. Blackburn, Caroline T. Clark, Lauren M. Kenney, and Jill M. Smith. New York: Teacher's College Press, 75–87.

Hinde, Elizabeth R. 2005. Revisiting curriculum integration: A fresh look at an old idea. *Social Studies* 96(3).

Horner, Sarah. 2011. Anoka-Hennepin school district stands by gay "neutrality" policy. *Twin Cities.com* (August 13), http://www.twincities.com/ci_18672082.

Kim, Robert, David Sheridan, and Sabrina Holcomb. 2009. *A report on the status of gay, lesbian, bisexual and transgender people in education: Stepping out of the closet, into the light.* National Education Association. http://www.nea.org/assets/docs/glbtstatus09.pdf.

Knudsen, Susanne V. 2005. Intersectionality: A theoretical inspiration in the analysis of minority cultures and identities in textbooks, 61–76. *Caught in the web or lost in the textbook?* Eighth International Conference on Learning and Educational Media. http://www.iartem.no/documents/caught_in_the_web.pdf.

Kosciw, Joe, Emily A. Greytak, Elizabeth M. Diaz, and Mark J. Bartkiewicz. 2010. *2009 National School Climate Survey: The experiences of lesbian, gay, bisexual and transgender youth in our nation's schools.* New York: GLSEN.

Kumashiro, Kevin K. 2002. *Troubling Education: "Queer" Activism and Anti-Oppressive Pedagogy.* New York: Routledge.

———. 2008. GLBT issues today—the framing of the GLBT movement, education, and politics. Speech given at NEA 2008 Summit. As cited in Kim, Sheridan, and Holcomb (2009).

Levy-Warren, Marsha H. 1996. *The adolescent journey: Development, identity formation, and psychotherapy.* Northvale, NJ: Jason Aronson.

Macgillivray, Ian K. 2004. *Sexual orientation and schools policy: A practical guide for teachers, administrators, and community activists.* Lanham, MD: Rowman & Littlefield Education.

Meyer, Elizabeth J. 2009. *Gender, bullying, and harassment: Strategies to end sexism and homophobia in schools.* New York: Teachers College Press.

Miner, Barbara. 1998. Reading, writing and censorship: When good books can get schools in trouble. *Rethinking Schools Online.* http://www.rethinkingschools.org/archive/12_03/cenmain.shtml.

Misawa, Mitsunori. 2010. Queer race pedagogy for educators in higher education: Dealing with power dynamics and positionality of LGBTQ students of color. *International Journal of Critical Pedagogy* 3(1): 26–35.

Monacelli, Nick. 2011. Sacramento lesbian student fights to wear tux at ball. *ABC News 10* (May 12, 2011), http://www.news10.net/news/article/137401/2/Sacramento-lesbian-student-fights-to-wear-tux-at-ball.

Nakkula, Michael J., and Eric Toshalis. 2006. *Understanding youth: Adolescent development for educators.* Cambridge, MA: Harvard Educational Publishing Group.

NMSA. 2002. *NMSA position statement on curriculum integration.* http://www.amle.org/AboutAMLE/PositionStatements/CurriculumIntegration/tabid/282/Default.aspx.

———. 2010. *This we believe: Keys to educating young adolescents.* http://www.nmsa.org/AboutNMSA/ThisWeBelieve/tabid/1273/Default.aspx.

Parker, Pat. 1999. Movement in Black. *Movement in Black*, 2nd ed. 1st ed., 1978. Ann Arbor, MI: Firebrand Books.

Pollock, Mica. 2008. *Everyday antiracism: Getting real about race in school.* New York: The New Press.

Pritchard, Mary E., and Gregory S. Wilson. 2003. Using emotional and social factors to predict student success. *Journal of College and Student Development* 44(1): 18–28.

Quillen, Ian. 2011. ACLU, Yale Law School run campaign against filtering LGBT content. *Digital Directions* 4(3): 13.

———. 2011. ACLU files first legal case of LGBT filtering campaign. *Education Week: Digital Education* (August 15), http://blogs.edweek.org/edweek/DigitalEducation/2011/08/aclu_files_first_case_of_lgbt.html.

Retired NBA star Hardaway says he hates "gay people." 2007. *ESPN* (February 16), http://sports.espn.go.com/nba/news/story?id=2766213.

Rhoden, William C. 2011. Bryant should have been forced to sit. *New York Times* (April 14), http://www.nytimes.com/2011/04/15/sports/basketball/15rhoden.html?scp=12&sq=kobe%20bryant%20apologize&st=cse.

Rich, Adrienne. 1986. Invisibility in academe. *Blood, Bread and Poetry.* New York: W.W. Norton.

Savin-Williams, Ritch C. 2005. *The new gay teenager.* Cambridge, MA: Harvard University Press.

Schopenhauer, Arthur. Attributed.

Stanglin, Douglas. 2011. Florida transgender teen crowned prom queen. *USA Today* (May 31), http://content.usatoday.com/communities/ondeadline/post/2011/05/fla-transgender-teen-crowned-high-school-prom-queen/1.

Teaching Tolerance. 2010. *Bullied.* DVD.

Weber, Tom. 2011. Anoka-Hennepin school district faces lawsuit over harassment of gays. *Minnesota Public Radio* (May 24), http://minnesota.publicradio.org/display/web/2011/05/24/anoka-hennepin-lawsuit/.

Vars, Gordon, and James A. Beane. 2000. Integrative curriculum in a standards-based world. ERIC Document ED 441618. http://www.nmsa.org/research/res_articles_integrated.htm.

Vossekuil, Bryan, Robert A. Fein, Marisa Reddy, Randy Borum, and William Modzelesky. 2002. *The final report and findings of the safe school initiative: Implications for the prevention of school at-*

tacks in the United States. Washington, DC: U.S. Secret Service and U.S. Department of Education. May 2002. http://www.secretservice.gov/ntac/ssi_final_report.pdf.

CHAPTER 8

American Psychological Association. 2005. *Based on the research, comprehensive sex education is more effective at stopping the spread of HIV infection*. http://www.apa.org/releases/sexeducation.html.

Boonstra, Heather. 2009. Advocates call for a new approach after the era of "Abstinence-only" sex education. *Guttmacher Policy Review* 12(1): 6–11.

Elia, John P., and Mickey Eliason. 2010. Discourses of exclusion: Sexuality education's silencing of sexual others. *Journal of LGBT Youth* 7(1): 29–48.

Forget swimming and riding a bike—young children today more likely to have mastered computer games: AVG study shows young kids learn tech skills before life skills. 2010. AVG.com (January 19), http://www.avg.com/us-en/press-releases-news.ndi-672.

Kirby, Douglas. 2007. Emerging answers: Research findings on programs to reduce teen pregnancy and transmitted diseases. Washington, DC: The National Campaign to Prevent Teen and Unplanned Pregnancy. http://www.thenationalcampaign.org/EA2007/EA2007_full.pdf.

Quillen, Ian. 2011. ACLU files first legal case of LGBT filtering campaign. *Education Week: Digital Education* (August 15), http://blogs.edweek.org/edweek/DigitalEducation/2011/08/aclu_files_first_case_of_lgbt.html.

Roffman, Deborah M. 2001. *Sex & sensibility: The thinking parent's guide to talking sense about sex*. Cambridge, MA: Da Capo Press.

SIECUS. 2010. State by state decisions: The Personal Responsibility Education Program and Title V Abstinence-Only Program. http://siecus.org/index.cfm?fuseaction=Feature.showFeature&FeatureID=1934.

SIECUS. 2009a.What the research says: Abstinence-only-until-marriage programs. http://www.siecus.org/_data/global/images/What%20the%20Research%20Says-Ab-Only-1.pdf.

SIECUS 2009b.What the research says: Comprehensive sex education. http://www.siecus.org/_data/global/images/What%20the%20Research%20Says-CSE-1.pdf.

Trenhom, C., B. Deyaney, K. Forston, I. Quay, J. Wheeler, and M. Clark. 2005. *Impacts of four Title V Section 510 abstinence education programs. Final report*. Princeton, NJ: Mathematica Policy Research.

Walters, Andrew S., and David M. Hayes. 2007. Teaching about sexuality: Balancing contradictory social messages with professional standards. *American Journal of Sexuality Education* 2(2).

Wingert, Pat. 2002. Periscope: Sex education "values trumps data." *Newsweek* (February 11).

CHAPTER 9

American Psychological Association. 2005. *Based on the research, comprehensive sex education is more effective at stopping the spread of HIV infection*. http://www.apa.org/releases/sexeducation.html.

Apple, M. 2005. Doing things the "right" way: Legitimating educational inequalities in conservative times, *Educational Review* 57(3): 271–93.

Asher, N. 2007. Made in the (multicultural) U.S.A.: Unpacking tensions of race, culture, gender and sexuality in education. *Educational Researcher* 36(2): 65–73.

Associated Press. 2008. Court upholds dismissal of suit over schools' same-sex teaching. *Boston Herald* (January 31), http://www.bostonherald.com/news/regional/general/view.bg?articleid=1070390.

DePalma, Renee, and Elizabeth Atkinson. 2010a. The nature of institutional heteronormativity in primary schools and practice-based responses. *Teaching and Teacher Education* 26(8): 1669–76.

———, eds. 2010b. *Undoing homophobia in primary schools: The No Outsiders Project.* Sterling, VA: Trentham Books.

Drago-Severson, Eleanor. 2009. Leading adult learning: Supporting adult development in our schools. Thousand Oaks, CA: Corwin.

Evans, R. 2001. *The human side of school change: Reform, resistance, and the real-life problems of innovation.* Jossey-Bass Education.

Gavin, Lorrie, Andrea P. MacKay, Kathryn Brown, Sara Harrier, Stephanie J. Ventura, Laura Kann, Maria Rangel, Stuart Berman, Patricia Dittus, Nicole Liddon, Lauri Markowitz, Maya Sternberg, Hillard Weinstock, Corinne Davide-Ferdon, and George Ryan. 2009. Reproductive health of persons aged 10–24 years—United States, 2002–2007. *CDC Morbidity and Mortality Weekly Report,* Surveillance Summaries, July 17, 2009.

Gruber, J. E., and S. Finneran. 2008. Comparing the impact of bullying and sexual harassment victimization on the mental and physical health of adolescents. *Sex Roles* 59: 1–12.

Heifetz, Ronald. 1998. *Leadership without Easy Answers.* Cambridge, MA: Harvard University Press.

Heifetz, Ronald A., and Marty Linsky. 2002. *Leadership on the line: Staying alive through the dangers of leading.* Boston, MA: Harvard Business School Publishing.

Hess, Amanda. 2010. Come for the pizza, stay for the deconstruction of masculinity. *Washington City Paper: The Sexist* (May 27), http://www.washingtoncitypaper.com/blogs/sexist/2010/05/27/come-for-the-pizza-stay-for-the-deconstruction-of-masculinity/.

Hostile hallways: Bullying, teasing and sexual harassment in school. 2001. Harris Interactive. Washington, DC: American Association of University Women.

Kelly, G. 2005. Re-visioning sexuality education: A challenge for the future. *American Journal of Sexuality Education* 1(1): 5–21.

Kosciw, Joseph G., Emily A. Greytak, Elizabeth M. Diaz, and Mark J. Bartkiewicz. 2010. *The 2009 National school climate survey: The experiences of lesbian, gay, bisexual and transgender youth in our nation's schools.* New York: GLSEN.

Leithwood, Kenneth, and Blair Mascall. 2008. Collective leadership effects on student achievement. *Educational Administration Quarterly* 44(4) (October): 529–61. As quoted in Wahlstrom (2008).

Lindsay, Jay. 2011. Catholic school won't admit gays' son. MSNBC.com (May 12), http://www.msnbc.msn.com/id/37113870/ns/us_new-life.

Macgillivray, Ian K. 2004. *Sexual orientation and school policy: A practical guide for teachers, administrators, and community activists.* Lanham, MD: Rowman & Littlefield Education.

Mayrowetz, David, Joseph Murphy, Karen Seashore Louis, and Mark A. Smylie. 2007. Distributed leadership as work redesign: Retrofitting the job characteristics model. *Leadership and Policy in Schools* 6(1) (February): 69–101.

McCarthy, Mike, and Kathy Baron. 2010. Ten big ideas of school leadership. *Edutopia* (March 15, 2010), http://www.edutopia.org/stw-maine-project-based-learning-ideas-principal-leadership.

Meyer, Elizabeth J. 2009. *Gender, bullying, and harassment: Strategies to end sexism and homophobia in schools.* New York: Teachers College Press.

———. 2011. *Gender and sexual diversity in schools.* Dordrecht: Springer.

Oster, M. 2008. Saying one thing and doing another: The paradox of best practices and sex education. *American Journal of Sexuality Education* 3(2): 117–48.

Patterson, Charlotte. 2009. Children of lesbian and gay parents: Psychology, law and policy. *American Psychologist* 64(8) (November): 727–36.

Powell, Brian, Catherine Bolzendahl, Claudia Geist, Lala Carr Steelman. 2010. *Counted out: Same-sex relations and Americans' definitions of family.* New York: Russell Sage Foundation.

Roffman, Deborah M. 2010. The puritans are dead: Long live the puritans? *Huffington Post* (February 18).

Sexy, inc.: Our children under influence. 2007. Directed by Sophie Bissonnette. National Film Board of Canada. Streamed from http://www.nfb.ca/film/sexy_inc/download.

Shih, Gerry. 2011. Clashes pit parents vs. gay-friendly curriculums in schools. *New York Times* (March 4), A21A.

Strategies for aligning board policy-making with education reform and program improvement. 2010. California County Superintendents Educational Services Association and the California School Boards Association. http://www.ccsesa.org/index/documents/School_Board_Leadership.pdf.

Terkel, Amanda. 2011.Tennessee anti-gay bill, backed by state chamber of commerce, puts big business in a tough spot. *Huffington Post* (May 25), http://www.huffingtonpost.com/2011/05/23/tennessee-anti-gay-bill-chamber-commerce-business_n_865581.html.

Thomas, Robert Murray. 2009. *Sex and the American teenager: Seeing through the myths and confronting the issues.* Lanham, MD: Rowman & Littlefield Education.

Trautner, Hanns, Diane Ruble, Lisa Cyphers, Barbara Kirsen, Regina Behrendt, and Petra Hartman. 2005. Rigidity and flexibility of gender stereotypes in childhood: Developmental or differential? *Infant and Child Development* 14: 365–81.

Trenhom, C., B. Deyaney, K. Forston, I. Quay, J. Wheeler, and M. Clark. 2005. *Impacts of four Title V Section 510 abstinence education programs. Final report.* Princeton, NJ: Mathematica Policy Research.

U.S. Department of Education Office for Civil Rights. 2010a. Dear colleague letter. October 26, 2010. http://www2.ed.gov/about/offices/list/ocr/letters/colleague-201010.pdf.

U.S. Department of Education Office for Civil Rights. 2010b. Dear colleague letter, harassment and bullying: Background, summary, and fast facts. October 26, 2010. http://www2.ed.gov/about/offices/list/ocr/docs/dcl-factsheet-201010.pdf.

Wahlstrom, Kyla L., and Karen Seashore Louis. 2008. How teachers experience principal leadership: The roles of professional community, trust, efficacy, trust, efficacy, and shared responsibility. *Educational Administration Quarterly* 44(4) (October): 458–95.

Walters, A. and D. Hayes. 2007. Teaching about sexuality: Balancing contradictory messages with professional standards. *American Journal of Sexuality Education* 2(2): 27–49.

Wright, Lisa L. 2008. Merits and limitations of distributed leadership: Experiences and understandings of school principals. *Canadian Journal of Educational Administration and Policy* (69) (February).

Yunger, J. L, P. R. Carver, and D. G. Perry. 2004. Does gender identity influence children's psychological well-being? *Developmental Psychology* 40(4): 572–82.

Zurbriggen, Eileen L., Rebecca L. Collins, Sharon Lamb, Tomi-Ann Roberts, Deobrah L. Tolman, L. Monique Ward, and Jeanne Blake. 2007. Report of the APA Task Force on the sexualization of girls. American Psychological Association.

CHAPTER 10

Akkerman, Sanne F., and Paulien C. Meijer. 2011. A dialogical approach to conceptualizing teacher identity. *Teaching and Teacher Education: An International Journal of Research and Studies* 27(2): 308–19.

Barr, Sebastian Mitchell. 2011. Personal communication.

DePalma, Renee, and Elizabeth Atkinson. 2009. Permission to talk about it. *Qualitative Inquiry* 15: 876–92.

Geijsel, Femke, and Frans Meijers. 2005. Identity learning: The core process of educational change. *Educational Studies* 31(4) (December): 419–30.

Kincheloe, Joe L. 2004. The knowledges of teacher education: Developing a critical complex epistemology. *Teacher Education Quarterly* 31(1) (Winter): 49–66.

Palmer, Parker. 2007. *The courage to teach guide for reflection and renewal, 10th anniversary edition*. San Francisco: Jossey-Bass. Kindle Edition.

Patai, Daphne. 1991. Minority status and the stigma of "surplus" visibility. *Chronicle of Higher Education* 38(10).

Rasmussen, Mary Lou. 2004. The problem of coming out. *Theory Into Practice* 43(2).

Riggs, Angela D., Amy R. Rosenthal, and Tina Smith-Bonahue. 2011. The impact of a combined cognitive-affective intervention on pre-service teachers' attitudes, knowledge, and anticipated professional behaviors regarding homosexuality and gay and lesbian issues. *Teaching and Teacher Education: An International Journal of Research and Studies* 27: 201–9.

Sanger, Matthew N., and Richard D. Osguthorpe. 2011. Teacher education, preservice teacher beliefs, and the moral work of teaching. *Teaching and Teacher Education* 27: 569–78.

Smith, Jill M. 2010. Overcoming an identity of privilege to support LGBTQ inclusivity in school. *Acting out: Combating homophobia through teacher activism*, eds. Mollie V. Blackburn, Caroline T. Clark, Lauren M. Kenney, and Jill M. Smith. New York: Teachers College Press, 114–26.

Thomas, Lynn, and Catherine Beauchamp. 2011. Understanding new teachers' professional identities through metaphor. *Teaching and Teacher Education* 27: 762–69.

Vavrus, Michael. 2008. Sexuality, schooling, and teacher identity formation: A critical pedagogy for teacher education. *Teaching and Teacher Education* 25(3): 383–90.

GLOSSARY

Gender/Sexuality Terms and Definitions

androgynous: having both male and female characteristics.

affirmed gender: a classification based on an individual's gender identity, which may be different/separate from assigned birth sex.

asexual: sexual orientation of an individual who does not feel sexual attraction or sexual desire.

assigned birth sex: a classification ("it's a boy"/"it's a girl") based on reproductive anatomy and physiology.

binary: a term used to describe that which relates to, is composed of, or involves *two* things. With respect to gender and sexuality diversity, the binary thesis organizes much of our either/or thinking about gender and sexuality (i.e., two sexes, two genders, two sexualities) and ignores those sexes, genders, and sexualities that do not lie in one of the two typically recognized categories.

biological sex: the biological state of having (1) female or male genitalia, (2) female (XX) or male (XY) chromosomes, and (3) a mixture of hormones: estrogen, progesterone, and testosterone.

bisexual: sexual orientation for an individual whose romantic, emotional, and sexual attractions and connections are with both males and females.

cisgender: a term describing individuals whose gender identity and gender expression match their biological and assigned birth sex. A cisgender person is someone who is *not* transgender.

comprehensive sexuality education: education about all matters relating to sexuality and its expression. Comprehensive sexuality education covers the same topics as sex education but also includes issues such as relationships, attitudes toward sexuality, sexual roles, gender relations and the social pressures to be sexually active, and it provides information about sexual and reproductive health services. It may also include training in communication and decision-making skills.

continuum of gender: a way of describing more than two genders.

continuum of masculinities/femininities: a way of describing more than two discreet forms of gender expression.

continuum of sexual orientation: a way of describing more than two sexual orientations.

developmentally appropriate practice (DAP): a method of teaching that incorporates knowledge of child development, identified strengths and needs of the specific children being taught, and the cultural backgrounds of each student.

female: one of the two recognized, primary biological sexes.

femininity: commonly understood to refer to a collection of qualities or attributes associated with women, as distinct from men; what qualities qualify as feminine is subject to debate, as is whether such qualities should be considered innate essences or cultural norms.

gay: an adjective describing an individual whose primary romantic, emotional, and sexual attractions and connections are with someone of the same sex. Specifically refers to men; also used as an umbrella term to describe all people with same-sex attractions.

gender: a socially constructed system of classification that ascribes qualities of *masculinity* and *femininity* to people. Gender characteristics can change over time and are different between cultures. Gender is not the same as *biological sex*, though the two are often conflated with each other.

gender and sexuality diversity (GSD): a broad construct that describes the continuums of biological sex, gender identity, gender expression, sexual orientation, sexual behavior, and sexual identity. GSD recognizes that gender identity and sexual identity are essential aspects of human identity for all people, and that gender and sexuality are inherently diverse. "Diversity" refers to the concept of biodiversity signifying the variety of genders and sexualities in the world. Gay, Lesbian, Bisexual, Transgender, Queer, Intersex (GLBTQI) identities are part of the larger gender and sexuality diversity construct.

gender expression: the way people externally communicate their *gender identity* to others through behavior, clothing, hairstyle, voice, etc.

gender identity: our innermost concept of self as male, female, queer—what we perceive and call ourselves.

gender identity (GI) development: a process of determining and consolidating one's gender identity, manifest first in toddlerhood, continuing through adulthood. Actual development of GI likely begins prior to toddlerhood.

gender identity instruction: the conscious and unconscious ways that teachers, parents, media teach children the "right" way to "be" a particular gender.

gender roles: the set of roles and behaviors assigned to females and males by a given society.

gender variant: a more contemporary term to describe those whose gender identity or expression differ from cultural expectations based on biological sex; it is increasingly applied to gender nonconforming children who may or may not develop a transgender identity. Gender variance does *not* indicate pathology.

genderqueer: a rejection of the gender binary (male/female) in favor of a more fluid, nontraditional gender identity.

gene: a segment of DNA; a unit of heredity.

heteronormativity: the binary view of gender and sexuality that assumes and privileges heterosexuality in individuals, couples and families, and supports traditional masculine and feminine gender roles and expression. It is the cultural and social "management" of gender and sexuality and is promoted and maintained by individuals and institutions.

heterosexuality: sexual, emotional, and/or romantic attraction to a biological sex other than one's own.

homosexuality: sexual, emotional, and/or romantic attraction to someone of the same biological sex.

intersectionality: theory that suggests that various social categories and axes of identity such as gender, race, class, and disability interact with each other on multiple levels. These interrelationships create a system of oppression that reflects the "intersection" of multiple forms of discrimination and is more complex than the simple conceptualizations of homophobia, sexism, racism, etc.

intersex: a range of physiological conditions in which a person is born with reproductive and/or sexual anatomy that do not conform to binary definitions of female or male biological sex.

lesbian: a woman who feels romantically, emotionally and sexually attracted to other women.

male: one of the two recognized, primary biological sexes.

masculinity: commonly understood to refer to a collection of qualities or attributes associated with men, as distinct from women; what qualities qualify as masculine is subject to debate, as is whether such qualities such be considered innate essences or cultural norms.

pansexual: describes those who are attracted to people across a spectrum of genders and sexes.

pedagogy: has several meanings. In this book pedagogy refers to (1) the art and science of teaching and instruction and (2) a particular approach to teaching based on educational theory.

polyamorous: refers to having honest relationships with multiple partners based on different types of intimacy, including sexual and/or romantic love.

queer: formerly a derogatory term and recently reclaimed as a positive umbrella term by many to describe those who do not conform to binary notions of gender and sexuality.

queer theory: an approach to literary cultural studies that rejects traditional categories of gender and sexuality.

reproductive sex organs: internal and external parts of the body that are involved in reproduction, e.g., penis, vagina, uterus, testicles, ovaries.

sex: the identification of biological and assigned sex.

"sex" hormones: hormones associated with uterine development of sex and gender (estrogen, progesterone, testosterone). A contested term.

sex reassignment surgery: surgical procedures that modify one's primary and/or secondary sex characteristics.

sexual behavior: what one actually does sexually. Sexual behavior is usually, but not always, consistent with one's *sexual identity* and *sexual orientation*.

sexual orientation: traditionally defined as the direction of one's sexual attraction to the same sex (homosexual), the opposite sex (heterosexual), both men and women (bisexual), or any sexual identity (pansexual). Asexual describes those who have no sexual attraction.

sexual identity: how we view ourselves sexually; what we call ourselves (e.g., gay, bi, queer, straight).

sexual identity development: a process of determining and consolidating one's sexual identity that is manifest first in early childhood and continues through adulthood.

sexuality: a broad construct that refers to the totality of sexual identity, orientation, and behavior.

socialization: the process by which people are taught or made to behave in a way that is acceptable to their society.

straight: a slang term for a person with a heterosexual orientation.

surgical correction: refers to an increasingly contested early treatment option for intersex individuals born with ambiguous genitalia.

trans: often used as substitute for transgender but it can also be used to include other gender identities, such as genderqueer and two spirit.

transgender: a broad term describing the continuum of individuals whose gender identity or gender expression, to varying degrees, do not conform to stereotypical masculine or feminine norms. Also used to describe those whose gender identity does not match their biological sex.

transsexual: an individual who does not identify with their birth-assigned gender and may alter their body hormonally and/or surgically.

two spirit: in Native American culture, this term generally means a person born with one biological sex who fulfills at least some of the gender roles assigned to both sexes; considered part male, part female.

INDEX

bolded page numbers are in text glossary definitions